The Dukes of Arenberg
and Music in the Eighteenth Century

The Story of a Music Collection

Marie Cornaz

Collectionner la musique / Collecting Music

The Dukes of Arenberg and Music in the Eighteenth Century

The Story of a Music Collection

Marie Cornaz

Translated from the French by Anna J. Davies

To
Michael Talbot

ISBN 978-2-503-55557-7
D/2015/0095/127

© 2015 Brepols Publishers n.v., Turnhout, Belgium

Printing and binding
by Grafikon, Oostkamp, Belgium

A PERSONAL NOTE

It was in the 1990s that Marie Cornaz began her exploration of the music collection held in the Arenberg family's private archives at Enghien (in the Belgian Hainaut region) – which since 1997 has been overseen by the non-profit organization The Arenberg Archives and its associated Cultural Centre (or AACC) – and ever since that time she has devoted herself assiduously to the analysis, classification, cataloguing, and promotion of this exceptional collection. A first visit arranged in 1995 with the then archivist, Capuchin friar Jean-Pierre Tytgat, marked the beginning of a long history of exchange between musicologist Marie Cornaz and the Arenberg family, centring on the wealth of early musical scores – both in manuscript and printed form – which at that time were still crying out to be identified. Encouragement to pursue this journey of discovery came in 1997, when Marie Cornaz was awarded the Arenberg Medal for Merit. With patience and enthusiasm, the riddle of this collection of musical works gradually began to be deciphered, and was brought to scholarly attention with the publication of two catalogues in the *Revue Belge de Musicologie*. The pages of music, which had been stored under the appropriate conditions for their conservation, together with the bound volumes, had emerged as a previously unknown source for nigh on two thousand works, the most significant dating from the eighteenth century. It was imperative that the most outstanding of these works be examined in greater depth, and the question needed to be asked: how had they found themselves in the family archives in the first place? 2010 saw the publication of *Les ducs d'Arenberg et la musique au XVIIIe siècle: Histoire d'une collection musicale*, a book representing the first outcome of this research process. The present study, which is a revised and updated version of the first edition, presents all the findings concerning music that have been made to date in the historical family archives relating to the eighteenth century, and compares these with the scores still preserved in the collection today. The subtitle of the study, 'The Story of a Music Collection', indicates that the book proposes also to retrace the steps which led to the gradual building-up of a music collection within what is a vast and diverse family library.

HSH Prince Pierre d'Arenberg, together with the Arenberg Foundation – an organization that seeks to promote European history as seen from the perspective of the Arts – were keen to support the publication of this new version in English in order to reach a more broadly international readership with a strong interest in music. The Arenberg family's own appreciation of musical life has led them to support a number of concerts, notably, since 2003, those associated with the Lauenen Chamber Concerts Association (see <www.arenbergfoundation.eu>). The chapters that follow serve to nurture musicological research while at the same time paving the way for further musical projects.

We congratulate Marie Cornaz on her remarkable work and wish her every success in her future undertakings.

HSH Duke Léopold d'Arenberg

PREFACE

The musicologist Marie Cornaz, Curator of the music collections at the Royal Library of Belgium and Senior Lecturer at the Université Libre de Bruxelles, has engaged all her talent, knowledge, patience, and commitment for what is, in several ways, a truly exceptional publication. This study is the product of an eager journey of exploration in the archives of the Arenberg family and the discovery of a surprising and unexpected musical treasure. The Arenberg family has in fact accumulated in the region of 600 music manuscripts and more than 900 printed works, including a number of extremely rare scores, hitherto unpublished and unique in the world. The earliest of these date to the seventeenth century, but the eighteenth century was the period when the Dukes of Arenberg and their families acquired the most exceptional of these musical gems, and the most significant in terms of European musical history. It is an undeniable fact that the prestige and influence of the Dukes of Arenberg contributed greatly to this very history. The Arenbergs were among the most influential aristocratic families in the Spanish Netherlands and Austria, with further possessions in Germany, France, Bohemia, and Italy. The Arenbergs have therefore been inseparably connected with the history of vast territories in Europe, including the lands that would give birth to Belgium as an independent and sovereign state. The historical presence of the Arenberg family – a truly pan-European family – is still visible today, thanks, among other things, to the châteaux and the other residences and monuments it has built and managed: notably, the Palace of Egmont in Brussels, where foreign guests to Belgium are received every day, the Château d'Arenberg at Heverlee (Kasteel van Arenberg, to use its Flemish name), near Louvain, which was bequeathed to the Catholic University of Louvain after the First World War, and, of course, the town of Enghien, where valuable archives of the Arenberg family are housed.

The Arenberg Archives at Enghien hold a very rich collection dating back over a millennium and contain numerous documents, deeds, registers, correspondence, maps, and engravings – running to over 1000 metres in length – relating to the House of Arenberg's history. The considerable historical, cultural, and political heritage that the Arenberg Archives represent has led to the creation of both the Arenberg Foundation and the non-profit organization The Arenberg Archives and Cultural Centre (AACC). The main aim of these institutions arises first and foremost from a duty to remember the great and influential reigning families who played a crucial role in the emergence of Europe and European civilization – a history characterized by rivalries, wars, and conflicts, but also by reconciliation, cooperation, synergies, and huge cultural legacies. The Arenberg family is one such remarkable example.

With this past in mind, it is important to promote not only European culture in its dynamic evolution, but equally, in a sense, the story of our present and of our future: a somewhat paradoxical formulation, but one that emphasizes the need to build an ever more unified Europe in what is an ever more globalized and, consequently, unstable and vulnerable world. The Arenberg Foundation seeks to encourage dialogue between the various European cultures, with due regard to their diversity, by applying to them the principle of subsidiarity, which is, moreover, enshrined in the most important European treaties. This is why the Arenberg Foundation and its Cultural Centre are striving to foster cooperation in the academic world, in the great libraries, public bodies at all levels, European authorities, state archives, and historical forums, and are aiming to encompass the whole socio-economic spectrum.

The discovery of this extraordinary musical treasure in the Arenberg family archives at Enghien should convince those families who possess archives of their own to join forces in order to ensure their preservation, dissemination, and publication, and their accessibility to a wide public.

Marie Cornaz's superb work thus sits within a vast and kaleidoscopic cultural context. It is useful to remember that, to date, the Arenberg Foundation and the Arenberg Archives and Cultural Centre have supported the publication of around twenty academic history books, shedding new light on our common past. Several academic prizes have also been awarded, among them the Duke of Arenberg History Prizes, the Arenberg-Coimbra European Prize, and the College of Europe-Arenberg European Prize. The present detailed academic publication dedicated to the Arenberg family and to music can only serve to diversify and 'multi-lateralize' the initiatives and activities of the Arenberg Foundation.

The extent of the Arenberg Archives is considerable. Among other items, they hold in manuscript form works by Jean-Baptiste Lully, composer to the King of France, Louis XIV, and also a manuscript of the Italian composer Pietro Torri, who came to Brussels in the last years of the seventeenth century. From the 1720s onwards Duke Léopold-Philippe d'Arenberg made the acquaintance of Italian musicians and singers visiting Brussels: notably, the performers of several operas by Antonio Vivaldi – which would explain the existence in the music collection of two manuscript arias for contralto from the opera *L'inganno trionfante in amore*, music that had been thought lost. It was also Duke Léopold-Philippe d'Arenberg who had the first private theatre built in 1732 at his residence at Enghien, which would be followed by a second at Heverlee in 1753. Between 1749 and 1752 the Duke of Arenberg was also Co-director at the Brussels opera house, the Théâtre de la Monnaie. These activities explain the accumulation of numerous manuscript scores in the ducal archives. The fact is that these archives represent an aspect of our musical and cultural life that has remained largely unknown until now.

The fifth Duke of Arenberg and his wife Louise-Marguerite, Countess de La Marck, stepped up the acquisition of musical works. The Countess had contact with the musical circles of Paris, something borne out by the presence within the collection of the sole extant copy of the *Second livre de pièces de clavecin* that the French composer Pierre Février had published in the French capital in the 1730s. In their private residences in Brussels, Enghien, and Heverlee Duke Charles-Marie-Raymond and his wife staged operas and hosted concerts of instrumental music. On studying the account books, Marie Cornaz learned that Duke Charles had come to the financial aid of several musicians, among them the Brussels musicians and composers Pierre van Maldere and Ferdinand Staes. Louis-Engelbert, the sixth Duke of Arenberg, whose expressive statue was erected at Heverlee, also took pleasure in musical performances. He made music a very important part of his life and activities, having lost his sight following an accident in 1775. Through his impetus the Arenberg music library continued to grow, notably through the purchase of scores by the violinist and music engraver Paul Mechtler, private music teacher to the family from 1771. On his visits abroad to Paris, London, Rome, and Vienna the

Duke attended numerous concerts (where he met musicians, including Haydn) and during this time acquired scores that would be added to his expanding music library.

I venture to suggest that Marie Cornaz was predestined to make these discoveries, whose immense importance she brings to light in this remarkable study, placing them with equal adeptness in their historical context. Yet this is hardly any surprise, given her distinguished background as a Doctor of Musicology – the subject of her doctoral thesis was music publishing and distribution in Brussels during the eighteenth century. Dr Cornaz's academic credentials are indeed impressive: research periods abroad, numerous conference papers and presentations at musicological symposia, membership of scholarly associations and of the boards of academic journals, and above all a long list of publications, among them several books, including a study of music and the Princes of Chimay (accompanied by a CD), as well as many articles. Marie Cornaz has also been awarded various prizes and distinctions, including awards from the Royal Academy of Belgium. She has been a Sulzberger Foundation prize-winner, as well as a recipient of the Duke of Arenberg's Medal for Merit. Marie Cornaz began her professional life as a researcher at the Université Libre de Bruxelles, moving to the Katholieke Universiteit Leuven and, later, the Musical Instruments Museum in Brussels, before joining the Royal Library of Belgium – an ideal itinerary that promises many further successes.

I offer Marie Cornaz my best wishes for her future research, hoping that she may make many more musical discoveries, as well as producing further first-rate publications that pay such brilliant homage to our beloved Europe.

Prof. Emer. Mark Eyskens
Minister of State
President of the Arenberg Foundation

FOREWORD

The story of a discovery, a catalogue, and the genesis of a study

It is often pure chance that explains how a hitherto unexplored topic is brought to the notice of a researcher – who, fired up, feels drawn by an irresistible urge to know more.

In 1995 Manuel Couvreur had become the managing editor of a volume on the history of the Théâtre de la Monnaie in the eighteenth century.[1] Aware of the privileged links that the Arenberg family had maintained with the Brussels opera house, he arranged a visit – along with several of the book's contributors – to the family's private archives at Enghien, then overseen by the Capuchin monks living in that small town in the Belgian province of Hainaut.[2]

As a contributor[3] to Manuel Couvreur's book but also as a doctoral student[4] and researcher at the Université Libre de Bruxelles – working on a project related to the study and inventory of musical manuscripts preserved in Belgium[5] – I had been invited to join the party to Enghien. It seemed a good idea to take advantage of the opportunity to view these archives and find out whether, perchance, they contained musical sources of any kind.

I will always remember that first visit. My presence at the archives at all had been more by chance than anything else, and I was without any idea of what awaited me. Having attended to some other members of the group, the Capuchin friar Jean-Pierre Tytgat (1942-2004), historian, chaplain, and archivist for the Arenbergs since 1979,[6] then asked me what it was that I was interested in seeing. I replied timidly that I would like to know whether the archives in his care contained any musical scores. He told me that indeed they did, and bade me follow him into the stock room, where, beckoning towards several sets of shelves, he informed me that the music collection had not been touched since its arrival at Enghien, and that no one had as yet set about classifying or studying it. He then allowed me to take a closer look at the contents of the shelves. By the evening I was exhausted, covered in dust, but above all amazed at what I had discovered that day. I asked Father Tytgat whether I could come back. This marked the beginning of a long story: over the next ten years and longer I would return to Enghien very often.

After an initial probe the music collection turned out to be first-rate, but a serious study was virtually impossible, since the collection had not been classified, nor had any inventory been taken of its contents. I therefore embarked on the long but fascinating task of classifying the material, very often having to reassemble parts of the same work that had become separated over time. Thanks to the support of my doctoral supervisor and director of research at the Université Libre de Bruxelles, Professor Henri Vanhulst, over the course of the following months I was able to spend many days classifying and making an inventory of the collection. This initial research led to the publication of an inventory that appeared in volume 49 of the *Revue Belge de Musicologie*[7] and listed 177 manuscripts and 678 printed documents. When it came to the earliest publications, this initial overview made reference to the *Répertoire International des Sources Musicales* (RISM) – the aim being, first, to draw attention to a number of printed scores, the examples of which, here at Enghien, were in fact the first to be recorded in Belgium, and, second, to stress that there were early editions in this collection not yet accounted for anywhere and whose existence had therefore been entirely unknown.[8] The huge amount of work already carried out up to this point prompted the Arenberg family to award me, in 1997, the Duke of Arenberg's Medal for Merit. This distinction meant a great deal to me, since it showed that the work to which I had passionately dedicated myself had met with recognition, and it encouraged me to forge ahead.

I had by now been awarded my doctorate in musicology, and from 1998 to 2002 held a postdoctoral research fellowship with the Belgian National Fund for Scientific Research (FNRS). My research during this time focused on the music archives at the Château de Chimay,[9] but the Arenberg Archives were never far from my mind. A certain amount of restructuring had in fact taken place at Enghien in the meantime, as a result of the definitive closure of the Capuchin Friary in August 1996[10], followed by the relocation to Brussels of the archivist at the time, who a few months later was relieved of his post as archivist of the House of Arenberg.[11] In November 1997 the family created a non-profit organization, the Arenberg Archives and Cultural Centre (or AACC), which was set up chiefly in order to manage the archives at Enghien.

Along with this new structure and the arrival in 2001 of archivists Lieve Bické and Guy Lernout, the archive's premises also underwent renovation, the main aim being to improve accessibility and the conditions of conservation. From 2002 I was keen to be involved in this new surge of activity, not least because I had recently stumbled upon a collection of scores that had previously escaped my notice. With the backing of the Arenberg family, I embarked on the definitive classification of the entire collection of musical documents in the archives with a view to drawing up a comprehensive inventory. Taking up each document one by one, and placing certain documents into folders or acid-free boxes, I decided to make a complete overhaul of my filing system, not only because the collection was practically doubling in size, but also because the subdivisions created in my first inventory now seemed, with the benefit of hindsight and experience, redundant.

When my fellowship at the FNRS drew to a close, I left research for some time to take up a post in the music publications service at the Brussels Centre for Fine Arts, and following that I worked as a researcher at the International Centre for the Study of Music in the Low Countries (Alamire Foundation) at the Katholieke Universiteit Leuven. In 2003 and 2004 the Centre gave me the opportunity to complete a definitive catalogue of the music collection at Enghien, which involved making significant modifications to the earlier catalogue. Apart from the fact that a greater number of musical sources appeared in the new catalogue than in the earlier version, it also gave or suggested (for certain sources) the identity of the composer and/or the work. Identification of the provenance of a number of the sources was made possible through a systematic consultation of the *Répertoire International des Sources Musicales*.[12] It should be mentioned here that among the newly discovered manuscripts were several Vivaldi arias, something I shall come back to later in this study. For the definitive catalogue, published in volume 58 of the *Revue Belge de Musicologie*,[13] I decided to allocate to the manuscript items a number from 1 to 578 (these could contain one or several works), preceded by the abbreviation 'Ms'. As regards the printed editions, these were given a classmark from 579 to

1084, preceded by the abbreviation 'I'. As a result, under these numbered printed items 960 different musical editions had been catalogued.

After all those years regularly spent at Enghien, I could at last fully grasp the nature of the music collection in its entirety, which, with its over 1500 printed and manuscript scores, represented one of the richest private music collections in Belgium.

But I did not want to leave it at that. This collection merited more than a mere catalogue, however well-researched this might be. It could serve as a point of departure for an innovative study of the place of music in the Arenberg family from the end of the seventeenth century onwards; it could serve to enrich our knowledge of the history of eighteenth-century musical life in the Austrian Netherlands, the family having its most important residences here at that time. Finally, this collection contained some extraordinary musical gems that deserved to be brought out of the shadows, so that performances of these works might be given by the musicians of today.

In 2005 I joined a research team at the Musical Instruments Museum in Brussels to participate in a project on Claudio Monteverdi's *Orfeo*. My connection with the Arenberg Archives did not stop here, either: how great was my surprise when, perusing the Arenberg family account books and receipts in the Arenberg Collection at the State Archives of Belgium, I came upon a document, entirely unknown to researchers, reporting the purchase of four violins from Cremona by Philippe-Charles de Croÿ (1587-1640), Prince of Arenberg, in 1624![14] Parallel to this research activity, I continued to broaden my knowledge of the Arenberg music collection and its history by searching for musical elements in a series of archival documents.

After several articles based on my Arenbergian research, the idea of an in-depth study naturally arose, leading first of all to a Belgian Royal Academy prize-winning essay in 2008,[15] followed in 2010 by the publication of my monograph *Les ducs d'Arenberg et la musique au XVIIIᵉ siècle: Histoire d'une collection musicale*. On 22 December of the same year, the American mezzo-soprano Vivica Genaux and the ensemble *Les Agrémens* (directed by Guy Van Waas) brought to life several arias from the Enghien archives at a memorable concert held at the Centre for Fine Arts in Brussels, during Belgium's presidency of the European Union.

But the story does not end there. Right from the day I discovered it in the private archives of the Dukes of Arenberg at Enghien, the music collection has never ceased to be present in my academic life, like a sort of electric current. In 2012 it even led to the equally fortuitous discovery of the Montagu Music Collection, at Boughton House in Northamptonshire, England.[16] That is why, with the support of HSH Duke Léopold d'Arenberg and HSH Prince Pierre d'Arenberg, the project of a revised and updated English edition, with a view to reaching a wider readership, logically asserted itself.

Acknowledgements

Before launching into the substance of this study, I should like to express my gratitude to the persons without whose help it could never have seen the light of day. For their constant and unwavering support, I must first extend my thanks to the Arenberg family: namely, † HSH Duke Jean-Engelbert d'Arenberg, HSH Prince Pierre d'Arenberg, HSH Prince Henri d'Arenberg, HSH Prince Étienne d'Arenberg, and especially HSH Duke Léopold d'Arenberg, who encouraged me again and again to persevere, despite the uncertainties of professional life. I must also stress the warm welcome given to me by successive archivists at Enghien: † Father Jean-Pierre Tytgat, already mentioned, Arnout Mertens, and more recently Lieve Bické and Guy Lernout. My wholehearted thanks go to Lieve and Guy, whose generosity with their time and readiness to help made the Arenberg Archives at Enghien a truly exceptional place to pursue this research.

I cannot continue, either, without mentioning Xavier Duquenne, whom I met so frequently at Enghien and in the State Archives Reading Room in Brussels. I wish to express my heartfelt appreciation for his kindness and constant readiness to show me the archival documents connected with music, many of which are kept in the section of the State Archives Arenberg Collection that he has recently catalogued.

I must also mention those who, from near or afar, have helped me both in my research and in the completion of this book: namely, Mario Armellini, Mia Awouters, Sebastian Biesold, Bruno Bouckaert, Anne-Emmanuelle Ceulemans, Manuel Couvreur, Sophie Dangreau, † Yves Delannoy, Louis Delpech, Jean-Marie Duvosquel, Frédéric Delaméa, Bruno Forment, Hervé Hasquin, Jean-Philippe Huys, Sandrine Jauneau, Kris De Baerdemacker, Patrick Lefèvre, Claude de Moreau de Gerbehaye, Maïté Morel de Boncourt, Denis Morsa, Peter Neu, Robert Nouwen, Peter Parren, Patrizia Rebulla,† Jan Roegiers, Sara Roegiers, Bernard Roobaert, Federico Maria Sardelli, Eugeen Schreurs, Louise K. Stein, Olivier de Trazegnies, Jean-Philippe Van Aelbrouck, Isabelle Vanden Hove, Henri Vanhulst, Anne Verbrugge, Olivia Wahnon de Oliveira, and Robert Wangermée.

My warm thanks go to the translator, Anna J. Davies, and also to musicologist Michael Talbot for reading and commenting on the English version of my book before publication, and for his ever-helpful advice.

For his constant support of my work, I owe especial thanks to Professor Mark Eyskens, Viscount, Minister of State, and President of the Arenberg Foundation.

Finally, for their unconditional support I cannot omit to thank my husband Thierry and my daughters Juliette and Louise, who have so often been regaled over the years with talk of the Arenberg music collection at Enghien.

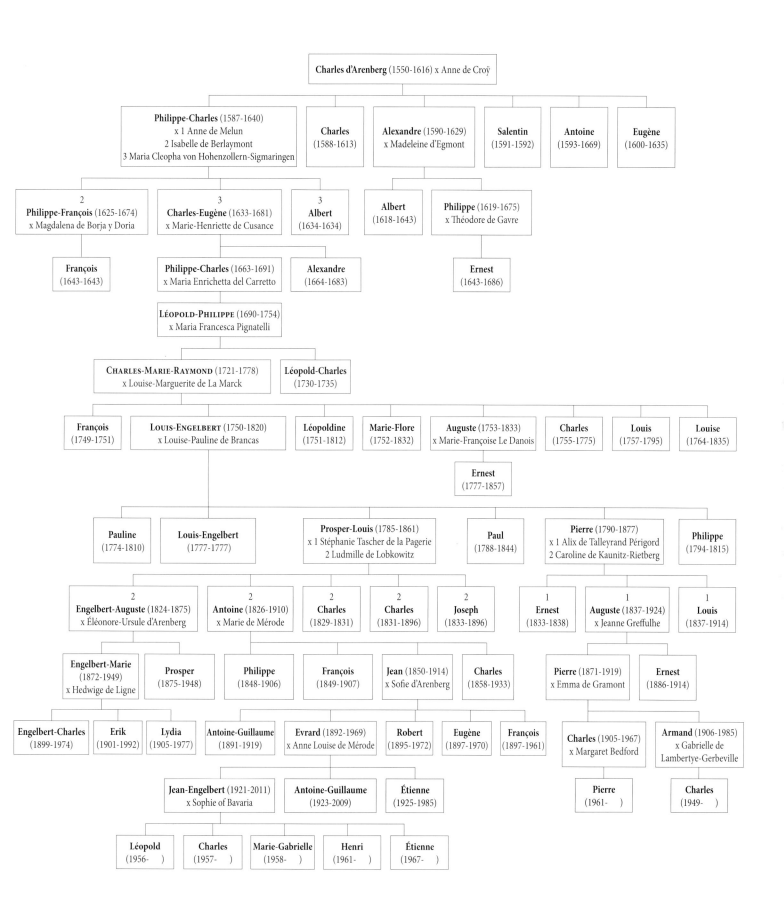

Charles d'Arenberg (1550-1616) x Anne de Croÿ

Philippe-Charles (1587-1640)
x 1 Anne de Melun
2 Isabelle de Berlaymont
3 Maria Cleopha von Hohenzollern-Sigmaringen

Charles
(1588-1613)

Alexandre (1590-1629)
x Madeleine d'Egmont

Salentin
(1591-1592)

Antoine
(1593-1669)

Eugène
(1600-1635)

2
Philippe-François (1625-1674)
x Magdalena de Borja y Doria

3
Charles-Eugène (1633-1681)
x Marie-Henriette de Cusance

3
Albert
(1634-1634)

Albert
(1618-1643)

Philippe (1619-1675)
x Théodore de Gavre

François
(1643-1643)

Philippe-Charles (1663-1691)
x Maria Enrichetta del Carretto

Alexandre
(1664-1683)

Ernest
(1643-1686)

Léopold-Philippe (1690-1754)
x Maria Francesca Pignatelli

Charles-Marie-Raymond (1721-1778)
x Louise-Marguerite de La Marck

Léopold-Charles
(1730-1735)

François
(1749-1751)

Louis-Engelbert (1750-1820)
x Louise-Pauline de Brancas

Léopoldine
(1751-1812)

Marie-Flore
(1752-1832)

Auguste (1753-1833)
x Marie-Françoise Le Danois

Charles
(1755-1775)

Louis
(1757-1795)

Louise
(1764-1835)

Ernest
(1777-1857)

Pauline
(1774-1810)

Louis-Engelbert
(1777-1777)

Prosper-Louis (1785-1861)
x 1 Stéphanie Tascher de la Pagerie
2 Ludmille de Lobkowitz

Paul
(1788-1844)

Pierre (1790-1877)
x 1 Alix de Talleyrand Périgord
2 Caroline de Kaunitz-Rietberg

Philippe
(1794-1815)

2
Engelbert-Auguste (1824-1875)
x Éléonore-Ursule d'Arenberg

2
Antoine (1826-1910)
x Marie de Mérode

2
Charles
(1829-1831)

2
Charles
(1831-1896)

2
Joseph
(1833-1896)

1
Ernest
(1833-1838)

1
Auguste (1837-1924)
x Jeanne Greffulhe

1
Louis
(1837-1914)

Engelbert-Marie
(1872-1949)
x Hedwige de Ligne

Prosper
(1875-1948)

Philippe
(1848-1906)

François
(1849-1907)

Jean (1850-1914)
x Sofie d'Arenberg

Charles
(1858-1933)

Pierre (1871-1919)
x Emma de Gramont

Ernest
(1886-1914)

Engelbert-Charles
(1899-1974)

Erik
(1901-1992)

Lydia
(1905-1977)

Antoine-Guillaume
(1891-1919)

Evrard (1892-1969)
x Anne Louise de Mérode

Robert
(1895-1972)

Eugène
(1897-1970)

François
(1897-1961)

Charles (1905-1967)
x Margaret Bedford

Armand (1906-1985)
x Gabrielle de
Lambertye-Gerbeville

Jean-Engelbert (1921-2011)
x Sophie of Bavaria

Antoine-Guillaume
(1923-2009)

Étienne
(1925-1985)

Pierre
(1961-   )

Charles
(1949-   )

Léopold
(1956-   )

Charles
(1957-   )

Marie-Gabrielle
(1958-   )

Henri
(1961-   )

Étienne
(1967-   )

INTRODUCTION

Sources

The present study focuses deliberately and above all on the content of the music collection itself. What kinds of eighteenth-century works do we have? By which composers? What is their geographical origin? While the study of the material was highly instructive in itself, it was also important to examine the archival documents with a view to gaining a better understanding of the connections that the Dukes of Arenberg – originally from the German Eifel region[17] – had with music in the Austrian Netherlands throughout the eighteenth century. We needed to discover why Dukes Léopold-Philippe (1690-1754), Charles-Marie-Raymond (1721-1778), and Louis-Engelbert (1750-1820) wished to cultivate the family's music collection, and how they went about this.

The systematic study of account books, the majority of which are preserved in the Arenberg Archives at Enghien,[18] allowed me to identify numerous payments made in relation to music, such as the purchase and upkeep of musical instruments, music lessons, support for singers, instrumentalists and musical institutions, and also subscriptions to the Théâtre de la Monnaie. By analysing a number of receipts, I was able to fill in the missing details, for the information given in the account books was often quite rudimentary. A multitude of other archival documents, most of which are kept either at Enghien or in the Arenberg Collection at the State Archives of Belgium, were also consulted, such as library catalogues, inventories, correspondence, and travel journals.

In order to grasp the music collection's place within the whole Arenberg archival corpus, it is worth tracing a brief history and overview of the various locations where the archives are held. In particular, the prominent position of the Arenbergs in the former Low Countries should be emphasized: since a large part of the family's possessions is concentrated in this region, the archives not only offer local historic interest but also shed considerable light on Belgian and European history in general.

The Arenberg Collection housed in the State Archives of Belgium (hereafter, SAB) was created, following the First World War, in 1918.[19] A large portion of the documents kept there comes from the Arenberg Palace in Brussels. The archive comprises mainly administrative and account records. Sequestered documents relating to Belgian property would not enter the SAB until 1935 on the initiative of Duke Engelbert-Marie d'Arenberg (1872-1949). In total, the Arenberg Collection at the SAB represents over a kilometre of archives, covering a period from the thirteenth to the twentieth centuries. In terms of geographical scope, the records relate mainly to north-western Europe.

Around 12000 documents arriving in 1918 were allocated an index card with a bibliographic description by Édouard Laloire (1870-1953), archivist to the ducal family before he joined the State Archives of Belgium in 1920. The catalogued documents were given a numerical classmark preceded by the letters 'LA'. One of Laloire's colleagues, Étienne Sabbe (1901-1969), later classified the documents that arrived in 1935, creating around 15000 catalogue cards essentially relating to documents from the nineteenth century and the beginning of the twentieth century. Here, the classmark given to the documents was prefixed by 'SA'. The archivist Arthur Cosemans (1897-1971) took a more specific interest in documents from the German domains belonging to the seventeenth to nineteenth centuries, producing almost 1000 bibliographic descriptions. From the 1950s onwards, several inventories relating to parts of the collection began to be published. In 2004, Xavier Duquenne began to draw up a brief description of a large, previously unstudied part of the collection, and numerical classmarks preceded by the letters MG (the initials of the archivist in charge, Claude de Moreau de Gerbehaye)[20] were applied to over 7500 documents.

As regards the Arenberg Archives at Enghien, these contain material delivered to the Capuchin Friars on 7 September 1964 by Duke Engelbert-Marie's three heirs Engelbert-Charles (1899-1974), Erik (1901-1992), and Lydia (1905-1977), following the wishes of their father. The late Duke wanted all the archival documents still in the family's possession after the donations to the State Archives of Belgium and to the University of Louvain to be given to a religious order that – as Engelbert-Charles emphasized in a letter of 19 October 1946 – had enjoyed close links to his family since the seventeenth century.[21]

A decision was made to house the archives in the Capuchin Friary at Enghien (where the family vault is also located). In 1965 an initial consignment of 162 boxes containing documents, registers, and books arrived in Enghien, and Father August Roeykens (1911-1979) embarked on the classification of deeds and registers, with reference to earlier inventories by J. Beauvoix (1750), P. Quittelier (1782), and É. Laloire (1910). In order to accommodate this material most effectively, Princess Lydia d'Arenberg and Duke Erik d'Arenberg had a building erected specifically for the archives, located next to the cloister. Father Roeykens was succeeded in his task by Father Jean-Pierre Tytgat, who, as mentioned above, would devote himself unstintingly to this work to the very end. When the Capuchin Friary eventually closed its doors for good, the Arenbergs once again became outright owners of the Enghien archives and created the NPO, the Arenberg Archives and Cultural Centre. Today this organization continues regularly to receive new archival documents from the family. In other words, it is a collection that remains open.

As at the SAB, the Arenberg Archives at Enghien hold documents pertaining to the management of the family property (such as the account books already mentioned) and archives relating to the family estates (at Enghien but also, among other places, Hal, Hautepenne, Hierges, and Brussels).[22] The Arenberg Archives additionally house personal family documents, such as certificates of baptism and marriage, wills, inventories of deceased persons' chattels, correspondence,[23] travel journals, various papers relating to the Arts, iconography (engravings, paintings, prints, photographs, etc), and … a music library!

The Louvain (Leuven) University Archives likewise contain a large Arenberg Collection, comprising documents given in 1939 to the university by the Duke Engelbert-Marie. This material comes from the family archives housed in the Arenberg château at Heverlee and pertains especially to the estates of the duchy of Aarschot from the sixteenth to the eighteenth centuries, as well as to the Benedictine Celestine monastery adjoining the Heverlee residence.

Historical sketch of the Arenberg family

In the eighteenth century the Dukes of Arenberg were heirs to a long family history – one worth surveying briefly here in order to give the reader an idea of how the Arenberg line came to hold the unrivalled position it did during this period, as much in the political as in the economic, financial, and cultural spheres.[24] Over the centuries the various branches of the family have held different titles, depending on the acquisition or the loss of lordships. The impressive hereditary estates acquired, and the revenue linked to them, rapidly created the basis for growing decision-making powers.

It is difficult to determine when exactly the family name first appeared, but we do know that in 1032 there was a lord of Cologne called Ulrich d'Arenberg, while numerous sources mention in 1166 a certain Henri d'Arenberg, who held the same title and who may be considered as the founding ancestor of the present-day House of Arenberg. Around this time the family built a fortress on a headland located on the river Ahr, a tributary of the Rhine, in the Eifel region, which was given the name Arenberg. On the marriage of Mathilde d'Arenberg to her cousin Count Engelbert II de La Marck in 1299, the county of La Marck (Westphalia) came into the family's possession. When the bride's brother Adolphe de La Marck became Prince-Bishop of Liège in 1313, the Liège Arenberg line became ever stronger. On his marriage to Marie de Looz, Mathilde's third son Evrard I acquired various properties in the principality of Liège and in the Ardennes. The Lord of Arenberg became also Lord of Neufchâteau, of Aigremont, of Warcq, and of Lummen. The House of Arenberg therefore became established in the Low Countries and in France during this period. Evrard III de La Marck-Arenberg was governor of the duchy of Luxembourg and the county of Chiny from 1478 to 1480. His son Evrard IV, Burgrave of Brussels and Mayor of Liège, held the title of Count de La Marck-Arenberg from 1509, whereby the lordship of Arenberg (in the Eifel) became a county. His brother Robert I married Mathilde de

1. Ruins of the château on Arenberg hill, c. 1800. Enghien, Arenberg Archives and Cultural Centre.

2. Marguerite d'Arenberg, wife of Jean de Ligne. University of Leuven, Kunstpatrimonium, Arenbergverzameling (Artistic and Cultural Heritage, Arenberg Collection).

Montfoort, hereditary *Maréchale* of Holland, allowing significant Dutch territories to enter into the family. Enjoying considerable prestige with the Holy Roman Emperor Charles V, Robert de La Marck-Arenberg was in 1517 named a member of the Privy Council of Margaret of Austria, Governor of the Netherlands. Robert de La Marck's grand-daughter Marguerite d'Arenberg (1527-1599) had extensive feudal possessions in the Northern and Southern Netherlands and held immediate sovereignty over Arenberg. Charles V therefore saw to it that the inheritance of a family that had always supported the Emperor did not fall into the wrong hands by arranging, in 1547, the marriage of Marguerite with Jean de Ligne. Widowed in 1568, Countess Marguerite d'Arenberg, who outlived her husband by thirty years, dedicated herself to her vast possessions, and especially to the county of Arenberg. In 1576 the Emperor Maximilian II raised her to the status of Princess-Countess of the Holy Roman Empire, making the county a principality. The eldest son Charles (1550-1616), first Prince-Count of Arenberg, excelled in diplomacy; a member of the Council of State, admiral, captain-general, and chamberlain of the Archduke Albert, he was the highest-ranking nobleman of the Spanish Netherlands. His high status was consolidated by his marriage in 1587 to Anne de Croÿ, Duchess of Aarschot and the heir to extensive property, including Heverlee and its château, after her brother Charles died childless in 1612, he being the last heir of the old princely house of Croÿ-Chimay.

The family's assets in the Spanish Netherlands were spectacularly increased by the union of the Arenberg and Croÿ fortunes, which allowed the family to gain more influence at Court and take precedence over other nobles. From then on, the Prince-Counts of Arenberg also became Dukes of Aarschot, a prosperous duchy located to the north of Louvain. In 1607 Charles d'Arenberg had acquired from the King of France, Henri IV, the town and lordship of Enghien, together with fourteen surrounding villages. The château and park became the principal residence of Charles and Anne, and the gardens would quickly become known in the seventeenth and eighteenth centuries as the handsomest in Northern Europe. Upon his first marriage to Isabelle de Berlaymont, Charles's son Philippe-Charles (1587-1640), who was Prince-Count of Arenberg, Duke of Aarschot, Prince of Porcéan and of Rebecq, Count of Seninghem, and Baron of Zevenbergen, acquired the county of Lalaing for the family. His son Philippe-François (1625-1674) became the first Duke of Arenberg: indeed, on 6 June 1644 Emperor Ferdinand III elevated the whole family to ducal status, the Principality-County becoming an Imperial duchy. Soon the custom was established for the title 'Duke of Arenberg' to be used only for the head of the family, whereas younger members of the family were known as 'Prince and Duke of Arenberg'. When Philippe-François died without an heir, his half-brother Charles-Eugène (1633-1681) inherited the estates. The latter brought with him the titles of Captain-General of the Southern Netherlands Fleet and High Bailiff of Hainaut, one of the most prestigious offices in the land. His eldest son Philippe-Charles (1663-1691), third Duke of Arenberg, died in combat in 1691; his widow Maria Enrichetta Felicita del Carretto, who brought the Italian lands of Grana, Monferrato, Roccavignale, and Savona into the family, was obliged to sell other family possessions in order to settle a series of debts. Fortunately, the financial situation of her son Léopold-Philippe (1690-1754), who became Duke in 1708, improved, thanks to the income from his military and governmental posts, as well as to better management of the hereditary estates.

Under Léopold-Philippe, and then under his son Charles-Marie-Raymond (1721-1778), the

3. Anne de Croÿ. University of Leuven, Kunstpatrimonium,
   Arenbergverzameling (Artistic and Cultural Heritage, Arenberg
   Collection)

Arenbergs' position reached its apogee. They enjoyed the full confidence of the Empire and held top posts in the Austrian Netherlands, which made them important players in political and diplomatic life. As wealthy landowners, their opinions were respected. They invested not only in commerce, becoming shareholders of the Ostend Company, active between 1721 and 1731, but also in industry, creating, notably, a silk factory at Enghien in the 1720s. They also had a strong commitment to the Arts, buying paintings and sculptures, keenly following the musical life of their time, and becoming patrons to numerous artists. Progressively and inevitably, the situation would change in the latter decades of the eighteenth century, affecting the destiny of Duke Louis-Engelbert d'Arenberg – known as the 'blind Duke' after an accident in 1775 which caused him to lose his sight. Having been asked to step down from his post of High Bailiff of Hainaut by Emperor Joseph II in 1787, the blind Duke lost all his titles, privileges, and prerogatives following France's annexation of the Austrian Netherlands

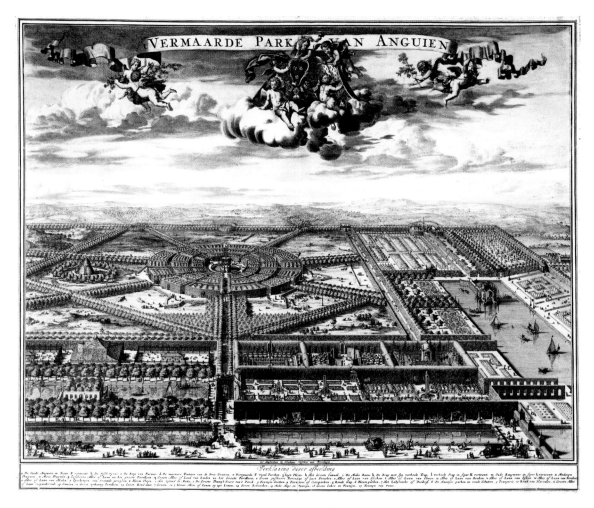

4. R. de Hooghe, *'t Vermaarde park van Anguien*, c. 1685. Private collection.

on 1 October 1795. He became a virtually landless Duke, even losing his German Arenberg duchy in 1801 following the Treaty of Lunéville. In 1803, moving from the status of emigrant and enemy alien (because of his status as an Imperial Prince) to that of French citizen, he was able to recover his Belgian and French properties but was forced to cede his former German possessions to his eldest son, Prosper-Louis (1785-1861), who was seeking to establish a new Arenberg duchy on the right bank of the Rhine. Duke Louis-Engelbert nonetheless remained a substantial landowner, developing mining and timber interests. Over the course of the nineteenth century members of the ducal family accumulated wealth by selling numerous possessions, and continued to acquire various estates and residences by purchase or through marriage, these acquisitions tending essentially to be in Belgium and France.

When the 1914-1918 War ended, the Belgian government decided to dispossess all German persons and companies of their property, rights, and interests. Considered German by the Belgian courts, the Arenberg family saw all of its property confiscated. In 1931 the Belgian State returned to their former owners the possessions that had not been sold. We shall now see how, very fortunately and *malgré tout*, the music collection managed to resist the shocks of history.

5. View of Heverlee with portraits of the Croÿ family. University of Leuven, Kunstpatrimonium, Arenbergverzameling (Artistic and Cultural Heritage, Arenberg Collection).

History of the library and its music collection

Today the music collection forms part of the Arenberg Archives and Cultural Centre at Enghien (hereafter, AACC), but the history of the collection is in reality closely related to the family library rather than to the family archives *per se*. Although the earliest musical works at the AACC stretch back to the end of the seventeenth century, the history of the Arenberg family library needs to be traced as a whole from the start of that century if we are to understand how the music collection as we know it today came into being.

The history of the Arenberg library's gradual expansion may be partially revealed through the inspection of a series of inventories. The earliest inventory in our possession was drawn up on the death of Charles de Ligne, Prince of Arenberg (1550-1616), and consists of a partial list of *livres de son Excellence* kept in the château at Enghien and containing thirty-four titles.[25] No musical work appears in this list, but another inventory relating to the Arenberg château's furniture drawn up in 1617 states that the residence possessed 'Toute sorte de livres tant plain chant qu'en musicque' (All manner of books from plainsong to [other kinds of] music),[26] among which we find several missals and a 'livre pour chanter les offices' (book for singing the Offices).

Charles d'Arenberg had possibly transferred to his own library a number of works inherited from his music-loving brother-in-law Charles de Croÿ, Duke of Aarschot (1560-1612), whose château at

6. Charles d'Arenberg. Enghien, Arenberg Archives and Cultural Centre.

Beaumont contained the largest and richest library of the former Low Countries. Charles de Croÿ had a greater interest in music than most of his contemporaries, having even learnt its rudiments as a student at the University of Louvain from the music publisher Pierre Phalèse II (c. 1545-1629). This is confirmed by Phalèse himself in his dedication to Anne de Croÿ (1564-1635), who was her brother Charles's heir, in his 1623 print of the *Cantiones sacrae* for eight voices by the Tournai-born composer Leonardus Nervius (c. 1585 - *ante* 1652). Indeed, in the dedicatory text Phalèse first of all praises the music by the Capuchin monk Léonard, then boasts of 'having had the honour to have served, and taught the art of playing instruments to, Monseigneur, his Excellency, your brother the late Duke of Arschot [*sic*] and de Croÿ, while he was still a student of Letters at the University of Louvain'.[27]

Following his second marriage in 1605 to his cousin Dorothée (1575-1661), Charles de Croÿ retired from public affairs, and thanks to his immense wealth was able to collect books, paintings,

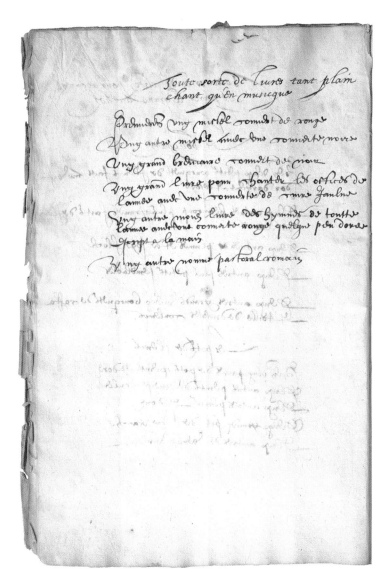

7. Inventory of furniture of the château d'Enghien, 1617. Brussels, State
Archives of Belgium, Arenberg Collection, LA 725.

tapestries, medals, coins, antiques, and works of art. Although his *Mémoires* tell us little about his
activities in the music world,[28] we do at least possess his manuscript lute tablature, which is today
housed at Valenciennes municipal library,[29] and bears the title 'Libvre de Musicque. Libvre tout escrit
de ma propre main appertient à moy, Charles Syre et Duc de Croÿ et d'Arschot' (Book of music.
Book entirely written by my own hand, Charles, Lord and Duke of Croÿ and Arschot). In addition to
containing various poems, this volume, which is largely in his own hand, brings together tablatures of
twenty songs for voice and lute, some of which are settings of poems by Desportes, Ronsard, Marot,
and Pontus de Tyard.

While some of Charles de Croÿ's books were doubtless added to the library of Charles d'Arenberg,
the husband of Anne de Croÿ, most of the contents of the library of the recently deceased Charles de
Croÿ's would come to be dispersed in 1612, since, once an inventory of its contents had been taken,

8. Village of Rocq in the *Albums de Croÿ*, volume 1, plate 45.

this library was sent by the heirs to Brussels to be sold by public auction in August 1614. The catalogue prepared for the occasion (an example of which is kept at the AACC) lists many musical works: one section with around thirty entries is entitled 'Libri Musici manuscripti', while another, 'Libri Musici impressi', lists around fifty works,[30] where we find the names of Orlande de Lassus, Jean de Castro, and Andreas Pevernage side by side with those of the Italians Andrea Gabrieli and Luca Marenzio.

A second inventory relating to the Arenberg library was drawn up in 1639 for books preserved in Brussels belonging to Anne de Croÿ's eldest son Philippe-Charles d'Arenberg (1587-1640), sixth Duke of Aarschot, who took as much pleasure in books as his uncle did. This list, not detailed enough to give us a clear idea of the content, mentions the existence of a box filled with printed music.[31] Thanks to several archival documents, we know that Philippe-Charles had been introduced to music at a very

9. Charles d'Arenberg, Anne de Croÿ and their children by Frans Pourbus the Younger. University of Leuven, Kunstpatrimonium, Arenbergverzameling (Artistic and Cultural Heritage, Arenberg Collection).

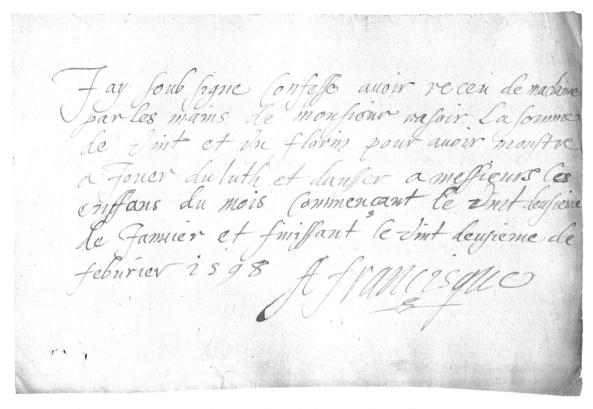

10. Receipt of Antoine Francisque. Brussels, State Archives of Belgium, Arenberg Collection, LA 6746.

young age. A receipt of 1598 that I discovered reveals that the latter, along with his brothers Charles (1588-1613) and Alexandre (1590-1629), took lute and dancing lessons from the lutenist and composer Antoine Francisque (d. Paris 1605), a native of Saint-Quentin.[32] This previously unpublished document sheds light on the life of this renowned lutenist; indeed, it confirms that Francisque was active in the Southern Netherlands before moving to Paris in 1600, the year in which his only work containing lute tablature, *Le Trésor d'Orphée*,[33] was published by Ballard. Alexandre, as well as Antoine (1593-1669), the future Count of Seneghem, and his sister Ernestine (1589-1653), would subsequently continue to receive lute lessons from an unspecified teacher, as evidenced in the account book of Anne de Croÿ for the months of March to December 1602.[34]

Married first to Anne de Melun (1610) and becoming sixth Duke of Aarschot in 1612 and third Prince of Arenberg in 1616, Philippe-Charles de Croÿ married his second wife Isabelle Claire de Berlaymont, Countess of Lalaing, in 1620. The French writer Jean Puget de la Serre (1595-1665), the inventor of many ballets performed at the Brussels Court, portrayed Philippe-Charles as Alidor in his work of 1628, *Le Roman de la cour de Bruxelles*: 'Generous Alidor, valiant as he is brave, is beloved of Ladies, feared by men, and admired by them all. The degree of his merit is connected to that of his birth, having acquired as much glory by his actions as by that which nature bestowed on him in the cradle'.[35]

In 1624 Philippe-Charles d'Arenberg acquired 'quatre violons de Crémone', as revealed in a handwritten expenses memorandum for payments made on his behalf by his adviser Gaspar

11. Charles Mouton by G. Edelinck. Royal Library of Belgium, Prints and
    Drawings Division, S IV 2697.

Dandeleu, which was drawn up in Brussels on 15 September of that year.[36] This purchase list is truly exceptional, because to date it represents the earliest source proving the acquisition of Cremonese violins in Brussels.[37] Indeed, ten years earlier the Governor of the Spanish Netherlands Archduke Albert (1559-1621) allocated 57 *philippes* to the lutenist Laurent van der Linden for the purchase of several stringed instruments in Italy, but this was for three lyres – probably *da braccio* – and two 'biguela bastarda', not violins.[38] The Brussels acquisition of 1624 at the very least bears witness to the renown that instruments from the Cremona school of violin-making enjoyed during this period. In fact, these instruments 'portez d'Italie'[39] (brought over from Italy) were bought at 48 florins apiece – a large sum showing that these were not simple violins but prestigious models of superior quality – actually much like those that appeared a year later in the inventory drawn up after the death of François Richomme, the King's Violinist and Master of Instrumentalists to the Kingdom of France (this last document also makes mention of four Cremonese violins, sold respectively for 90, 60, 36, and 24 livres).[40] In both instances the instruments were intended for use in the higher echelons of society. While the excellence of Cremonese instrument-making came about in the first half of the seventeenth century, the Cremonese model was in fact already known in the North in the second

12. Expenses memorandum of Gaspar Dandeleu. Brussels, State Archives of Belgium, Arenberg Collection, MG 3558.

13. Violin by H. Amati, 1611. Brussels, Musical
Instruments Museum, M 4160.

half of the sixteenth century. There is evidence that from the 1570s onwards Cremonese violins were well-known to Parisian violin-makers and that they were making copies of them. It also seems that a distinction was made between instruments for common usage crafted by local violin-makers and prestigious models bought directly from Italy. To date it has not been possible to trace any instrument that belonged to the Arenberg family during this period.

The list of purchases from 1624 also mentions the repair of a 'coffre des violes et une viole rompue': that is, both a chest of viols and a broken viol. Payment to the organ-builder Matthijs Langhedul (active from 1592 to 1636) is also mentioned, the sum amounting to a little over 4 florins for 'repair[ing] the organs on several occasions'.[41] A member of a family of organ-builders from Ypres, Langhedul was one of the most famous organ-builders of the time; he had been organ-tuner and organ-builder at the royal chapel in Madrid from 1592 to 1599 before arriving in Paris, where he stayed until 1605, contributing towards the creation of the classical French organ. By 1611 Langhedul was back in Brussels, employed once more at court, and in 1618, under the auspices of the English organist and composer John Bull, he embarked on the construction of a new organ for Antwerp Cathedral.

Finally, the memorandum specifies the purchase of music books. First of all, there are 'livres de Mortaro a 12'. What this mention probably refers to is the 1595 Venetian print of the *Missa, motecta,*

14. H. Amati by J. Lecurieux. Royal Library of Belgium,
Prints and Drawings Division, S III 25163.

cantica B. Mariae Vir. qui partim octonis, partimq. duodenis vocibus modulantur, liber secundus,[42] 'a 12' denoting the number of voices.[43] The Italian composer Antonio Mortaro, who was appointed to the post of organist at the Franciscan monastery of Milan in 1598, composed both sacred and secular works that were very popular and widely circulated for over forty years in a number of anthologies.[44] The Duke also paid 12 florins for 'les livres de musicqz de Praetorius' supplied by 'Phalesius selon son billet', the latter being the Antwerp-based publisher mentioned earlier, Pierre Phalèse II, who during this period played a major part in the distribution of Italian music in the Southern Netherlands.[45] The music acquired in 1624 may therefore have been contained in the box of printed music mentioned in the 1639 inventory. But what is certain is that it disappeared at some point from the family library, as is the case for all the music acquired before the end of the seventeenth century.

The library built up during the second half of the seventeenth century at the palace in Brussels appears considerable, for when Philippe-Charles, third Duke of Arenberg (1663-1691), died, his widow Maria Enrichetta Felicita del Carretto (1671-1744) sold part of it in order to settle debts.[46] Later on, when circumstances improved, the Dowager Duchess and subsequently her son Léopold-Philippe (1690-1754), who became fourth Duke of Arenberg in 1708, acquired vast numbers of books, especially from Brussels-based dealers.

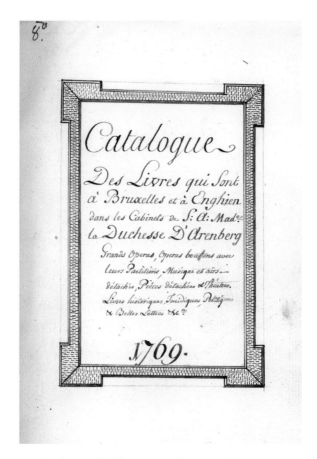

15. Catalogue of books, 1769. Enghien, Arenberg
Archives and Cultural Centre, 29/12.

Coming to the following generation, Charles-Marie-Raymond d'Arenberg (1721-1778), who became the fifth Duke of Arenberg in 1754, resolved to create a library not only with bibliophilic appeal but also encompassing a broad field of knowledge. Many works were bound in vellum, and a gilt supralibros with the Duke's coat of arms was applied to the covers. Many musical works in the collection still retain these insignia today. When the Royal Library in Brussels opened its doors to the public for the first time in June 1772, the Duke donated a series of works to the institution, as well as two enormous globes, the work of the Venetian cartographer Vincenzo Maria Coronelli.[47]

In the decade 1760-1770 several inventories from the family library in Brussels explicitly mention the existence of musical works: the *Catalogue des livres qui sont à la Bibliothèque de S.A.S.me Monseigneur le Duc D'Arenberg* (compiled in Brussels in 1768);[48] the *Catalogue des livres qui sont à Bruxelles et à Enghien dans les cabinets de S.A. Mad.e la Duchesse d'Arenberg. Grands Operas. Operas bouffons avec leurs Partitions, Musique et airs détachés, Piéces détachées & Théatres, Livres historiques, Juridiques, Politiques & Belles Lettres &a.* (compiled in Brussels in 1769);[49] the *Catalogue des livres de la Bibliothèque de S.A.S.M. le duc d'Arenberg Bruxelles 1777;*[50] and the *Catalogue des livres de la Bibliothèque de S.A.S. Monseigneur le Duc d'Arenberg à Bruxelles*, produced in two volumes in 1778.[51]

The last two catalogues were compiled by the bibliographer Jean-Noël Paquot (1722-1803) from Florennes, who was in the service of the Duke of Arenberg from 1772, having previously held the post of Librarian at the University of Louvain.[52] Paquot was known as the author of *Mémoires pour servir à l'histoire littéraire des dix-sept Provinces des Pays-Bas, du pays de Liège et de quelques contrées voisines*.[53] His work for the family library was extensive. Having created an index card with a bibliographical description for each work, he classified each card by category, and then drew up the inventory in two volumes, completing it in 1778.[54]

While in the Duchess of Arenberg's library catalogue of 1769[55] the categories 'French Grand Opera scores', 'Opéra bouffon scores', and 'Various music and detached airs' are specified, in the other library catalogues, under the rubric of 'music', only theoretical works on music are listed. Scores and other musical items therefore have to be sought elsewhere, variously under the subject headings 'Liturgy', 'Theology', 'Italian poets', 'modern French poets', 'Greek, Latin, and Italian theatre', 'Prose comedies, dramas', and 'Manuscripts'. Where the latter are concerned, the classification is not systematic, and musical manuscripts are listed also under other headings. As regards works relating to instrument-making, these are filed under the heading 'Arts, Crafts, and Manufacture'.

These various catalogues illustrate the character of the library at a given moment and allow us to estimate the total stock at over 12000 items.[56] By examining them, we are also able to establish that a number of musical sources present in the music collection as it is preserved today in Enghien formed, from the middle of the eighteenth century onwards, part of the vast family library in Brussels. This was housed in the Grand Hôtel d'Egmont, which became the Hôtel d'Arenberg, in the Sablon district of that city. Other musical works in the AACC Collection, though absent from the above-mentioned lists, must in all likelihood have already belonged to it, since they display characteristics linking them by date to certain works recorded in the catalogues.

Louis-Engelbert (1750-1820), who became Duke in 1778, had an even keener interest in books than either his father or grandfather, and this interest only increased after the accident in 1775 that caused him to go blind: indeed, prevented by his handicap from pursuing many of the activities associated with his position, he invested large sums of money in the acquisition of books and newspapers of all kinds, which were read to him by a person he called 'his eye'. In other words, he procured works in order for them to be read and consulted, and not simply in order to possess them for the sake of mere ownership. The account books and receipts are testimony to the colossal number of books bought from dealers in Brussels and abroad, or at auction. We discern here a good deal of interest in the sciences, Freemasonry, French literature, and musical scores. Management of the family library was entrusted to the Abbé Nepper in 1784, and in 1789 François Lenssens, a former Jesuit, succeeded him.[57]

The French Revolution put a halt to the library's growth, some books being dispatched to Vienna in 1794, along with a series of archival documents. Nevertheless, a large part of the collection remained in Brussels, and when the Duke moved back to the capital in 1804, he brought the library back to life, employing Voncken from 1807 to take charge of its administration.[58]

In the early part of the nineteenth century the majority of the musical works appear to have been kept in Brussels. A number of volumes listed in the Duchess of Arenberg's library catalogue of 1769 appear in the catalogue drafted in 1818 at the Hôtel de la Porte de Hal, which had been the Duchess's residence since 1778,[59] following the death of her husband, Duke Charles-Marie-Raymond.[60]

16. The librarian Charles de Brou photographed by
E. Fierlants.

Although not specifying any locality, two later, undated inventories from the music library deserve a mention here. The first[61] records works from Porte de Hal as well as many others, classifying them under the subject headings 'Orchestral scores', 'Scores with piano accompaniment', 'Oratorio, cantatas', 'Scholastic works', 'Sacred music', 'Various vocal works', 'Instrumental music, Concert pieces', and 'Piano'. Over forty pages in length, the second catalogue is written in the hand of Prince Paul d'Arenberg (1788-1844),[62] son of the blind Duke, who took as keen an interest in music as his father had done. His catalogue does not encompass the whole music collection as it exists today at the AACC, but it does describe very precisely a large number of works acquired around the end of the eighteenth century and during the period 1810-1820.[63] Over 160 publications detailed in Paul d'Arenberg's catalogue are still present in the music collection today.

On his father's death in 1820, Duke Prosper-Louis d'Arenberg (1785-1861) decided to rethink the role of the family library, which by now numbered over 15000 volumes.[64] In 1822 renovations were carried out with the aim of creating a new library on the ground floor at the heart of the Brussels palace, facing the main entrance; this would be capable of housing – in thirty glass-fronted cabinets – some 50000 volumes.[65] The Duke called upon the Dijon artist Sophie Frémiet (1797-1867), wife of the sculptor François Rude and a pupil of David, to create designs for the glass doors of the book cabinets, in the form of thirty female allegorical figures, each representing the nature of the books stored in it. Among these figures, one portrayed Euterpe, Muse of Music in Greek mythology, a detail allowing us to affirm that at least a part of the library's musical works was indeed kept in the Brussels library at this time.[66] The *Catalogue de la Bibliothèque du château d'Heverlé* (Château of Heverlee Library Catalogue), compiled mid-way through the nineteenth century, includes no references to music. As for Enghien, we know that a botanical library existed there, as evidenced by the *Catalogue de la bibliothèque des serres de S.A. Mons.gr le Duc d'Arenberg à Enghien* (Catalogue of the Glasshouse Library of HSH Monseigneur the Duke of Arenberg at Enghien) compiled at the same time as the Heverlee catalogue.[67]

Like his great-grandfather, his grandfather, and his father, Prosper-Louis was an art collector. His holdings grew in 1833 on the death of his uncle Prince Auguste of Arenberg, Count de La Marck (1753-1833), who had accumulated an exceptional collection. The gallery of paintings, housed in a newly constructed left wing looking on to the main courtyard of the Brussels palace, boasted canvases by Frans Hals, Rembrandt, Van Dyck, Jordaens, and even Rubens, while on the ground floor of the same main building visitors could enjoy the many sculptures and other works of art on display.[68] Some other works from the late Prince Auguste d'Arenberg's library, housed in the rue Ducale in Brussels, opposite the park, were likewise added to the Duke's library.

With Duke Prosper-Louis d'Arenberg, bibliophilic interest in old books really became ingrained in the family; this tendency was confirmed very clearly when administration of the library and the art collection was entrusted to the Brussels-based painter and writer Charles de Brou (1811-1877).[69] On behalf of the family, de Brou set about acquiring thousands of engravings, coins, and medals, as well as manuscripts, incunabula, and various other works from well-known dealers in Paris, London, and Vienna.

This love of books did not cease after Duke Prosper-Louis's death in 1861. Assisted until 1871 by Charles de Brou,[70] his son Engelbert-Auguste (1824-1875) continued to add to the collection, acquiring ancient manuscripts and valuable prints – with an emphasis on works related to Belgian history. Purchases were made of incunabula, post-incunabula, Flemish and Dutch illuminated Books of Hours, psalters, breviaries, engravings, and also medals, which were acquired either from private individuals or from dealers both in Belgium and abroad.[71] These acquisitions were never in reality concerned with works that would come to stock the music collection as we see it today, since collectors of the second half of the nineteenth century were not on the whole very interested in eighteenth- or early nineteenth-century scores. The death of Duke Engelbert-Auguste in 1875 put an end to this frenetic acquisition of prestigious works. The collection at that time included over 1800 medals and over 7000 engravings, and the *Collection spéciale d'incunables et de livres rares et précieux* contained over 1300 works. As for the general library, it comprised over 30000 volumes!

In 1896 Duke Engelbert-Marie (1872-1949), son of Engelbert-Auguste, had an inventory taken of his collections and his library – possessions that had hardly been augmented since his father's death. The great library now contained forty-five book cabinets, while eight further cabinets in an adjoining room housed journals and almanacs, sales catalogues, and also printed musical scores.[72] During this period both the Heverlee and the Enghien libraries were absorbed into the library at the Brussels palace. Several sales held in 1901 and 1902 caused a fair proportion of this exceptional patrimony to be broken up; yet the music collection remained intact, for at that time it aroused no interest whatsoever.

Coincident with this dispersal of material, the book collections of the family actually grew in 1903, thanks to the purchase of Schloss Nordkirchen in Westphalia, a residence with an extensive library of over 7000 volumes, among them a series of German and Italian incunabula. All its books display an ex-libris displaying the Nordkirchen coat of arms. No volume in the music collection as it exists today at Enghien carries this book-plate. Although the majority of the books at Nordkirchen remained where they were, a few volumes, as well as some Dürer engravings, were added to the shelves of the great library in Brussels.

Around 1903 the bookcases bearing Sophie Frémiet's designs were dismantled, probably as a space-saving measure, and were re-installed at the Arenbergs' château at Heverlee. They were then filled with what had until then constituted the Brussels *Collection spéciale*. During these years the family became increasingly open to the idea of allowing researchers access to the archives and the library at their palace in Brussels. In 1910 the first international congress of librarians and archivists actually organized a visit to the palace archives and library. In 1912 the Duke's archivist, Édouard Laloire, was given the additional responsibility of looking after the library. But the First World War brought all projects to a juddering halt. During the first few months of the war the Heverlee library's contents were boxed up and stored safely away. The same happened to a number of works from the Brussels library. In November 1918 the palace in Brussels was sold to the City of Brussels,[73] but the library's contents, as was the case for the rest of the Arenberg family possessions, were, on account of the family's origin, considered to be German property and were therefore placed under sequestration by a law of 17 November 1921.[74] In 1928 some items from the former library were removed by Victor Tourneur (1878-1967), a civil servant attached to the Royal Library of Belgium. These included some 800 printed works, seven manuscripts, and also several sets of engravings and lithographs. The remaining library collection, some 20000 volumes, was sold on 3 and 4 January 1929 for the benefit of the Ministry of Finance at the Salle Mens in Brussels.[75]

In the summer of 1939 Duke Engelbert-Marie informed the Rector of the Catholic University of Louvain of his intention to offer to that university 'the cream of the old library of Arenberg': that is, a collection of boxes containing more than 1500 incunabula and other precious works from the former *Collection spéciale* and the cabinets of the great library. The family had excellent relations with the university, having made a gift of the Heverlee château to the institution. The start of the Second World War caused negotiations to be suspended – and fortunately so, since the library could all have gone up in smoke in the second fire at the Louvain University library in May 1940! In 1949 the Duke donated a collection of paintings to the University of Louvain, mainly family portraits which previously adorned the Heverlee residence and the palace in Brussels; remaining parts of this collection can still be seen today in the drawing rooms at Heverlee.[76]

From 1951 onwards the remainder of the Arenberg family library was disposed of by Duke Engelbert-Charles (1899-1974), and the library at Schloss Nordkirchen was sold almost in its entirety to the Brussels antique dealer Paul van der Perre. The manuscripts and old prints from the great library in Brussels were also sold, and today are to be found on the shelves of various major libraries, including the Library of Congress in Washington, the Bibliothèque Nationale de France, and the Royal Library of Belgium. A few works from the Nordkirchen collection were donated by Duke Engelbert-Charles to the University of Louvain. Finally, a part of the book collection still in the family's possession, plus the music collection, joined the Arenberg Archives at Enghien.

It is therefore something of a miracle that the music collection that I discovered at Enghien at the heart of a library of such exceptional richness has managed to survive the passage of time, escaping damage or dispersal!

Let us now look more closely at how and why the Dukes Léopold-Philippe, Charles-Marie-Raymond, and Louis-Engelbert d'Arenberg sought to contribute, each in their turn, to the enrichment of the family's music library throughout the eighteenth century.

17. Léopold-Philippe d'Arenberg. University of Leuven, Kunstpatrimonium, Arenbergverzameling (Artistic and Cultural Heritage, Arenberg Collection).

CHAPTER I

LÉOPOLD-PHILIPPE, FOURTH DUKE OF ARENBERG
(1708-1754)

This study begins by looking at the very earliest musical scores held by the AACC Collection, which date to around 1700, tracing the beginnings of this music collection as well as the life and accomplishments of Duke Léopold-Philippe d'Arenberg – a personality who would make his mark for almost half a century, not least in the musical circles of his time.

A Prince's childhood and French operatic repertoire

Léopold-Philippe-Charles-Joseph d'Arenberg, Duke of Aarschot and Croÿ, Prince of Porcéan and Rebecq, was christened at the collegiate church of Saints-Michel-et-Gudule in Brussels on 14 October 1690.[77] The son of Philippe-Charles (1663-1691), third Duke of Arenberg from 1681,[78] and Maria Enrichetta Felicita del Carretto (1671-1744), Marchioness of Savona and Grana,[79] Léopold-Philippe had an elder sister, Marie-Anne, who had been baptized in the same church on 30 August 1689.[80]

Léopold-Philippe had not reached his first birthday when his father Philippe-Charles died – on 25 August 1691, aged just 28 – near Petrovaradin, Serbia, following injuries sustained during the Battle of Salankemen against the Turks. Little is known of Philippe-Charles's musical tastes apart from the fact that, as was the norm for those of his rank, he had taken dancing lessons from an early age. This dancing master had been Adam-Pierre de La Grené (1625-1702) in Brussels, as La Grené himself tells us in his manuscript *Livre de raison*.[81]

Léopold-Philippe and his sister Marie-Anne were thus left with their mother, a young woman of twenty, who was now quite alone, since both her parents had died several years earlier.[82] In order to settle certain debts, the young widow – obliged to assume management of the family affairs until her son came of age in 1708 – had to sell a number of her possessions, among them a section of the family library.[83] Two musical works, printed in the second half of the seventeenth century and probably belonging to the old library, seem nonetheless to have remained in the family, because they appear later on in the catalogues of 1768 and 1777. Although these two volumes no longer form part of the music collection today, they deserve a mention here.[84] The earliest work, published in Halle in 1662, is the Swabian Andreas Hirsch's translation into German of extracts from the *Musurgia universalis, sive ars magna consoni et dissoni*[85] by the German scientist Athanasius Kircher (1601-1680), the original Latin

18. Philippe-Charles d'Arenberg. Enghien, Arenberg Archives and Cultural Centre.

19. Maria Enrichetta Felicita del Carretto. University of Leuven, Kunstpatrimonium, Arenbergverzameling (Artistic and Cultural Heritage, Arenberg Collection).

edition of which had been published in two volumes in Rome in 1650.[86] In this *magnum opus*, which is one of the central treatises on music of the seventeenth century, notable theoretical topics examined by Kirchner include certain acoustic phenomena and the invention of a machine for music composition.

The other work that is today lost but is cited in the catalogues is the 1676 Paris print of the *Paraphrase des pseaumes de David par Godeau* in the version 'en vers francais et en musique' adapted by the French composer Thomas Gobert (d. 1672).[87] This arrangement of the *Paraphrase* by the poet Antoine Godeau (1605-1672), first published in 1659 and continually reprinted up to 1686, contains pieces for two voices intended for 'ceux qui connaissent seulement un peu de musique' (those who know only a little music).[88]

Apart from these two publications, no trace exists of any work dating from before the 1680s, either in the catalogues or in the current music collection. It was only from the end of the 1690s that a new library would truly start to be built up, thanks to successive purchases made by the Duchess and afterwards by her son, and also via donations.

The earliest dated music print still preserved today at the AACC bears the year 1682. This is a copy in score of *Persée*, the 'tragédie en musique' by Jean-Baptiste Lully (1632-1687), published by Christophe Ballard in Paris.[89] Also present is a 1684 print of Lully's 'tragédie en musique' *Amadis de Grèce*, which belonged to a certain Mademoiselle Choiseau, an actress whose first name is unknown but who is cited as being employed in Brussels at the Théâtre de la Monnaie in 1705.[90] The collection also contains other prints that emerged from Christophe Ballard's presses prior to 1700: a score of the masterpiece *Thétis et Pelée* (1689) by Pascal Collasse (1649-1709);[91] *Les Amours de Momus* (1695)[92] by the

20. Léopold-Philippe d'Arenberg as a young boy. Private collection.

21. J.-B. Lully, *Persée*, Paris, Ballard, 1682, title page. Enghien, Arenberg Archives and Cultural Centre, I 1035.

Parisian Henry Desmarest (1661-1741); *Ariane et Bacchus* (1696)[93], a 'tragédie en musique' by the viol-player Marin Marais (1656-1728); and two scores by the composer and cleric André Campra (1660-1744): the *divertissement* entitled *Vénus, feste galante* (1698)[94] and the 'opéra-ballet' *L'Europe galante* (1699).[95] Finally, we have the first volume of the *Recueil des meilleurs airs italiens* published by Ballard in 1699,[96] which includes several Italian arias inserted into French operatic works as well as a movement from the cantata *Sconsigliato consiglio* for soprano and basso continuo by Giovanni Bononcini (1670-1747).[97]

Many volumes copied during these years offer in manuscript form an identical repertoire, devoted solely to scores by Lully. Choiseau's name also reappears on manuscript copies of two more 'tragédies en musique' not yet mentioned: *Alceste*[98] and *Cadmus et Hermione*.[99] Two further manuscripts are marked on the front cover with a gilt supralibros bearing the name 'Belligny'. One of these is *Amadis de Grèce*,[100] already mentioned; the other, *Atys*.[101] Additionally, there are three contemporary manuscript scores (without any indication of ownership) of the 'tragédies en musique' *Thésée*[102] and *Bellérophon*,[103] as well as of the ballet *Le Temple de la Paix*.[104]

We cannot be sure how or when the scores mentioned above, whether in printed or manuscript form, were added to the family's music library. Some of them may have been among the volumes that survived the sale of the old library by the paterfamilias Philippe-Charles. These scores nevertheless took their place in the Duchess's library during the last years of the seventeenth century when these

22. J.-B. Lully, *Thésée*. Enghien, Arenberg Archives and Cultural Centre, Ms 8.

23. Maximilian II Emanuel of Bavaria by J. Vivien. Royal Library
of Belgium, Prints and Drawings Division, S II 34598.

operas were being performed in Brussels at the Académie de Musique on the Quai au Foin, a theatre predating La Monnaie, which opened in 1700. Indeed, the newspaper *Relations véritables* reveals that the Brussels premières of *Amadis*, *Bellérophon*, and *Thésée* were given at the Quai au Foin respectively in January 1695,[105] November 1696,[106] and December 1697.[107]

At the time when these operas were performed in Brussels, Léopold-Philippe d'Arenberg was still only a boy, but his mother Maria Enrichetta Felicita del Carretto was among the 'high society' ladies close to the Governor of the Spanish Netherlands, Maximilian II Emanuel of Bavaria (1662-1726). The Duchess was indeed in attendance on 26 March 1692 when the sovereign (a man with a keen interest in music) made his official entry into Brussels. A pupil of the Saxon organist and composer Johann Caspar Kerll (1627-1693), Maximilian Emanuel would soon become acquainted with such musicians as Marc-Antoine Charpentier, Marin Marais, and Tomaso Albinoni, and he actively contributed to the development of a richer musical life in the regions he governed.[108] Maria Enrichetta Felicita del Carretto was all the closer to the political élite in being herself the daughter of Ottone Enrico del Carretto, governor of these same regions from 1682 until his death in 1685.[109] She made the acquaintance of the Italian organist and composer Pietro Torri (c. 1650-1737), who was initially Master of the Chamber Music at the Brussels court of Maximilian Emanuel of Bavaria, but afterwards (from 1695) kapellmeister – a post that he would hold until his departure for Munich in March 1701, and which he would regain

24. P. Torri, 'Quante pompe ha la bellezza'. Enghien, Arenberg Archives and Cultural Centre, Ms 3/7.

upon his return to Brussels in 1705 and 1706. Torri already had a long career behind him, having been organist and kapellmeister in Bayreuth from 1684 onwards at the court of Christian Ernst (1644-1712), Margrave of Brandenburg-Bayreuth, before arriving in 1689 at the court of Bavaria in Munich, where he was appointed organist of Maximilian Emanuel of Bavaria.[110] A composer of around twenty operas, ten or so oratorios, twenty Masses, and motets, plus a few sonatas, this musician from Peschiera, a small town on Lake Garda, also tried his hand at small-scale secular vocal works, leaving in manuscript form around thirty or so *duetti da camera* and around thirty cantatas.

Although we cannot be sure in which precise year this happened, Pietro Torri gave the Duchess of Arenberg a bound volume (classmark Ms 3 in the AACC Music Collection) of fifty-two gilt-edged, numbered folios containing nineteen of his compositions. No indication is given about the genre of these compositions, but they appear at first sight to be free-standing Italian arias without recitatives. They are preceded by a dedication in French signed by the composer:

> Madame.
>
> Vous m'avez fait la grace d'ecouter quelqu'uns de mes ouvrages avec plaisir, un goust aussi seur, et un discernement aussi juste que le vostre est asseurement l'applaudissement le plus glorieux que je leurs puisse procurer … Permettez moy donc, Madame, d'avoir l'honneur de vous les offrir pour servir de temoignage eternel a la reconnoissance infinie et aux respects profonds avec lesquels j'ay l'honneur d'estre Madame. Vostre tres humble. et tres hobeissant serviteur P. Torri.

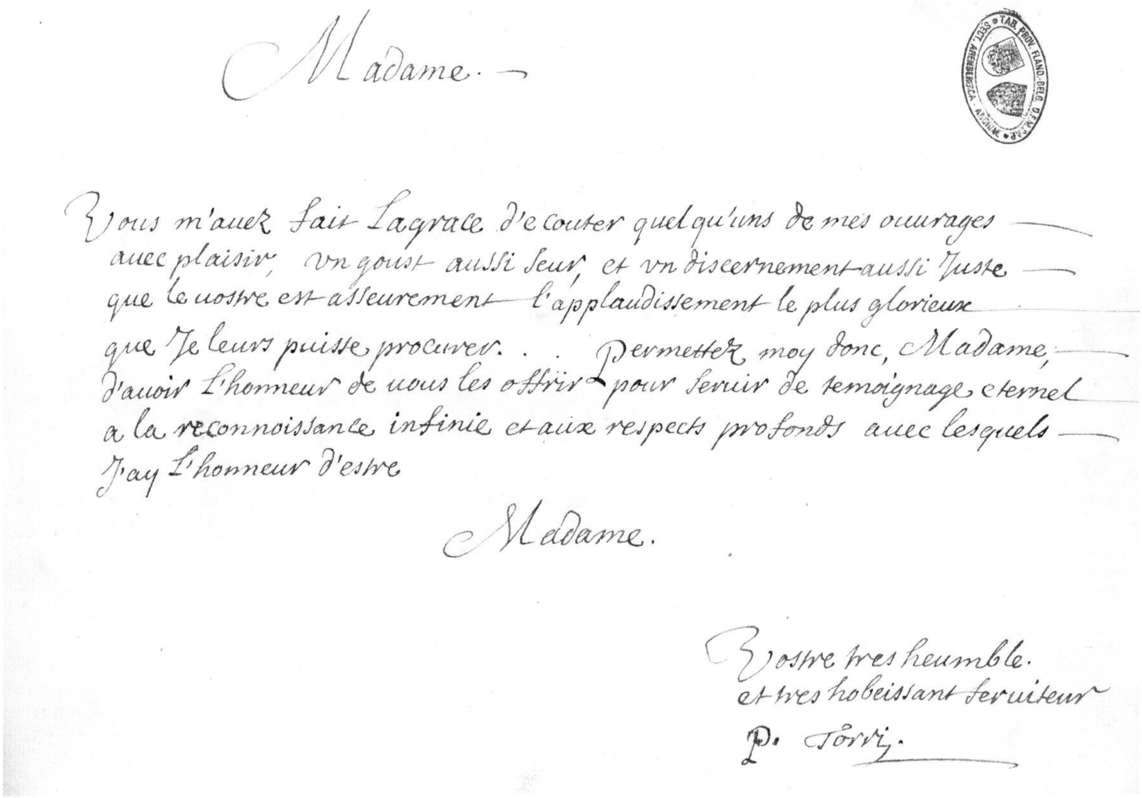

[handwritten letter in French]

25. P. Torri's dedication to the Duchess of Arenberg. Enghien, Arenberg Archives and Cultural Centre, Ms 3.

[Madam,

You have honoured me by listening to some of my works with pleasure [.] A taste as assured and a discernment as sound as yours is surely the greatest approval that I could obtain for them … Allow me, then, Madam, the honour of offering these works to you as an everlasting testimony to the infinite gratitude and deep respect with which I have the honour of being, Madame, Your very humble, and very obedient servant P. Torri.]

These lines suggest that the dedicatee had had the opportunity of hearing some of the pieces in the volume. We do not know whether this performance took place at the court of the governor or in private; but it seems that, in contrast with other musicians employed at the Brussels court, Torri was not employed by the Arenberg family.[111] The watermark discernible on the pages of the collection suggests that the volume was indeed compiled while Torri was staying in the Spanish Netherlands, since it appears on a number of varieties of Dutch paper used in these regions.

The volume is made up of seven pieces written for soprano or bass, oboe or flute, and basso continuo, plus twelve other pieces for soprano and basso continuo; the latter is never figured. A similarity can be observed between the handwriting of the dedication opening the manuscript and that of the text underlaid to the musical notes, as well as in the great homogeneity existing between the textual and musical scripts. Lettering of this kind is found elsewhere on most of the manuscripts considered to be in Torri's hand that are held by the Bavarian State Library in Munich – sources that nevertheless have neither signature, nor date, nor dedication.[112]

Whatever the case, the volume Ms 3 remains exceptional in containing several pieces not otherwise recorded today in any other source. This does not apply to the first seven compositions, since these appear again in a manuscript collection preserved in the Bavarian State Library under the title *Trastulli*. This collection of musical *divertissements*[113] in four volumes brings together sixty arias and cantatas. Having long been attributed to Agostino Steffani (1654-1728), director of chamber music at Maximilian Emanuel of Bavaria's court in Munich from 1681 to 1688, it is considered today to be an autograph of Torri, even though the manuscript does not mention him by name.[114] The *Trastulli* have the instruction 'da capo' at the end of each piece, whereas in the Arenberg volume the section to be repeated is written out in full.

The first four pieces, scored for soprano, melody instrument, and basso continuo, appear in the second and third volumes of the *Trastulli*, no details being given there of the melody instrument to be employed. These pieces are: 'Il sospiro è una parola' (*Trastulli* III/2) – with 'hautbois' (oboe), the Arenberg volume specifies; 'Spero sì dagli aspri marmi' (*Trastulli* II/9); 'Dì, pastorella, oh quanto è bella' (*Trastulli* II/8); and, 'Luci serene, se per voi moro' (*Trastulli* II/7).

As for the fifth, sixth, and seventh pieces, these can all be found in the first volume of the *Trastulli*, each with a recitative absent from the Belgian source. Thus 'Le rose odorose' (Ms 3/5) with 'flauto' (meaning the *flûte douce*, or recorder) is in fact the aria that follows the recitative 'Dalle spine da i Numi' (*Trastulli* I/2). 'Per te sola sorge l'alba' (Ms 3/6) is the aria preceded by the recitative 'Bella diva' (*Trastulli* I/9); here, the Munich manuscript specifies that the melody instrument should be the viola da gamba or else the 'fluste allemand': that is, the transverse flute. As for 'Quante pompe ha la bellezza' (Ms 3/7), this is the aria placed after the recitative 'Seguono i tuoi vestigi' (*Trastulli* I/10). The Arenberg manuscript stipulates that this piece – the only composition by Pietro Torri assigned to a solo bass voice – should be accompanied by a transverse flute.

The twelve following pieces that complete Ms 3 are all written for soprano and basso continuo without melody instrument accompaniment. In order, they are: 'Vuò morir, o cieco arciero', 'Tutti i tuoi dardi, Amore', 'Occhi videnti sogli d'amor', 'Il bacio che s'incontra con l'avido sospir', 'Larve, sogni e ombre nere', 'Finché liete raddop[p]iar le colombe amorosette', 'Ai prieghi nulla nieghi', 'Non più vezzi ma diletti', 'Intendere non so com'essere', 'Di viole, di gigli e di rose', 'Vezzose pupille', and 'Si resisterà'. To date, these compositions have not been found in any source other than the Arenberg volume – apart, that is, from the penultimate piece, 'Vezzose pupille', which reappears in two manuscript collections preserved in the British Library, albeit not under Torri's name but instead under that of the Italian composer, singer, and theorist Pier Francesco Tosi (1654-1732), the misattribution probably arising from orthographic confusion.[115] While some pieces from the Ms 3 collection appear in fact to be movements from cantatas, in the absence of concordances it is difficult to know whether the same can be said of the unpublished 'arias'. Whatever the case, they exhibit, like those in the *Trastulli*, a strong stylistic affinity with the Italian masters of the cantata Alessandro Scarlatti (1660-1725) and Giovanni Bononcini, both of whom composed literally hundreds of such works. The pieces also evidence the infiltration of this Italian vocal genre into the Brussels musical world of the late seventeenth century.[116]

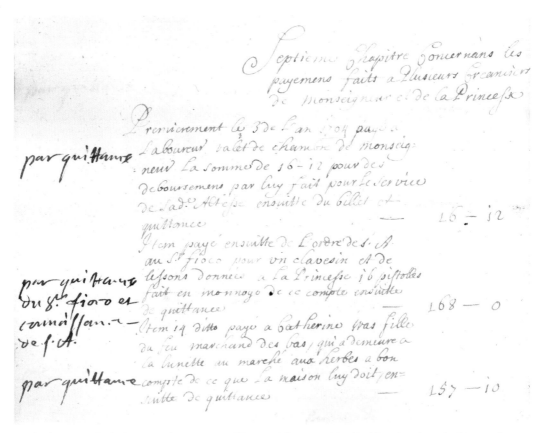

26. Reference to P. A. Fiocco in the accounts of Domis, 3 January 1704. Enghien, Arenberg Archives and Cultural Centre, 64/28/II.

Another Italian musician who was very influential in Brussels, the Venetian Pietro Antonio Fiocco (1654-1714), met the Duchess of Arenberg towards the end of the seventeenth century. Having arrived in the metropolis in 1682, he became in 1687 musical director at the ducal chapel of the church of Notre-Dame du Sablon.[117] Fiocco fathered many children, all of whom were born in Brussels; these included several sons who would become musicians, among them Jean-Joseph and Joseph-Hector Fiocco. The AACC Collection contains a manuscript miscellany that belonged (as instanced in an inked annotation on the first folio) to 'Don Andrez de Curse, secretaire de Sa Majesté imperial et Catolique de la par de Flandre' (secretary to his Imperial and Catholic Majesty of Flanders).[118] This collection contains: an instrumental trio for two treble parts and a bass part by a composer described in the source as 'Signore Louigy Alfogor', but who is otherwise unrecorded; airs by French composers including Jean-Baptiste Matho (1663-1746); the Italian duet 'Del mio cor la cara pena' ('Se crudel che m'incatena') by a composer who remains anonymous; and a sacred work identifiable from the single part for alto plus basso continuo as the motet for alto, two violins, and bass in D minor *Ad caelicas* by Pietro Antonio Fiocco, the composer of around thirty motets, four Masses, the pastorale *Le Retour du printemps*, and two sonatas.[119]

In 1694 the Italian bankers Francesco Gasparini and Gio Paolo Bombarda, in association with Fiocco, decided to hire the Quai au Foin opera house in Brussels (where no performances had taken place since 1689), thereby becoming its new directors. They were assisted in their enterprise by

Governor Maximilian Emanuel, a strong supporter of musical performances, and they staged Lully's operas mentioned above. But Fiocco also composed some new prologues for these works, the original prologues having been in honour of the King of France, Louis XIV, who in August 1695 had laid siege to Brussels. Indeed, the Hôtel d'Arenberg, which stood in the rue des Peaux (the present-day rue d'Arenberg), was among the buildings destroyed during the French assault.[120]

When, in 1696, Torri left Brussels for some time to stage his opera *Briseide* in Hanover, Fiocco took up a deputizing post as the Governor's 'lieutenant de la chapelle'.[121] He would retain this post after the definitive departure of Maximilian Emanuel from Brussels in May 1706, and would remain attached to it until his death.[122] The Arenberg family account records inform us that from 1703, the year when Pietro Antonio Fiocco became musical director at court, and at Notre-Dame du Sablon in Brussels, he was giving private harpsichord lessons to the fourteen-year-old Princess Marie-Anne, elder sister of the future Duke Léopold-Philippe d'Arenberg. Indeed, on 3 January 1704, the sum of 16 pistoles (equivalent to 168 florins) was paid to the musician for a series of lessons given during the preceding weeks, and also for a 'clavesin' (harpsichord) delivered to the family.[123] We do not know whether the future Duke Léopold-Philippe also had lessons with the Venetian; the preserved archival documents are mute on this subject. At this time, Fiocco was also active as a harpsichord merchant,[124] and the instrument that he supplied to the family perhaps came from the Brussels-based workshop of the harpsichord-maker Jérôme Mahieu (d. Brussels 1737), or may have been selected from a stock of older instruments, such as those built by the Antwerp makers Joannes (1578-1642) and Andreas Ruckers (1579-1645), which were very sought-after in the eighteenth century.[125]

27. A. Ruckers, harpsichord. Brussels, Musical Instruments Museum, M 2935.

28. J.-B. Lully by N. Mignard. Chantilly, Musée Condé.

The 1695 edition by Ballard of *Les Amours de Momus* by Henry Desmarest was perhaps added to the shelves of the Arenberg family library in 1699, when the French composer, who had been 'ordinaire de la musique du Roy' of France since 1680, arrived in Brussels from France. Following the death of his wife in 1696 Desmarest wished to marry his new companion Marie-Marguerite de Saint-Gobert without her parents' consent – a capital crime. He began his exile in Brussels, where he was welcomed by Governor Maximilian Emanuel of Bavaria, who commissioned some sacred music from him.[126] In 1701 Desmarest came to the Spanish court of King Philip V with the assistance of his friend, the Breton composer and singer Jean-Baptiste Matho,[127] whom he had known at the Chapelle royale as a singer (*chantre*). We may note that Matho's airs *Petits oiseaux, est-ce le jour qui vous éveille* and *Aussitôt que Tircis* plus the duet *Le Vin, charmante Iris* appear in the manuscript collection Ms 27 containing the motet by Fiocco already mentioned.

From 16 October 1700, the date of a rehearsal of Lully's *Atys*,[128] the Théâtre de la Monnaie would quickly start to take its place as the leading opera house in Brussels. Built by the Venetian architects Paolo and Pietro Bezzi on the orders of Maximilian Emanuel of Bavaria and his treasurer Bombarda, this new institution enjoyed the support of various aristocrats, notably the Duchess of Arenberg. However,

29. J.-B. Matho, *Le Vin, charmante Iris*. Enghien, Arenberg Archives and Cultural Centre, Ms 27.

30. Anonymus, *Vue de la place de la Monnaie à Bruxelles*, engraving. Archives of the City of Brussels, Iconography Collection, D 881.

the political situation was particularly delicate for the Governor, who, following the successive deaths of his son Joseph Ferdinand and King Charles II of Spain, switched allegiance by signing a treaty with France, which obliged him to leave Brussels on 22 March 1701. Nevertheless, the French defeat at Höchstädt forced Maximilian Emanuel to take up residence again in Brussels in 1704, before the Battle of Ramillies on 23 May 1706 forced him to move his court to Mons, where he resided until 1709.

Consistent with the inaugural performance of *Atys* on 19 November 1700, the first few years of La Monnaie bore Lully's stamp, with Brussels performances of *Acis et Galatée*, *Alceste*, *Persée*, and *Bellérophon* directed by Fiocco. During this time the Arenberg family continued to add to their music library, acquiring scores (published by Ballard) not only by Lully (*Proserpine*, 1707)[129] but also by his contemporaries Campra (*Hésione*, 1701[130] and *Tancrède*, 1702)[131] and Louis de Lacoste (c. 1675-c. 1750), represented by his 'tragédie en musique' *Philomèle* (1705).[132] During these years the nine volumes of the *Recueil general des opera representez par l'Academie royale de musique, depuis son etablissement*, published by Ballard between 1703 and 1710, allowed the Arenberg family to read the librettos of a good number of operas, among them those of Lully.[133] The Duchess of Arenberg provided tangible financial support to the Brussels opera house: the accounts from February 1707 reveal that she paid the director of the institution, Joseph de Pestel, employed there since July 1706,[134] 'pour du charbon à l'opéra' (for coal needed by the opera), as well as 'pour un petit ballet'[135] performed as part of the dances that took place 'les Dimanches, Mardis, & Jeudis pendant le Carneval'.[136]

A final source, undated but assignable, on account of its codicological characteristics, to the period during which the Duchess had sole management of the family affairs, must also be mentioned. This is an oblong bound manuscript collection bearing the classmark Ms 1 which brings together – in ninety-three folios, of which the first fourteen are numbered – twenty anonymous Italian pieces for soprano and basso continuo, all written in a careful hand, probably that of a copyist. The part of the watermark that is visible on the pages is unfortunately not sufficiently clear to allow us to identify the origin of the paper used. The volume bears its successive owners' names: on the first folio, by way of a heading to the first musical staves, appear the words 'Mademoiselle De Quinones', which have been crossed out; below are added the words: 'Ce livre appartient a Monsieur Brodor'. Although the last name remains a mystery, the first probably refers to a member of the Spanish noble family, the Quiñones, perhaps connected with Don Geronimo de Quiñones, who became Spanish Governor of the region of Franche-Comté in 1671 in succession to Charles-Eugène d'Arenberg (father-in-law of the Duchess of Arenberg). Among the anonymous pieces in the Ms 1 collection two have been identified through consultation of the *Répertoire International des Sources Musicales* (RISM). One is the piece opening the collection, 'Il dardo ho nel core', which is in fact an extract from the opera *L'incoronazione di Serse* by the Bolognese composer Giuseppe Felice Tosi (1619-1693). This opera was first performed in Venice at the Teatro San Giovanni Grisostomo on 26 December 1690 with a libretto by Adriano Morselli after Corneille's tragedy *Rodogune*.[137] This soprano aria appears, in a version for alto, also in a set of manuscripts held by the rich Santini Collection in Münster. As regards the third piece in the collection, this is the aria 'Amor, dove mi guidi', a movement from the 'dramma per musica' *L'inganno scoperto per vendetta* by the Bolognese composer Giacomo Antonio Perti (1661-1756), first staged in Venice on 28 December 1690 at the Teatro San Salvatore[138] with a libretto by Francesco Silvani; this

31. G. F. Tosi, 'Il dardo ho nel core' [*L'incoronazione di Serse*]. Enghien, Arenberg Archives and Cultural Centre, Ms 1.

32. G. A. Perti, 'Amor, dove mi guidi' [*L'inganno scoperto per vendetta*]. Enghien, Arenberg Archives and Cultural Centre, Ms 1.

piece is found in other sources: besides the volume in the Santini Collection just mentioned, there is a complete manuscript of the opera in the Biblioteca Estense e Universitaria in Modena.

Thanks to research carried out in 2012 by the American musicologist Louise K. Stein,[139] sixteen other pieces from Ms 1 can be identified as coming from *La Psiche o vero Amore innamorato*, a 'dramma per musica' in three acts by Alessandro Scarlatti in Naples (then under Spanish control) intended for the artistic circle of Gaspar Méndez de Haro y Guzmán, seventh Marquis of Carpio and Viceroy of Naples from 1683 to 1687. According to the libretto published in Naples in 1683,[140] this opera was performed at the Palazzo Reale on the birthday of Mariana of Austria, mother of King Charles II of Spain (22 December 1683); but other documents seem to indicate that the first performance was delayed, finally taking place in January 1684. The arias preserved in the collection Ms 1 are: 'Che in pianti gl'amanti', 'Per temprare gli sdegni del seno', 'Non poter nel duol morire', 'Non ti stancar, fortuna', 'Ch'io non pensi al bell'idolo mio', 'Se fede non presti', 'Non più tormenti', 'Così dolce e così mite del mio cor', 'Vaghe schiere a cui ride nel viso', 'Se quando di pace Cupido è foriero', 'Sei pur simile a un amante', 'Se di Psiche le guancie vezzose', the recitative 'Fra tante pene' followed by the aria 'In dolce riposo', and finally the arias 'Tu scherzi col periglio' and 'Fieri dardi acuti strali'. Several of these arias, sung by the characters Amore, Psiche, Anteo, Astrea, and Arsida in the three acts of the work, are also included in other manuscript sources, of which the most important is preserved in the library of Pavia University. The two other pieces from Ms 1 need further investigation but appear to be from *Il Maurizio* by the Bolognese composer and cellist Domenico Gabrielli (1659-1690); this is an opera that had several productions, the first occurring in Venice in December 1686.

A Duke in close association with musicians

The year 1708 marked a turning point in the life of the young Léopold-Philippe d'Arenberg, who on 10 January 1700 had been raised to the rank of Knight of the Order of the Golden Fleece by King Charles II of Spain.[141] Indeed, on 14 June of that year, a few months before his eighteenth birthday, Léopold-Philippe was declared Duke, assuming de facto responsibility for the destiny of his family.

During these first few years of the eighteenth century, Brussels' importance as a capital city grew ever greater, becoming the centre of public life in the Southern Netherlands, a territory seeing out its final years under the Spanish regime. The young Duke, who at the time resided for the most part at

33. Léopold-Philippe d'Arenberg, engraving. Private collection.

34. F. Mancini, 'Empia stella nemica' [*Gli amanti generosi*]. Enghien, Arenberg Archives and Cultural Centre, Ms 362.

35. Léopold-Philippe d'Arenberg. University of Leuven, Kunstpatrimonium, Arenbergverzameling (Artistic and Cultural Heritage, Arenberg Collection).

36. Maria Francesca Pignatelli. University of Leuven, Kunstpatrimonium, Arenbergverzameling (Artistic and Cultural Heritage, Arenberg Collection).

Enghien and Heverlee, resolved to take a more active part in the metropolis, and rented a patrician house for the first time there (the family, we recall, having been dispossessed of their Brussels residence in 1695).[142] In March 1709 a musician who was both a lutenist and violinist came to perform at the Duke's residence, but we do not know his name, nor what he played.[143] In the city the Duke, together with the musician Pietro Antonio Fiocco, became one of the principal patrons of the Brotherhood of St Anthony of Padua, founded at the Sablon church in September 1709 or May 1710 by the banker Francesco Gasparini.[144]

In October 1709, Léopold-Philippe was named Governor of the city of Mons, while the following month he succeeded to the title of High Bailiff of Hainaut, which meant that he became the leading figure in local political life.[145] On 19 January 1710 a pastorale, *Philandre*, was performed in his honour 'by the college of the company of Jesus at Mons', as stated in the libretto published by Laurent Preud'homme in Mons.[146] Since at that time 'pastorale' often denoted a pastoral opera, it is probable that this Jesuit work was accompanied by music.

On 29 March 1711 Duke Léopold-Philippe d'Arenberg married a girl of thirteen, Maria Francesca Pignatelli (1696-1766), Countess of Egmont and Princess of Bisaccia (in the kingdom of Naples), at the church of Saint-Jacques-sur-Coudenberg in Brussels. The Pignatelli family was at that time one of the most powerful in the kingdom of Naples. The young bride's father Nicola Pignatelli (1658-1719) was the nephew of Antonio Pignatelli (1615-1700), who was Pope Innocent XII from 1691 until his death. Maria Francesca Pignatelli, daughter of Marie-Claire Angéline, Countess of Egmont (1669-1714), would quickly become known in Brussels circles as 'Madame de Bisache'. Her father was associated with Bombarda and Gasparini through a business in Italian grain;[147] quite naturally, therefore, the new Duchess, like her mother-in-law, was well acquainted with the large Italian community that had settled in Brussels. Speaking Italian as competently as she did French, the young wife had a great passion for music.[148] The couple would go on to have six children: Marie-Victoire, Marie-Adélaïde, Charles-Marie-Raymond (the future duke), Marie Flore Charlotte Thérèse, Marie Eulalie Augustine, and Léopold-Charles.

Among various anonymous French airs and Italian arias, the incomplete manuscript miscellany Ms 362 held by the AACC Collection contains the soprano aria 'Empia stella nemica', which is identifiable as a movement from the 'dramma per musica' *Gli amanti generosi* by the Neapolitan composer Francesco Mancini (1672-1737), on a libretto by Giovanni Pietro Candi. This was first performed in Naples at the Teatro San Bartolomeo during the carnival of 1705. The previous year, Mancini had become principal organist at the royal chapel of the Viceroy of the Kingdom of Naples. This aria, which we know from various other sources, was taken up again by the composer himself in his new version of the opera entitled *L'Idaspe fedele* that was performed for the first time at London's Haymarket Theatre on 23 March 1710 – the second wholly Italian opera staged in England after Giovanni Bononcini's *Almahide*.[149] In 1720 Mancini would become director of the Conservatorio di Santa Maria di Loreto in Naples, training a whole new generation of composers, before succeeding Alessandro Scarlatti in 1725 in the post of *maestro di cappella* at the royal chapel in Naples. We may suppose that volume Ms 362 was added to the family library by the Duchess or her family – all the more so since the AACC is the only collection in Belgium today that still possesses a source containing music from this operatic work.[150]

Field Marshal Duke Léopold-Philippe d'Arenberg witnessed at first hand the War of the Spanish Succession, which ended on 11 April 1713 with the Treaty of Utrecht, whereby the Southern Netherlands were ceded to Austria. Charles VI of Habsburg (1685-1740), Emperor from 1715 to 1740, named a governor general to represent him in the Austrian regions. This function was initially entrusted to Eugène-François de Savoie (1663-1736), who would never actually reside in the Low Countries, before being conferred on Archduchess Maria Elisabeth (1680-1741).

In these early years of Austrian rule the library of the Duke of Arenberg grew in size, with purchases made not only through Brussels dealers such as the brothers Simon and François t'Serstevens,[151] but also through foreign dealers, notably Johannes Van Duren in The Hague.[152] The archival documents unfortunately do not give details of the works thus acquired, so we cannot establish precisely which works were added to the music section of the library. Nonetheless, the AACC Collection contains a series of prints that were added during this period to the scores already present.

The French repertoire available in the Christophe Ballard editions continued largely to hold sway. Purchase was made of the 1713 print of *Les Amours déguisés* by the Hainault composer and singer working in Paris, Thomas-Louis Bourgeois (1676-1750),[153] an 'opéra-ballet' with a prologue and three entrées that was first performed in Paris at the Théâtre du Palais-Royal on 22 August of that year.[154] The collection also contains the 'tragédie en musique' *Télémaque et Calypso* by the Parisian composer André Cardinal Destouches (1672-1741) which was premiered on the same stage on 29 November 1714 and published that same year.[155] Since our knowledge of the programming for the Théâtre de la

Monnaie during these years is only fragmentary,[156] it is hard to know whether these two works were performed there or not. Indeed, these prints may have been acquired by the Duke during his long stay in Paris in 1715.

On 13 November 1718 Duke Léopold-Philippe became Military Governor of Hainaut and the city of Mons.[157] He made his official entry into the city on the following 11 April, being received with great pomp by the nobility and the bourgeoisie of the town as well as by the garrison troops, as related by the Mons writer and librettist Gilles-Joseph de Boussu (1681-1755) in his *Histoire de la ville de Mons ancienne et nouvelle*.[158] During this period of celebration de Boussu signed and dedicated the libretto of the little opera *Le Retour des plaisirs* to the Duke, who as Grand Bailiff of Hainaut had appointed him to a city magistrate's post in 1714. This occasional work set to music by André Vaillant had been known until now principally through the survival of its printed libretto.[159] Since December 2013 this unique musical manuscript has been preserved in the music collections of the Royal Library of Belgium[160] and appears to have been the personal copy of Gilles-Joseph de Boussu. When this librettist wrote *Le Retour des plaisirs* he had already penned several tragedies, including *Hedwige, reine de Pologne*, published in Mons in 1713 and likewise dedicated to the Duke of Arenberg.[161] As regards André Vaillant, his work as a composer is attested from 1698 onwards at the *Chapelle musicale* of the Municipality of Valenciennes: a group of around ten singers and the same number of instrumentalists who shaped the musical life of that city. After *L'Immaculée conception* (1698), a sacred work performed by the pupils of the Convent of Notre-Dame in Valenciennes, Vaillant is known for *Les Plaisirs de Mariemont* (1708), a pastorale performed in Mons before its dedicatee, Maximilian Emanuel of Bavaria, as well as for the 'concert' *Le Gouvernement de Valenciennes*, given on 11 March 1711 at Valenciennes to celebrate Christian-Louis de Montmorency-Luxembourg's appointment to the post of governor of that city. Following his collaboration with the librettist Foucquier,[162] André Vaillant set to music *Le Retour des plaisirs*, but we do not know under what circumstances he met Gilles-Joseph de Boussu, with whom he collaborated on this work alone. As for the Duke of Arenberg, while we know that he knew Boussu, did he have the opportunity to make Vaillant's acquaintance? The question remains unanswered, yet it is very possible that this was indeed the case, since the account books reveal that the Duke regularly visited Valenciennes at this time, and, moreover, starting in 1715, paid an endowment to the 'Pauvres Ladres de Vallenciennes': that is, the lepers of the city.[163]

Le Retour des plaisirs is written for four solo singers who play the roles of Pallas, the city of Mons, la Renommée, and Hainaut – in the tessituras of soprano, alto, tenor, and bass, respectively. These soloists are joined by a chorus of four voices, called a 'troupe de jeux et de plaisirs'. No indication is given in the score regarding instrumentation except for the annotations 'violons' and 'b.c.' for the basso continuo, the latter being partially figured.[164] The opera's prologue begins with a symphony with the structure 'vite – lentement – vite' (in the Italian style) in which, during the slow movement, Pallas, goddess of wisdom, sings the glory of the Duke of Arenberg, who is compared to the mythical figure of Alexander the Great as a person of culture and a military hero. Following the prologue, the opera proper commences with a purely instrumental overture. The work continues with a succession of solo passages, instrumental passages for strings, and choral interventions that symbolize the voice of the people celebrating the return of the hero – that is, the Duke of Arenberg – bringing renewed peace.

37. J.-B. Lully by Hesse. Royal Library of
Belgium, Music Division,
II 68.938 D Mus.

The Duke is depicted as a shepherd, while the shepherdesses, keen to see their shepherd again, embody the city of Mons and the region of Hainaut – all of this therefore falling within the pastoral tradition. The title of this little *opéra de circonstance* itself doubtless makes reference to the eponymous prologue preceding the five acts of Lully's *Alceste*, a work which, as we have seen, was among the musical works known to the ducal family. In Lully's prologue the Nymph of the Seine hails the hero, who has gone off to war and whose return is eagerly awaited – in this case, the King. La Gloire next announces the return of the King, and the nymphs and gods of the woodlands then celebrate the significance of this return: the renewal of prosperity, of pleasure. Finally, it is probable that *Le Retour des plaisirs* was also conceived by Vaillant as a sort of response to the pastorale *Les Plaisirs de Mariemont*, which he had composed in 1708 on a libretto by Foucquier. Even if a musical comparison cannot be made, it must be noted that *Les Plaisirs de Mariemont*, like *Le Retour des plaisirs*, includes a chorus assigned to a 'troupe de jeux et de plaisirs' and pays tribute to a Prince 'que l'Hiver ramène en cet azyle' (whom Winter brings home to this sanctuary). Following *Le Retour des plaisirs*, the Jesuit College of Mons dedicated to the Duke of Arenberg the pastorale *Daphnis*, a work whose libretto, published in Mons in 1719, mentions the name neither of an author nor of a composer.[165] None of these pieces appears today in the AACC Collection.

The account books of Duke Léopold-Philippe show that on 8 September 1719 the family came into possession – via an individual in Brussels named Souvé – of 'quattre opera d'Arcangelo Corelli', costing 14 florins, and of 'trois Livres de trio de Petz', costing 4 florins and 4 sols, and acquired in manuscript form four unspecified volumes and four small books of 'pieces allemandes'.[166] By this time the Italian violinist and composer Arcangelo Corelli (1653-1713) had died; but his œuvre, solely instrumental and

38. Souvé's receipt of 8 September 1719. Enghien, Arenberg Archives and Cultural Centre, 64/27/II.

39. Arcangelo Corelli by E. Snell. Royal Library of
Belgium, Music Division, II 38.325 B Mus.

of an exceptional quality, was being circulated throughout Europe, thanks to the flourishing music printing business. The Arenbergs at this time acquired 'four operas' by this master: probably the first four published works, each presenting a collection of twelve *Sonate a tre* for two violins and bass. The first editions of Corelli's Opp. 1, 2, 3, and 4 emerged from the presses in Rome in 1681, 1685, 1689, and 1694 respectively,[167] but each opus was republished around twenty times before 1719 in locations as varied as Bologna, Venice, Modena, Amsterdam, London, Paris, and even Antwerp; it is therefore not possible to know precisely which Corelli prints were acquired by the Duke of Arenberg in 1719. Additionally, works by the Munich composer and singer Johann Christoph Pez (1664-1716) were purchased at this time. As a member of Maximilian Emanuel of Bavaria's circle, Pez worked as a musician at his court in Munich in 1688, before moving to Bonn in 1694 to enter the service of Maximilian Emanuel's brother Joseph Clemens, Prince-Bishop of Liège. The 1719 purchase must have been of three separate *parts* for a work, and not three works by the composer, since – apart from the more modest amount spent – the reference is to 'livres' (books), not to 'opera' (in the sense of collections). It is probable that either Pez's Op. 2 or his Op. 3 was acquired, each collection having been issued by the Amsterdam publisher Étienne Roger under the title of *Sonate da camera a tre, due flauti e basso*.[168] Pez's compositions are clearly influenced by Corelli, who was his teacher in Rome. Corelli's and Pez's publications sadly no longer exist in the AACC Music Collection: in fact, they seem to have been in the Arenberg family for only a short time, since they did not even appear in the library inventories drawn up in the second half of the eighteenth century.[169]

On 14 May 1720 the instrument maker Jérôme Mahieu in Brussels delivered a harpsichord 'à double clavier', costing 25 pistoles,[170] while in August of the same year a Matthieu and a Germain are listed as employed by the Duke as domestic servants, both being referred to as 'valet de pied musicien' (footman musician).[171] Also in the employ of the Duke was a certain 'S.r. Fioco' – in all probability, the Brussels organist and composer Jean-Joseph Fiocco (1686-1746), who in 1714 (on the death of his father Pietro Antonio) succeeded to the directorship of the Royal Chapel.[172] Jean-Joseph Fiocco may have been engaged as a gesture to commemorate his deceased father, who was close to the family, but what his actual duties were while employed by the Arenbergs remains unclear.

During this period the Duke of Arenberg increasingly established himself as a friend of the Sciences and Arts, accommodating the Parisian lyric poet Jean-Baptiste Rousseau (1670-1741) at his Brussels residence while the poet was in exile. It was through the Duke (in Brussels in 1722) that Rousseau met the French writer and philosopher François-Marie Arouet, better known as Voltaire (1694-1778) – with whom he would quickly fall out. Voltaire had met Léopold-Philippe d'Arenberg in Paris in 1715, an encounter that inspired an Epistle, which begins as follows:

> D'Aremberg, où vas-tu? Penses-tu m'échapper?
> Quoi! Tandis qu'à Paris on t'attend pour souper,
> Tu pars, et je te vois, loin de ce doux rivage,
> Voler en un clin d'œil aux lieux de ton bailliage!
> C'est ainsi que les dieux qu'Homère a tant prônés
> Fendaient les vastes airs de leur course étonnés,
> Et les fougueux chevaux du fier dieu de la guerre
> Franchissaient en deux sauts la moitié de la terre.
> Ces grands dieux toutefois, à ne déguiser rien,
> N'avaient point dans la Grèce un château comme Enghien;
> Et leurs divins coursiers, regorgeant d'ambroisie,
> Ma foi, ne valaient pas tes chevaux d'Italie.
> […][173]

The ducal account books from the years 1723 and 1724 abound in musical references. Under the date of 5 February 1723 'joueurs de hautbois et violons' are paid handsomely for a private concert given, receiving 250 florins 10 sols.[174] On the following 11 September the Duke pays 317 florins 16 sols to the doorman of the Théâtre de la Monnaie, Antoine Petit, thereby defraying costs incurred notably by 'S. Miees',[175] which refers to the director Jean-Baptiste Meeûs, owner of the theatre since 1717. A few weeks later, on 9 November, 'deux corne de chasse', 'deux basson', 'trois hautbois', 'deux basse', and 'cinque violons' performed for the Duke in Mons.[176]

In early 1724, on two occasions in January[177] and February,[178] 210 florins were paid by the Duke for 'le loyer de la loge' of 'l'abonnement de la Comedie'; this sum was paid in person directly to 'S. Dulondel Comedien': that is, the French actor Jean-Baptiste-Joseph Duhautlondel, known as Dulondel, who had quitted the Parisian stage for the provinces in 1722.[179] At the same time the dancing master, violinist, and composer François Hanot (1698-1770), originally from Dunkirk and at that point living in Mons, was giving dancing lessons to the Duchess, probably at Enghien.[180]

After spending some time in Vienna the Duke made the decision, in June 1725, to host at his château at Enghien a series of concerts, as well as a private theatrical performance ('en société').[181] The 26 June 1725 issue of the newspaper *Relations véritables* gave an account of the occasion:

> Vendredi passé Mr. le Duc d'Arenberg aiant invité Mrs. les Ambassadeurs Plenipotentiaires de l'Empereur & d'Espagne, avec plusieurs autres Seigneurs & Dames de la premiere qualité, les traitta à son Château d'Enghien avec beaucoup de magnificence, & leur donna plusieurs concerts de musique, avec une piece de Theatre intitulée, le *Triomphe de la Paix*, qui eut beaucoup d'applaudissement.

> [Last Friday, Monsieur the Duke of Arenberg, having invited Messieurs the Ambassadors Plenipotentiary of the Emperor and of Spain, with several other Lords and Ladies of the highest rank to their Château at Enghien, hosted them magnificently, offering several musical concerts, as well as a play entitled *Le Triomphe de la Paix*, which was received with great applause.]

The Duke paid 1412 florins 18 sols 4 deniers for the costs 'qui concernent la feste donnée à Enghien en juin 1725'. The *divertissement* to a prologue *La Fête d'Enghien ou le Triomphe de la Paix* was performed on a makeshift stage, since the château did not yet have a theatre at that time. We know that it was penned by a member of the Fiocco family,[182] thanks to the description, in the Duchess of Arenberg's library catalogue of 1769, of the composition manuscript, which unfortunately has not come down to us.[183] The Fiocco here in question seems to be the Jean-Joseph Fiocco already mentioned rather than his younger brother Joseph-Hector (1703-1741), whose career did not really take off until 1726,

40. The Duchess of Arenberg's catalogue of books. Enghien, Arenberg Archives and Cultural Centre, 29/12.

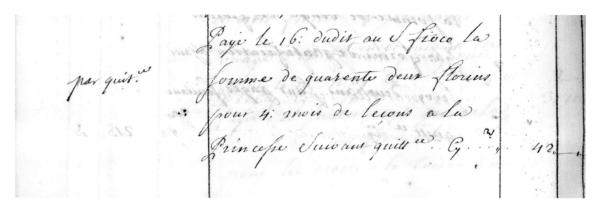

41. Reference to J.-H. Fiocco in the accounts of Bureau de St André, 16 March 1726. Enghien, Arenberg Archives and Cultural Centre, 63/22-28.

and who, according to the works that have survived, did not compose any occasional music (*musique de circonstance*) – unlike his brother, who composed in particular the oratorios *La morte vinta sul Calvario* (1726) and *La tempesta de' dolori* (1727), which were commissioned by the Archduchess Maria Elisabeth from her *Maître de chapelle*.

That same year (1725) the Duke bought 'les œuvres de molieres en huit volumes' from the Brussels book-dealer Antoine Claudinot,[184] while on 19 November he sponsored a ball held in Mons in honour of Archduchess Maria Elisabeth, who had assumed her governorship of the Austrian Netherlands and made her public entry into Brussels a few weeks earlier, on 9 October. The twenty musicians employed for the occasion were directed by a Daniel Schenkel, about whom we know nothing.[185]

Fiocco's name appears again in the account records for 1726 in connection with the payment of four months of harpsichord lessons given to 'la Princesse',[186] which most likely refers to the ducal couple's eldest daughter Marie-Victoire, then aged eleven.[187] After Pietro Antonio and Jean-Joseph, it is very likely that the young harpsichordist Joseph-Hector, aged twenty-three, in his turn entered the service of the ducal family.

A love of Italian opera

The Peruzzi and Landi troupes

The Archduchess Maria Elisabeth, who governed the Austrian Netherlands from 1725 onwards, had a particularly lively interest in Italian opera.[188] Her brother, the Emperor Charles VI, was also an eager proponent of Italian music, and especially admired the works of Antonio Vivaldi, whom he had the opportunity to meet in Lipica (home of the Imperial Stud) and in Trieste in September 1728; Vivaldi would dedicate the concertos of his *La cetra* Op. 9 to Charles VI.[189] In 1727 the Archduchess invited to Brussels the company of the Venetian impresario Antonio Maria Peruzzi, who had perhaps attracted her attention in Prague in 1724,[190] when that company was also directed by the Venetian tenor and impresario Antonio Alvise Denzio (1689 - after 1763) and performed in the theatres of Count Franz Anton von Sporck in Kuks and Prague. Antonio Maria Peruzzi, son of Giovanni Maria Peruzzi

42. Governor Maria Elisabeth by F. Harrewijn. Royal Library of Belgium, Prints and Drawings Division, S III 19427.

43. Anonymus, *Orlando furioso*, Brussels, [1727], title page. Royal Library of Belgium, Rare Books Division, VB 6464/24 A.

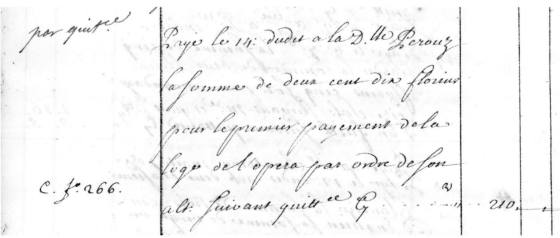

44. Reference to A. Peruzzi in the accounts of Bureau de St André, 14 October 1727. Enghien, Arenberg Archives and Cultural Centre, 63/22-28.

(d. 1735), was probably Antonio Denzio's cousin. In Venice, in 1688, the latter's father, Pietro Denzio, had married the singer Teresa Peruzzi, who was born in Brussels in 1667 of a certain Antonio Peruzzi, who was probably also Giovanni Maria Peruzzi's father.[191] Research carried out by Louis Delpech reveals that as from May 1718 Antonio Maria Peruzzi played an ill-defined musical role, but one linked to the opera at the Saxon court in Dresden; on 30 May he married in Dresden a certain Anna Henriette. Often referred to as 'Ariette', the latter was born around June 1697 in Mons and was the daughter of Robert du Hautlondel (more commonly known as 'La France'), a musician employed by this same *Kapelle* since 1708. Antonio Maria Peruzzi and his wife stayed only a short time in Dresden, however, since they were expelled at the end of 1719 following a murder trial.[192] After Dresden and Prague the impresario moved to Breslau in 1725, and then to Köln the following year.[193]

On 9 January 1727, in Brussels, Antonio Maria Peruzzi signed a lease with the owner of the Théâtre de la Monnaie, Jean-Baptiste Meeûs (referred to above). Taking effect on Easter Monday (14 April) and set to end at carnival the following year, it was agreed in the contract that a new production would be given each month. On 27 April Peruzzi staged his first production: the 'dramma per musica' *Orlando furioso*. The libretto (printed for the occasion in Brussels in a bilingual Italian-French edition) mentions neither the composer, nor the librettist, nor the performers, but does include a printed dedication signed 'Antonio Peruzzi' addressed to Archduchess Maria Elisabeth.[194] On consulting it, however, it appears that we are looking at a Brussels version of *Orlando* that is a combination of a version by Antonio Vivaldi performed in Venice in 1714 (RV 819) and a different version by the Venetian Antonio Bioni (c. 1698 - after 1739) that had been staged in Prague on 23 October 1724, with Antonio Denzio in the principal role.[195] The overture of this Brussels version, identified in April 2014 by the English scholar Michael Talbot as possibly authored by Bioni, is preserved in the Sainte-Gudule Collection at the Royal Conservatory of Brussels.[196] A classification of this music collection in the church of Sainte-Gudule was undertaken by the Brussels canon Jean Bernard Vanden Boom (1688-1769), who had embarked on a tour to Italy in 1725.[197]

From July 1727 to January 1728 Peruzzi's troupe achieved great success on the Brussels stage with the pastorale *Amor indovino* by Antonio Cortona (?1680 - after 1740) as well as the 'drammi per musica' *La costanza combattuta in amore* by Giovanni Porta (c. 1675-1755), *L'Arsace* by Domenico Sarro (1679-1744), *Faramondo* by Nicola Porpora (1686-1768), and *Alba Cornelia* by Francesco Bartolomeo Conti (1681-1732).[198] In Brussels librettos both in Italian and bilingual French-Italian versions (in quarto format) were produced for the performances of these transalpine works (these do not give a publisher's name), allowing the audience to follow the plot. The librettos further show that the Brussels versions of these operatic works were in fact pasticcios combining original arias with borrowings from other works.[199] Although no trace of these booklets is found in the AACC, we do know that the Duke and Duchess of Arenberg were in the audience, since they paid the impresario's wife Anna Peruzzi a subscription for a box in the sum of 210 florins.[200] Some manuscripts may have been acquired by the Arenberg family following these performances, such as a copy of one among the 130 cantatas by Porpora: *La viola che languiva,* for soprano or alto and basso continuo, a work also found in other sources,[201] or that of an unidentified *Duetto* by the composer of Neapolitan operas Domenico Sarro, of which only two separate instrumental parts for first violin and viola are preserved.[202]

45. N. Porpora, *La viola che languiva*. Enghien, Arenberg Archives and Cultural Centre, Ms 99.

One of the notable members of the Peruzzi company was the Bolognese contralto Anna Vincenza Dotti (active 1711-1728), who had only a short time before, during the three preceding seasons, caused a sensation in London, where she had taken several roles in operas by Handel written for the company of the Royal Academy of Music.[203] Another Handelian artist in the troupe was the Bolognese tenor Luigi Antinori (c. 1697-1734), who had performed with Anna Dotti in *Rodelinda* in London in 1725 and in Porpora's *Imeneo in Atene* in Venice the following year.[204]

Despite his success in Brussels, Peruzzi managed his affairs badly. Deep in debt, he was obliged to leave the city at the end of January 1728, continuing on to Frankfurt-am-Main in 1731 and Augsburg two years later.[205] One of his colleagues, Gioacchino Landi, a musician from a Florentine family who had distinguished himself in Madrid, Paris, and London,[206] took over the lease agreement of the Monnaie opera house on 9 March 1728 – for the lofty sum of 600 pistoles per annum (the equivalent of over 6000 florins): the amount that Peruzzi had also paid.[207] Landi in fact quickly left Brussels for Milan to form a new troupe, and during his absence the Italian performances continued under the artistic direction of one of his assistants, the Venetian composer Francesco Corradini (c. 1690-1769).[208]

At the beginning of April 1728 the Duke of Arenberg invited an Italian violinist, who has not been identified, to appear in a concert at one of his residences;[209] perhaps this was a musician who belonged to Landi's interim troupe. From April to July 1728 Landi offered Brussels audiences the 'drammi per

46. Leonardo Vinci by C. Biondi. Royal Library of Belgium, Music Division, Fétis 4710 B Mus.

musica' *Ernelinda* by Leonardo Vinci (c. 1696-1730) and *Archelao* by Conti – also in hybrid versions, as evidenced by the librettos printed in Brussels for each occasion.[210] The AACC Music Collection holds no numbers from these works, but does possess (in an incomplete contemporary manuscript) the vocal part accompanied by basso continuo of the aria 'Sento l'ombra del mesto Germano', identified as a number from another of Vinci's 'dramma per musica', *Medo*, based on a libretto by Carlo Innocenzo Frugoni.[211] This work was commissioned from Vinci to appear in the festival programme at the ducal palace in Parma on the occasion of the wedding of Antonio Farnese and Enrichetta d'Este. In order to oversee his production, staged in May 1728, the composer must have had to abandon his post of *vicemaestro* at the royal chapel in Naples for a few weeks, a position he had held since Alessandro Scarlatti's death in 1725 and in which he worked alongside Francesco Mancini (referred to earlier). This aria ('Sento l'ombra') sung by the character Perse in act III, scene 10, was performed by the Italian tenor Giovanni Paita (active from 1708 to 1729), one of the celebrated singers of the era and admired in equal measure for his singing and his acting.[212] Among Paita's fellow performers were Antonio Bernacchi (Medo), Costanza Posterla (Asteria), Vittoria Tesi (Medea), Dorotea Lolli (Artace), and Carlo Broschi – known as Farinelli (1705-1782) – who considered Giasone from *Medo* to be one of his

47. M. Falco, *Ninfa crudele e bella*. Enghien, Arenberg Archives and Cultural Centre, Ms 461.

favourite roles.[213] At the time Leonardo Vinci was one of the most influential opera composers in Italy, appreciated for his richly melodic vocal and orchestral writing. The pages in the Arenberg family's possession may have been acquired either via one of the artists recruited in Italy for the Brussels opera house, or by Landi himself, or even via the Neapolitan contacts of the Pignatelli family.

Gioacchino Landi had returned to Brussels in August 1728, as the *Relations véritables* newspaper reports on the 20th of that month:

> M. Landi, entrepreneur des opéras au service de S.A.S., est retourné en cette ville [Brussels] depuis avant-hier. Il a amené plusieurs sujets, tant pour le théâtre que pour l'orchestre, et entre autres le célèbre Pasi, qui est le plus habile de tous les musiciens d'Italie, la Rosa Ungarelli et Ristorini, pour les intermèdes, et Martinetto dal hautbois; et on prépare l'opéra de Griselide, pour célébrer, le 29 de ce mois, le jour de naissance de l'impératrice régnante.

> [M. Landi, the impresario of the operas in the service of H.S.H., returned to this city [Brussels] the day before yesterday. He has brought several persons, both for the theatre and for the orchestra, and among others the famous Pasi, who is supreme among Italian musicians, Rosa Ungarelli and Ristorini for the intermezzi, and Martinetto the oboist; and they are preparing the opera *Griselda* in order to celebrate, on the 29th of this month, the birthday of the reigning empress.]

48. A. Pasi, 'Il suo dolce'. Enghien, Arenberg Archives and Cultural Centre, Ms 469.

On 29 August the new company indeed took part in the festivities celebrating the birthday of Empress Elisabeth Christine of Brunswick-Wolfenbüttel (1691-1750), consort of Emperor Charles VI. They performed *Griselda* by the Florentine, Giuseppe Maria Orlandini (1676-1760),[214] a 'dramma per musica' that had premiered in Venice at the Teatro San Samuele on 8 May 1720,[215] as well as the comic intermezzi *Vespetta e Pimpinone*.[216] This lighter part of the performance allowed the audience to admire the talents of the soprano Rosa Ungarelli, well-known in Italy (active 1709-1732),[217] and of her husband, the tenor Antonio Maria Ristorini (active 1690-1732).[218] The day after this performance the same artists performed the intermezzi *Don Micco e Lesbina*.[219] Among the musicians engaged by Landi was the Milanese oboist and composer Giuseppe 'Martinetto' Sammartini (1695-1750) (elder brother of Giovanni Battista Sammartini), who stayed in Brussels for a few months before arriving in London in May 1729.[220]

Three anonymous arias for voice and basso continuo preserved in manuscript in the AACC Collection have been identified as coming from two operas staged by Orlandini in Venice at the Teatro San Giovanni Grisostomo.[221] 'Se giammai da speco l'eco' is Teonoe's aria from act III scene 4 of the five-act tragedy *Ifigenia in Tauride*, first performed during the carnival of 1719 by the soprano Francesca Cuzzoni (1696-1778).[222] As for 'Non può più saldarsi' and 'Struggerà l'argivo foco',[223] these are arias from act I of *Paride*, a 'dramma per musica' in five acts composed for the carnival of 1720. Polide's aria in scene 4, 'Non può più saldarsi', was sung by the soprano Antonia Pelizzari, while

Cassandra's aria, 'Struggerà l'argivo foco', appears in scene 6 and was first performed by the Venetian contralto Diana Vico.[224] These items were perhaps owned by the artists employed by Landi and may have been used to perform some pastiche work or other.

Ungarelli and Ristorini may, in turn, have travelled with the manuscript score of the cantata for soprano and harpsichord in G minor, *Ninfa crudele e bella*, by the Neapolitan composer and pioneer of *opera buffa* Michele Falco (?1688 - after 1732).[225] This source (Ms 461 in the AACC Collection) is genuinely exceptional for bringing to light an entirely unknown cantata by this composer; indeed, up till now his only known work was the cantata for soprano and basso continuo *Verdi colli e piaggie amene* appearing in a manuscript collection in the library of the Conservatorio di Musica San Pietro a Majella in Naples.[226] Like its counterpart, the cantata *Ninfa crudele e bella* is written in a style recalling Alessandro Scarlatti. It is perfectly feasible that the seven pages possessed by the library of the Duke of Arenberg are in fact the autograph manuscript of this cantata. Indeed, although the original handwriting of Falco is not known to us, these pages appear not to be a final, edited copy – especially at the end of the piece, where several notes have been corrected by scratching out the ink, while one measure has been completely erased. As in the case of the Orlandini manuscripts, the paper used for the piece by Falco bears no trace of a watermark that would allow us to confirm its origin as Italian.

In the company performing on the Brussels stage from the summer of 1728 there was also the Bolognese castrato mezzo-soprano Antonio Pasi (active 1704-1732), a celebrity in Italian opera houses whose career had begun some time between 1704 and 1708 in Venice, Modena, and Florence.[227] The singer's name appears on the verso side of the last of the three manuscript folios, which are unbound and lack page numbers; these are catalogued under the classmark Ms 469. Furthermore, the incomplete aria for soprano and unfigured bass beginning with the words 'Il suo dolce' and numbered '9a' contains the introductory remark 'del signore Pasi'. The other folios contain four arias (likewise for soprano and unfigured bass): numbered '5a', 'S'io vedessi un augelletto' comes from *La costanza combattuta in amore* by Giovanni Porta, a 'dramma per musica' premiered at the Teatro San Moisè in Venice on 17 October 1716;[228] the aria '6a', 'Non lascia il ben che brama' 'Del Sig.re Nicola Porpora', is an extract from the opera *Siface*; the aria '7a', whose text is missing, is 'Del opera di Lucio Papiro', from the 'dramma per musica' by Orlandini;[229] while under '8a' we find 'Non trova mai riposo' 'del Sigr Antonio Vivaldi', an aria from *Farnace* RV 711.[230]

Although Porpora's *Siface*, which had premiered at Venice's Teatro San Giovanni Grisostomo on 26 December 1725, was not staged at the Monnaie by the Landi company, Porta's *La costanza combattuta in amore* had been performed by Peruzzi's troupe on 28 August and 21 September 1727.[231] As for Orlandini's *Lucio Papirio*, performed in Brussels on 4, 7, 14, and 21 November 1728,[232] this was certainly among the works presented by Landi's company: a printed bilingual libretto tells us that the first performance, given on the feast-day of St Charles, was to 'rappresentarsi in Brusselle gli 4 novembre 1728 per solennizzare il nome di Carlo VI' – i.e., the Habsburg Emperor Charles VI.[233] Duke Léopold-Philippe d'Arenberg seems to have attended one of these performances, having acquired a copy of the libretto, as shown by the library catalogues compiled in the second half of the eighteenth century.[234] The 'dramma per musica' *Lucio Papirio* had received its première at the Teatro San Bartolomeo in Naples on 11 December 1717. *Maestro di cappella* of the Grand Duke of

49. A. Vivaldi, 'Non trova mai riposo' [*Farnace*]. Enghien, Arenberg Archives and Cultural Centre, Ms 469.

Tuscany since 1711, Orlandini built up a strong reputation as a composer of operatic works, and more particularly of comic intermezzi, the most famous of these being *Bacocco e Serpilla*, which was presented in Verona in 1715, the three component parts of which were staged as interludes during performances of *Lucio Papirio* in Brussels. The Brussels libretto reveals that the version of *Lucio Papirio* given at the Théâtre de la Monnaie included not only arias by Orlandini but also a new overture and two arias by Giuseppe Sammartini; although the music of the two arias 'Scrivi la morte mia' and 'Sangue, amore in doppio affetto' by 'Mr. St. Martin qui joue de l'Hautbois' is today lost, the music of his overture is preserved at the Brussels Conservatory in five separate manuscript parts, held in the original file from the Sainte-Gudule Collection, where we read the inscription: 'Lucio Papirio del Sig.or Giuseppe San Martini'.[235] As for the Neapolitan composer Porpora, he was at this time an internationally renowned personality, both as a composer and as a singing teacher, the castrato Farinelli having been one of his pupils. Composed on a libretto by Pietro Metastasio, his 'dramma per musica' *Siface, re di Numidia* marks, after a period spent in Vienna in the service of the Emperor, the beginning of his period in Venice, an era of success that would see him enter into rivalry with first Vinci and then Hasse. The work would quickly become recognized as the composer's most successful. The aria 'Non lascia il ben che brama' is sung in the second scene of act I by the character Viriate, the bride destined for the King of Numidia, Siface, and was assigned to the soprano Marianna Benti from Rome ('La Romanina') during the original performance in Venice.

The 'dramma per musica' *Farnace* by Antonio Vivaldi, composed on a libretto by Antonio Maria

50. Anonymus, *Antonio Vivaldi*. Bologna, Museo
internazionale e biblioteca della musica.

Lucchini, is also closely bound up with the city of the Doges, having had its first performance at Venice's
Teatro Sant'Angelo on 10 February 1727. The work met with favour and prompted Vivaldi to compose
several other versions. Teaching the violin to the young ladies of the Ospedale della Pietà from 1703,
Vivaldi was a composer celebrated all over Europe for his chamber and concert music, which was
widely disseminated through publications from 1705 onwards. He ventured into opera for the first
time in 1713, at the age of 35, offering *Ottone in villa* in Vicenza, followed by *Orlando finto pazzo* at
the Sant'Angelo theatre in November 1714. Several operas were subsequently performed in Florence,
Mantua, and Rome. For the première of *Farnace* the aria 'Non trova mai riposo' was sung in scene 13
of act I by the contralto Anna Girò (c. 1710 - after 1748), who played the role of Tamiri, Farnace's wife.
The aria appears at the crucial moment when Tamiri is saved from suicide by her mother, Berenice.
From her first appearance on the stage in Venice during the autumn of 1724, Anna Girò was close to
the composer, who gave her roles in twenty or so productions between 1726 and 1740;[236] she had in fact
been in contact with Vivaldi since at least 1723, the year when she appeared in Treviso in a pasticcio
entitled *La ninfa infelice e fortunata*, a work for which the composer seems to have written several
arias.[237] The other performers in *Farnace*, cited in the libretto published for the occasion in Venice
by Marino Rossetti, were: Maria Maddalena Pieri (Farnace), Angela Capuano (Berenice), Lucrezia
Baldini (Selinda), Lorenzo Moretti (Pompeo), Filippo Finazzi (Gilade), and, as Aquilio, Domenico
Giuseppe Galletti[238] – who would next join Landi's company in Brussels. One may therefore imagine
that the folios making up Ms 469 could have been added to the Duke of Arenberg's music library via
this artist, or via Pasi, or indeed via any other member of the Italian company; we may even suppose
that they were copied out in Brussels by the very hand of one or other of these men, for the paper used
gives every indication of belonging to a type manufactured in the Austrian Netherlands.[239] As for the

51. The Grand Canal and the Rialto Bridge in Venice by N. Chapuy. Royal Library of
Belgium, Prints and Drawings Division, S II 77265.

version of *Farnace* given by the Italian troupe at the Théâtre de la Monnaie on 30 January, 24 February, and 1 March 1729,[240] this was not the version by the *Prete rosso* (as Vivaldi was known, thanks to his red hair), since the libretto published in Brussels, which differs from that of Lucchini, mentions the name of the composer Antonio Cortona. However, this does not rule out the possibility that the Vivaldi aria 'Non trova mai riposo' was sung in Brussels in one of the Peruzzi or Landi productions, as may have been the case with the other arias linked to Antonio Pasi preserved under Ms 469.

Probably via the same dissemination route two manuscript arias for contralto by Vivaldi likewise came into the Arenbergs' ownership. These have been identified as sung by the character Stesicrea, the rejected wife of King Antiochus, in act II of *L'inganno trionfante in amore* RV 721. As mentioned in the libretto published in Venice by Marino Rossetti in 1725, this three-act 'dramma per musica' was staged in Venice at the Teatro Sant'Angelo during the autumn of that year, with, in the role of Stesicrea, Costanza Posterla, who would sing in the 1728 production of Vinci's *Medo*, mentioned earlier.[241] The première of *L'inganno* may be dated more precisely to shortly before 15 December 1725, preceding *Turia Lucrezia* by Antonio Pollarolo (1676-1746) from Brescia, which was performed on 27 December to open the carnival season, which began at the end of the Christmas festivities.[242] In contrast with the Venetian libretto of *Farnace*, which indicates that the music 'è del celebre Sig. D. Antonio Vivaldi', the libretto of *L'inganno* gives no composer's name. The reason for this omission is that *L'inganno* is in reality an adaptation of an earlier opera, *Laodicea e Berenice*, by the Bolognese composer Giacomo Antonio Perti, based on a libretto by the Venetian Matteo Noris; this was staged on 26 December 1694 at the Teatro San Salvatore in Venice, and its music remains untraceable. The identification of these unpublished extracts in the AACC Collection as coming from Vivaldi's *L'inganno* has enabled us to discover two more arias from an opera whose music had hitherto remained effectively lost.[243]

52. Antonio Vivaldi by J. Caldwall in J. Hawkins, *A General History of Music*. Royal Library of Belgium, Music Division, 3190 B Mus.

To be precise: no more or less complete score of the work has been found to date, and only two other arias have been identified, in Berlin manuscripts – these forming part of a serenata called *Die gecrönte Beständigkeit* (Constancy rewarded) which was performed in Hamburg at the Gänsemarkt Theatre on 7 December 1726 by the Italian soprano and impresario Maria Domenica Polone and other, unnamed singers. With arias in Italian and recitatives in German, this work was advertised in the local press as presenting music 'Von dem Welt-bekannten Italiänischen Virtuosen Signor Vivaldi'.[244]

As with the majority of Italian operatic works of the period, Vivaldi's operas were not destined, unlike much of his instrumental music, to know the blessing of a printed edition, for they were composed to be performed in the context of an ephemeral production for which only the text, the libretto, was printed. In the case of the Venetian composer, the complete or partial autograph scores of twenty-two operas have survived: notably that of *Farnace*, which is contained in the Giordano Collection at the National and University Library in Turin. This collection, together with the complementary Foà Collection, holds manuscripts that were originally also part of a single library: that of the Venetian senator and Count Jacopo Soranzo, as attested in an inventory of 1745.[245] As with *L'inganno*, many other operas by Vivaldi have come down to us only in very piecemeal fashion, thanks to the survival in manuscript of the music of several arias, the remaining arias being known only through their texts, thanks to the surviving librettos.

The libretto of Vivaldi's *L'inganno* of 1725 is attributed to the amateur composer Giovanni Maria

53. A. Vivaldi, 'Langue il fior sull'arsa sponda' [*L'inganno trionfante in amore*]. Enghien, Arenberg Archives and Cultural Centre, Ms 460.

Ruggieri and exhibits numerous modifications when compared with the original Noris text, one of these being that the two female roles of Laodicea and Berenice are now renamed Stesicrea and Cleonice. Examination of this libretto allows us to associate the two arias from the AACC with the opera. The aria in A major 'S'odo quel rio che mormora', from act II scene 2, is housed in two folios under the classmark Ms 411, one being the vocal part with unfigured bass and the other the second violin part. The aria in F major 'Langue il fior sull'arsa sponda' appears later on, in act II, scene 13. Catalogued as Ms 460, this is preserved in two separate parts: a pair of folios containing the part for voice and unfigured bass, and a single folio containing the part named 'violetta (i.e., viola). The discovery of this source allows us to reveal the identity of a score containing this same aria, which is copied into a manuscript collection of Dresden provenance belonging to the collections of the Royal Conservatory of Brussels.[246]

L'inganno tells the story of the King of Asia, Antiochus, who, having rejected Stesicrea (now living on the banks of the Euphrates), decides to marry Cleonice, who had previously been promised to Teramene, King of Numidia. Stesicrea suggests to Teramene that they go to Antiochus's palace in disguise, passing themselves off as the shepherdess Eurilla and shepherd Silano in order to regain the hearts of those who have rejected them. At the start of act II, Cleonice welcomes her new servant Eurilla, who speaks to her of Stesicrea. The aria 'S'odo quel rio che mormora' appears at this point in the story. On seeing Stesicrea, Antiochus decides that he wishes to renew his relationship with her.

54. A. Vivaldi, 'S'odo quel rio che mormora' [*L'inganno trionfante in amore*]. Enghien, Arenberg Archives and Cultural Centre, Ms 411.

Having attempted to attack Cleonice, Stesicrea reveals to her rival her true identity and sings the aria 'Langue il fior'. At the end of act III, the two couples – Antiochus and Stesicrea, Teramene and Cleonice – are reconciled and reunited.[247]

Only the folios containing the vocal part of the two arias of *L'inganno* give an indication of the composer's name. It is probably written by the same hand, even if the handwriting of the attribution 'Del Sr Ant.o Vivaldi' is not strictly identical. The paper used for these folios displays the *tre lune* (three moons) watermark, which is visible on a good many specimens of Venetian paper used for copying music.[248] Even though no performer in the Venetian production would have belonged to Landi's company in Brussels, we may nonetheless assume that the folios were copied in Venice by one of the scribes working for the Teatro Sant'Angelo or for Vivaldi himself before arriving in the Austrian Netherlands, where they were perhaps used in the pasticcios performed by the Peruzzi and Landi companies.

In the Italy of the *Settecento*, and particularly in Venice, the trade in manuscripts of operatic music had become very well established and made the owners of Venetian copying shops rich men. Music copyists were attached to one or several theatres in the city, and it was their duty to prepare the material needed for performances, both by instrumentalists and by singers. They also worked with the city's composers, who would pass them their original manuscripts so that they could undertake various transcriptions: complete scores, parts, individual movements, or short scores. The autograph manuscript had only a limited function, therefore, since it had (mandatorily) to be copied professionally in order for the work finally to make itself known. Some manuscript copies, prestigious or otherwise, emerged from the circle of musical professionals and were bought by amateur enthusiasts, collectors, and travellers, who enjoyed acquiring a memento of operas they had seen. The Venetian pages in the Arenberg library are clearly copies made originally for professional use. They have been realized without any particular care, are unbound, and include instrumental parts, which are generally absent from copies intended for amateurs, who were content with a transcription of the vocal part with basso continuo.

Like other composers of his era, Antonio Vivaldi regularly re-used material. Research carried out by the Italian musicologist and orchestral conductor Federico Maria Sardelli shows that the *Prete rosso* used a musical theme in 'S'odo quel rio che mormora' that had already appeared in the aria 'Lascierà l'amata salma' from his opera *Il Tigrane* RV 740, staged in Rome in 1724, as well as in the aria 'Al seren d'amica calma' from *La Gloria e Himeneo* RV 687, a serenata in honour of the marriage of Louis XV performed in Venice on 12 September 1725. As for the aria 'Langue il fior sull'arsa sponda', this shows similarities with a later aria appearing in the cantata *Vengo a voi, luci adorate* RV 682.[249]

Catalogued under Ms 329, two manuscript pages written on the same kind of Venetian *tre lune* paper offer twenty-two opening bars from the vocal part, as well as the complete forty-seven bars of the second violin part of the soprano aria 'Fedel la pena mia', which comes from the 'dramma per

55. Antonio Pollarolo, 'Fedel la pena mia' [*Turia Lucrezia*]. Enghien, Arenberg Archives and Cultural Centre, Ms 329.

musica' *Turia Lucrezia* by Pollarolo, a work that followed *L'inganno* at the Teatro Sant'Angelo.[250] Once again, the folios held by the AACC are truly remarkable, for they represent, even if incompletely, the sole documented musical item so far recovered from this opera, which is otherwise known only from its libretto. As the printed libretto states, this aria is sung by the protagonist in act II scene 8, and in the performance at Sant'Angelo this role was taken by the same Costanza Posterla.[251] The son of the opera composer Carlo Francesco Pollarolo (c. 1653-1723), Antonio is explicitly identified in the source by the precise words 'Del Sig.r Antonio Polaroli'. Here, too, it is plausible to imagine that these pages arrived in the Austrian Netherlands thanks to one or other of the Italian artists; their codicological characteristics show such strong similarities with the Vivaldi manuscripts Ms 411 and 460 that one could well imagine that they all belonged to one and the same dismembered whole.

In addition to *Lucio Papirio* and *Farnace*, mentioned above, between December 1728 and March 1729 Landi's troupe offered Brussels audiences the comic intermezzi *Il malato immaginario* by Conti, *Bacocco e Serpilla* by Orlandini, and *La Truffaldina* by Ungarelli and Ristorini, as well as Pietro Torri's 'dramma per musica' *La Merope*.[252]

Riding on the crest of successful productions, the Landi company enjoyed a reputation that quickly spread beyond the 'Belgian' frontiers. On 7 June 1729 it was invited to make its début at the Paris Opera with *Bacocco e Serpilla*, an event devised by Victor Amadeus I of Savoy, Prince of Carignano and Inspector of the Royal Academy of Music, who had initially hoped to bring London's Italian opera company (directed at the time by Handel) to the French capital. Parisian audiences were won over by Landi's artists, who gave four performances of *Serpilla* as well as presenting the intermezzi *Don Micco e Lesbina*.[253]

The Italian company afterwards returned to Brussels, giving further performances of 'drammi per musica' between August 1729 and February 1730: Porpora's *Temistocle*, Sarro's *Alessandro Severo*, and the unattributed *Armida abbandonata* and *Attalo*.[254] Although we know that these works were given in pasticcio form, it seems that *Armida* may have been produced by the Italian troupe in a version inspired by that of the Venetian composer Antonio Bioni, for they had been the first to perform Bioni's *Armida* (at Prague in November 1725). As for *Attalo*, this could well be a pasticcio drawing on Porpora's *La verità nell'inganno*, a 'dramma per musica' presented in Milan during the carnival of 1726.[255]

Among the Landi company's members in Brussels were also the singer Girolama Valsecchi Madonis (d. 1740) and her husband, the Venetian violinist Giovanni Antonio Madonis (c. 1690-c. 1770), who was probably a pupil of Vivaldi, and was the concertmaster of the Peruzzi company from 1725 onwards.[256] Girolama Valsecchi Madonis had been among the performers in the first version of Vivaldi's *Orlando furioso* in 1714.[257] It is probably no coincidence that the music library of Duke Léopold-Philippe d'Arenberg holds a manuscript of a sonata for violin and basso continuo by 'S.r Madonis'.[258] Examination of the three manuscript folios reveals that this is the sonata which would be published as *Sonata X* in the 1731 Parisian edition of his *XII sonates à violon seul avec la basse* dedicated to the Abbé de Pomponne,[259] 1731 being also the year when this violinist entered the service of the Venetian ambassador in France. The manuscript held by the AACC, written on paper lacking an identificatory watermark, includes numerous crossings-out and two bars that have been entirely deleted by cross-hatching. Could this in fact also be an autograph manuscript? Without knowing

56. Madonis, *Sonata*. Enghien, Arenberg Archives and Cultural Centre, Ms 459.

what Madonis's handwriting looked like, this is of course difficult to verify. But what is noticeable is that, in contrast to the Parisian edition, the source in the AACC includes many variants, most especially the addition of ornaments and passing notes.

After the carnival of 1730 the Italian company disbanded, opening the way for French repertoire to taken centre-stage again. Some Italian singers returned to Prague to rejoin Denzio's troupe, one of whose highlights, in the spring of 1730, was a production of Vivaldi's *Farnace*, the first of five Vivaldi operas performed in Prague between 1730 and 1732.[260] As for Landi, he spent some time in a debtors' prison, before being released.[261] In 1731, according to the account books for that year, Landi had a private audience with Duke Léopold-Philippe d'Arenberg; they tell us that on 12 December the impresario was paid 4 guineas (over 50 florins) for 'avoir joüé et chanté au concert' (having played and sung in a concert).[262] Landi probably did not perform alone, but we cannot be sure who accompanied him during this concert. In February 1732 he was paid one pistole by the Duke for 'un mois de leçon de musique qu'il a donné a la D.elle Desgrois' (a month of music lessons that he has given to Mlle Desgrois), a young woman in service with the family.[263]

Wishing to pursue a career as a clergyman, but not in possession of sufficient funds to take holy orders, Landi sought financial assistance from Archduchess Maria Elisabeth, who, recalling the

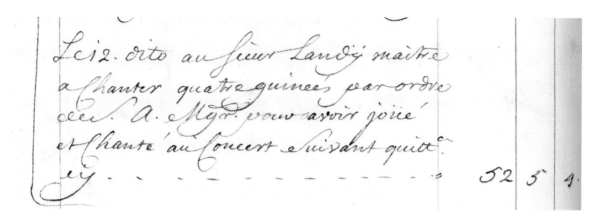

57. Reference to Landi in the accounts of Pascal Henrion, 12 December 1731. Enghien, Arenberg Archives and Cultural Centre, 63/29-35.

excellence of his performances in Brussels, had no hesitation in granting him, on 5 October 1732, a pension for life of 250 German florins.[264] Landi would eventually leave the Austrian Netherlands; we have records of his presence in Vienna in 1737 and Milan in 1739.

The AACC Collection's manuscript miscellanies Ms 491 and Ms 371 contain other Italian arias of the same kind, but, chronologically speaking, these collections cannot have been acquired via members of Landi's company; nor do they seem to be connected to Italian performances at the Théâtre de la Monnaie. In all likelihood, they were added to the Duke of Arenberg's music library during the years following the Italians' departure from the capital of the Austrian Netherlands. As with other manuscripts already mentioned, these collections, unbound and containing sets of instrumental parts, do not share any characteristics whatsoever with the copies intended for sale to wealthy music-lovers. The paper used for the two collections exhibits no identifiable watermark.

Two collections of Italian arias

The incomplete collection Ms 491 consists of twelve arias on pages that were copied by two different scribes. While two of these arias remain anonymous,[265] the other ten have been identified as connected with operas staged between 1723 and 1734. Among these we find, first of all, a score of the aria 'Destrier ch'all'armi usato' for alto, two violins, bass, and trumpets – sung by the character Poro, King of India, who has been conquered by Alexander the Great and is in love with Cleofide – which closes act II scene 10 of *Alessandro nelle Indie*. Based on a libretto by Pietro Metastasio, this 'dramma per musica' is by the Venetian composer Giovanni Battista Pescetti (c. 1704-1766), as the scribe marks on the manuscript. This opera was first staged at Venice's Teatro Sant'Angelo on 30 January 1732, with the castrato Gaetano Valetta in the role of Poro.[266] Since 1725, this composer, a pupil of Antonio Lotti, had been presenting his operas in various Venetian opera houses, sometimes in collaboration with Baldassare Galuppi. A number of arias from this opera survive in other locations, notably at the Library of the State Archive of Bologna.

'Sciolga dunque al ballo', which follows in the collection and likewise takes the form of a score, has been identified as the aria sung by the character Mirtillo, Amarilli's lover, in the final scene of the third and final act of Handel's *Il pastor fido* HWV 8, an opera based on a libretto by Giacomo Rossi,

58. G. B. Pescetti, 'Destrier ch'all'armi usato' [*Alessandro nelle Indie*]. Enghien, Arenberg Archives and Cultural Centre, Ms 491.

after Giovanni Battista Guarini, which had its first performance at London's Haymarket Theatre on 22 November 1712, to little acclaim. Preceding the final ballet scene, this aria (scored for soprano, two violins in unison, and bass) was included without modification in the second, revised version of the work, which the composer staged thirteen times at the same theatre, starting on 18 May 1734. This aria, given its first outing in 1712 by the castrato Valeriano Pellegrini (c. 1663-1746), known as 'Valeriano', was entrusted in 1734 to the castrato Giovanni Carestini (c. 1705-c. 1760), nicknamed 'Cusanino', a singer notable for having participated in the Venetian première of Vivaldi's *Siroe* in 1727.[267]

The aria 'Priva del caro bene', likewise appearing in score in the manuscript collection, comes from the 'dramma per musica' *Dalisa* by Johann Adolf Hasse (1699-1783). Resident in Naples from 1722, Hasse was a pupil of Porpora and later of Alessandro Scarlatti in that city, and from 1725 this musician from Bergedorf (near Hamburg) enjoyed a high reputation as a composer of opera, quickly becoming known as 'Il Sassone' (the Saxon). In 1727 Hasse moved to Venice, where he remained for several years, and in 1731 was invited to the court of Dresden, becoming kapellmeister there two years later. 'Priva del caro bene', created for the singer in the title role, appears in act II scene 5, and at its first performance at the Teatro San Samuele in Venice on 17 May 1730 was performed by the Venetian mezzo-soprano Faustina Bordoni (1697-1781), who on 20 July of the same year would become the composer's wife. Preserved in many locations, this aria would be recycled in several of Hasse's later operatic works.[268]

The aria 'Non mi chiamar crudele' 'Del Sr Hasse detto il Sassone' likewise appears in the collection, and includes parts for soprano and instrumental bass, as well as for second violin. It comes from

59. J. A. Hasse, anonymous engraving. Royal Library of Belgium, Music Division, Fétis 4892 A Mus.

act I scene 7 of the 'dramma per musica' *Euristeo*, which was similarly performed at the Teatro San Samuele on 21 May 1732.[269] The libretto published in Venice indicates that Ormonte, played by the castrato Gaetano Majorano ('Caffarelli') (1710-1783), had to sing this aria instead of the aria 'Torna al padre';[270] the aria 'Non mi chiamar crudele' was in actual fact a borrowing, having already appeared in act II scene 14 of one of Hasse's earlier operas, *Cajo Fabricio*, staged in Rome on 12 January of the same year. On that occasion it was performed by the castrato Angelo Maria Monticelli (c. 1712 - ?1758) in the role of Sestia. It is noteworthy that the AACC manuscripts Ms 81 and Ms 82 also contain two Hasse arias taken from operas written after librettos by Metastasio, both staged in 1731. These are 'Che sorte crudele' from *Cleofide*, based on *Alessandro nell'Indie* and presented in Dresden on 13 September, and 'So che pietà non hai', an aria from *Catone in Utica*, performed in Turin on the following 26 December.[271] The two sources can be attributed with certainty to a single copyist, whose handwriting differs completely from the two styles encountered in the Ms 491 collection. The unbound pages of music also contain (for aria 1) a separate viola part, and (for aria 2) the first violin, second violin, and viola parts. Here we have two famous arias, copied in a careful and clear hand, that were performed in their day by renowned artists. Indeed, 'Che sorte crudele', sung by the protagonist (act I scene 3 of *Cleofide*), was entrusted to Faustina Bordoni, while the second aria (from act II scene 3 of *Catone*), sung

60. J. A. Hasse, 'Non mi chiamar crudele' [*Euristeo*]. Enghien, Arenberg Archives and Cultural Centre, Ms 491.

by the character Arbace, Prince of Numidia and an ally of Catone, was performed on that occasion by Carlo Broschi, more popularly known as 'Farinelli'.

Next in the Ms 491 collection appears the aria 'Stando accanto all'idol mio', a number from *Gianguir* by Geminiano Giacomelli (c. 1692-1740), which was premiered at the Teatro San Cassiano in Venice on 27 December 1728 with Faustina Bordoni in the role of Semira, who sings this aria in act III scene 5.[272] The Royal Conservatory of Brussels holds a manuscript score of the whole of this 'dramma per musica' in three acts,[273] while separate arias survive in various libraries, including the Bibliothèque Nationale de France.[274]

After Giacomelli, Pescetti reappears (spelled 'Percetti' by the second copyist) with the aria 'Saria piacer, non pena, la servitù d'amore' (sung by Cleonice's confidante Barsene, who is in love with Alceste) from act II scene 14 of his opera *Demetrio*, the première of which was given in Florence during the carnival of 1732. Pescetti was in London from 1736 and staged this work again, at the Haymarket on 12 February of the following year, with Farinelli, who had been in London since 1734, in the title role of Alceste (who is none other than Demetrio). Pescetti next directed the 'Opera of the Nobility', the rival company to Handel's in the British capital, having succeeded Porpora in this post.[275] The famous castrato's name appears additionally in a heading ('Sung by Sig:r Farinelli') found on another manuscript in the AACC (classmark Ms 384), a handwritten score for voice and instrumental bass of the aria 'Amor, dover, rispetto' from *Adriano in Siria* by the Florentine composer Francesco Maria Veracini (1690-1768). Farinelli indeed performed the title role of this work at the King's Theatre in London on 26 November 1735 before an audience that included, notably, Handel.[276]

61. J. A. Hasse, 'So che pietà non hai' [*Catone in Utica*]. Enghien, Arenberg Archives and Cultural Centre, Ms 81.

Duke Léopold-Philippe d'Arenberg made the acquisition, probably during this period, of an engraved portrait of Farinelli, dated 1735, made in Venice by the German engraver Joseph Wagner (1706-1780) after an original painting by the Italian painter Jacopo Amigoni (or Amiconi) (1682-1752) who had met the castrato several times in London.[277] This engraving of the well-known singer perhaps came into the Duke's ownership while he was holding the post of Ambassador Extraordinary of the Empress during a stay in London from May to September 1742.[278]

The Ms 491 collection also includes three individual parts (soprano and instrumental bass, 'violino unis', and 'violetta') for the aria 'Amato ben, tu sei la mia speranza', which is sung by Ippolita in act III scene 7 of Vivaldi's *Ercole su'l Termodonte* RV 710. In the story Ippolita is sister of the Queen of the Amazons, Antiope; she falls in love with the Greek Teseo, a member of the expedition led by Ercole. This 'dramma per musica' composed on a libretto by Antonio Salvi was written while the *Prete rosso* was residing in Rome (from October 1722 onwards), and its first performance took place in January 1723 at the Teatro Capranica, a theatre to which Vivaldi was attached as a composer during the carnival seasons of 1723 and 1724.[279] Even though in *Ercole* the Venetian composer creates a pasticcio of his own compositions, recycling over twenty arias from his previous works, the aria 'Amato ben' is in fact a new piece. Although no folio among the manuscript parts of this aria held by the Arenberg Library actually gives the title of the work or the composer's name, it is not difficult to identify the aria, since

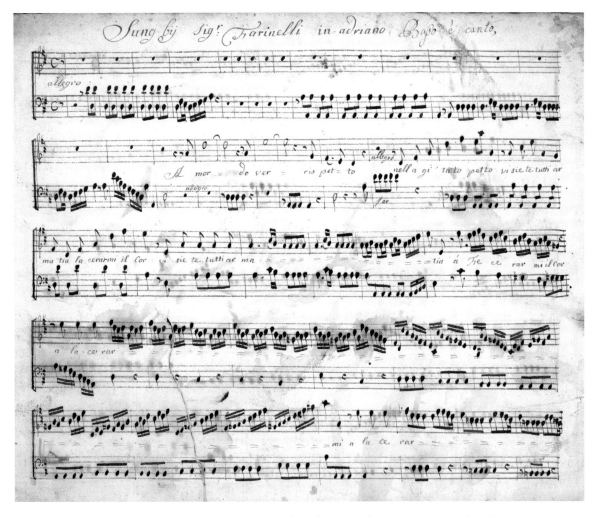

62. F. M. Veracini, 'Amor, dover, rispetto' [*Adriano in Siria*]. Enghien, Arenberg Archives and Cultural Centre, Ms 384.

it appears in various other sources, most notably in the Santini Collection in Münster.[280] Its abundant survival in manuscript copies is easily explained by the fact that this was the opera's 'signature' aria, enthusiastically received by audiences. In the first performance Ippolita was played by the Italian castrato soprano Giacinto Fontana, or 'Farfallino' (active 1712-1735), a singer who dominated Rome opera stages in travesty roles during the 1720s.[281] The other roles in this opera, even the female ones, were all performed by male singers, as papal restrictions required: Giovanni Ossi (Antiope), Giovanni Dreyer (Orizia), Girolamo Bartoluzzi (Martesia), Giovanni Battista Pinacci (Ercole), Giovanni Battista Minelli (Teseo), Giovanni Carestini (Alceste), and Domenico Giuseppe Galletti (Telamone), who would later travel to Brussels with the Landi company.

The composer who appears next in the collection is Leonardo Vinci, represented by his aria for soprano and instrumental bass 'Deh, respirar lasciatemi qualche momento', sung by the character Artaserse, Prince and later King of Persia, in act I scene 11 of the eponymous opera.[282] This 'dramma per musica' was first staged in Rome at the Teatro delle Dame on 4 February 1730, then performed in Milan and in Ferrara, with Farinelli in the role of Arbace, Artaserse's friend. We may note that the Ms 306 collection includes the manuscript aria 'Per quell'affetto che l'incatena', which has been identified as coming from the same opera and is sung by the character Semira (sister of Arbace and lover of Artaserse) in act II scene 13.[283] Although the format of the pages differs between the collections Ms 491

63. Carlo Broschi, or 'Farinelli', by Wagner, engraving after J. Amigoni.
Enghien, Arenberg Archives and Cultural Centre, Biographies of
musicians, 9/1.

and Ms 306, the hand of the two sources shows similarities to that of one of the two copyists of Ms 491.

The final two arias that have been identified from the Ms 491 collection are by the Bolognese composer Gaetano Maria Schiassi (1698-1754) and Porpora. Schiassi's aria for soprano and instrumental bass 'Chi vive amante sai che delira', sung by Poro's sister Erissena, who is in love with Alessandro, appears in act I scene 4 of *Alessandro nelle Indie*. This opera was staged in Bologna during the 1734 carnival, shortly before the definitive departure of Schiassi for the royal court of Lisbon. From Porpora we have a score for soprano, two violins, bass, and oboe of the aria 'Pietoso ciel difendimi', Carilda's aria from act II scene 9 of *Arianna e Teseo*, which was sung by the soprano Benedetta Soresina at the Teatro San Giovanni Grisostomo in Venice during the carnival of 1727.[284]

As regards the Ms 371 collection, consisting of unbound pages, this contains four arias, of which one remains anonymous.[285] The score of the aria 'Qui l'augel di pianta' may be connected with *Aci, Galatea e Polifemo* HWV 72, a cantata that Handel composed in Naples in 1708. This aria was to be reused by the composer a few years later in his masque *Acis and Galatea* HWV 49/b (1718). There follow parts for soprano and instrumental bass, as well as for second violin, of the aria 'Non ha ragione, ingrato' which

64. A. Vivaldi, 'Amato ben, tu sei la mia speranza' [*Ercole su'l Termodonte*]. Enghien, Arenberg Archives and Cultural Centre, Ms 491.

appears to be an extract from the end of scene 17 in act I of *Didone abbandonata*, the 'dramma per musica' by Vinci staged in Rome at the Teatro delle Dame for the opening of the carnival season on 14 January 1726. This aria is sung by the title character Dido, Queen of Carthage, who is in love with the Trojan Aeneas. Vinci set to music the first-ever opera libretto written by Metastasio, which was used for the first time by Domenico Sarro in 1724, and then in the following year by Porpora. The aria for soprano and instrumental bass that follows, 'Ritorna a lusingarmi', does not mention the composer's name but specifies 'in Didone'. By studying the textual incipit and the music itself we can establish that this extract is in fact the fifth Vivaldi aria in the AACC Collection. It is a soprano aria sung by Costanza at the end of scene 7 in act I of *Griselda* RV 718, a 'dramma per musica' based on a libretto by Carlo Goldoni (after Apostolo Zeno) that opened in Venice at the Teatro San Samuele on 18 May 1735. For Vivaldi this opera had particular significance, since it was the only work of his commissioned by a Venetian theatre owned by the Grimani family, who were the proprietors of the San Giovanni e Paolo and San Giovanni Grisostomo theatres in addition to the San Samuele. By writing 'in Didone', the manuscript's copyist, who transcribed only the part for voice and basso continuo, seems at first glance somehow to have become distracted, repeating as he did the provenance of the preceding aria. In fact, no aria entitled 'Ritorna a lusingarmi' appears in Metastasio's libretto of Vinci's *Didone abbandonata*.[286] Moreover, a comparative study of all the arias in *Didone* with 'Ritorna a lusingarmi' permits us to conclude that Vivaldi did not draw inspiration from his contemporary for the composition of this aria.

During the first performance of Vivaldi's *Griselda*, whose autograph manuscript is preserved in the Foà Collection in Turin, the role of Costanza, the daughter of Griselda and Gualtiero who was taken

65. Carlo Broschi, or 'Farinelli', by Jacopo Amigoni. Bucharest, Muzeul Naţional de Artă al României.

66. A. Vivaldi, 'Ritorna a lusingarmi' [*Griselda*]. Enghien, Arenberg Archives and Cultural Centre, Ms 371.

away at birth, was played by Margherita Giacomazzi. She was joined by Gregorio Balbi (Gualtiero), Anna Girò (Griselda), Gaetano Valetta (Roberto), Lorenzo Saletti (Ottone), and Elisabetta Gasparini (Corrado). The opera tells the story of Gualtiero, King of Thessaly, who is forced to renounce his wife Griselda, in order to marry someone whom he does not know to be actually his daughter, Costanza. The aria arrives at a moment when Costanza, welcomed by Gualtiero as his betrothed, is with her beloved, Roberto, whom she thinks she must leave for ever, and sings 'Ritorna a lusingarmi la mia speranza infida' (fickle hope returns to flatter me). The story turns out well for everyone in the end, since Griselda regains the love of Gualtiero, and Costanza and Roberto can marry.

This virtuoso aria, marked *Allegro non molto* in the autograph manuscript and *Allegro* in our copy, was conceived by Vivaldi as a demonstration piece for the Venetian soprano Margherita Giacomazzi, who made her début on the Venetian opera stage in this role. Handel would in fact include this aria in his pasticcio opera *Didone abbandonata* HWV A12, performed at London's Covent Garden theatre on 13 April 1737.[287] This therefore clarifies the remark 'In Didone' made in the ducal library manuscript, which is a reference to the borrowing of the Vivaldi aria in Handel's *Didone*.

It is remarkable to reflect that Belgian libraries listed by RISM hold no contemporary manuscripts of a Vivaldi vocal work or extract from an operatic work – with two exceptions, both held by the Royal Conservatory of Brussels: the aria 'Un guardo, un vezzo, un riso' from act III scene 5 of *La costanza trionfante degl'amori e degl'odii* RV 706, a 'dramma per musica' staged in Venice during the carnival of 1716;[288] and the aria 'Langue il fior sull'arsa sponda', already mentioned. One important collection of

67. D. Bigaglia, *Udite e sospirate*. Enghien, Arenberg Archives and Cultural Centre, Ms 412.

Italian repertoire, namely the music library of François-Joseph Fétis (Mons, 1784-1871), which has been in the Royal Library of Belgium's possession since 1872, surprisingly also lacks any manuscript arias by the Venetian composer. With no fewer than five Vivaldi arias in its possession, the ducal library is therefore exceptional in more ways than one.

Duke Léopold-Philippe d'Arenberg completed the Italian baroque repertoire of his library with a contemporary manuscript score of four unnumbered pages, consisting of one sheet of paper folded in two, on which the previously mentioned *tre lune* watermark can be discerned. This is a manuscript of the cantata in A minor for soprano and instrumental bass *Udite e sospirate* by Diogenio Bigaglia (c. 1676-c. 1745).[289] On the front page of the music we find the description: 'Cantata / Del P. D. Diogenio Bigaglia / Monaco Cassinense'. The last detail alludes to the fact that this composer had been a monk at the Benedictine 'Cassinese' monastery of San Giorgio Maggiore in Venice since 11 March 1694; he became subdeacon in 1698, priest on 22 August 1700, and deacon on 12 June 1704 (or 1706), before succeeding to the position of Prior in 1713.[290] Numerous manuscripts of Bigaglia's works carried the epithet 'monaco cassinense', as is the case for a collection in the Royal Conservatory of Brussels and another belonging to the Fétis collection at the Royal Library of Belgium.[291] Almost all the music by this composer has remained in manuscript – Masses, motets, oratorios (all lost bar one), and cantatas alike: only a single instrumental collection, his Op. 1, *XII Sonate a violino solo o sia flauto e violoncello o basso continuo*, was published; this was in Amsterdam during the 1720s.[292] Bigaglia seems to have been held in high regard by his contemporaries if we are to believe Jean-Benjamin de La Borde, who writes in his

Essai sur la musique ancienne et moderne (1780) that he (Bigaglia) 'sest distingué au point que les maîtres allaient le consulter, & faisaient le plus grand cas de ses conseils' (made such a mark that the masters sought him out, and took his advice very seriously).[293] Leaving aside the Arenberg manuscript, the study of *Udite e sospirate* can today refer to only one other source: a manuscript collection of twenty-two cantatas by the composer held by the Bibliothèque Nationale de France.[294] Around fifty other cantatas by Bigaglia are preserved in libraries across Europe; yet with no benchmarks for comparison, it is not possible to confirm whether the pages of Ms 412 are in the composer's hand or that of a scribe contemporary with him.

Instrumental music and private theatre

During the period of the strong Italian presence on the operatic stage of La Monnaie and subsequently, Léopold-Philippe d'Arenberg's music collection grew as he acquired the transalpine operatic repertoire in vogue at the time; yet this was also accompanied by an interest in furthering his family's practical musical instruction at home, with lessons in dancing and music forming part of his children's education. Instrumental music gradually accumulated on the shelves of the library, and it would not be long before a private theatre was built at the Duke's home.

In 1727 the organist, harpsichordist, and composer Josse Boutmy (1697-1769), originally from Ghent but at the time living in Brussels, became harpsichord teacher to Maria Francesca Pignatelli, the Duchess of Arenberg.[295] Boutmy was at this time organist of the collegiate church of Saints-Michel-et-Gudule, having in 1719 succeeded his eldest brother, Jacques-Adrien, in that post. Speaking of this period in a letter of 1756 to Governor Charles of Lorraine, Boutmy wrote 'qu'il a eu le bonheur d'avoir pour Ecoliers tous les jeunes Seigneurs et Dames de la Cour, ce qui lui faisoit un bénéfice considérable et l'a mis à même d'élever sa famille sans jamais avoir demandé ni gratification ni augmentation' (that

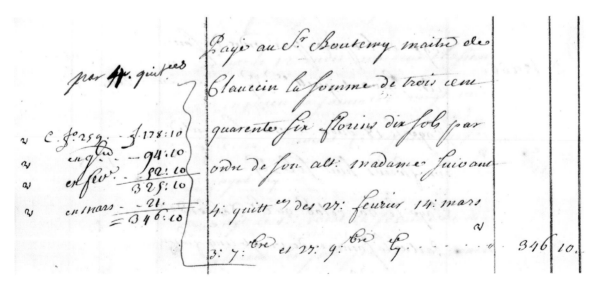

68. Reference to Josse Boutmy in the accounts of Bureau de St André, 1727. Enghien, Arenberg Archives and Cultural Centre, 63/22-28.

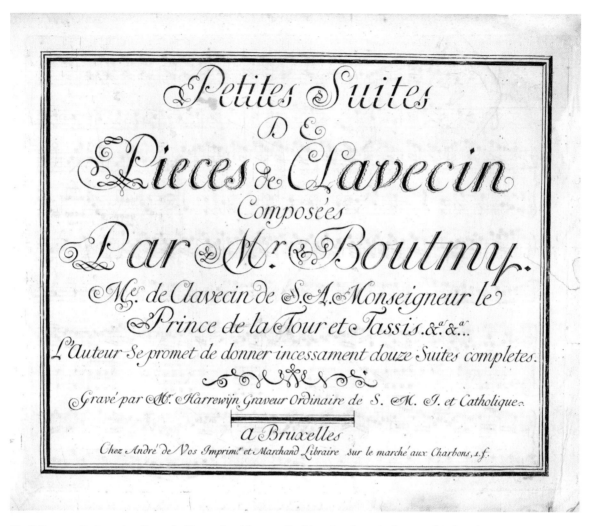

69. J. Boutmy, *Petites suites*, Brussels, Harrewijn, title page. Enghien, Arenberg Archives and Cultural Centre, I 691.

he had had the pleasure of having as his pupils all the young lords and ladies of the court, something that brought him considerable profit, giving him the means to raise his family without ever having to ask for a gratuity or a salary increase).[296] The work *Principes de l'accompagnement du clavecin* by the Parisian composer Jean-François Dandrieu (1682-1738) was probably acquired by the Duke at this time.[297] Published in Paris by Foucault in 1718, this practical guide, which established the reputation of its author and went through several reprints, includes a few explanatory pages, followed by twenty-one lessons. This volume is no longer held by the AACC Collection.[298]

The family would closely follow the career of Boutmy, whose first published works would be added to the music library when Boutmy was (from 1 January 1736) in the service of Prince Anselm Franz of Thurn and Taxis (1681-1739). The AACC therefore holds the sole known copy of the print of the *Petites suites de pièces de clavecin*, which was produced jointly by the music engraver François Harrewijn and the printer André de Vos in Brussels.[299] Since de Vos commenced his activity in December 1736, we may reasonably assume that this publication came off the presses during the course of 1737 as a prelude to the *Premier livre de clavecin*, published in Paris by Veuve Boivin in 1738.[300] Unfortunately, the

70.   J. Boutmy, *Petites suites*, Brussels, Harrewijn, inside cover of the title page. Enghien, Arenberg Archives and Cultural Centre, I 691.

preserved copy of the *Petites suites* cannot enlighten us about Boutmy's early attempts at composition, comprising as it does merely the title page and the back cover, presenting the start of an *Allegro* in G major. The Collection contains two copies of the *Premier livre* of 1738,[301] yet the *Troisième livre de pièces de clavecin*, engraved in Brussels in 1749 and dedicated to Charles of Lorraine, is missing, although it once belonged to the family library, as attested by the Duchess of Arenberg's catalogue of 1769.[302] Indeed, the list of subscribers to this last work mentions four members of the Arenberg family: the then Duchess and three of her four children still living: Marie-Adélaïde, Charles-Marie-Raymond, and Flore.[303] On the title page of this Op. 3, the composer mentions his post of organist at the Brussels court chapel, a position he had held since 1744. Throughout the six suites of the *Troisième livre*, Boutmy, as in the two first works, does not observe the usual sequence of the suite (*Allemande, Courante, Sarabande,* and *Gigue*), but instead presents – in the French style of François Couperin (1668-1733) in his 'Ordres', or of Jean-Philippe Rameau (1683-1764) in his *Suites* – a free alternation between pieces of a choreographic nature and others sometimes alluding to sonata movements (*Allegro, Andante, Vivace*) or else giving an indication of character (*Naïvement, Fièrement*). In contrast

71. J.-P. Rameau by Delatre. Enghien, Arenberg Archives and Cultural
Centre, Biographies of musicians, 9/1.

to previous works, no names of individuals are attached to the pieces. If the French contributions of Couperin and Rameau are obvious throughout the six suites, Handel's influence is also felt, melded with Italianizing formulae in the manner of Domenico Scarlatti. But even though Boutmy takes inspiration from the great masters, he also adds a very personal touch, which both surprises and moves in equal measure.[304] It was perhaps Boutmy who suggested to the Duke that he acquire for his library Rameau's *Traité de l'harmonie réduite à ses principes naturels*, a work published in Paris by Jean-Baptiste Christophe Ballard in 1722.[305] This ground-breaking publication in the history of European music theory indeed represents more than a work of pure theory, since it also contains elements of a treatise on composition.[306]

Between 1728 and 1734, Prince Charles-Marie-Raymond and Princess Marie-Adélaïde were receiving regular dancing lessons from Pierre Deschars, a dancer at the Paris Opera who had moved to Brussels (the city where he remained until his death on 12 May 1734).[307] Deschars had been dancing master to the Archduchess Maria Elisabeth's page-boys from 1726 and was paid 21 florins a month for his lessons.[308]

72. J.-H. Fiocco, *Pièces de clavecin* Op. 1, Brussels, Krafft, title page. Bibliothèque Nationale de France, Music Department, Vm [7] 1909.

On 30 October 1729 the ducal family rented the Grand Hôtel d'Egmont (the large Egmont mansion) in the Sablon district of Brussels, the owner of which was the Duchess's own brother, Procope d'Egmont-Pignatelli. Between 1730 and 1732, the Duke ordered renovation work to be carried out on this building, at a cost exceeding 4000 florins, notably in order to instal something that was rare for the era: a bathroom.[309]

In 1731, Joseph-Hector Fiocco dedicated his *Pièces de clavecin* Op. 1 to Léopold-Philippe d'Arenberg. At this time 'vice-maître de la musique de la cour' (assistant director of court music) alongside his brother Jean-Joseph, this composer, organist, and harpsichordist from Brussels had not forgotten the Duke, who had assisted his career by employing him in 1726 (see above) as his daughter's harpsichord teacher. The print of Fiocco's *Pièces de clavecin*, which in all certainty was held by the music library at this time, is not recorded in the catalogues of the second half of the eighteenth century.[310] The surviving copies of this publication reveal a superb title page embellished with a frontispiece depicting two lions, a crest of the Duke's coat of arms, and four cherubs – the work, like the rest of the volume, of the Brussels master-engraver Jean-Laurent Krafft (1694-1768).[311]

The dedication reproduced in the second folio of the edition, which is written in the declamatory style typical of this kind of text, conveys the sincere recognition of the musician towards his noble patron:

> A son Altesse Monseigneur Le Duc D'arenberg, Prince du St. Empire, Cher. de la Toison d'Or, Grand d'Espagne de la Pre. Classe. General d'Artillerie de sa Mté. Imp. & Cathe. Colel. d'un Regiment d'Infanterie allemand, &c. Grand Bailly Officier souverain du Pays & Comté d'Hainau, Gouverneur & Capne. Genal. de ladte. Province, &c. &c.
> Monseigneur La liberté que je prens ne seroit point pardonnable, si les extrêmes obligations que je dois A. V. A. ne sembloient me le permettre. Quoi que né dans la Musique, & pour ainsi dire élevé par elle même; Elle m'eût peut être refusé ses faveurs si la generosité de V. A. ne m'avoit mis en état de les meriter. De cette maniere Monseigneur, C'est plutôt le fruit de vos bontez que j'ôse Vous presenter, que mon propre travail. Agréez s'il vous plait le temoignage de ma reconoissance, il me sera toujours chèr, puisqu'il me procure la satisfaction de publier partout ce que je vous dois, aussi bien que la soumission profonde & respectueuse avec laquelle j'ai l'honneur d'être Monseigneur De Votre Altesse Le très humble & très obéissant serviteur J.H. Fiocco.

> [To His Highness Monseigneur Le Duc D'Arenberg, Prince of the Holy Roman Empire, Knight of the Golden Fleece, Grandee of Spain of the First Class, General of Artillery of His Imperial and Catholic Majesty, Colonel of a Regiment of German Infantry etc., Grand Bailiff, Sovereign Officer of the Land and County of Hainaut, Governor and Captain General of the said Province, etc., etc.
> Sir, the liberty that I am taking would be unpardonable if the extreme obligation that I owe to Your Highness did not appear to permit me it. Although born into music and, so to speak, raised by it, I would perhaps have been denied its favours if Your Highness's generosity had not put me in a condition to deserve them. In this light, Sir, it is rather the fruit of your own bounty that I am daring to present to you than my own work. Please design to accept this token of my thanks, which I will always cherish, since it procures me the satisfaction of broadcasting everywhere my debt to you, as well as the deep and respectful submission with which I have the honour to sign myself Your Highness's very humble and obedient servant J.H. Fiocco.]

Fiocco presented the Duke with his first musical publication before leaving Brussels for Antwerp, where he had been offered the post of Master of the Cathedral Music, not least thanks to a recommendation given him by the Duke of Arenberg.[312] He would return to Brussels in 1737 to take up the position of musical director at the collegiate church of Saint-Gudule. Comprising two suites, Op. 1 is stylistically close both to the French tradition of François Couperin and to Italian music, with its sonata movements. Enjoying some success, the collection next received an edition published in Amsterdam, and it remained popular for several years, for in 1757 the *Mercure de France* announced the release of a new edition, today lost, in Paris 'aux adresses ordinaires', stating 'que le nom de l'auteur fait l'éloge des *Piéces* et [...] dispense d'en dire davantage' (the composer's name alone is sufficient recommendation for the *Pièces*).[313]

Another volume that could not pass the ducal family by was an example of the *Pièces de clavecin* Op. 1 by the leading Brussels-based organist and harpsichordist Charles-Joseph van Helmont (1715-1790).[314] This publication, likewise engraved by Krafft, was advertised in the newspaper *Relations véritables* on 17 December 1737. Succeeding Josse Boutmy as organist of the collegiate church of Sainte-Gudule, van Helmont became choirmaster at the parish church of Notre-Dame de la Chapelle during that year of 1737.[315] In his *Pièces*, similarly comprising two suites, van Helmont came closer to the French style than

73. C.-J. van Helmont, *Pièces de clavecin*, Brussels, Krafft, title page. Enghien, Arenberg Archives
and Cultural Centre, I 859.

Fiocco and appreciated brusque changes of tonality.[316]

The music library of Duke Léopold-Philippe also benefited during these years from the acquisition
of a work of instrumental music which is no longer part of the AACC Collection: the *Sonates mêlées
de pièces pour la flûte traversière avec la basse* by the French virtuoso flautist and composer Michel
Blavet (1700-1768), published in Paris in 1732.[317] The previous year, the Paris publishing house Ballard
had issued *La Première hirondelle du printemps ou petits airs légers, pour la harpe, le clavecin & les
autres instruments*, a work by a certain Frederic G. Hauck. This print is among the *unica* in the AACC
Collection, since no copy of this publication exists in any library in the world, nor any other printed
work by this totally forgotten composer.[318] Unlike many Ballard editions, this one in the Duke's library
was not bound in leather, but instead had a marbled paper cover. This sixteen-page volume contains
(from pages 3 to 13) seven airs for voice and instrumental bass part: *Oui je veux aimer, Qu'un jeune
amant est dangereux, Qu'il est charmant de vous voir* (described as a 'Menuet d'Allemagne'), *À tout
moment, Iris, je me blâme, Le Doux pèlerinage* (termed a 'Contre-Danse'), *Dans nos bois tout se
renouvelle*, and *Embarquez-vous avec nous*. A table of the volume's contents appears after the pieces;
underneath can be seen the publication authorization given to the publisher 'à Paris le 16. Avril 1731'
by the official bodies. The volume closes with a reproduction of the official text pertaining to the issue
of the royal music printing licence granted to Jean-Baptiste Christophe Ballard in 1715, following the
death of his father Christophe Ballard.

After the departure of the Italian artists the programming of the Théâtre de la Monnaie would be

LA PREMIERE
HIRONDELLE
DU PRINTEMPS,
O U
PETITS AIRS LEGERS,

POUR LA HARPE, LE CLAVECIN,
& les autres Inſtruments.

Par Monſieur F R E D E R I C G. H A U C K.

DE L'IMPRIMERIE
De J-B-Christophe Ballard, Seul Imprimeur du Roy, & de l'Academie
Royale de Muſique. A Paris, ruë Saint Jean-de-Beauvais, Au Mont-Parnaſſe.

M. D C C X X X I.
AVEC PRIVILEGE DU ROY.

74. F. G. Hauck, *La Première hirondelle*, Paris, Ballard, title page. Enghien, Arenberg Archives
and Cultural Centre, I 761.

dominated by the great French tragic and comic repertoire, notably under the impetus of Jean-Richard Durant, known as Le Roux, an actor from the Comédie-Française, who commenced his directorship of the Brussels stage in the Easter of 1730.[319] The Duke attended these performances, leasing an annual box for 630 florins from Durant and subsequently from his successor, the Parisian Joseph Bruseau de La Roche (d. Brussels 17 July 1750).[320] In October 1731 he also attended a *spectacle* at the Théâtre du Coffy, paying 20 escalins (around 7 florins) 'pour voir les singes' (to see the monkeys).[321] This Brussels theatre, located in rue de la Colline, near the Grand-Place, played host in particular to tight-rope walkers, acrobats, and marionettes.[322]

Between 1730 and 1733 the Duke of Arenberg and audiences at La Monnaie were able to see the great tragedies of Jean Racine (*Britannicus, Andromaque, Mithridate, Iphigénie,* and *Phèdre et Hippolyte*) and Pierre Corneille (*Médée, Horace, Polyeucte martyr, Pyrrus roi d'Épire, Rodogune, princesse des Parthes, Le Comte d'Essex,* and *Nicomède*). Among the comedies performed was *Démocrite amoureux* by Jean-François Regnard, as well as two works by Philippe Néricault ('Destouches'): *Le Philosophe marié ou le Mari honteux de l'être* and *Le Glorieux*.[323] While the theatre dominated at this time, music was welcomed at some performances; thus on 1 October 1730 there was a staging of the comedy *Le Nouveau monde* by the Abbé Simon-Joseph Pellegrin (1663-1745), a play interspersed with musical interludes by the singer and actor Jean-Baptiste Maurice Quinault (1687-1745),[324] whose *Musique du Triomphe du temps* (a work published in Paris by Flahault in 1725) was owned by the Duke of Arenberg.[325] Another instance was Racine's tragedy *Athalie*, performed on 5 November 1730 in Brussels, with choruses composed in 1691 by Jean-Baptiste Moreau (1656-1733).[326]

75. J.-B. M. Quinault, *Musique du Triomphe du temps*, Paris, Flahault, title page. Enghien, Arenberg Archives and Cultural Centre, I 838.

On 1 March 1732 Duke Léopold-Philippe d'Arenberg began to invest in a private theatre[327] at his château at Enghien.[328] A succession of cabinet-makers, painters, and founders were employed, and on April 1732 Jean de La Fontaine's comedy *Le Florentin* was staged.[329] However, construction continued over the next few months.[330] On 11 August 1732 the Duke paid the person who provided lodging for several musicians engaged to play at a reception held at Enghien, but the register does not give their names.[331] While this development enabled the Arenberg family to enjoy a veritable private theatre of their own, it seems that as early as the seventeenth century makeshift theatres had been erected for one performance or another at the Enghien residence. So on 1 September 1625, during the events held as part of the wedding celebrations of Caroline d'Arenberg and Ernest, Count of Issenbourg, a play entitled *La Prise de Bréda* was performed by some pupils from the school attached to the Augustine monastery in Enghien on a 'théâtre dressé au chasteau'.[332] Like the château itself, the private theatre built in 1732 was demolished in 1806, having suffered the depredations of the French occupiers.

In 1733 Duke Léopold-Philippe, wishing to have a permanent pied-à-terre in the imperial capital, purchased a house in Gumpendorf on the outskirts of Vienna. Having returned to Brussels, the Duke left the city again in August 1733 to take command of his troops in the Rhineland. He would not return to the Austrian Netherlands until 1736. During his absence his Egmont residence in Brussels was leased to the Viennese Count Friedrich August von Harrach, who since 1732 had held the post of Minister Plenipotentiary of Governor Maria Elisabeth.[333]

While the Duke was away at on campaign some performances nonetheless took place at Enghien. On 30 May 1733 a certain Gilles Ladron delivered two tambourines 'pour la Commedie d'Enghien';

these percussion instruments, often used to supply rhythm to dances, were probably intended to accompany a performance at the private theatre.[334] The following month the Brussels dancing master Jacques Perez (1688-1760), son of the dancer André Perez,[335] also appeared on the Arenberg private stage;[336] at one of these performances *mirlitons*, or onion flutes, also known as eunuch flutes – tubular woodwind instruments – were played.[337]

On 24 April 1736 the Duke's elder sister Marie-Anne died in Utrecht. She had married François-Egon de la Tour d'Auvergne, Duke of Bouillon (1671-1710),[338] in Brussels in 1707. Widowed, she became married again in February or March 1712 to Martin Maisy, her late husband's equerry – a scandalous *mésalliance* that became the talk of Europe. Léopold-Philippe d'Arenberg was at that time a close adviser to Emperor Charles VI, before being appointed by the latter, on 23 February 1737, Commander-in-Chief of the troops in the Austrian Netherlands.[339]

On 25 November 1737, the Duke bought the Petit Hôtel d'Egmont in the Sablon district – the *hôtel de Luxembourg* – thereby enjoying the use of a permanent pied-à-terre in Brussels once again.[340] A few months prior to this the family's harpsichords had been reconditioned by an instrument-maker in Brussels called Louis Bizant, who later would join the staff of the court of Governor Charles of Lorraine.[341] As regards the bass singer at the royal chapel, Jacques-Antoine Godecharle (father of the Brussels composer Eugène Godecharle),[342] the Duke assigned to him the task of copying and converting 'a la clef du violon 180 menuets a l'usage des Commedies'[343] – although it has not been possible to trace this task of clef alteration, which was probably carried out in connection with the activities organized for the Enghien private stage.

Meanwhile, during the period 1733-1739, the Théâtre de la Monnaie continued to see its directorship change continuously, some companies going bankrupt within a matter of weeks. The French repertoire of tragedies and comedies remained dominant, although the 'dramma per musica' *Lucio Papirio* (performed several times in 1728 by the Landi company) was staged again on 10 October 1734.[344] In terms of operatic repertoire, we must mention the first-known Brussels performance of Lully's 'tragédie en musique' *Cadmus et Hermione*, which took place on 14 November 1734;[345] of this score (as already mentioned) the ducal library holds a manuscript copy.[346] The Duke of Arenberg also acquired the two first volumes of the first edition of the reference work by the Parisian brothers François and Claude Parfaict *Histoire du théâtre françois, depuis son origine jusqu'à présent. Avec la vie des plus célèbres poëtes dramatiques, des extraits exacts & un catalogue raisonné de leurs pièces, accompagnés de notes historiques & critiques*, a fifteen-volume work published in Amsterdam between 1735 and 1749.[347]

Corneille and Racine continued to delight Brussels audiences, but other playwrights appeared: notably, Marivaux, whose comedy *La Double inconstance* premiered at La Monnaie on 24 February 1734. But the man who stood out between 1733 and 1739 was unquestionably Voltaire. His tragedies *Brutus, Zaïre, Alzire ou les Américains*, and *Hérode et Mariamne*, and his comedy *L'Enfant prodigue ou l'École de la jeunesse* were all box office successes.[348]

The Duke of Arenberg held the French author and philosopher in particular regard, and invited Voltaire to stay with him again in 1739. Voltaire and his companion Gabrielle Émilie Le Tonnelier de Breteuil, Marquise du Châtelet, arrived in Brussels on 28 May of that year, and over the following

Fig. 3.

Fig. 11.

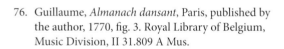

Après la passe croisée, Le Cavalier s'etrouve, le bras droit derriere et le gauche élevé.

Le Cavalier tenant sa Dame à la 3ᵉ. position, lui fait faire deux tours sans la lacher.

76. Guillaume, *Almanach dansant*, Paris, published by the author, 1770, fig. 3. Royal Library of Belgium, Music Division, II 31.809 A Mus.

77. Guillaume, *Almanach dansant*, Paris, published by the author, 1770, fig. 11. Royal Library of Belgium, Music Division, II 31.809 A Mus.

months the couple visited the Duke often, both in the capital and at Enghien.[349] In a letter he addressed to Helvétius on 6 July 1739 from Enghien, Voltaire wrote:

> […] Je suis actuellement avec madᶜ du Chastelet à Anguien chez m. le duc d'Aremberg, à 7 lieues de Bruxelles. […] Je suis actuellement dans un château où il n'a jamais eu de livres que ceux que madᶜ du Châtelet et moi avons apportés. Mais en récompense, il y a des jardins plus beaux que ceux de Chantilly, et on y mène cette vie douce et libre qui est l'agrément de la campagne. Le possesseur de ce beau séjour vaut mieux que beaucoup de livres. Je crois que nous allons y jouer la comédie, on y lira du moins les rôles des acteurs […].[350]

> [[…] I am currently with Mme du Chastelet at [E]nghien with the Duke of Arenberg, 7 leagues from Brussels. […] I am staying in a château where there have never been any books save those which Mme du Châtelet and I have brought ourselves. But, to make up for this, there are gardens here which in beauty outshine those of Chantilly, and we are enjoying a peaceful and free existence which is the agreeableness of the countryside. Our host is worth more than many books. I think we are going to put on a play – at least we shall read aloud the actors' lines […].]

In these few lines the writer appears somewhat harsh in his observation about the Duke's library, but stresses that he has given the latter some books – these possibly being the first volumes of the

Amsterdam edition of his *Œuvres*, which first began to appear in 1738.[351] He describes the beauty of the gardens at Enghien but speaks also of the fact that a private theatrical performance is about to take place. The play in question was Molière's *L'École des femmes*, with Anne-Charlotte de Rouvroy (1675-1755), Princess of Chimay, in the role of Agnès, the Marquise du Châtelet as Georgette, and Voltaire as Arnolphe.[352] Poquelin, better known by his stage name Molière (of whose new 1725 edition of the *Œuvres* the Duke owned a copy),[353] had featured at the Monnaie in 1735 with his *Misanthrope*, and the following year with *La Princesse d'Élide*.[354]

Among the 'opéra-ballets' likely to have been added to the shelves of the Duke of Arenberg's music library during this period we find the Paris prints of *Le Ballet de la Paix* and *Zaïde, reine de Grenade*.[355] The first, a work by the Parisian composers François Francoeur (1698-1787) and François Rebel (1701-1775), was premiered in Paris at the Palais-Royal Theatre on 29 May 1738 and published the same year.[356] Pancrace Royer (c. 1705-1755) composed the second 'opéra-ballet', which audiences at the Palais-Royal saw, likewise for the first time, on 3 September 1739;[357] this was a work which for the composer – harpsichord teacher to the royal children of France since 1735 – marked a very successful return to the operatic genre. Because we have only a fragmentary picture of the programming of the Théâtre de la Monnaie for these years, it is hard to know whether these two ballets were performed at the Monnaie or not.[358] The prints were perhaps acquired by the ducal family during a visit to Paris; the family may even have attended one or other of these performances.

The Duke and Governor Charles of Lorraine

Emperor Charles VI died on 20 October 1740, and his daughter Maria Theresa became Empress. When Governor Maria Elisabeth died on 26 August 1741, Charles Alexander of Lorraine (born 12 December 1712 at Lunéville) became Governor General of the Austrian Netherlands, remaining in that post until his death on 4 July 1780. Charles Alexander was brother-in-law to Empress Maria Theresa in a double sense, being both the brother of Maria Theresa's husband Emperor Francis I and the husband of Maria Theresa's sister, Archduchess Maria Anna of Austria, whom he married in Vienna on 7 January 1744. Engaged in a combat triggered by the War of the Austrian Succession, the Governor would not arrive in the Austrian Netherlands until 1744, making his entry into Brussels with his wife on 26 March of that year. In April 1742 Maria Theresa sent the Duke of Arenberg to The Hague and to London as Ambassador Extraordinary. After the Duke fulfilled his mission successfully the Empress made him a Privy Councillor. In 1743 he took command of the troops of George II of England, in Hanover. On 27 June of that year these battalions defeated the French at Dettingen in Lower Franconia, a military victory celebrated by Handel in his 'Dettingen' *Te Deum* in D major HWV 283.

During this troubled period the Duke's children continued to receive dancing lessons. From October 1742 until March 1743[359] these lessons were given by a certain 'Tabary', probably the Tabari recorded in 1736 in Paris as a dancer with the Opéra-Comique at the annual Foire Saint-Laurent (St Lawrence Fair).[360] Despite the difficult political context Duke Léopold-Philippe arranged the marriage of his daughter Flore, on 12 January 1744 at the Arenberg château at Heverlee, to Jean-Charles Joseph, Count

78. Charles of Lorraine by F. Harrewijn. Royal Library of Belgium,
Prints and Drawings Division, S I 23106 plano.

of Mérode-Montfort and Marquis of Deynze (1719-1774). A few weeks later the Duke's mother died: the Dowager Duchess Maria Enrichetta Felicita del Carretto passed away at Drogenbos on 22 February,[361] making her son heir to her Italian possessions of Grana, Monferrato, Roccavignale, and Savona, while Drogenbos and a house situated near the Porte de Hal in Brussels were also added to his estate.

In March 1744 Duke Léopold-Philippe was probably in Brussels to attend the official entry of the new governor. He may have taken advantage of the occasion to admire in the hall at the Serment de Saint-Georges (in the Place de Bavière) the famous automata by the inventor from Grenoble Jacques de Vaucanson (1709-1782),[362] which, the newspaper the *Gazette de Bruxelles* tells us in effusive tones, 'ont fait l'admiration de tout Paris, Londres, & de la Hollande', and are 'autant de Chef-d'Œuvres & Miracles de l'art, qui sont uniques dans le monde'.[363] Whether or not he saw the automata, the Duke certainly acquired for his library the pamphlet *Mécanisme du flûteur automate, présenté à Messieurs de l'académie royale des sciences. Avec la description d'un canard artificiel [...] Et aussi celle d'une autre figure, également merveilleuse, jouant du tambourin & de la flute*, published in Paris in 1738.[364] The

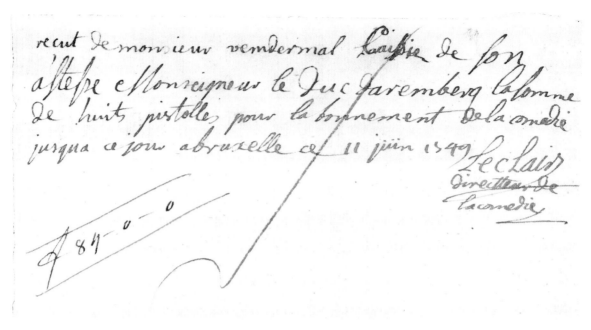

79. Receipt signed J.-B. Leclair, 11 June 1749. Enghien, Arenberg Archives and Cultural Centre, 64/34/I.

tambourine- and flute- player mentioned above 'imite par art tout ce que le plus habile Joüeur est obligé de faire'.[365]

On Sunday 5 April 1744, Easter Day, the new Governor and his wife for the first time attended Mass at the collegiate church of Sainte-Gudule, presided over by court musicians under the direction of Jean-Joseph Fiocco.[366] But after two months Charles of Lorraine found himself obliged to leave the territories he governed to return to the battlefield and the armies in the Rhineland. At that time the imperial troops were under the high command of Léopold-Philippe d'Arenberg.[367] From that period onwards, the Duke would maintain a close relationship with the Governor, a bond that would outlast the end of the war.

After their victory at Fontenoy the French occupied the Austrian Netherlands, and on 11 May 1745 Brussels was placed under siege by the Maréchal de Saxe, head of the French armed forces. In June 1745 the Duke was given command of the troops in Silesia. From 4 to 9 May 1746 King Louis XV stayed at the Grand Hôtel d'Egmont in Brussels. On the first evening after his arrival he held a gathering to which he invited the actor Charles-Simon Favart (1710-1792);[368] Favart was asked to direct the Brussels operatic stage, a post he would retain until the French departure from the city. With a large company at his disposal, Favart put on many of the works he had staged in Paris at the Opéra-Comique. He also brought to the stage his own works, such as Cythère assiégée, an 'opéra-comique' in one act, a fragment of which survives in the ducal library. Indeed, a contemporary manuscript transmits just the (unaccompanied) vocal line of the air 'Habitants de ce doux empire' from Favart's work (a parody of Lully's Armide), which was performed in Brussels 'le 7 juillet 1748'.[369] This aria was apparently copied directly from the libretto printed in Brussels for the occasion.[370] Containing thirty pages of engraved music, this publication states on its title page that the work was 'Représenté à Bruxelles pour la premiere fois le 7 juillet 1748 par les comédiens de S.A.S. monseigneur le comte de

80. Charles of Lorraine by Deforgues, 1756. Royal Library of Belgium,
     Palace of Charles of Lorraine.

Saxe, marechal général des camps & armées du Roy, & commandant general des Pays-Bas';[371] this date is further reproduced in the upper right-hand corner of the first of the four pages of the manuscript belonging to the ducal collection.

The Treaty of Aix-la-Chapelle was signed on 18 October 1748, restoring the Southern Netherlands to Austria. The French troops departed, and the Duke of Arenberg returned to Brussels on 28 January 1749. Over the subsequent weeks he led the commission of the provisional government, which continued its operations until Charles of Lorraine's arrival in Brussels in April of that year.[372]

Now returned to his Brussels residence, the Duke could once again devote some of his time to his books and to music. In February 1749 the volumes in the library were catalogued, numbered, and put back on the shelves,[373] while a few days later the large harpsichord underwent repairs and was tuned by Louis Bizant.[374] As in the past, the Duke was also pleased to be able to attend performances at the Monnaie, paying his subscription to the director, the French musician and dancer Jean-Benoît Leclair (1714 - after 1759), who was the younger brother of the violinist and composer Jean-Marie Leclair.[375] On 27 April 1749 the Duke saw the younger Leclair's ballet *Le Retour de la Paix*, based on a libretto by Joseph Bruseau de La Roche,[376] to celebrate the return of Charles of Lorraine to the Austrian Netherlands.[377] The libretto, printed for the occasion by the Brussels-based Jean-Joseph Boucherie,[378] states on its title page that the work was dedicated to the Governor and that he attended the performance.[379]

The Duke as co-director of the Théâtre de la Monnaie

Freed from the constraints of his military career, Duke Léopold-Philippe d'Arenberg decided to take an active part in the operatic world of Brussels, becoming co-director of the Théâtre de la Monnaie in succession to Leclair, who left Brussels to take up positions directing the Liège, Ghent, and Utrecht opera houses, before settling in Holland. From 21 June 1749 until 1 April 1752 the Duke shared the management of the institution with Duke Charles-Élisabeth-Conrad d'Ursel (1717-1775) and Jean-Charles Joseph, Count of Mérode and Marquis of Deynze (also the Duke's son-in-law since 1744). The licence stipulated that the Duke of Arenberg and his two co-directors agreed 'de tenir la Redoutte, faire representer les Opera, Commedies et donner des Bals, faisant defense a tous Autres d'en representer qui puissent faire tort a ceux qui ont faite la dite Soumission […]'.[380] Further on, the official document required that 'Les trois soussignés s'engagent de procurer une troupe des Commediens beaucoup meilleure que l'on est accoutumé d'en avoir dans cette Ville' and that Charles of Lorraine, who would select the boxes intended for the court and draw up the list of persons 'qui doivent entrer sans payer', support the enterprise by paying an annual sum of 6000 florins; this sum would be greater if the Governor wished the company to include extra singers or dancers.[381]

Although the print does not specify this, it is probable that the *divertissement* entitled *Le Retour désiré*, composed by Charles-Joseph van Helmont in Brussels, was performed at La Monnaie while it was co-directed by Léopold-Philippe d'Arenberg. The engraved publication, which is today in the Duke's music collection,[382] mentions the year 1749 but gives neither the place nor the date of the first performance. Van Helmont was at that time musical director at the Sainte-Gudule collegiate church, a post mentioned on the title page, whose attractive frontispiece depicts five cherubs encircling

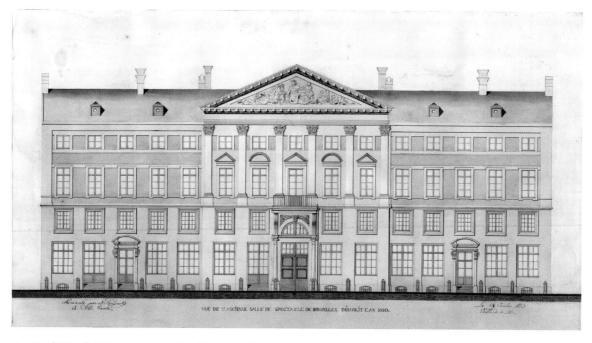

81. *Le Théâtre de la Monnaie*, drawing. Museum of the City of Brussels-The King's House.

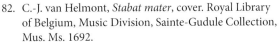

82. C.-J. van Helmont, *Stabat mater*, cover. Royal Library of Belgium, Music Division, Sainte-Gudule Collection, Mus. Ms. 1692.

83. C.-J. van Helmont, *Le Retour désiré*, Brussels, 1749. Enghien, Arenberg Archives and Cultural Centre, I 766.

the coat of arms of Charles of Lorraine. The volume includes eight airs and a duet, but omits the composition's three symphonies, three ballets, and two choruses. As was often the case with *pièces de circonstance* (occasional works with social-political relevance), recourse to mythological characters (Jupiter, Mercury, Minerva, and Venus) allowed power to be extolled through allegory. A nymph of the Netherlands comes to sing the praises of Jupiter, embodied in the person of Charles of Lorraine himself.[383]

During the summer of 1749 the co-directors invited to Brussels an Italian company that had not long before staged a series of 'opere buffe' in London but which, on account of debt, had been forced to make a rapid departure from the English capital. The principal singer of this company directed by the impresario Giovanni Francesco Crosa (c. 1700 - after January 1771),[384] which came to Brussels on 5 August for two months,[385] was the Florentine tenor Filippo Laschi (active 1739-1789), who had achieved great success in Venice in the 'opera buffa' repertory.[386] The *Gazette de Bruxelles* reported on the first performance, which was attended by Governor Charles of Lorraine:

> Le Sr. Grosa, Entreprenneur de l'Opera Comique Italien donnera aujourd'hui la premiere Répresentation, où le Sr. Lasky joüerea le Rôle de Bouffon. Cette troupe est aussi parfaite que nombreuse, tant pour les Voix que pour les Instrumens, dont l'Orchestre est de plus accomplies. Le Sr. Grosa ne donnèra ses Répresentations que pendant deux mois de suite, étant obligé de retourner pour le mois de Novembre à Londres, où il y eut un concours extraordinaire de monde.[387]

> [Sr Grosa, the Director of the Italian Opéra Comique company will today give its first performance, with Sr Lasky in the comic role. This company is as perfect as it is numerous as regards both its voices and its instruments, and its orchestra is among the most accomplished. Sr Grosa will give performances during only two consecutive months, being obliged to return by November to London, where there was an extraordinarily large audience.]

Several manuscripts were added to the Duke's music library via these artists. Ms 399 contains three separate parts (voice and instrumental bass, first violin, and second violin) of the aria 'Madam lasciatemi in libertà' from the 'dramma giocoso' *Li tre cicisbei ridicoli* by Natale Resta (*maestro di cappella* in Milan in 1748), which was performed in Bologna during the carnival of 1747 and staged by Crosa's company in London and afterwards Brussels in 1749. The vocal part states that the movement is 'cantata da Laschi', the singer who performed the role of one of the three *cicisbei*, or *chevaliers servants*, required by the plot. The Duke also owned a copy of the bilingual Italian-French libretto published for the performance by the Brussels printer and bookseller Jean-Joseph Boucherie; this publication states that the work was destined 'Per il gran teatro di Brusella' but does not give an exact date.[388]

Although no Brussels libretto confirms this, *Don Calascione*, by the Italian composer Gaetano Latilla (1711-1788), was likewise among the works performed at the Théâtre de la Monnaie by the Italians. This 'dramma giocoso', which is the third, revised version of *Il Gismondo*, similarly by Latilla (the performance of which took place in Naples in the summer of 1737), had been staged in London on 21 January 1749 by the Crosa company.[389] As for the second version of the work, *La finta cameriera*, this had been premiered at the Teatro Valle in Rome during the summer of 1738. Mss 363, 373, 380, and 398 in the AACC library contain three numbers from *Don Calascione* that are clearly the work of three different copyists. Ms 363 and 373 bring together the five separate parts of the 'con tre stromenti' duet 'Quando senti la campana' (tenor *travesti*, bass, first violin, second violin, and instrumental bass), which is sung in act II scene 3 by Giocondo, a young man disguised as a servant, and Pancrazio, an elderly Florentine man. Only the title page of the bass part mentions the composer's name, rendered in misspelt form as 'Del Signor Cattila'. The aria 'Colà sul praticello' for tenor *travesti* and instrumental bass is kept under classmark Ms 380. Performed by the character Dorina, Pancrazio's (female) gardener, this number appears a little later on in the same act, in scene 10. As for Ms 398, this contains two separate parts, for tenor plus instrumental bass and first violin, of the aria 'La frivoletta, la violetta' (and not 'fravoletta', as written on the manuscript), sung by Don Calascione, a young maverick from Rome, in scene 5 of the third and final act. The two parts, with their annotation 'Sig.r Laschi', tell us that the title role was indeed performed by the Florentine tenor in Brussels, whereas in performances of earlier versions of the work this role had been taken by Francesco Baglioni. The success of *Il Gismondo* and its later versions allowed Latilla to establish his reputation as an opera composer, which contributed towards his appointment in 1753 as *maestro di coro* at the Ospedale della Pietà in Venice.

Among the members of Crosa's Italian company in Brussels was also the castrato Gaetano Guadagni

84. Gaetano Latilla, 'La frivoletta, la violetta' [*Don Calascione*]. Enghien, Arenberg Archives and Cultural Centre, Ms 398.

(1728-1792), who had just made his name in London with Handel's support and would become famous in 1762 as Orpheus in Gluck's *Orfeo ed Euridice*. Also present were the Florentine *primo buffo* Pietro Pertici (c. 1700-1768) and the soprano Eugenia Mellini, an Italian singer who would afterwards move to Amsterdam (the city where she died, in 1755).[390] Under the classmark Ms 89, the manuscript score of the aria 'Giovinotti d'oggidì' for soprano and instrumental bass includes the information 'cantata dalla Signora Laschi', referring to the Bolognese singer Anna Maria Querzoli Laschi (active 1737-1768), wife of the tenor Laschi and likewise a singer with the Crosa company. This same aria appears in a manuscript held by Neuchâtel University Library, with the heading 'Signre Pertici', a detail absent from the manuscript in the ducal collection. This could suggest that the singer was the author of the text, a hypothesis supported by the fact that he did indeed rework and translate a series of librettos. Another name, that of Eugenia Mellini, appears in the upper left- and right-hand corners of the first of the two pages of the manuscript score Ms 72 in the Music Collection, where we discover the aria 'Questo non sarà mai' by Baldassare Galuppi, who was also known as 'il Buranello' (1706-1785),[391] a reference to his place of birth, Burano. In contrast to the many manuscripts scant in introductory detail, this score, once again written on paper with the Venetian *tre lune* watermark, not only gives the name of the interpreter of the role and its composer but also mentions the year 1745 and the city of Venice. This is in fact an aria from the 'dramma giocoso' *La forza d'amore* performed at the Teatro San Cassiano on 30 January 1745, where it is sung in act I scene 7 by Talestri, a role that was indeed performed by Eugenia Mellini.[392]

85. B. Galuppi, 'Questo non sarà mai' [*La forza d'amore*]. Enghien, Arenberg Archives and Cultural Centre, Ms 72.

The Laschi couple and Eugenia Mellini also performed in the Brussels production of *Orazio*, a 'dramma giocoso' by Pietro Auletta (c. 1698-1771), as indicated in the bilingual libretto published in The Hague by the printer Pierre Gosse, which states on its title page: 'Per il gran teatro di Brusella'.[393] The Brussels performance of this work took place on 21 September 1749, as reported in the *Gazette de Bruxelles*.[394] Performed in Naples during the 1737 carnival season, *Orazio* had many more successful runs, both in Italy and in Munich, before being staged at the King's Theatre in London on 29 November 1748, where it was absorbed in part into a pasticcio entitled *Il maestro di musica* with arias by Giovanni Battista Pergolesi (1710-1736).

It is more than probable, even if the accounts are mute on the subject, that such personalities as Laschi performed in private at the Duke's residence (as in the time of Landi), and that some of the manuscripts mentioned were donated on those occasions. After a period in Brussels Crosa's company returned to London, where it went bankrupt;[395] it then moved to The Hague in June 1750, and subsequently to Leiden, before finally performing in Amsterdam from August to October that same year.[396]

On 3 October 1749 the Duke and his associates played an active role in organizing the fireworks launched from the ornamental lake in Brussels Park by the Italian pyrotechnicians Gaetano Ruggieri and Giuseppe Sarti by suggesting that the vocal and instrumental concert accompanying the rockets, girandolas, and other cascading fireworks be provided by the musicians of the orchestra of La Monnaie. The event was attended not only by Charles of Lorraine and his court but also by 'un concours infini de peuple', the *Gazette de Bruxelles* tells us.[397] The same pyrotechnical masters had recently dazzled London (on 27 April of that year) with a display commemorating the Treaty of Aix-la-Chapelle, accompanied

Baldassare Galuppi

86. Baldassare Galuppi by G. Bernasconi. Royal Library of Belgium, Music Division, II 31.657 A Mus.

by Handel's famous Royal Fireworks Music. The Saxon composer's music was therefore possibly used again in Brussels Park.

When the Italian company left, the Monnaie's co-directors invited to Brussels the brothers François (1695 - before 1774) and Barthélemy (1699 - after 1763) Hus from Rouen, French actors and theatre directors[398] who staged performances in the city for several weeks from November 1749.[399] The *Almanach historique et chronologique de la comedie françoise etablie à Bruxelles* (1754) tells us:

> La Cour, voulant avoir un Spectacle à Bruxelles, Monseigneur le Duc d'Aremberg, qui a toujours honoré les Talens de sa Protection, engagea Monsieur le Marquis de Deims & Monsieur le Duc d'Ursel, de se joindre à lui pour attirer la troupe des Freres His, qui étoit pour lors à Rouen. Elle ne put se refuser aux Conditions avantageuses qui lui furent proposées. Elle arriva en cette Ville, & y fit sa première Représentation au Mois de Novembre 1749. Sur la fin de cet Hyver une partie de cette Troupe se dispersa, & fut remplacée par differens sujets, sous la Direction de ces mêmes Seigneurs qui la continuerent ainsi pendant trois années.[400]

> [The Court being desirous of entertainment in Brussels, his Lordship the Duke of Arenberg – who has always honoured the talent under his patronage – entreated Monsieur the Marquis of Deims and Monsieur the Duke of Ursel to join him in bringing to the city the [Hus] Brothers, whose opera company was then based in Rouen. They could not but accept the advantageous conditions offered. The company arrived in this city, and gave its first performance in the month of November 1749. At the end of that winter, some members of the company disbanded, and were replaced by new artists, under the direction of the same gentlemen, who continued to direct productions there for the next three years.]

The Hus company performed a solely French repertoire, although it is not certain which works were staged. On 6 November 1749 Charles of Lorraine attended one of their performances for the first

87. Project for antique stage scenery with figures from the *commedia dell'arte* by G.-F.
Blondel (?). Royal Library of Belgium, Prints and Drawings Division, S III 16797.

time – not at the Monnaie but at the Théâtre du Coffy, where he saw a 'réprésentation de la Comedie Françoise'.[401]

A bilingual libretto printed by Jean-Joseph Boucherie tells us that *La serva padrona* by Giovanni Battista Pergolesi was to be performed 'nell' [*sic*] grande teatro in Bruxelle l'anno 1751', but we do not know who the actors were for this performance, nor exactly when it took place.[402] With this choice of programming, the Duke of Arenberg and his partners continued to affirm their affinity with the transalpine operatic repertoire. The intermezzi *La serva padrona*, which had been staged by the composer for the first time on 28 August 1733 at the Teatro San Bartolomeo in Naples during the intervals of Pergolesi's own 'opera seria' *Il prigionier superbo*, had, as we know, rapidly become a work in its own right, with enduring international success. The Brussels performance came only a short time before the Parisian one on 1 August 1752 – the event that would ignite the famous *Querelle des Bouffons*. During this period the Duke of Arenberg also acquired the score, engraved by John Walsh in London in 1749, of Pergolesi's celebrated *Stabat mater*, which the gifted Italian composer completed in 1735 before succumbing to tuberculosis on 16 March the following year at the age of 26.[403]

The Arenberg family account books preserve the evidence of numerous financial transactions completed 'pour la Comédie' during the seasons managed by the Duke, notably with Veuve Nettine, a state banker.[404] We find listed: the purchase of 'habits de comédie venus de Paris';[405] payments to the French actor Jean-François Fieuzal, alias Durancy (d. Brussels, 16 February 1769);[406] those to the dancer Louise Paran;[407] those to the French ballet master Jean-Baptiste Dutrou, alias Lemaire (d. Brussels, 31 October 1761);[408] and payment for a stage curtain painted by Jacques-Denis Dubois (c. 1720-1776), who was also an actor.[409]

88. G. B. Pergolesi by E. von Heinrich. Bibliothèque Nationale de France, Music Department, Prints Collection, Pergolesi G. 001.

89. G. B. Pergolesi, *Stabat mater*, London, Walsh. Enghien, Arenberg Archives and Cultural Centre, I 804.

Even if the Duke invested much of his time in managing the Brussels opera house, he did not neglect the private theatre at his château in Hainaut, where artists from the Monnaie also gave performances. Thus the *Gazette de Bruxelles* of 4 August 1751 reported that Charles of Lorraine 'va faire une promenade au château d'Enghien, appartenant au Duc d'Aremberg, où ce seigneur la régalera de la représentation d'une comédie exécutée par les Comédiens de cette ville'[410] (will make an excursion to the Château d'Enghien, seat of the Duke of Arenberg, where His Lordship will entertain his esteemed guest with a comedy performed by the actors of this city).

During his directorship Duke Léopold-Philippe d'Arenberg organized several musical masquerades involving the principal members of the nobility, which Charles of Lorraine attended. These festivities, which took place during carnival, allowed participants to metamorphose into actors and dancers for one night. Costumes were made specially for the occasion, as attested by one preserved inventory.[411] The *Gazette de Bruxelles* gives an account of one such masquerade that took place in the streets of Brussels on the night of 6-7 February 1752. The event began at the residence of the Duke of Arenberg, and concluded later on with a ball at the Monnaie opera house, the procession perfectly symbolizing the close ties existing at that time between the private and public spheres.

> S.A.R., les Seigneurs & Dames, de la principale Noblesse, ont fait la nuit du six au sept une Mascarade *Venetienne* composée de quatre Quadrilles, chacune de quatre Dames & quatre Seigneurs. La premier représentoit quatre Jardiniers & Jardinieres, la second quatre Matelots & Mattelottes, la troisiéme quatre Paysans & Paysannes, la quatriéme quatre Pelerins & Pellerines. L'Assemblée s'est faite chez M. le Duc d'*Aremberg* où l'on à soupé masqué. Ces Seigneurs & Dames sont sortis à minuit deux a deux dans des Caleches ouvertes, & ont fait une Promenade dans les principales ruës de la Ville, toutes ces Voitures se suivoient a la file: Il y avoit auprès

de chacune deux Palfreniers a Chéval qui portoient des flambeaux tous different masqués de même que les Cochers. Il y avoit a la tête un *Woorst* chargé de Timballes & Trompettes, cette Mascaradc sc fermoit par un autre *Woorst* chargé de Musiciens tous different masqués. La marche a continuée dans cet ordre jusqu'au *Grand Théatre* ou le Bal a commencé par une Contre-Danse relative a cette Mascarade.[412]

[H.R.H. and the lords and ladies of the principal nobility on the night of the sixth to the seventh [February 1752] held a *Venetian* masquerade ball comprising four quadrilles, each for four ladies and four lords. The first quadrille represented four gardeners and their partners; the second, four sailor couples; the third, four peasant couples; and the fourth, four pilgrim couples. The assembly took place at the residence of the Duke of Arenberg, where a masked supper was held. At midnight these lords and ladies came out two by two in open carriages and toured the main streets of the city in single file in a long procession: next to each carriage rode two grooms on horseback bearing torches, each wearing a different mask, as did the coachmen. At the head of the parade was a *Woorst* [float] carrying kettledrummers and trumpeters. A *Woorst* at the rear conveyed musicians, all of them wearing different masks. The procession continued up to the Grand Theatre, where the ball began with a *contredanse* alluding to this masquerade.]

The Duke must have felt gratified to be able to offer hospitality to his friends at his new Egmont residence (the Grand Hôtel d'Egmont), which had been his official property for only a matter of weeks, the deed of sale having been signed on 22 January 1752.[413] He entrusted his refurbishment projects for the house to a renowned artist, the Florentine painter, theatre designer, and architect Giovanni Niccolò Servandoni (1695-1766). The latter had already established a prestigious career, having been the painter-designer and technical director of the Académie Royale de Musique in Paris from 1728 to 1742, before leaving France (on account of debt) to serve at various European courts. Although it might be surmised that he created decorative designs for the Théâtre de la Monnaie during his time in Brussels, no evidence yet allows us to corroborate this.[414]

On 1 April 1752 the Duke of Arenberg and his associates handed over the directorship of the Brussels opera stage to the actor Durancy, who had come to the Austrian Netherlands with Favart. Over the next three years Durancy managed a first-class troupe that specialized in the plays of Molière, Regnard, and Marivaux as well as the tragedies of Racine and Corneille.[415]

Although the Duke attended productions by the new director,[416] he now invested much energy in private performances, succumbing to the Parisian trend of 'théâtromanie'.[417] Thus the Duke of Arenberg's residence in Brussels hosted private productions of Molière's *Le Misanthrope* and Regnard's *Le Retour imprévu*, which were staged, respectively, on 3 November 1752 (feast-day of St Hubert), and the following day, the feast-day of St Charles, the Governor's patron saint:

Vendredi jour de *Saint Hubert*, S.A.R. alla selon la coutume prendre le divertissement de la Chasse aux Environs de *Tervueren*, & vers le soir Elle se rendit à l'Hôtel du Duc d'*Aremberg*, pour y voir une représentation de la Comédie du *Misantrope*, exécutée par les Seigneurs & Dames de cette Ville. Samedi, Fête de *Saint-Charles*, dont S.A.R. porte le Nom, il y eut *Gala* à la Cour. M. l'Abbé de *Coudenberg* y entonna le *Te Deum* & célébra une Messe solemnelle chantée par la Musique ordinaire; après laquelle S.A.R. reçut les Complimens de la principale Noblesse à cette occasion. Il y eut ensuite un grand Dîner chez S.Ex. le Marquis de *Botta-Adorno*, auquel S.A.R. se trouva. A cinq heures les Comédiens ordinaires donnerent une représentation de la Comédie de l'*Important*, suivie d'un divertissement de Danses & de Chants allégoriques à la Fête du jour. Après souper la Noblesse régala encore S.A.R. à l'Hôtel du Duc d'*Aremberg* de la Comédie du *Retour Imprévû*; & la nuit les Comédiens donnerent un Bal *gratis* au Grand-Théâtre.[418]

[On Friday, the feast-day of St Hubert, H.R.H. undertook his customary hunting in the Tervueren region, and towards the evening he arrived at the Duke of Arenberg's residence to see a performance of the play *Le Misanthrope* given by the ladies and gentlemen of this city. On Saturday, the feast-day of St Charles, the patron saint of H.R.H., there was a gala held at court. The Abbé de Coudenberg sang the *Te Deum* and celebrated a solemn Mass sung by *la Musique ordinaire* [the musicians of the court]; after which H.R.H. received the compliments of the principal Nobility on this occasion. There followed a grand dinner at the residence of H. E. the Marquis of Botta-Adorno, which was attended by H.R.H. At five o'clock the actors [of the Théâtre de la Monnaie] performed the comedy *L'Important*, which was followed by a *divertissement* of dances and allegorical songs alluding to the feast-day. After supper the Nobility treated H.R.H. again to a performance, at the Duke of Arenberg's residence, of the play *Le Retour imprévu*; and during the night the actors gave a ball, gratis, at the Grand Theatre.]

On 28 February 1753 a new version of Favart's 'opéra-comique' *Cythère assiégée* was staged in Brussels,[419] while in May audiences enjoyed *Le Devin du village* – intermezzi by the Swiss writer, philosopher, and composer Jean-Jacques Rousseau (1712-1778) – which had seen a successful run the previous year in France at Fontainebleau and later at the Académie Royale de Musique.[420] The Duke of Arenberg was closely following the debate surrounding the *Querelle des Bouffons*, which exploded in Paris in August 1752 after a performance of Pergolesi's operatic divertimento *La serva padrona* (see earlier). He acquired Rousseau's famous *Lettre sur la musique française*, which appeared in November 1753, where that author pours scorn on French music, whereas Italian music is presented as a model of melodic excellence.[421]

The Brussels residence of Léopold-Philippe d'Arenberg also resonated with the sound of music. Thus in March 1753 the oboist A. Vanderhagen (first oboe in the royal band of Charles of Lorraine)[422] received payment for private recitals given on eight occasions.[423]

While around 1752 a quotation was made for a theatre construction project (never completed) at the Brussels residence,[424] the end of 1753 saw the building of a theatre at the Arenberg château at Heverlee. The account books from 1754 show that on 9 January the Duke paid 691 florins 7 sols for 'les decorations du Theatre qui est a heverlé'.[425] Since the room was fairly narrow, the Duke had the walls painted with a *trompe-l'œil* effect, adorned with characters from the *commedia dell'arte*.[426] Some elements of this design (at ceiling level) have survived, and make the theatre at Heverlee the only private theatre conceived in the eighteenth century by the ducal family still in existence today. As at Enghien, it seems that as early as the seventeenth century theatrical performances were given at the Heverlee residence. In 1611, Charles d'Arenberg had a troupe of English actors play there on several occasions.[427]

At the Théâtre de la Monnaie, in the month of November 1753, Durancy's troupe staged a parody of *Le Devin du village* called *Les Amours de Bastien et Bastienne*, with music by the Italian composer Carlo Sodi (1715-1788). Next, Crosa's Italian company were back at the Monnaie (having made a stealthy return to Brussels), one of their prestige productions, on 30 November, being Galuppi's *Il mondo della luna*, an 'opera buffa' that had premiered at the Teatro San Moisè in Venice on 29 January 1750.[428] *Il Buranello*, who had become one of Venice's most renowned composers after Vivaldi's death, thanks in particular to the great success of his operas composed on librettos by Goldoni such as *Il mondo della luna*, was a composer in whom the ducal family took a great interest, collecting several manuscripts of his works for the music library. Among these we find scores containing two numbers from the 'opera

Château d'Heverlé   *Le théâtre*

Nels, Bruxelles Serie 36 No. 89

90. Theatre at the Heverlee château, post card from the beginning of the twentieth century.
Enghien, Arenberg Archives and Cultural Centre.

seria' *L'Olimpiade*, after a libretto by Pietro Metastasio, which was staged in Milan at the Teatro Regio Ducale on 26 December 1747 as the opening work of the carnival season. These are two arias sung by the character Megacle: 'Superbo di me stesso',[429] from act I scene 2, and 'Se cerca, se dice',[430] from scene 10 of the following act. The role is written for castrato, and we know that during the Naples production, which occurred shortly after the Milan first performance, the singer was Angelo Maria Monticelli, who had a short time before (in 1746) delighted London audiences.

In addition to operatic works and pieces for keyboard, Galuppi composed over 200 sacred works, including motets as well as several Masses, written mostly during his time as *vicemaestro* of the *Cappella ducale* of San Marco in Venice from 1748 onwards. The Duke of Arenberg indeed acquired (perhaps through a member of Crosa's troupe) separate manuscript parts for one of Galuppi's two Masses in G major – a significant acquisition, since sacred music was, with this single exception, entirely absent from the ducal collection at that time. Held under the classmark Ms 29, the preserved parts (alto voice, first violin, second violin, viola, organ, and bass) give only a fragmentary picture of this work, which was actually composed 'con violini, viole, oboè, corni e basson cioè fagotto obbligato, trombe, timpani, e bassi', as the title page of the separate 'organo e basso' part mentions. While these copies may have been acquired with a view to performance, they actually appear more as collectors' pieces, to judge from the careful way they have been kept and from their hard-cover binding embellished with colourful floral motifs. This Mass, written for four solo voices, and of which only the alto voice part is preserved here, can be found in other, contemporary manuscript sources.

On 9 January 1754 the 'opéra bouffon' *Les Troqueurs* by Antoine Dauvergne (1713-1797), first staged in Paris at the Saint-Laurent Fair on 30 July 1753, was performed in Brussels. At some point during the period of these performances in the French and 'Belgian' capitals a copy of the score published in Paris was added to the Duke's music library.[431] He thereby acquired a work that was highly emblematic in

91. B. Galuppi, *Messa a 4°*. Enghien, Arenberg Archives and Cultural Centre, Ms 29.

relation to the *Querelle des Bouffons*, since Dauvergne's creation had been commissioned by Monnet, director of the Saint-Laurent Fair, with the aim of confusing partisans of Italian music by leading them to believe that this was the work of an Italian composer. The work was so successful in Paris, especially when Monnet revealed the identity of the composer, that it was withdrawn after numerous performances in September 1753, because it was seen to be casting a shadow on the venerable institution of the Opéra. In Brussels, as in Paris, the work met with great success and was performed three times within the space of a month: between 9 January and 12 February 1754.

At Heverlee, on the following 4 March, Duke Léopold-Philippe died. Music and performance had played a constant part in his life. After a childhood cradled in the French operatic repertoire of Lully performed from 1700 at the Théâtre de la Monnaie, and by the Italian music of Pietro Torri and Pietro Antonio Fiocco, Duke Léopold-Philippe had manifested a marked taste for Italian opera, an inclination probably strengthened by his marriage to a princess from the kingdom of Naples. His love of music and his contacts with a series of Italian musicians either passing through or living in the Austrian Netherlands allowed the Duke's music library to be endowed with a range of exceptional manuscripts, the like of which simply did not exist in other libraries of his era. The Théâtre de la Monnaie was a place of musical discovery for the Duke, but also a forum for social interaction that he supported financially. It did not take him long to co-direct the theatre, where he would meet artists and musicians whom he soon recruited for performances given in private in the theatres especially built for him at his residences in Enghien and Heverlee.

92. Charles-Marie-Raymond d'Arenberg. University of Leuven, Kunstpatrimonium, Arenbergverzameling
     (Artistic and Cultural Heritage).

CHAPTER II
CHARLES-MARIE-RAYMOND, FIFTH DUKE OF ARENBERG
(1754-1778)

Like his father, Charles-Marie-Raymond d'Arenberg would be both a soldier and a friend of the Arts, attending events at the Théâtre de la Monnaie, supporting musicians, and organizing private performances. He would dedicate himself particularly to his library, to which would be added a wealth of musical works.

A fortunate alliance

The eldest son of Duke Léopold-Philippe d'Arenberg and Maria Francesca Pignatelli, Charles-Marie-Raymond was born in Enghien on 31 July 1721. He was christened in the chapel at the château on the following 2 August, while further official baptismal ceremonies were held in Vienna on 12 March

93.   Charles-Marie Raymond d'Arenberg as a child.
University of Leuven, Kunstpatrimonium,
Arenbergverzameling (Artistic and Cultural Heritage).

94.   Louise-Marguerite de La Marck by Angelica Kauffman.
Private collection.

1746.[432] Brought up in one of the most influential families of the Austrian Netherlands, the young Prince was fortunate to receive an education second to none, which, as we have seen, included lessons in dancing and probably also music.[433] In 1739 the Prince embarked on a military career and four years later commanded a Walloon regiment.[434] Alongside his father he fought at the Battle of Dettingen, and in 1746 was promoted to Major General of the Imperial Army.[435]

In Paris, on 18 June 1748, Charles-Marie-Raymond d'Arenberg married Louise-Marguerite (1730-1820), Countess de La Marck, a young woman of almost eighteen.[436] This union was of particular significance for the ducal family, since it was the first marriage between an Arenberg and a member of the French nobility, and it took place in the political context already mentioned: the War of the Austrian Succession. The marriage increased the family's assets, with possessions gained most notably in Brittany. The bride was the only daughter of Louis-Engelbert de La Marck (1701-1773), Count of Schleiden and Marquis of Vardes, and of Marie-Anne Hyacinthe de Visdelou, Dame de Bienassis (1712-1731).[437]

Louise-Marguerite was still an infant when her mother died, and a young girl when her father married again, at Versailles on 2 April 1744. His new bride was Marie-Anne Françoise de Noailles (1719-1793), the daughter of Adrien Maurice de Noailles and Françoise Charlotte Amable d'Aubigné.[438] It was well known that Louise-Marguerite's new step-mother loved music and in Paris was considered an accomplished harpsichordist. In 1746 Jean-Marie Leclair (1696-1764), the violinist and dancer from Lyon, dedicated his one and only opera, *Scylla et Glaucus*, to Marie-Anne Françoise, this work being performed on 4 October of that same year.[439] Around 1750 the organist, harpsichordist, and composer Pierre Février (1696-1760) similarly dedicated to her the edition of his cantata *Le Rossignol*.[440] Originally

95. Harpsichordist, in J. Haydn, *Differentes petites pieces faciles […]*, Vienna, Artaria, title page.
Royal Library of Belgium, Music Division, Mus. 1277 C.

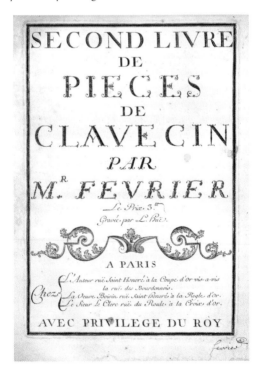

96. P. Février, *Second livre de pièces de clavecin*,
Paris, published by the author, title page.
Enghien, Arenberg Archives and Cultural
Centre, I 861.

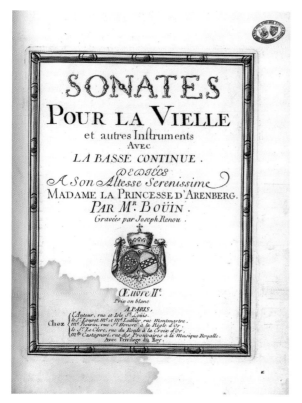

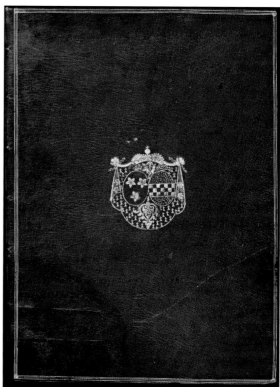

97. J.-F. Bouin, *Sonates pour la vielle*, Paris, published by the author, title page. Enghien, Arenberg Archives and Cultural Centre, I 988.

98. J.-F. Bouin, *Sonates pour la vielle*, supralibros. Enghien, Arenberg Archives and Cultural Centre, I 988.

from Abbeville (Picardie, N. France), Février moved to Paris around 1720 and made his name there as a master of the harpsichord, giving a series of recitals in the salons of high-society Paris.

Pierre Février probably taught the harpsichord to Louise-Marguerite de La Marck, for among the scores she brought with her from Paris following her marriage was a print of the *Second livre de pièces de clavecin*, published in the French capital by the composer shortly before 1737.[441] This volume was added to the family's music library and is today among the *unica* of the collection.[442] Comprising two suites, the collection fits perfectly into the French harpsichord repertoire of this period, being reminiscent of Jean-François Dandrieu, Jean-Philippe Rameau, and Michel Corrette.

Another publication that seems to have travelled with the young bride to the Austrian Netherlands is the *Sonates pour la vielle et autres instruments avec la basse continue dédiées à son Altesse Serenissime Madame la Princesse d'Arenberg* Op. 2, by the Parisian *vielle à roue* (hurdy-gurdy) master and publisher Jean-François Bouin (d. 1767).[443] The *Mercure de France* of August 1748 announced the publication of this print, published by its author on the occasion of the Duke's marriage. Having acquired a bad name in the seventeenth century, the hurdy-gurdy saw an extraordinary ascent in the 1720s, when many works were composed for the instrument; some aristocratic ladies even set about learning it.[444] We do not know whether Louise-Marguerite took lessons with Bouin, who had published as his Op. 1 *Les Muses, suittes à deux vièles, muzettes avec la basse on peut les jouer sur la flûte à bec, traversière, violon, hautbois.* Bouin's Op. 2 is, at any rate, the only score for the hurdy-gurdy held by the library.

99. Louvet, Hurdy-gurdy. Brussels, Musical Instruments Museum, M 521.

100. Palace of Charles of Lorraine (Brussels), musical instruments with hurdy-gurdy, mural detail. Royal Library of Belgium, Palace of Charles of Lorraine.

Charles-Marie-Raymond and his wife would go on to have eight children: François-Marie-Thérèse, Louis-Engelbert (the future Duke), Marie-Léopoldine, Marie-Flore, Auguste-Marie-Raymond, Charles-Joseph, Louis-Marie, and Marie-Louise.

When the war ended, in 1749, and French troops withdrew from the Austrian Netherlands, Duke Léopold-Philippe decided to step down from his post of Governor of Mons, passing on the post to his son Charles-Marie-Raymond, who had already been appointed High Bailiff of Hainaut.[445] On the death of his father on 4 March 1754, Charles-Marie-Raymond became the fifth Duke of Arenberg.

A love of music and performances

On 28 June 1754 the new Duke of Arenberg paid 252 florins to Durancy, director of the Monnaie opera house, 'pour une demi-année en avance de deux lorgnettes'.[446] From July of the following year, the family occupied three boxes and supported the French actor Jean-Nicolas Servandoni, better known as D'Hannetaire (1718-1780), in his management of the Brussels theatre,[447] paying for painting works undertaken by Jacques-Denis Dubois.[448] The family attended new performances of *Les Troqueurs* and *Le Devin du village*, as well as the pastorale *Titon et l'Aurore* by the French violinist and composer Jean-Joseph Cassanéa de Mondonville (1711-1772) on 23 October 1754,[449] and *Le Ballet de la rose* by Louis Devisse on 13 April 1755[450] – the same evening, in fact, as a performance of the work that had inspired Devisse: Rameau's 'opéra-ballet' *Les Indes galantes*, two movements from which the Duke owned in an unidentified print.[451] A dancer at the Paris Opera, the ballet master Louis Devisse had recently been engaged at the Monnaie, together with his wife, likewise a dancer.[452] His performance in the role of Boreas was well received by the Duke, who rewarded him with a gift of over 100 florins.[453] In June 1755, Racine's tragedy *Esther* was staged at La Monnaie, with choruses composed by Jean-Baptiste Moreau. During this same period the 1750 Parisian edition of Racine's *Œuvres* in three volumes was added to the ducal library.[454]

On 15 July 1754 Charles-Marie-Raymond became official owner of the Grand Hôtel d'Egmont in Sablon district of Brussels, formerly the Hôtel d'Arenberg,[455] where in March 1756 a group of musicians (who have not been identified) played in concert on two occasions.[456] Five months later

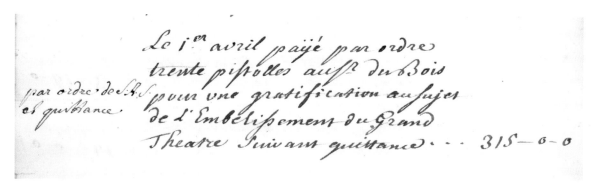

101.   Reference to Dubois in the accounts of Jacques Gaillard, 1755. Enghien, Arenberg Archives and Cultural Centre, 64/1-7.

JEAN JOSEPH CASSANEA

DE MONDONVILLE

Maitre de musique de la Chapelle du Roi

Né a Narbonne

Dessiné par C.N. Cochin 1768   Gravé par Delatre

A Paris chés Esnauts et Rapilly rue St Jacques a la Ville de Coutance A.P.D.R.

102. J.-J. Cassanéa de Mondonville by Delatre, after C.-N. Cochin. Enghien,
      Arenberg Archives and Cultural Centre, Biographies of musicians, 9/1.

103. Empress Maria Theresa by G.-E. Petit, after M. de Meytens. Royal
Library of Belgium, Prints and Drawings Division, S II 87714 plano.

the Seven Years War began, sparked off by the siege of Saxony by Frederick II of Prussia. The Duke of Arenberg and Governor Charles of Lorraine had to leave for the campaign. The alliances had in the meantime changed, with Great Britain, Prussia, and Hanover now in coalition against France, Austria, and Russia. During this conflict Charles-Marie-Raymond distinguished himself in battle and was soon judged to be one of the Empress of Austria's best generals. Raised to the rank of Knight of the Golden Fleece in 1757, he was granted in the following year the highest Austrian military honour: the Grand Cross of the Military Order of Maria Theresa, following the Battle of Hochkirch (Saxony) on 14 October 1758, which ended in bitter defeat for the Prussian armies.[457]

Although the Duke was in the Austrian Netherlands only sporadically during the first few years of the war, which ended in 1763, the Duchess (considered a very pretty woman by Prince Charles-Joseph de Ligne)[458] did not hesitate to take on the organization of private concerts,[459] attending performances at the Théâtre de la Monnaie[460] and overseeing the purchase from Brussels booksellers of a series of newspapers, including the *Mercure de France* and gazettes from Brussels and Utrecht.[461]

104. Hôtel d'Arenberg, c. 1754. Archives of the City of Brussels, plans of Brussels, 'grands plans' 3.

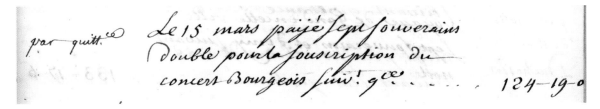

105. Reference to the Concert Bourgeois in the accounts of Jacques Gaillard, 1759. Enghien, Arenberg Archives and Cultural Centre, 64/1-7.

Public concert societies

Charles-Marie-Raymond supported not only the Brussels opera stage but also the music societies and associations being set up in the capital. The first public concert society in Brussels, the Concert Bourgeois, was established in the winter of 1753-1754, and in 1756 moved into the renovated Petite Boucherie building located in Place de Bavière, today Place de Dinant.[462] The society took its inspiration from the Parisian Concert Spirituel founded in 1725, which held concerts of sacred and instrumental music for the general public. The Concert Bourgeois scheduled its concerts only during La Monnaie's period of annual closure, as well as on Mondays, Wednesdays, and Fridays – days off during the theatrical season.[463] At this time another society was mentioned in the press: the Concert Noble, which in its first few years arranged concerts only very infrequently. On 20 March 1754 Charles of Lorraine attended a concert held by 'une compagnie de la noblesse' at the King's House, or 'Broodthuys', on the Grand-Place, which was attended by 'un grand nombre de Personnes de la premiere Distinction',[464] among whom, in all likelihood, would have been the Duke of Arenberg.[465]

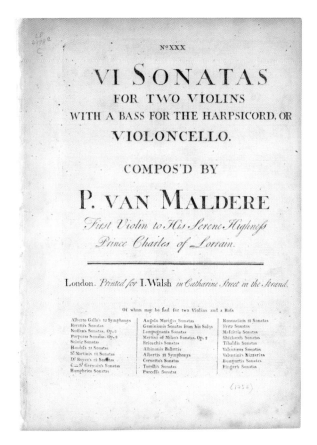

106. P. van Maldere, *VI Sonatas for two violins with a bass*,
London, Walsh. Royal Library of Belgium, Rare Books
Division, LP 4.498 C.

The concerts arranged 'par une Compagnie de Bourgeois' between the end of 1753 and November 1756 took place at unspecified Brussels venues in the presence of Charles of Lorraine and many other 'personnes de distinction',[466] among them presumably Duke Charles-Marie-Raymond.[467] The first official performance at the Petite Boucherie, which had been leased to the Concert Bourgeois from December 1755, took place on 4 November 1756, the feast-day of St Charles, in the presence of the Governor, who became the association's patron. For this inaugural concert the musicians performed 'différens morceaux de Musique vocale & instrumentale des mieux choisis',[468] and a prologue by the Brussels composer Pierre van Maldere (1729-1768), who since 1749 had been principal violinist of the court orchestra, directed by Henri-Jacques de Croes.[469] Van Maldere, who had been a pupil of Jean-Joseph Fiocco (discussed above), clearly appears to have been the association's kingpin – which can only have been an indicator of quality when we consider that this musician, a protégé of Charles of Lorraine, would later enjoy great success as a composer and virtuoso violinist: notably in Vienna, where on 8 March 1757 he performed before Empress Maria Theresa.[470]

The Concert Bourgeois's activities did not always necessarily take place in the concert hall of the Petite Boucherie; the press tells us, for instance, of a concert held on 30 June 1757 at the Jesuit church, to celebrate the Austrian military victory of 18 June over the Prussians at the Battle of Kolin (about 50 kilometres from Prague). A *Te Deum* was sung on this occasion, as well as a Mass during which the Milanese oboist Giuseppe Besozzi (1686-1760) met with resounding success.[471] On the following 8 July two other members of the Besozzi family, Antonio (1714-1781) and his son Carlo (1738-1791), performed at the Théâtre de la Monnaie's first-ever instrumental concert.[472] A few months later Charles of Lorraine was once again at war, as was his General, the Duke of Arenberg.[473]

In 1759 Charles-Marie-Raymond became an active member of the Concert Bourgeois. The family account books mention that the sum of 124 florins was paid for 'la souscription du concert bourgeois'.[474] This amount was apparently for a registration fee, for over the next few years it became reduced to two double-sovereigns, the equivalent of 35 florins 14 sols.[475] During that year the Duke's eldest son Louis-Engelbert was at school in Paris.[476] The education of the young Prince and his brothers and sisters included prominently harpsichord lessons and dancing lessons.[477] In the French capital Jean-François Béate (1728-1781), a dancer with the King of France's Ballets, was one of their teachers.[478] In Brussels the Parisian dancing master Jean-Jacques Bigot (c. 1730-1767) taught the ducal children from 1760,[479] the year in which he was appointed to the court of Charles of Lorraine as *maître de danse* to the page-boys, replacing the lately deceased music publisher and dancer Joseph-Claude Rousselet.[480]

The Duke of Arenberg is mentioned by name in a little, anonymous manuscript composition of thirty-two bars written for cello, called 'menuet du ducq d'Aremberg'. This minuet appears on the

107. *Menuet du ducq d'Aremberg*. Royal Library of Belgium, Music Division, Ms II 2780 Mus.

first page of a vellum-bound collection containing 131 instrumental pieces of this kind (minuets and marches): a volume entitled 'Principes de Musique pour le Violoncelle'. This belonged to François-Bonaventure-Joseph Dumont, Marquis de Gages (1739-1787), a Freemason from Hainaut, as the ex-libris on the upper inside cover shows, the volume having joined the collections of the Royal Library of Belgium in 1901.[481] After the first sixteen bars in F major a second minuet of the same length appears in the same key. The performer must then repeat the first minuet, as signalled by the direction 'da capo il primo'. The first part of this collection, comprising thirty-eight folios, ends with the handwritten inscription 'finis le 17 de maÿ / 1759', which leads one to suppose that the minuet for the Duke was composed, or at the very least copied out, at the beginning of 1759.

Seriously wounded at the Battle of Torgau in Saxony on 3 November 1760, Charles-Marie-Raymond d'Arenberg had to cease fighting. After a four-month period of convalescence in Prague and Vienna[482] he returned to the Austrian Netherlands and to his family at the Brussels residence

108.   I. Vitzthumb by A. Cardon. Royal Library of Belgium, Prints and Drawings
       Division, S I 2293.

on 20 April 1761, as related by the First Secretary to the Duke, Jérôme Debiefvre (d. 1802).[483] As a member of the Concert Bourgeois, the Duke attended, on 3 June 1761 at the Petite Boucherie, the prologue *Le Temple des arts*, a work by the Brussels-based Austrian composer Ignaz Vitzthumb (1724-1816) celebrating the return of Charles of Lorraine to Brussels;[484] the latter had likewise been absent from the Austrian Netherlands, sojourning in Vienna between April 1760 and May 1761.[485] Among the performers of this *œuvre de circonstance* were Marie-Anne Nonancourt (1741-1819) and the Frenchmen Louis Compain-Despierrières (b. 1733) and François-Antoine-Joseph Rousseau, known as Chatillon (1729-1802): three important figures at the Théâtre de la Monnaie. Pierre van Maldere played the violin, the Abbé Massart the cello.[486]

Born in Baden near Vienna, Ignaz Vitzthumb had moved to Brussels as an eleven-year-old boy in 1735, joining the court chapel as a chorister; and it was here that he met van Maldere. In 1742 he enlisted in a regiment fighting in the War of the Austrian Succession. Upon his return to Brussels six years later he rejoined the court chapel as a composer, singer (he was a tenor), and violinist. The year 1761 was marked not only by the performance of his *Temple des arts*, whose music and text remain lost, but also by his association with La Monnaie, where he held the post of teacher to the children of the troupe. At the Monnaie he staged in succession his 'opéra-comique' *La Fausse esclave*, first performed on 20 October 1761, and his pastorale *L'Éloge de la vertu ou le Tribu des cœurs*, given on the following 4 November, the feast-day of St Charles – two works whose music is similarly lost.[487]

Performances in public and in private

In the 1760s the family continued to pay for the boxes at La Monnaie.[488] The family attended not only performances included in the subscription rate, but also non-subscription performances ('abonnements suspendus') for which subscribers had to pay for their seats in the same way as the rest of the audience.[489] The family encouraged Pierre van Maldere when he agreed to commit himself to the management of the Brussels opera house, starting in the 1763 season and co-directing the institution with Guillaume Charliers de Borghravenbroeck, Superintendent of the Willebroek canal and Treasurer of the City of Brussels, and Pierre Gamond, steward of the property of Charles of Lorraine. The Duke of Arenberg also held theatrical and musical performances at his château in Heverlee,[490] hired musicians to entertain guests at a supper party,[491] and attended performances of 'comédie flamande' at the Monnaie.[492] French operatic works were indeed staged at the Monnaie in Dutch translation: one such play was the comedy *Ninette à la cour*, which was performed in December 1761 in a translation by Jean-François Cammaert (1710-1780).[493] The boundary between private and public performances was very often blurred, since artists, musicians, singers, and actors appeared both on the Brussels stage and in the Duke's private residences, as had already been the custom in Léopold-Philippe d'Arenberg's day.

At the conclusion of the Seven Years War Brussels became one of the cities visited by Leopold Mozart (1719-1787) with his son Wolfgang (1756-1791) and daughter Maria Anna (Nannerl) (1751-1829). Both born in Salzburg, the young virtuosos were introduced between September and December 1762

109. Wolfgang Amadeus Mozart by Pietro Antonio Lorenzoni (?), 1763. Salzburg, Mozarteum Foundation.

110. The Mozart family by Carmontelle. Chantilly, Musée Condé.

at the Viennese Court, where they performed before Empress Maria Theresa, Emperor Francis I, and the couple's daughter, Archduchess Marie Antoinette, the future Queen of France. Returning to Salzburg in January 1763, the Mozart family set off again on the following 9 June for a tour through Europe, which would last three and a half years. They arrived in Brussels on 4 October 1763 and stayed there, awaiting an opportunity to appear before Governor Charles of Lorraine, until 15 November. On 14 October little Wolfgang composed the *Allegro* of his harpsichord sonata with violin accompaniment KV 6, known as the 'Brussels sonata', which would be completed in the French capital a few weeks later.[494]

In his journal Mozart's father wrote that while staying with his young children in the capital of the Austrian Netherlands he met 'Monsgr: Le Duc d'Arenberg avec Sa Familie',[495] although we cannot be sure whether a private concert took place as a result of that meeting. The Mozarts also came across the van Maldere brothers: that is, Pierre, but also Guillaume and Jean-Baptiste, who were both employed as musicians at the court chapel, directed at the time by Henri-Jacques de Croes. The acquaintance was certainly made of Ignaz Vitzthumb, who since 1763 had been assisting his friend Pierre van

Maldere in running the Théâtre de la Monnaie as 'maître de musique et de chant'.[496] In Vienna the Mozart family had surely heard of the famous violinist and of Vitzthumb, just as they cannot have failed to learn that the most important family in the Austrian Netherlands and the closest to Empress Maria Theresa was that of the Arenbergs – a fact that would amply justify their making the Duke's acquaintance. A review in the newspaper *Augspurgische Ordinari-Post-Zeitung*[497] tells us that a 'grosse Concert' took place in the Concert Bourgeois concert room, probably on Wednesday 9 November, in the presence of Charles of Lorraine and 'viele Noblesse' (many members of the nobility – therefore in all probability including the Duke of Arenberg). The Mozarts soon left Brussels for Paris, where the children would play before the King, Louis XV, on 1 January 1764.[498] During this time the harpsichord-tuner Jean-Baptiste Numans (d. Brussels, 15 August 1784), Louis Bizant's successor at the Brussels court since 1758,[499] adjusted and tuned 'le clavecin des princes';[500] the latter tried their hand at the organ, too.[501] Sadly, no instrument of this period showing signs of having belonged to the ducal family has come down to us, so we do not know from which workshop this harpsichord came.

Charles-Marie-Raymond's abundant and detailed correspondence includes two letters that shed considerable light on the amateur theatre company set up by the Duke and Duchess, in which the roles were taken by ladies and gentlemen of the local nobility. An anonymous letter addressed to Duke Charles-Marie-Raymond d'Arenberg from Brussels and dated 3 December 1764, which could be in the hand of the Duke's secretary Jérôme Debiefve, gives details of this particular troupe. At the

111. W. A. Mozart, *Allegro* from the sonata KV 6. Salzburg, Mozarteum Foundation.

112. L. Mozart, *Violinschule*, Augsburg, Lotter, 1770. Royal Library of Belgium, Rare Books Division, Fétis 6.215 B.

113. Pierre-Alexandre Monsigny by Carmontelle. Chantilly, Musée Condé.

time the letter was written, the Duke had been in Vienna since 1 May primarily in order to attend, in the following January, the wedding of Joseph II, son of Empress Maria Theresa, to Maria Josepha of Bavaria.

> Le retardement de votre retour a mis nos Dames Comiques dans la plus grande desolation Mons. Le Duc; elles s'étoient appliqué a l'envie dans l'espoir de se produire pendant le courant du mois, et l'emulation s'en etoit si bien marcé, qu'on ne peut pas dire qu'il y en ait une qui ne joue bien; je ne puis pas comprendre dans le nombre de celles que j'ai entendu Mad.e la Princesse de hornes, parcqu'elle ne fait que revenir de la campagne, et qu'elle ne s'est pas produit encore a aucune repetition. Je sais que Mad.me la Duchesse vous a fait un detail exact du point ou en est la noble trouppe. Dieu veuille que le degré de perfection ne diminue d'ici a votre retour, pour l'epoque duquel ces dames font de paris. Mad.e la Comtesse de Merode soutient que vous serez tres decidé à passer votre carnaval a Vienne, et que la Comedie ne sera joué qu'après paques, elle a fait la dessus un pari avec Mad.e de Bonléz. Le sujet de la Comedie absorbe toute la conversation, hormis les moments qu'on s'occupe de l'evenement du mariage du Roi des Romains, que l'on dit fixé au 15. de janvier, comme vous scaurez mieu que nous. [...] La santé et l'humeur de Mad.e Votre mere sont beaucoup meilleurs depuis qu'elle a pris le parti de voir du monde; elle est la plus occupée de la Comedie, et personne de la trouppe ne va chez elle qu'elle ne lui fasse repeter son role [...].[502]

> [The delay in your return has plunged our actresses into the deepest despair, Lord Duke; they had marvellously applied themselves in the hope of putting on a performance this very month, and their spirit of emulation was so marked that one cannot say that any of them does not play her part well; I cannot include in the number of those I have heard the Princess of Hornes, since she is only now returning from the countryside and has not taken part in any rehearsal. I know that Madam the Duchess has kept you precisely informed about the stage the noble troupe has reached. God grant that their degree of perfection does not decrease between now

and your return, on the time of which these ladies are laying bets. The Countess of Mérode maintains that you will be very firmly committed to spending your carnival in Vienna, and that the comedy will have to wait until after Easter; she has made a wager on it with Madame de Bonlez. The subject of the comedy absorbs all the conversation, except for those moments when the talk comes round to the forthcoming marriage of the King of the Romans, which they say has been fixed for 15 January, something about which you will know better than we do. [...] The health and mood of Madam your mother are much better since she decided to see people; she is the person most taken up with the comedy, and no one from the troupe may visit her without having to recite her part [...].]

In another letter dated the following 14 December, the same person writes to the Duke:

[…] Il ne se presente ici rien d'essentiel. Depuis la nouvelle du retardement de votre retour, les repetitions comiques languissent et sont pour ainsi dire suspendues; il devoit y en avoir une mardi passé chez Md.e de Bonléz pour la piece du Philosophe marié, lorsque tout le monde etoit assemblé, Mad.e de hornes ne voulut pas repeter […] Je suppose que Mad.me la Duchesse vous rendra de ceci un meilleur compte que moi qui n'en suis instruit que legerement ou pour mieux dire a demi […].[503]

[[...] Nothing important is happening here. Since the news of the delay in your return the theatrical rehearsals have languished and, so to speak, are suspended; there should have been one last Tuesday at the home of Madame de Bonlez for the play *Le Philosophe marié*, when everyone was there, but Madame de Hornes refused to rehearse [...] I suppose that Madam the Duchess will give you a better account of this than I can, since I am only slightly informed or, more accurately, half-informed [...].]

The play referred to here is the comic masterpiece in five acts *Le Philosophe marié ou le Mari honteux de l'être* by Philippe Néricault Destouches, the première of which took place in 1727 and which was first performed at the Théâtre de la Monnaie on 14 September 1732, later performances taking place there in 1753 and 1762.[504] Among the 'noble trouppe' gathered together at the ducal palace in Brussels were Duchess Louise-Marguerite (who had returned from Vienna without her husband on 2 November 1764);[505] her sister-in-law Marie Flore, Countess of Mérode; her mother-in-law Maria Francesca Pignatelli;[506] and lastly Princess Élisabeth Philippine de Hornes and Countess Marie-Thérèse de Sart, Baroness de Bonlez, who was the daughter of the Minister Plenipotentiary Charles of Cobenzl. As a letter addressed by the latter to Doctor Gerard van Swieten on 25 February 1765 states, the ladies of the troupe, too, convened at Heverlee and put on sixteen to eighteen plays in which 'la duchesse d'Arenberg joue joliment'.[507] Evidence of these performances is also provided by an inventory compiled at the château at Heverlee in 1776 that takes the form of an 'Etat des decorations du théâtre'.[508] The ducal family had costumes especially made for these private performances.[509]

In the absence of her husband (he would not return from Vienna until 14 April 1765) the Duchess supported the public opera stage of La Monnaie, paying for the lighting used in some rehearsals. On 4 February 1765 'chandelles et lampions' provide light for the artists[510] preparing for the Brussels première, the following day, of *Les Deux cousines ou la Bonne amie*, a play interspersed with *ariettes* by the French actor and composer Robert Desbrosses (1719-1799). On the following 22 February[511] a rehearsal took place for the Brussels première of the 'opéra-comique' *Le Roi et le fermier* by the French composer Pierre-Alexandre Monsigny (1729-1817). This work met with great success in the capital of the Austrian Netherlands, where it played on numerous occasions between 1765 and 1792.[512] The 'opéra-comique' genre was largely dominant in theatres at that time, both in Paris and Brussels, and the works of Monsigny, as well as those of Duni and Philidor, were very popular with audiences. In December 1765 the Duke took the opportunity to engage the Parisian dancing master Michel Billion ('Billioni') (1729-1795), a member of the Monnaie company, to give his children private tuition. These lessons only lasted three months, however, since, embroiled in an action for debt, Billioni was forced to leave Brussels in March 1766 for Paris, where he took up the post of ballet master with the troupe of the Comédie-Italienne.[513] After Billioni's departure the dancing master Saint-Léger, previously active in Paris and Amsterdam,[514] became teacher to the Duke's children,[515] in addition to his role as ballet master at La Monnaie, this theatre now once again directed by D'Hannetaire. Mlle Nogentelle, a *danseuse figurante* on the Brussels stage, who would go on to make a career at the Paris Opera, also was among Charles-Marie-Raymond d'Arenberg's protégés.[516]

In February and March 1767 a number of events were held to mark Charles of Lorraine's recovery from severe gout. The members of the Concert Bourgeois took this opportunity to resume their musical activities, which had been put on hold for three years. On 16 February[517] the Petite Boucherie building, adorned for the occasion with thousands of lanterns, hosted a sumptuous evening concert, described thus in the *Description des fêtes données à Bruxelles [...] à l'occasion de la Convalescence de Son Altesse Royale Monseigneur le Duc Charles-Alexandre de Lorraine:*[518]

> [...] il y a plusieurs années qu'il s'est établi ici, sous la Protection de S.A.R. un Concert Bourgeois composé non seulement d'honorables Citoyens de cet Ordre, mais aussi de plusieurs Seigneurs de la première distinction, & qui enfin à la gloire d'avoir pour premier Membre Son Auguste Protecteur. Ce Concert semble être un Hommage qui lui est particulièrement consacré: il n'a lieu que lorsqu'il peut se flatter d'être honoré de la Présence de S.A.R., &, après avoir été fermé pendant trois ans, il se rouvrit avec un éclat qui a fait un honneur infini à ses membres & à l'intelligence de ses Directeurs. Leur zéle & leur joie ne se renfermérent pas dans les bornes de la Salle. L'extérieur du Batiment étoit illuminé avec autant d'art que de gout [...] Ces illuminations, dont on avoit peine à soutenir l'éclat, étoient dans leur degré de perfection à l'arrivée de LL.AA.RR. & si elles les surprirent agréablement, Elles ne furent pas moins touchées de voir une foule immense, qui occupoit non seulement toute la rue, mais aussi les Fénêtres & jusqu'aux Toits des Maisons, qui étoient toutes éclairées par des Flambeaux. Des acclamations unanimes se joignirent au son des Timbales & Trompettes placées sur l'avant Corps du Bâtiment du Concert, & l'on eut dit que tout ce peuple avoit gravé dans son cœur le chiffre que l'illumination présentoit à ses yeux [...]. Toute la capacité de la Salle étoit remplie. Les Dames de la première qualité, richement parées, ornoient ce beau Spectacle, où LL.AA.RR. furent reçues au bruit des Timbales & Trompettes de l'Orchestre mêlé à celui des applaudissemens qui se répeterent jusqu'à 3 fois avec la plus grande vivacité. Ils ne cesserent que pour faire entendre une Cantate composée à l'occasion de la Convalescence de Monseigneur, & mise en musique par un Maître auquel nous sommes redevables de la célébrité de nos plaisirs dans ce genre. Ce prélude, si intéressant par son objet et par la beauté de la Musique, plût infinement par celle de l'éxécution, & tout le Concert mérita les mêmes suffrages par le choix des airs & des simphonies. On y entendit des voix qui sont en possession de nos applaudissemens, des Instrumens qui ont donné à notre Orchestre la reputation la plus distinguée, & enfin un Violon qui a été admiré des meilleurs Juges des pays les plus éclairés de l'Europe.

> [[...] Several years ago there was established here under the protection of H.R.H. a Concert Bourgeois composed not merely of honourable citizens of that estate but also several lords of the highest distinction, and which even gained the glory of having as its first member its August Protector. This concert society appears to be an act of homage towards him especially:

114.   Project for a theatre set with arbour by G.-F. Blondel (?). Royal Library of Belgium, Prints and Drawings Division, S III 16798 plano.

it puts on events only when it can flatter itself to have the honour of the presence of H.R.H., and having ceased operations for three years, it reopened its doors with a brilliance that did infinite honour to its members and to the good sense of its directors. Their zeal and joy were not confined within the bounds of the hall. The outside of the building was lit up with equal art and taste [...] These illuminations, which were almost overpoweringly brilliant, reached their height of perfection just when Their Royal Highnesses arrived, and if they surprised the latter pleasantly, the latter, in their turn, were no less touched to see a huge crowd that filled not only the entire street but also the windows going right up to the rooftops of the houses, which were all lit up by torches. Unanimous cheers mingled with the sound of the trumpets and kettledrums placed at the front of the concert hall, and one might have said that all these people had engraved in their hearts the figure that the illuminations presented to their eyes. [...]. The hall was filled to capacity. The ladies of the highest quality, richly bejewelled, adorned that fair spectacle, where Their Royal Highnesses were received to the sound of the trumpets and drums of the orchestra allied to that of the cheering, which was repeated up to three times with the greatest vigour. This stopped only in order to make way for a cantata composed on the occasion of Monseigneur's convalescence and set to music by a master to whom we are indebted for the fame of our pleasures in that art. This prelude, so interesting on account of its subject and the beauty of the music, pleased infinitely through that of its performance, and the whole concert merited the same plaudits for the choice of the airs and symphonies. We heard voices that have earned our applause, instruments that have given our orchestra a most distinguished reputation, and, finally, a violinist who has been admired by the best judges in the most enlightened countries of Europe.]

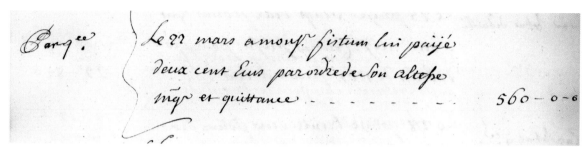

115. Reference to Vitzthumb in the accounts of Jacques Gaillard, 1768. Enghien, Arenberg Archives and Cultural Centre, 64/1-7.

At this grand re-opening concert audiences heard a cantata composed especially for the event by 'un Maître auquel nous sommes redevables de la célébrité de nos plaisirs dans ce genre': that is, Ignaz Vitzthumb.[519] 'Le violon qui a été admiré des meilleurs juges des pays les plus éclairés de l'Europe' was Pierre van Maldere; this was in fact to be van Maldere's last concert with the Concert Bourgeois, for he died during the following year.[520] The account books of Charles-Marie-Raymond d'Arenberg show clearly that the Duke paid 22 florins 10 sols for 'une partie des frais du Concert Bourgeois à l'occasion du rétablissement de S: A: R:'.[521] The Duke was probably in the audience a few days later at the King's House, on the Grand-Place, for the 'Concert des Nobles', where an as yet unidentified cantata was performed in the same spirit and circumstances.[522]

When Pierre van Maldere died, the Austrian Netherlands lost not only an outstanding musician and concert director but also a composer with a Europe-wide reputation: the creator of five operatic works, chamber music, and several symphonies, of which editions were published both in France and in England. Curiously, the AACC Music Collection preserves no work by van Maldere, and the ducal library inventories drawn up in the eighteenth century are equally silent.

Among the musicians playing in the Concert Bourgeois performances was the Brussels harpsichordist and composer Ferdinand Staes (1748-1809), a pupil of Ignaz Vitzthumb, who was also harpsichordist at La Monnaie in 1767.[523] That same year he was recruited in turn by the Duke as harpsichord teacher to the family, and he provided the Arenbergs with some music about which we unfortunately know nothing.[524] He became acquainted at the Duke's home with the music teacher and cellist Philippe-Jean Doudelet,[525] who would later confirm having 'dirigé avec succès les Concerts Noble et Bourgeois',[526] and with a dancing master from Brussels, Pierre Trappeniers (1734-1794), who had replaced the late Jean-Jacques Bigot as teacher of this accomplishment to the page-boys of Charles of Lorraine.[527]

Being close to the higher echelons of power, Duke Charles-Marie-Raymond d'Arenberg often invited Governor Charles of Lorraine to his private performances, as attested by the latter in his *Journal secret*. On 16 March 1767 the Governor noted: 'Après dîné, été à Evre [Heverlee] voir la comédie';[528] in the same place a few days later, on 6 April, he saw *Le Misanthrope*, which had already been staged by the Arenbergs in Brussels in 1752, while the following day he watched a performance of another Molière comedy, *Les Femmes savantes*.[529]

Ignaz Vitzthumb's name appears for the first time in the ducal account books in 1768. Having been forced to give up his post of orchestral director at the Monnaie at the start of 1766,[530] as a result of certain differences, Vitzthumb decided on 10 September 1767 to set up his own company with assistance from some of his friends and colleagues from the Monnaie:[531] namely, the actor, chorus member, head machinist, and set designer Jacques-Joseph Debatty, the tenor and violinist Paul Mechtler,[532] the musicians Benoît Gehot and Charles-Joseph Lartillon, and the Brussels actor Alexandre-Florentin Bultos (1749-1787). On 22 March 1768 Vitzthumb received 'par ordre de Son Altesse Mgr' the hefty sum of 560 florins[533] in order to prepare a performance in Dutch with his troupe. This took place in the following month of November at the Duke's château at Heverlee, and required the further payment of 400 écus: that is, the substantial sum of 1120 florins.[534] In the meantime the company had performed between May and September 1768 under the name of 'Brusselse Muzikanten' in various Dutch cities including Utrecht, The Hague, Delft, and Amsterdam.[535] The existence of this company of actors and musicians was nonetheless fairly short-lived, for on 25 February 1769 an inventory was drawn up of the clothes, decorations, and other effects previously belonging to it.[536]

On 8 January 1769 Charles of Lorraine dined at the ducal residence in Brussels and saw the masquerade *Le Tableau mouvant*.[537] There once more, on the following 7 March, he saw the three-act drama *Les Amants malheureux ou le Comte de Comminges* by François-Thomas-Marie de Baculard, known as Baculard d'Arnaud (1718-1805), noting that this play was 'assez mauvaise et très triste'.[538] A few days later Charles-Marie-Raymond d'Arenberg met the Governor twice at the Concert Bourgeois concert room, to celebrate Charles of Lorraine's twenty-five-year tenure as Governor. The Duke supported concerts on 26 and 31 March, a prologue composed by Vitzthumb being among the works performed.[539] The Duke did indeed pay – in addition to his annual subscription fee of 2 double-sovereigns – 105 florins 'pour les fraix occasionnés par rapport au jubilé de S: A: Roÿal'.[540] Among the other pieces performed on this occasion were two songs: the air *Voilà ce que c'est qu'aller au bois* by the Abbé Jean-Pierre Pagès (1715-1806) of Paris, Prince Charles-Joseph de Ligne's librarian from the 1760s onwards;[541] and *Amis, pour la fête, que chacun s'apprête*, with music taken from the *Rondeau de chasse* by the Frenchman Pierre de La Garde (1717 - after 1792). Several of de La Garde's compositions are indeed present in the music library of the Duke: most especially, the duet *Hé quoi tout sommeille* in the form of separate manuscript parts[542] and, in its Parisian edition, the 'pastorale héroïque' in one act *Aeglé*, first staged in 1748 at the theatre of Madame de Pompadour and the work that established its composer's reputation.[543]

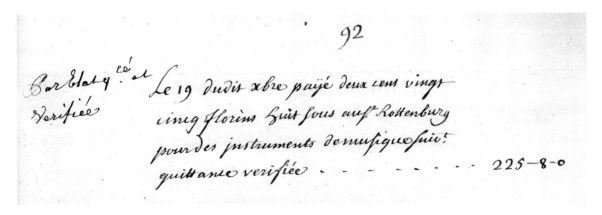

116. Reference to Rottenburgh in the accounts of Jacques Gaillard, 1769. Enghien, Arenberg Archives and Cultural Centre, 64/1-7.

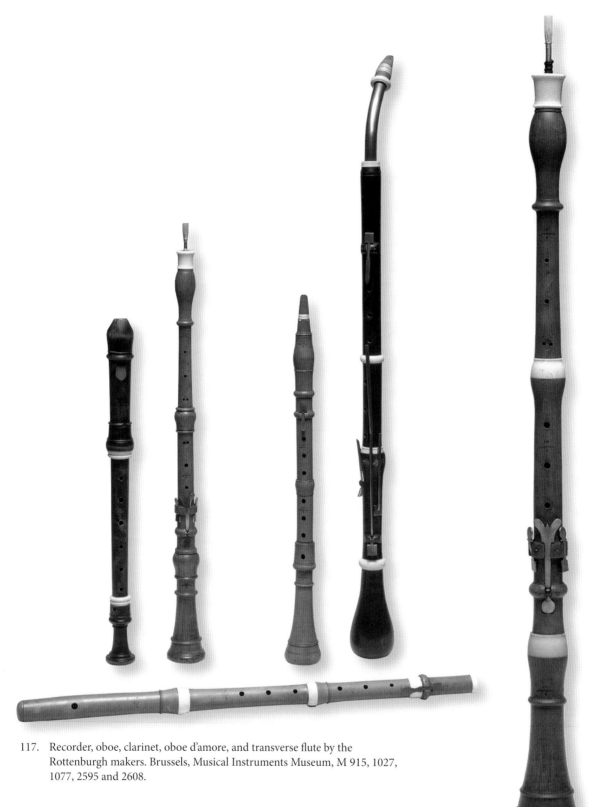

117. Recorder, oboe, clarinet, oboe d'amore, and transverse flute by the
     Rottenburgh makers. Brussels, Musical Instruments Museum, M 915, 1027,
     1077, 2595 and 2608.

118. Jean-Hyacinthe II Rottenburgh,
     oboe. Brussels, Musical
     Instruments Museum, M 2609.

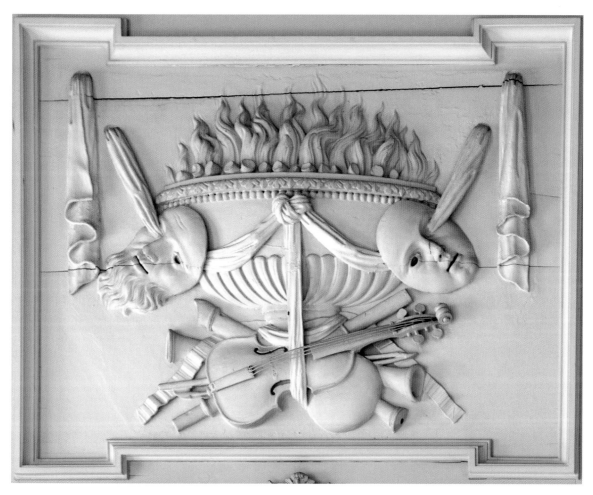

119. Palace of Charles of Lorraine (Brussels), masques and musical instruments, mural detail. Royal Library of Belgium, Palace of Charles of Lorraine.

In 1769 the Duke of Arenberg declared himself a patron of the Academy of Fine Arts in Brussels[544] and continued to support Vitzthumb, engaging him for a series of concerts during the carnival season and financing the appointment of five clarinettists for his orchestra.[545] In funding these instrumentalists – endowing the institution with clarinettists in residence – he was enabling the clarinet to make its way on to the Brussels operatic stage. The clarinet was first used in opera in France in 1751, for Rameau's *Acante et Céphise*, and was at this time a relatively recent arrival on the operatic stage. Over the course of that year Charles-Marie-Raymond d'Arenberg purchased several (unnamed) musical instruments, from the Brussels stringed-instrument and woodwind-instrument maker Jean-Hyacinthe II Rottenburgh (1713-1783),[546] these acquisitions being testimony to the Arenbergs' active interest in music-making. We may suppose that some of the instruments bought from Rottenburgh – who, in addition to clarinets, made oboes, recorders, and flutes (stamped with 'I. H. ROTTENBURGH') – were intended to be lent to musicians of the Théâtre de la Monnaie orchestra. A handful of instruments by this important Austrian Netherlands maker are today held by the Musical Instruments Museum in Brussels.

The Duke also supported artists at the Monnaie by attending non-subscription performances ('abonnements suspendus') whereby particular performers benefited directly from ticket sales, the subscription being temporarily suspended for these performances. The performance of 29 September 1769 was organized to support the French actor Jean-Claude-Gilles Colson, or Bellecour (1725-1778),[547] who was another protégé of Charles of Lorraine,[548] and on 6 December the French actress Marie-Suzanne-Joseph Artus Truyart (1741-1787), wife of Defoye, was the artist in the limelight.[549] This last soirée saw the revival of Monsigny's opera *Le Déserteur*, which had first been performed in Brussels on 9 September 1769, six months after its première in Paris,[550] and from which several airs in manuscript were added to the music collection.[551]

The Library and printed musical works

As mentioned earlier, Charles-Marie-Raymond d'Arenberg was very attached to his library, which he sought to expand with thought and care so that it would become a gateway to a broad range of knowledge. He desired to order his books by subject, and to ensure that the right conditions were

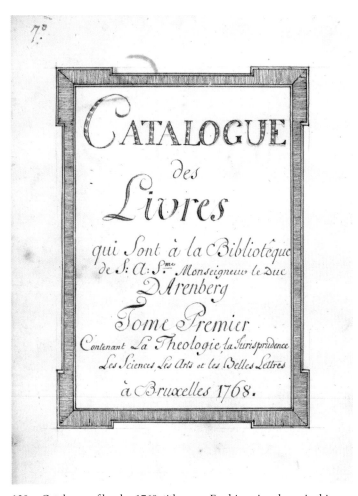

120. Catalogue of books, 1768, title page. Enghien, Arenberg Archives and Cultural Centre, 29/10.

121. J.-J. Mouret, *Les Festes de Thalie*,
      supralibros. Enghien, Arenberg Archives
      and Cultural Centre, I 1021.

122. Ex-libris of A. Cardon (in J.-J. Mouret, *Les Festes de Thalie*).
      Enghien, Arenberg Archives and Cultural Centre, I 1021.

provided for their conservation. Accordingly, he drew up a first inventory of his Brussels library in 1768: the *Catalogue des livres qui sont à la Bibliothèque de S.A.S.me Monseigneur le Duc D'Arenberg*,[552] of which the first volume (the only one preserved) lists only a few musical works. During the same period the Duke embarked on the cataloguing of his painting collection. From 1756 until 1772 a bookbinder named Étienne was in the Duke's service, having the responsibility of binding not only the books but also the inventories, specifically 'pour les archives d'Enghien'.[553] In 1769 Étienne was commissioned to emblazon the book covers of a series of volumes in the collection with the Duke's coat of arms. This depicted three medlar flowers in the centre of a shield surrounded by the collar of the Order of the Golden Fleece, set on the cross of the Military Order of Maria Theresa.[554] Many of the musical volumes given this uniform vellum binding still retain today this distinctive supralibros. Most often, they also display an ex-libris designed by the Brussels engraver Antoine-Alexandre-Joseph Cardon (1739-1822) to show the book's possession by the 'Duchesse D'Arenberg', Louise-Marguerite de La Marck.

The first volumes of music embossed in this way were engraved operatic scores printed in Paris, where one finds the names of such composers as François-Joseph Gossec (1734-1829) from Hainaut and the Frenchmen Pierre-Alexandre Monsigny and François-André-Danican Philidor (1726-1795). Gossec's *Les Pêcheurs* was included in the Parisian edition that came out from La Chevardière in 1766,[555] which was probably acquired by the Duke after the Brussels première of this 'comédie mêlée d'ariettes' on 19 September 1767. In 1766 the Brussels printer and bookseller Jean-Joseph Boucherie (who printed the *Gazette des Pays-Bas* from 1759 to 1768) published a libretto of *Les Pêcheurs* that contained in addition the music for two of its *ariettes* printed in movable type – a publication not inventoried in the ducal library but which may quite feasibly have been part of the library at one time.[556] *Le Maître en droit* by Monsigny appears in its edition of 1760,[557] while the same composer's operas *Le Cadi dupé* and *On ne s'avise jamais de tout* date from 1761.[558] A printed score of Monsigny's *Rose et Colas* was once held by the family library, before it disappeared. This *comédie* had been staged for the first time in Paris on 8 March 1764 and was performed in Brussels on 16 June 1765[559]. As for

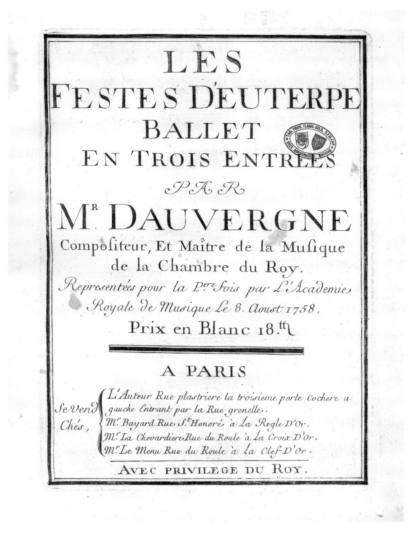

123. A. Dauvergne, *Les Fêtes d'Euterpe*, Paris, published by the author. Enghien,
      Arenberg Archives and Cultural Centre, I 1060.

the printed scores of Philidor's works marked with the Duke's coat of arms, these are *Blaise le savetier* (1759),[560] *Le Jardinier et son seigneur* (1761),[561] *Le Maréchal ferrant* (1761),[562] *Sancho Pança dans son île* (1762),[563] and *L'Amant déguisé ou le Jardinier supposé* (1769).[564] These five operas were performed in Brussels in 1760, 1763, 1765, 1770, and 1769, respectively.[565] Three Philidor scores, which are listed in the section 'A Bruxelles Operas Bouffons en Partitions' of the *Catalogue des livres qui sont à Bruxelles et à Enghien dans les cabinets de S.A. Mad.e la Duchesse d'Arenberg. Grands Operas, Operas bouffons avec leurs Partitions, Musique et airs détachés, Piéces détachées & Théatres, Livres historiques, Juridiques, Politiques & Belles Lettres &a. 1769*,[566] no longer appear in the collection. These works are: *Le Bûcheron ou les Trois souhaits*, *Le Sorcier*, and *Tom Jones*, first performed in Paris on 28 February 1763, 2 February 1764, and 27 February 1765, respectively, and in Brussels on 28 July 1765, 13 June 1765, and 26 July 1766.[567]

The inventory of 1769 reveals that the music-loving Duchess owned her own music library located at the Arenberg residence in Brussels. The section 'Grand operas françois en partition' lists the prints of two ballets first performed in Paris in 1758: *Les Fêtes de Paphos* by Mondonville[568] and *Les Fêtes d'Euterpe* by Dauvergne,[569] works that seem not to have been performed on the Brussels stage. Eleven other prints not yet mentioned also appear in the inventory under 'Operas Bouffons en Partitions'. Prominent among these are works by the Italian composer Egidio Duni (1709-1775), who lived in Paris: *L'Île des fous* (1760),[570] *Mazet* (1761),[571] *Les Deux chasseurs et la laitière* (1763),[572] *Le Milicien* (1763),[573] *La Fée Urgèle ou Ce qui plaît aux dames* (1765),[574] *La Clochette* (1766),[575] and *Les Moissonneurs* (1768).[576] Only the second work listed above is still present in the music collection today.[577] Finally, we have *Le Serrurier* by the Paris-based Bohemian composer Josef Kohaut (1738-?1793),[578] a work that once appeared alongside three other scores today missing: *La Servante maîtresse* (1754), a translated version by Pierre Baurans of Pergolesi's *La serva padrona*,[579] *Le Tonnelier* (1765)[580] by Gossec, Philidor, and their associates, and *Toinon et Toinette* (1767), also by Gossec.[581]

The bookbinder Étienne was in charge of the uniform binding not only of the volumes cited above, which were recent acquisitions, but also of a number of older Paris prints (Ballard, essentially) already on the library shelves – works by Campra, Destouches, Francoeur, Lully, and Rameau. The sole instrumental publication included in this binding exercise was Bouin's *Sonates pour la vielle et autres instruments*, a work dear to the Duke and Duchess.[582]

By studying both the newspapers and account books it is possible to attempt to answer, at least in part, the question of who supplied the Arenberg family with the opera scores listed in the Duchess's library catalogue. In the 1760s the Duke was a loyal client of the Brussels booksellers Pierre Vasse, Jean-Joseph Boucherie, Jean-François Horgnies, and Josse Vanden Berghen. From these sellers he bought not only newspapers, such as the *Mercure de France*, and gazettes from the Low Countries, Amsterdam, Cologne, and Frankfurt, but also books. The account books regularly mention payments for 'livrance de livres' (delivery of books), but the receipts giving details of the books delivered are not all preserved, so we still cannot tell if any musical scores formed part of a consignment.

Several scores inventoried in 1769 seem to have been acquired from Jean-Joseph Boucherie.[583] Indeed, on 14 June 1764 Boucherie placed an advertisement in the *Gazette des Pays-Bas* to say that he was selling 'les Partitions' (scores) of a series of *opéras-comiques* and *comédies mêlées d'ariettes*, among them *Mazet*, *Le Maître en droit*, *Rose et Colas*, and *L'Île des fous*.[584] A few weeks later he announced that he had just acquired some new scores, among them *Le Sorcier*,[585] while in April 1765 he also offered *Le Serrurier*.[586] Boucherie himself stated in one of his press announcements that he had obtained these engraved scores in Paris.[587] Other scores were perhaps bought by the Duke in the French capital without the help of an intermediary, for the family regularly visited the city, as in 1764, on their way to Vienna. In 1766, a box 'de livres venus de Paris', the contents of which are not known, was delivered to the ducal residence in Brussels.[588] As for the scores of *Les Moissonneurs* and *Toinon et Toinette*, they may have been supplied by Jean-Louis de Boubers (1731-1804), the Brussels-based printer and bookseller originally from Lille,[589] for the latter announced in the *Gazette des Pays-Bas* of 23 June 1768 that he was selling 'La Partition des Moissonneurs, de Toinon & Toinette & des meilleurs Opéra nouveaux, ainsi que des assortimens de Musique'.[590] The separate parts of a few airs from *Toinon et Toinette* would later be re-transcribed, probably from the printed score, for use at one or other private performance.[591]

124.   C. P. E. Bach, *Sechs Sonaten*, Berlin, Winter. Enghien, Arenberg Archives and Cultural Centre, I 1073.

Over the course of the Arenbergs' travels and through contacts made throughout Europe the ducal library also expanded during the 1760s through the acquisition of a series of printed instrumental music scores, which did not receive Étienne's special binding. The 1763 Berlin edition of *Zweyte Fortsetzung von Sechs Sonaten fürs Clavier* by Carl Philipp Emanuel Bach (1714-1788)[592] was probably used in harpsichord lessons, while the *Sonates en trio pour le clavecin avec accompagnement de violon et basse ad libitum* Op. 7 by Johann Schobert (c. 1735-1767), published by Bailleux in Paris, no doubt livened up chamber music sessions,[593] just as the first *Suite de contredances pour les violons flutes hautbois avec accompagnement de basse ou basson telles qu'elles s'executent au bal de l'opera* by Pierre Just Davesnes, a cellist in the orchestra of the Paris Opera from 1750 to 1766, will also have done.[594]

Musical manuscripts

As we have seen, the various inventories in the ducal library essentially list the printed and bound musical works. The Duke of Arenberg and his family did continue, however, to acquire manuscript music, loose-leaf or bound, of scores or individual parts, including both operatic and instrumental music.

From around the 1750s, all over Europe, more and more people started to take up music. Musical manuscripts therefore ceased to serve solely for the use of professionals or as a mark of prestige among wealthy amateur collectors: they became commercial products, genuine consumer items, produced with an ever-wider circulation. Music copyists provided operatic extracts for amateur musicians to be performed at private concerts and recitals. At the same time, the rise in instrumental music helped music publishing to prosper and gave rise to a proliferation of manuscript copies for the performance of this repertoire.

Charles-Marie-Raymond, as well as his wife and later their children, were no exception to these developments. As a result, the AACC Collection contains a large number of manuscript copies that

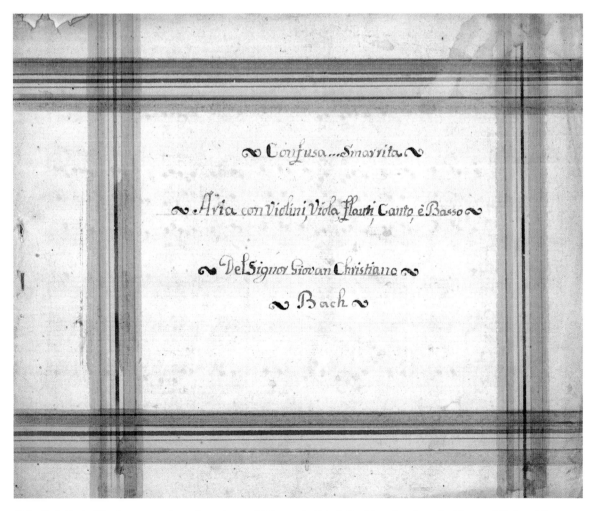

125. J. C. Bach, 'Confusa, smarrita, spiegarti vorrei' [*Catone in Utica*]. Enghien, Arenberg Archives and Cultural Centre, Ms 60.

126. Johann Christian Bach by T. Gainsborough.
Bologna, Museo internazionale e biblioteca
della musica.

doubtless were used for private performances, where the performers were musicians in the Duke's service, or recruited on an *ad hoc* basis, or else members of the Duke's family. So even if a manuscript was by definition unique, it no longer enjoyed the same status as it would have had in Léopold-Philippe d'Arenberg's time during the first half of the eighteenth century, since many manuscripts constituted, from then on, typical specimens of the innumerable copies of works disseminated commercially in printed and manuscript form throughout most European countries.

Among the ducal library's operatic holdings is a manuscript score of the aria 'Se possono tanto due luci' from the opera by Johann Christian Bach (1735-1782) *Alessandro nell'Indie*.[595] This work, which premiered at the Teatro San Carlo in Naples on 20 January 1762, comes from the composer's Italian period, as does the aria 'Confusa, smarrita, spiegarti vorrei', also present in manuscript form,[596] from the 'dramma per musica' *Catone in Utica*, performed for the first time at the same venue a few months earlier, on 4 November 1761. Appearing in the second scene of the third act, it was no coincidence that 'Confusa' was copied out, since it is the opera's most celebrated aria.

Other manuscript scores present movements from works by Italian composers produced in various European cities in the 1750s and 1760s. Thus the duet 'Ma tu piangi?' sung by the characters Ipodamia and Pelope in *Pelope* by Niccolò Jommelli (1714-1774)[597] was associated with the court of Stuttgart, for this 'opera seria' played there on 11 February 1755, when the composer was kapellmeister in the city. At that time Jommelli was well known all over Europe for his sacred music (composed especially while he was *maestro di cappella* at St Peter's in Rome), and also for his operas, which were commissioned for Italian theatres as well as Viennese and London stages.[598] The music library also contains an aria written by a rival of Jommelli at the Vatican: the Neapolitan David Perez (1711-1778). This is 'Il mio dolor vedete', an aria from *L'eroe cinese*,[599] whose first performance was on 6 June 1753 at the court of the King of Portugal, where, since the previous year, the composer had been director of the musical establishment and teacher to the royal princesses. This aria appears in act II scene 2 of the opera and is written for the character Siveno, son of Leango, Regent of the Chinese empire. There was little chance that Niccolò Piccinni (1728-1800), one of the central figures of Italian and French opera in the second half of the eighteenth century, would fail to be added to the Duke's music collection, here in the form of a manuscript score of the soprano aria 'Una povera ragazza' from the composer's successful 'dramma giocoso' *La buona figliuola*. Written on a libretto by Goldoni, this work was first performed at the Teatro delle Dame in Rome on 6 February 1760, before being taken to Paris in June 1771, and to Brussels the following January.[600] Of works by Tommaso Traetta (1727-1779), the library holds a contemporary copy of Demetrio's aria 'Già che morir degg'io'[601] occurring in act III scene 7 of the 'opera seria' *Antigono*, which premiered at the Teatro Nuovo in Padua on 16 June 1764. The composer had since 1758 been at the helm of the court musicians at Parma, while writing operas for the Turin, Vienna, and Mannheim stages. The Venetian Francesco Zoppis (c. 1715 - after 1781) also appears in the collection, with the aria 'Dirò che fida sei', sung by Selene, Dido's sister, in act I scene 3 of *Didone abbandonata*, first staged in 1758 while the composer was employed at the Italian Opera House of St Petersburg.[602] Alongside these scores, the collection also holds nine separate manuscript parts of the aria 'Recagli quell'acciaro', an extract from *Ezio* by Ferdinando Bertoni (1725-1813), given during the carnival of 1767 at the Teatro San Benedetto in Venice, where the composer held the post of choirmaster at the Ospedale dei Mendicanti.[603]

As regards instrumental music, we find among others the name of the Italian composer and cellist Luigi Boccherini (1743-1805), together with a manuscript part for violin from his sonata for keyboard

127. Luigi Boccherini by A.-A. Bourgeois de
La Richardière, after Lefèvre. Bibliothèque
Nationale de France, Music Department,
Prints Collection, Boccherini 003.

and violin Op. 5 no. 3, in two movements: a work that corresponds to number 27 in Yves Gérard's thematic catalogue.[604] In actual fact, what we have is a copy of the print of the *Sei sonate di cembalo e violino obligato* Op. 5, which the composer published with Venier in 1768 after his sojourn in Paris. This collection is dedicated to Anne Louise Brillon de Jouy (1744-1824), whom Boccherini considered to be one of the greatest harpsichordists of her day. It was so successful that it quickly established the reputation of its author: numerous manuscript copies were made, and several new editions of the work were produced up to the beginning of the nineteenth century. This Parisian publication, which perhaps once belonged to the ducal library, no longer forms part of the AACC Collection.

The Duke's final years

1770 marked the return of Ignaz Vitzthumb as conductor of the orchestra of the Théâtre de la Monnaie. The Duke of Arenberg continued to advance Vitzthumb 315 florins every three months for the remuneration of five clarinettists in the orchestra.[605] From 1771 until his death he also granted the Austrian a bonus of 630 florins at the start of each year as a gesture of thanks for his work throughout the previous year.[606] The Duke also recruited Paul Mechtler (a native of the small town of Stranzendorf, some forty kilometres from Vienna), principal violinist at La Monnaie from 1771,[607] to give 'leçons de musique' – in particular, violin lessons – to his children.[608] Books were purchased from Jean-Louis de Boubers, who since 18 October 1769 had held the position of bookseller within La Monnaie itself,[609] dealing solely in dramatic works.[610]

At this time Princesses Marie-Léopoldine and Marie-Flore were receiving harpsichord lessons from Godefroid Staes, son of their former teacher Ferdinand Staes. The new harpsichord master produced copies of scores for the family, too,[611] while the upkeep of the two instruments used by the family was entrusted to a certain E. Borremans,[612] a musician attached to the orchestra of La Monnaie.[613] From March 1771 the young ladies were also learning a new instrument, the harp, under the instruction of Antoine Pallet – second violinist and harpist in the orchestra of the Théâtre de la Monnaie since 1767.[614] An unprecedented craze for this instrument was sparked off in 1770 when the future Queen, Marie Antoinette, herself a harpist, triggered the influx of numerous instrument-makers into Paris, together with the composition of specific pieces for harp.[615] The Duke's daughters had two instruments at their disposal: a large harp loaned by Pallet's intermediary, at the cost of up to 3 florins and 3 sols per month, and a small harp that was already in the family's possession and whose repair the music master took it upon himself to carry out.[616] The Princesses had lessons once a week with Pallet, and he provided them with scores as well as new strings.[617]

It was probably Pallet who suggested that the family acquire the *Nouvelle Méthode pour l'accompagnement du clavecin et bon pour les personnes qui pincent de la harpe* by Honoré Garnier, who, as the page title specifies, was an 'accompagnateur du roi de Pologne'.[618] It was above all through this work, published in Paris in 1766, that Garnier made his name three years before he died (at Nancy).[619]

From July 1771, Antoine Pallet had just one pupil within the Duke's family: Marie-Léopoldine,[620] since Marie-Flore had decided to stop her lessons shortly after her marriage (on 18 April 1771 in Heverlee)

128.   Harp by J.-H. Naderman. Brussels, Musical
Instruments Museum, M 3174.

to Guillaume d'Ursel (1750-1804),[621] son of Duke Charles d'Ursel, who was co-director of La Monnaie together with Léopold-Philippe d'Arenberg. After the wedding celebrations the Arenberg family held a concert in Brussels on 29 April, which was attended by Charles of Lorraine,[622] and on 1 May some 'musiciens extraordinaires' were engaged by the Duke to play at his residence and, three days later, at the Duke d'Ursel's home.[623] In the first few days of June, finally, a performance was given at the Duke's private theatre at Heverlee; if we go by the number of tickets printed by Antoine Cardon, the family expected to receive an audience of up to eight hundred and fifty![624] In 1773 Carlo Boni dedicated to Marie-Flore his *Six quatuor pour harpe ou clavecin, violon, alto & basse*, a work published in Paris at the 'Bureau d'abonnement musical'. This print sadly no longer exists in the AACC Collection and has not been located in any other library; nor is it cited in the old inventories of the ducal collection. Its existence is in fact attested only by the advertisements that appeared in the Parisian press upon its publication in March 1773.[625] The composer himself remains an enigma, since we know absolutely nothing about him.

129. Marie-Flore d'Arenberg, Duchesse d'Ursel. University of Leuven, Kunstpatrimonium, Arenbergverzameling (Artistic and Cultural Heritage).

On 5 June 1771 Charles-Marie-Raymond d'Arenberg departed for England, together with the Brussels botanist Eugène Joseph Charles d'Olmen, Baron de Poederlé (1742-1813),[626] and the English naturalist and physician John Turberville Needham (1713-1781), who had moved to Brussels in 1769. Although the main aim of the trip was to visit English gardens and acquire exotic trees and plants, the trio also attended performances at the London theatres, as we are told in Poederlé's manuscript travel journal *Journal du voiage que je fis en Angleterre avec Monsieur le Duc d'Arenberg et Mr. Needham membre de la Société Royale de Londres &c. en 1771 étant parti de Bruxelles le 5 juin et revenu le 11 août au château d'Enghien.*[627]

During this period, several London parks and gardens were beginning to offer refreshments and entertainments of all kinds, as well as concerts. The Duke, de Poederlé, and Needham visited two of these: Vauxhall and Marylebone.[628] The Baron notes on 11 June that at the Vauxhall Gardens 'il y a un orchestre, on y chante en anglais';[629] two days later he writes that Marylebone also has an orchestra and that they attended, 'sur le théâtre qui s'y trouve dans les jardins', a performance of Pergolesi's *La serva padrona* in English.[630] On 29 July the three gentlemen attended a ball in London, during which minuets were played and *contredanses* danced; the Baron observes in the journal that these were lively ('vives') and that 'il y a toujours un tambourin et une petite flûte mêlée avec la musique'.[631] The Duke does not seem to have taken advantage of his stay to purchase musical prints in the British capital, because the only volume that could have been brought back to Brussels at this time was *The Favourite Songs in the Opera Orfeo*, published in London in 1770 by the Scot Robert Bremner (c. 1713-1789). This publication is a score containing several numbers from *Orfeo ed Euridice* (1762) by Christoph Willibald Gluck (1714-1787) in the version reworked by Johann Christian Bach and Pietro Alessandro Guglielmi (1728-1804) that was first presented at London's King's Theatre on 7 April 1770.[632] A manuscript contemporary with the print re-transcribes the two famous arias 'Che farò senza Euridice' and 'Chiamo il mio ben così' sung by Orfeo.[633]

Back in Brussels, the Duke continued to attend performances at the Théâtre de la Monnaie, notably the 'abonnements suspendus'. On 23 September 1771 he went to a performance of Corneille's tragedy *Rodogune*, followed by the 'comédie mêlée d'ariettes' *Silvain* by André-Ernest-Modeste Grétry (1741-1813), a composer from Liège. This work had received its première in Paris on 19 February 1770, and its Brussels première arrived three months later, on 5 June.[634] The whole evening was intended to promote the French actress Jeanne-Louise-Élisabeth Pitrot, known as Mme Verteuil, and was attended by both the Duke[635] and Governor Charles of Lorraine.[636] On the evening of 22 December, both the young French actor Jean Mauduit, or Larive (1747-1827) (future husband of Eugénie D'Hannetaire[637] and a bright light at the Comédie-Française)[638] and a certain Dugué were centre-stage, performing in the comedy *Turcaret* by Alain-René Lesage and the 'parodie en musique' *Les Amours de Bastien et Bastienne*.[639] These performances were also attended by the Duke and Charles of Lorraine. On 1 February 1772, the comedies *Le Dissipateur ou l'Honnête friponne* by Néricault Destouches and *Les Méprises* by Pierre Rousseau[640] were given for the benefit of the Parisian actor Jean-Baptiste Fauchard, or Grandmesnil (Grand-Ménil) (1737-1816), and Louis Compain-Despierrières.[641] On the following 2 March, the Duke also attended a soirée intended to support the orchestral conductor Vitzthumb, the actors Jacques-Denis Dubois, and Larive, as well as the actress Defoye.[642]

130. *The Favourite Songs in the Opera Orfeo*, London, Bremner, page 15. Enghien, Arenberg Archives and Cultural Centre, I 985.

131. Mandolin player in P. Denis, *Méthode raisonnée pour apprendre à jouer de la mandoline*. Royal Library of Belgium, Music Division, Fétis 6204 B Mus.

On 20 April 1772 Ignaz Vitzthumb began his first season as director of the Théâtre de la Monnaie, a role he shared with Louis Compain-Despierrières until December 1774. Since 14 August 1771, however, when their official licence was granted, the two associates had been receiving the monies paid each quarter in subscriptions – as attested by the printed receipt concerning the two boxes numbered '1.er Rang N° 17' relating to the Duke of Arenberg.[643] Vitzthumb put all his energies into quickly making the institution he directed an opera house of the highest quality, surpassing that of Paris. The 'abonnements suspendus' performances continued to be numerous,[644] and some concerts of instrumental music were also programmed, such as one featuring the Italian mandolin player Giovanni Battista Gervasio (1725-1785) on 7 December 1774, a concert attended by the Duchess of Arenberg.[645] The mandolin was at that time a much-prized instrument in Brussels, following the example of Paris; the French capital regularly hosted concerts for this instrument, notably in the concert room of the Concert Spirituel.

Brussels audiences had heard Grétry's works for the first time on 17 June 1769, with *Lucile*,[646] but it was principally under Vitzthumb that this composer came to the fore. The Brussels premières of *Zémire et Azor* (8 July 1772), *L'Ami de la maison* (11 November 1772), *Le Magnifique* (9 July 1773), and *La Fausse magie* (12 May 1775) were performed in quick succession and punctuated by many other works by the *Liégeois* composer. Thus the schedule of May 1772 offered, in that month alone, four revival performances: *Les Deux avares* (3 May), *Silvain* (7 May), *Le Huron* (17 May), and *Le Tableau parlant* (31 May).[647] If they wished, audience members could purchase from the Monnaie bookshop copies of the libretto, printed by Josse Vanden Berghen, such as that of *Silvain*, published in 1770, which contains two *ariettes* printed in movable type.[648]

The Arenbergs fell in with the general enthusiasm for Grétry's works, with the result that printed scores from Paris, such as *L'Ami de la maison*[649] and *Les Deux avares*,[650] were added to the music library. The second work seems to have been obtained via Jean-Louis de Boubers, for a note of 5 May 1772 states that he had 'Les deux avares' delivered to the Duchess, though without specifying which edition this was.[651] Manuscript copies of certain airs from *Les Deux avares*, as also from *Lucile*, *Le Tableau parlant*, *Silvain*, *Zémire et Azor*, *La Rosière de Salency*, and *Le Magnifique*, were gradually added to the

132.   Grétry by É.-L. Vigée-Lebrun. Versailles, Musée national des châteaux
de Versailles et de Trianon.

133.   A.-E.-M. Grétry, *L'Ami de la maison*, Paris, Houbaut. Enghien, Arenberg Archives and Cultural Centre, I 967.

library's shelves, either in the form of a score or as separate parts, and these must have be used for one or other private musical performance.[652]

The Concert Bourgeois continued to be supported by the Duke during the 1770s. He kept up his subscription and attended scheduled performances there.[653] As an organizer of public concerts, the Concert Bourgeois produced entrance tickets, some of which came in the form of playing cards.[654] It also had receipts printed[655] and, to mark the new year, greetings cards decorated with musical instruments[656] or, like playing cards, with red diamonds.[657]

From 1772 the Duke's children were increasingly involved in music-making. Marie-Léopoldine continued to take harpsichord lessons with Staes (until 1774), harp lessons with Pallet (until 1776),[658] and singing lessons,[659] while the young Prince Charles-Joseph, aged seventeen, began singing lessons with Jean-François Dewinne[660] and transverse flute lessons with René-Joseph Gehot, a member of the Monnaie orchestra.[661] The vocal exercises were soon abandoned, but the Prince continued with the flute, several instruments being acquired from the flute maker Rottenburgh.[662] The eldest Prince, Louis-Engelbert, resumed dancing lessons with the Frenchman Laurent Bocquet, who was also the ballet master of Vitzthumb's company at the Monnaie;[663] in 1773 Prince Charles was also taught by that dancer and choreographer.[664] The family's music teacher continued to be the violinist Paul Mechtler, who would maintain this post after the Duke's death in 1778. A certain P. M. Hinne was engaged by the Duke in 1772 to copy music scores, both for harp and for harpsichord, intended for Princess Marie-Léopoldine.[665] In 1774 the latter became one of the first people in the Austrian Netherlands to pride themselves on owning not only a harpsichord but also a 'forte piano'.[666] This pianoforte (tuned by Borremans) was probably acquired from the Tournai harpsichord-maker Henri-Joseph Van Casteel (1722-1790),[667] who in 1770 became the first maker to build this type of instrument in the region. That year he announced in the *Gazette de Pays-Bas* that he had just finished 'un Clavecin à Marteau, autrement dit Forte Piano, de la plus grande harmonie, justesse d'expression & force, & qui a été approuvé par les meilleurs Musiciens de cette ville. Cet instrument contrefait le luth & la harpe, & a un registre qui contrefait l'orgue. Le Forte Piano se touche avec une grande facilité. Il est tout monté en grosses cordes de laiton'.[668] A number of Van Casteel's instruments have been preserved and attest

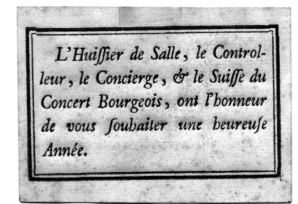

134. Printed greetings card of the Concert Bourgeois in the form of a playing card. Enghien, Arenberg Archives and Cultural Centre, folder 'divers musique/1', front and back.

to the quality of his craftsmanship – notably a pyramid-shaped pianoforte made in 1771 that is owned by the Musical Instruments Museum in Brussels.

In the last few years of his life Duke Charles-Marie-Raymond continued to hold balls, concerts, and theatrical and operatic performances at his private residences. Thus in June 1772 the stage designer-decorator and actor Jacques-Denis Dubois was appointed at the private theatre in Brussels to paint forestage scenery, a side panel, and also the decorations for a performance of the tragedy *Le Comte de Comminges* by Baculard (a work that had already been staged at the Duke's residence in 1769) and for a 'petit opera qui fut joué après', the title of which we unfortunately do not know.[669] When musicians worked simultaneously at La Monnaie and in the service of the Duke, this could sometimes pose problems. Indeed, in October 1772 Vitzthumb was obliged to wait for his musicians all to be back together in order to present Philidor's opera *Ernelinde, princesse de Norvège*, which was finally performed on the fifteenth day of that month.[670] In December 1773, Antoine Albanese

135. Pyramid-shaped pianoforte by Henri Van Casteel. Brussels, Musical Instruments Museum, M 2000.013.

(1729-1800) appeared in concert at the Duke's Brussels residence.[671] This French composer and singer of Italian origin, employed at the *Chapelle royale* of France, regularly sang at the Concert Spirituel in Paris and came to perform in Brussels on several occasions.[672] In the music library his name appears on a manuscript prepared a few years after the performance at the Duke's home.[673] On 11 April 1774 someone named Petit received from Charles-Marie-Raymond d'Arenberg the sum of 178 florins 10 sols 'pour avoir chanté au Concert a l'hotel de son Altesse'.[674]

Masquerades were still held, and on 27 February 1773 the Duke hosted one at his Brussels residence with the theme *Le Triomphe de Bacchus*. The next day, the *Gazette des Pays-Bas* gave this account of the event:

> Hier, dernier jour du Carnaval en ce pays, la principale Noblesse exécuta une mascarade très-ingénieusement inventée qui représentoit *le Triomphe de Bacchus*. Après un char de Musiciens étoit Silene entouré de Satires, & suivi d'un autre char portant Bacchus avec divers Bacchans & Bacchantes. Dix ou douze Birouches [*sic*] suivoient, & étoient accompagnés d'une foule de Silvains & de Faunes très-proprement vêtus. Cette belle Mascarade après avoir été à la Cour, traversa différentes rues de la Ville, & revint à l'Hôtel d'Arenberg; d'où elle étoit partie, & où elle soupa.
>
> [Yesterday, the last day of carnival, the high nobility performed a very ingeniously devised masquerade representing *The triumph of Bacchus*. After a chariot with musicians came Silenus surrounded by satyrs, followed by another chariot carrying Bacchus with various Bacchantes of both sexes. Ten or twelve barouches followed, being accompanied by a crowd of sylvans and fauns very fittingly dressed. This beautiful masquerade, having visited the court, travelled along different streets of the city and returned to the Arenberg residence from which it had come and where the masqueraders supped.]

These celebrations brought together not only the Duke and his wife but also their children, for the accounts tell us that the young Prince Charles participated in some of them[675] and had outfits specially made.[676] Festivities taking place in the ducal houses continued to be attended by Governor Charles of Lorraine, and on 7 February 1774 the latter noted in his *Journal* that he had 'Eté au spectacle et au bal chez le duc d'Aremberg'.[677] A few months later, on 23 November, the Duke was at the wedding of his second son, Auguste (1753-1833), Count de La Marck since 1773, and Marie-Françoise Le Danois, Marquise de Cernay (1757-1810). Entitled *Festes de Raisme*, a canvas painted on the occasion of this marriage that includes actors and musicians underlines the fact that the Raismes estate passed thereby into the hands of the Arenberg family.[678]

In 1775, in recognition of the popularity the Governor enjoyed, the Estates of Brabant decided to erect a statue of him. The official inauguration of the sculpture, which was created (at the Duke's instigation) by Pierre Verschaffelt (1710-1783) from Ghent, took place on 17 January 1775 with much pomp. Music evidently played a large role in the festivities, the Concert Bourgeois not neglecting the opportunity to perform at this prestigious event glorifying its patron. On 24 January the same concert society performed a prologue composed by Vitzthumb, who had been in sole charge of La Monnaie for several weeks following the departure of his associate Louis Compain-Despierrières.[679] The work was written for large choir and two solo voices, and was performed by Compain and Angélique D'Hannetaire (1749-1822), daughter of Jean-Nicolas Servandoni D'Hannetaire and a

136. *Festes de Raisme*. University of Leuven, Kunstpatrimonium, Arenbergverzameling
(Artistic and Cultural Heritage).

member of the company at the Monnaie since 1766.[680] The concert continued with the song *Amis, pour la fête, que chacun s'apprête*, which had already been presented at the Concert Bourgeois during the celebrations of 1769; this piece preceded a round sung on the air of Philidor's vaudeville in *Tom Jones* by Angélique D'Hannetaire and Compain, as well as by Françoise-Claudine de Clagny (1753-1780) and Mlle Saint-Quentin, both employed in Brussels since the 1774-1775 season. This concert was financed by the Duke, who paid not only the Concert Bourgeois's annual subscription fee but also a supplementary fee for the event.[681] Keeping up the spirit of the celebrations, Charles-Marie-Raymond d'Arenberg invited Charles of Lorraine to his home again on the following 6 February to take part in a masquerade entitled *Les Vendangeurs*, which was choreographed by Pierre Trappeniers, dancing master to the pages of the Governor and steward of the balls and *redoutes* (assemblies) at the Monnaie since 1773.[682] Count Jean-Népomucène de Clary, son-in-law to Prince Charles-Joseph de Ligne after marrying the latter's daughter Christine on 31 January, described the festivities of 1775 in a series of letters, dwelling especially on this masquerade, in which he took an active part, and which was held again at the Monnaie on the 12 February. He reports that four quadrilles were danced there, and that 'la princesse d'Arenberg' (that is, the young wife of Prince Louis-Engelbert d'Arenberg, Louise-Pauline de Brancas) 'était à la tête du premier, en blanc et bleu'. The other actors mentioned by Clary are Princess Élisabeth-Philippine-Claude de Stolberg, the Princess of Hesse, his own wife Princess Christine de Ligne, Countess Lucie-Thérèse de Liedekerke, the Countess de Clary, and Count Charles-Florent de Maldeghem.[683]

At the start of 1775 Vitzthumb formulated an editorial concept that was totally new for Brussels: the publication in separate parts of arrangements of operatic *ariettes* for voice, two violins, and basso continuo, these vocal pieces originally having had orchestral accompaniment. For this enterprise he joined forces with the brothers Pierre-Joseph Théodore and Philippe-Henri Van Ypen at their headquarters in the rue de la Madeleine in Brussels (where they had been music publishers since 5 July 1774), together with the French copper-engraver, Abraham Salomon Pris (1740-1800). Pris was recruited by Vitzthumb from the orchestra itself, for he was also a trumpeter and horn player.[684] The associates quickly brought out a collection of *Six ariettes de differens operas arrangèes* [sic] *pour être exécutées à deux violons avec la basse continue* taken from *Berthe* by Gossec, *La Rosière de Salency* and *La Fausse magie* by Grétry, Philidor's *Le Bon fils*, and Gluck's *Le Cadi dupé*. The Duke was quick to acquire a copy, which is today among the *unica* of the collection, for no other recorded library in the world holds this publication.[685] It was at this time that Vitzthumb suggested to Charles-Marie-

137. The statue of Charles of Lorraine, 1775.
Royal Library of Belgium, Prints and
Drawings Division, S II 22896.

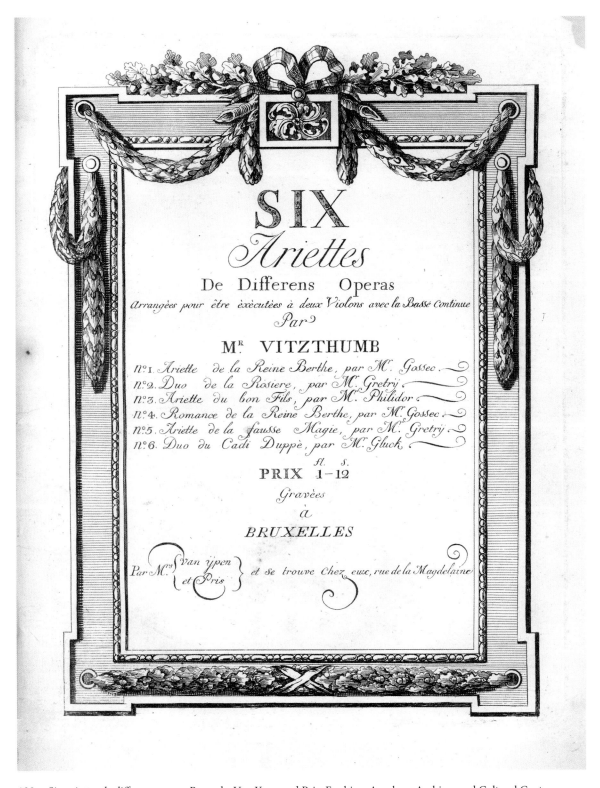

138. *Six ariettes de differens operas*, Brussels, Van Ypen and Pris. Enghien, Arenberg Archives and Cultural Centre, I 949/1.

139. Charles-Joseph de Ligne by A. Cardon. Royal Library of
Belgium, Prints and Drawings Division, S II 7539 f°.

Raymond d'Arenberg that he subscribe to the *Premier recueil d'ariettes d'opéra arrangées par Mr. Vitzthumb avec premier et second violon et la basse continue sous le chant*, before even a subscription notice had been placed in the *Gazette des Pays-Bas* (which occurred on 18 May 1775).[686]

To potential customers Vitzthumb offered, for 3 couronnes (9 florins 9 sols), to deliver thirty-six *ariettes* in one year, with three *ariettes* at the start of each month, between July 1775 and June 1776. The publication was also available abroad: from Jean-François Horgnies, purveyor of gazettes, in all post offices in the Southern Netherlands, Liège, Cologne, Frankfurt, Augsburg, and London, as well as from bookshops in The Hague and Amsterdam.[687] The formula was a success and, following the same principles, the Austrian produced a second volume (1776-1777) and then a third one (1777-1778), which, like the first volume, came to be added to the shelves of the Duke's music library.[688] The Van Ypen brothers, who were joined in 1776 by the musician Paul Mechtler, produced pre-printed receipts for their customers.[689]

The *ariettes* arranged in the collections come from all the operas that were popular with audiences at the Monnaie, such as Monsigny's *La Belle Arsène*,[690] Grétry's *Les Mariages samnites*,[691] the French version of Gluck's *Orfeo* (*Orphée et Eurydice*), and Sacchini's *L'Olympiade*. Vitzthumb did not fail, either, to include his own works, publishing in the three collections of *ariettes* numbers from *La Foire de village* and *La Statue*, operatic works written on librettos by the Abbé Jean-Pierre Pagès, as well as his 'opéra-comique' *Céphalide ou les Autres mariages samnites*. Composed in collaboration with the Italian singing teacher and mandolin player Giovanni Cifolelli on a libretto by Prince Charles-Joseph de Ligne (1735-1814), this last work was conceived by Vitzthumb as a musical riposte to the 'drame lyrique' *Les Mariages samnites* by Grétry, a composer with whom he had fallen out for good during the summer of 1776. The work – whose autograph manuscript survives today in the music collection of the château of the Princes de Ligne in Belœil – received its première at La Monnaie on 30 January 1777, with the librettist's mistress Angélique D'Hannetaire in the title role.[692] The airs appearing in

140.   I. Vitzthumb, *Heureux qui près de toi*, Brussels, Van Ypen. Enghien, Arenberg Archives and Cultural Centre, I 616.

141. J. T. Brodeczky, *Trois sonates*, Brussels, Van Ypen and Pris, title
page. Enghien, Arenberg Archives and Cultural Centre, I 868.

the different collections of *ariettes* were so popular that these prints served as a basis for manuscripts probably copied for the use of amateur musicians.[693] Another Brussels publication signed 'P. Van Ypen' is among the unique pieces of the AACC: this contains, in three separate parts, the *ariette* by Vitzthumb entitled *Heureux qui près de toi*, a piece that was not included in the subscription volumes and is unknown from other sources.[694]

In April 1776 the Van Ypen brothers, Pris, and Mechtler dedicated their edition of Johann Theodor Brodeczky's *Trois sonates pour le clavecin ou le pianoforte avec accompagnement d'un premier et second violon & violoncelle* Op. 2 to Duke Charles-Marie-Raymond. Brodeczky was an obscure Bohemian composer residing in Brussels in 1774. The title page of this publication, which the engraver Pris signed with the inscription 'pris d. & Sc. Scrip', features a medallion adorned with the coat of arms of the dedicatee. This print, which was added to the Duke's music library,[695] was sold not only in the Austrian Netherlands but also abroad: in Amsterdam, Frankfurt, The Hague, Lyon, Mainz, and Paris.[696] It is significant that the dedication is not penned by the composer himself, as was usually the case, but is by the publishers, who had been close to the Arenberg family for years.

In addition to his professional activity as an arranger, Vitzthumb continued to direct the Théâtre de la Monnaie and its orchestra. In the orchestra he worked alongside Antoine Pallet, who had similarly

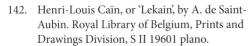

142. Henri-Louis Caïn, or 'Lekain', by A. de Saint-Aubin. Royal Library of Belgium, Prints and Drawings Division, S II 19601 plano.

143. Gluck by Quenedey. Enghien, Arenberg Archives and Cultural Centre, Biographies of musicians, 9/1.

called on the Van Ypen brothers and the engraver Pris to publish his *Recueil de petits airs arrangès [sic] pour la harpe*, which were extracts from Grétry's *Le Magnifique*, *Zémire et Azor*, and *La Rosière de Salency*, and Monsigny's *La Reine de Golconde* – all successful productions at the Brussels opera house. With this volume, the harpist Pallet was presenting the very first Brussels publication devoted to the harp.[697] Pallet must surely have given copies of his compositions to his pupil Marie-Léopoldine d'Arenberg, yet the print is no longer to be found in the AACC Collection; nor is it listed in the library catalogues prepared in 1777 and 1778.

The performances staged by Vitzthumb were still being enthusiastically attended by the Duke and Duchess, who each had a private box at the Monnaie: ground-level box 16 and box 17 of the second tier in the left-hand balcony.[698] Financial assistance to artists remained a constant, and when the French tragedian Henri-Louis Caïn, known as Lekain (1729-1778), a 'comédien du roi', stayed in Brussels in May 1775, the family covered his costs.[699] In 1776, when Étienne Lecocq succeeded Jacques Gaillard as manager of the family accounts, he created a specific section for 'les Spectacles & la Musique', demonstrating the ever-greater role that these played over the years. In 1776 alone expenditure for this category amounted to an eye-watering 2690 florins and 2 sols! On 15 February 1777, the non-subscription performance of the day, which was seen by the Duchess of Arenberg, was 'donné au profit de Mlle. Angelique': that is, Angélique D'Hannetaire.[700] The work performed that night was Vitzthumb's *Céphalide*, given for the fifth and final time since its première at the end of January, plus the comedy *Le Français à Londres* by Louis de Boissy, known as Bonnefoy (1694-1758).[701]

On 31 May 1777, the director Vitzthumb, in debt, had to cease his activities and announced to his audiences that as from the next day there would be no more performances until further notice. But three associates quickly took over the theatre's management. These were the Parisian actor Louis-Jean Pin (b. 1734), the Brussels actor Alexandre Bultos, and the Parisian dancer and actress Marguerite-Louise Odiot de Montroty, known as Sophie Lothaire. Even though bankrupt, the Austrian continued to be supported by Duke Charles-Marie-Raymond d'Arenberg: the annual allowance of 630 florins scheduled at the beginning of 1778 to thank the artist for his loyal service over the previous year would indeed be paid a final time after the Duke's death in order to respect the 'ordre verbal de feu Mgr.' (the verbal instruction of the late Duke).[702] However, the new Duke, Louis-Engelbert, immediately stopped this gift, as he did also that awarded to the clarinettists in the orchestra.[703] Ignaz Vitzthumb, an artist of genius with a complex personality, thus became definitively ousted from the Arenbergs' close circle.

On the death of Charles-Marie-Raymond d'Arenberg the family library in Brussels contained, as I have mentioned, over twelve thousand volumes. The musical acquisitions, like the others, grew during the 1760s, these consisting for the most part of repertoire connected with performances at the Théâtre de la Monnaie. Duke Charles-Marie-Raymond was a man curious about a multitude of subjects, from the plastic arts to literature, as well as natural science, and he also allotted a place to music. But his interest in music took the form chiefly of private music-making by members of the family, or by artists who came to perform in private concerts and recitals. Some volumes were bound: in 1776 a man named Le Clerck took over the role of book-binder from Étienne,[704] and the following year De Groot.[705] In 1777 the librarian Jean-Noël Paquot finished his first library catalogue, aided by an assistant.[706] The following year, he completed a second catalogue in two volumes, dividing the works into thematic categories. In December 1778 Paquot would be paid 1255 florins 'pour deux ans un mois et trois jours de ses apointemens'; like Vitzthumb, he was subsequently given notice by Duke Louis-Engelbert d'Arenberg, leaving the family's service for good on 9 December.

Apart from the many scores and works already cited above, the catalogues of 1768, 1777, and 1778 list a few works that have not yet been mentioned, and which are no longer held in the AACC Collection. In the first inventory[707] the section 'Arts Métiers et Manufactures' was completed *a posteriori* with a mention of the two first parts already available from *L'Art du facteur d'orgues*, published in 1766 and 1770. This monumental work by the French Benedictine monk, scholar, and organ-builder Dom François Bédos de Celles (1709-1779),[708] which in 1778 comprised four parts, was mentioned again in the catalogues of 1777[709] and 1778[710] in the section 'Metiers ou Arts Mecaniques'. In the section 'Theatre des Grecs, des Latins, des Italiens' of the catalogues of 1777 and 1778 three prints appear that seem to refer to musical works, but we cannot tell from the descriptions whether these are scores or librettos. The first publication is a Viennese print (1765) of the 'commedia per musica' *Madama l'umorista, o Gli Stravaganti* by Giovanni Paisiello (1740-1816); the other two date from 1770: one printed in Pressburg (present-day Bratislava) for the 'opera buffa' *Il finto pazzo per amore* by Niccolò Piccinni; the other (Viennese) for Gluck's 'tragedia per musica' *Alceste*. Piccinni and Gluck were at the heart of a *querelle* that in Paris, a few years later, would set the so-called Gluckistes and Piccinnistes at loggerheads. The Duke also acquired a pamphlet published in 1777 entitled *Problème: Si Gluck est plus grand musicien que Piccini*.[711] In the same vein the catalogue section 'Supplément aux Sciences

& aux Arts' of 1778 cites the *Essai sur les révolutions de la musique en France* by the French author and critic Jean-François Marmontel (1723-1799). In this work, published in 1777, Marmontel favours Italian music, declaring himself to be anti-Gluckist and thereby taking a full part in the tussle between the partisans of Gluck and of Piccinni.[712]

It was on 17 August 1778 that Duke Charles-Marie-Raymond d'Arenberg died at his château in Enghien, having succumbed to smallpox. The title thereupon passed to his eldest son, Louis-Engelbert. Whereas his father Léopold-Philippe had been especially attracted to the Italian operatic repertoire and developed privileged contacts with musicians in the Austrian Netherlands, Charles-Marie-Raymond d'Arenberg maintained slightly different connections with music. His marriage to a music-loving French Countess alone could have instigated the expansion of French repertoire seen in his music collection, both operatic and instrumental. Parisian prints of French operas came to fill the shelves of the family library, inspired by performances seen both in Brussels and in other European capitals. Manuscript copies intended for private use were subsequently made from the published works. Undoubtedly through his social position, and probably thanks also to his personal tastes, Charles-Marie-Raymond became an important patron of musical life in the Austrian Netherlands – even more so, in fact, than his father – by supporting the first society for public concerts in Brussels, the Concert Bourgeois, as well as the Théâtre de la Monnaie. The Monnaie was no longer a place of *ad hoc* recruitment for artists: it became more a space for the coming together of musicians and dancers – artists who were employed variously (whether alternately or simultaneously) at the court of Governor Charles of Lorraine, on the public stage, or in the private circle of the Duke for music lessons or performances. More than ever before, the private and public spheres became closely connected, as exemplified by the activities of the Austrian musician Ignaz Vitzthumb, who was supported financially not only at the Concert Bourgeois and the Théâtre de la Monnaie but also in his private initiatives. Instrumental music was not forgotten, either: in parallel with the purchase of the most diverse musical instruments from local makers (woodwind instruments, harpsichord, then pianoforte and harp), printed scores were acquired for performance by the family, notably the Duke's children, while manuscript copies of instrumental works were also executed.

144.   Louis-Engelbert d'Arenberg as a young man. Enghien, Arenberg Archives and Cultural Centre.

CHAPTER III
LOUIS-ENGELBERT, SIXTH DUKE OF ARENBERG
(1778-1820)

The lot of Louis-Engelbert d'Arenberg would turn out to be quite different from that of his father and grandfather, and yet the Duke would still take great pleasure in musical performances, just as they had also done. After he was blinded in an accident music would in fact become very much more important to him than might have been foreseen, and it would hold a particular interest for him during his various travels. It was on account of the impetus he provided that the Arenberg music library continued to grow.

A Crown Prince

Prince Louis-Engelbert, born in Brussels on 3 August 1750, was the second son of Duke Charles-Marie-Raymond d'Arenberg and Louise-Marguerite de La Marck. He was given the same Christian name as his maternal grandfather. Chance would make Louis-Engelbert the eldest son and potential heir to the title of Duke after the death, on 31 March 1751, of his brother François-Marie-Thérèse, an infant of just twenty months. The young Prince had an all-embracing education, with languages, drawing, and riding taught alongside the harpsichord, organ, violin, and dance. In his lessons he was instructed by some of the leading musical figures of the court of Charles of Lorraine and the Théâtre de la Monnaie – among them, Staes, Doudelet, Trappeniers, and Mechtler.[713]

In 1764 Louis-Engelbert first experienced life at court in Vienna, and three years later he began a career in the military, soon becoming a sub-lieutenant. He studied at the University of Strasbourg, an institution he left in 1771 in order to continue his army training.[714] In 1772 he rose to the rank of major, and the following year lieutenant-colonel. Louis-Engelbert would later remark that his military experience did him the greatest good, because it taught him to cope more easily with life's hardships.[715]

On 17 January 1773 the King of France, Louis XV, and the Royal Family attended the signing of the marriage contract between Louis-Engelbert d'Arenberg and a young woman from one of the most prominent families of France: Louise-Pauline de Brancas (1755-1812), Countess de Lauraguais, the eldest daughter of Louis-Léon-Félicité de Brancas (1733-1824)[716] and Élisabeth Pauline de Gand-Vilain de Mérode (1737-1794), Princess of Isenghien. Two days later the religious marriage service took place in Paris in the private chapel of Louise de Gand-Vilain (1717-1773) *née* de Roye de La Rochefoucauld, grandmother of the bride.[717] This marriage allowed new properties to enter the family estate, such as Charleroi, Gilly, and Châtelineau, plus the Hôtel d'Isenghien, a mansion in the Sablon district in Brussels. The same year, Louis-Engelbert became a member of the Brussels Masonic Lodge of *L'Heureuse rencontre*, which had been founded in 1772, although he was not yet officially listed as a member. In the years that followed he would join other Lodges, together with his wife, who also sought involvement in these kinds of association. In 1778 they would both become members of the Lodge *Vraie et Parfaite Harmonie* in Mons, while four years later the Duchess would become *Grande maîtresse* at the Lodge in Brussels of *Les Vrais Amis de l'Union*.[718]

The financial means allocated by the Duke to the young bridegroom was considerable, since for the year 1774 alone the pension paid to him amounted to 12000 florins.[719] The couple were to have six children: Pauline, Louis-Engelbert, Prosper-Louis (the future Duke), Paul, Pierre, and Philippe.

On 12 June 1774 Louis-Engelbert took part with his younger brother Charles in the masquerade *Les Tableaux*, held at the Théâtre de la Monnaie in honour of the Archduke Maximilian, youngest son of Empress Maria Theresa. The masquerade's final dance, choreographed by the dancing master Trappeniers, was modelled on *tableaux vivants* inspired by Rubens and Van Dyck. The *Gazette des Pays-Bas* gave an account of the guests in attendance at the ball, citing among these 'le Prince d'Aremberg' and 'le Prince Charles d'Aremberg'.[720]

On 9 September 1775, in the park at Enghien, Prince Louis-Engelbert, then aged twenty five, was involved in a hunting accident, in which he suffered facial scarring and the permanent loss of his sight. Less than two years later another tragedy struck: his son Louis-Engelbert, who was born on 19 August 1777, died just three days later. On the following 11 October the young father, on account of his blindness, was forced to abandon his military career in the Empress's Austrian army.[721] A new life had therefore to be forged.

The music-loving 'blind Duke'

When Charles-Marie-Raymond died, on 17 August 1778, his son Louis-Engelbert – who would acquire fame as 'le duc aveugle' ('the blind Duke') – became the sixth Duke of Arenberg. Despite his condition he also succeeded his father as High Bailiff of Hainaut, this office having been bestowed on him by Empress Maria Theresa on 15 April 1779. From this time onwards musical performances played a significant part in the Duke's life. He continued to attend performances at the Théâtre de la Monnaie (which was still being directed by the trio of Pin, Bultos, and Lothaire), paying a subscription for two boxes.[722] He continued to employ a number of artists who had been in the service of his father, giving notice to others, such as Vitzthumb; but he also called upon new performers.

As music master to the family since 1771, the Austrian Paul Mechtler was among his most loyal employees. Mechtler gave lessons to the Duchess, Pauline de Brancas, while continuing to instruct her sister-in-law, Princess Marie-Léopoldine.[723] For his lessons this musician regularly provided scores for his pupils to work from, not least his own: in particular, the new volumes containing the series of collections of *ariettes* that had been published on the initiative of Vitzthumb. Indeed, Mechtler had become the official engraver of the Brussels firm, Van Ypen, and had created, under the new imprint 'Van Ypen et Mechtler',[724] the *Quatrième recueil de 36 ariettes d'opéra par année avec premier, second*

145. Louise-Pauline de Brancas. Enghien, Arenberg
Archives and Cultural Centre.

violon et la basse continue sous le chant. This publication, in which the arrangements, uncredited, are probably Mechtler's work, would appear monthly each year until the fourteenth volume, the series finally ending in June 1789. The Arenberg family were keen subscribers to this series, for today the AACC Collection still holds the twelve first volumes.[725] We do not know whether the subscription lapsed after the twelfth volume, or the final volumes were later removed from the music library.

A pianoforte made by Henri-Joseph Van Casteel was delivered to the ducal home in Brussels at the end of 1778.[726] The receipt tells us that the instrument cost 326 florins and was intended for the Duchess's use. We do not know whether it was meant to replace the one acquired in 1774 or was bought as an additional instrument. A few weeks later, during a public sale, the Duke acquired various pieces of furniture as well as a harpsichord.[727]

When the Duke and his wife visited Vienna at the end of May 1779, Duke Louis-Engelbert asked his secretary to write down his account of their stay. The secretary noted that the ducal couple went to the Burgtheater to see the singspiel *Die Bergknappen* by the Viennese composer Ignaz Umlauf (1746-1796). Written on a libretto by the Viennese writer Paul Weidmann (1747-1810), this popular work had been chosen a few months earlier to mark the opening of the Burgtheater, an institution founded for the purpose of promoting German-language opera (the *Singspiel*), which would be so fervently supported by the future Emperor Joseph II.[728] Regarding this work, the Duke noted (via his secretary) that 'la musique est en verité tout à fait agreable'.[729] After Umlauf's singspiel the Duke and Duchess saw Grétry's opera *La Fausse magie*, 'en allemand qui fut parfaitement exécutée'.[730] The Duke also remarked that he especially enjoyed the voice of 'Cavaglieri', the Viennese soprano Catarina Cavalieri

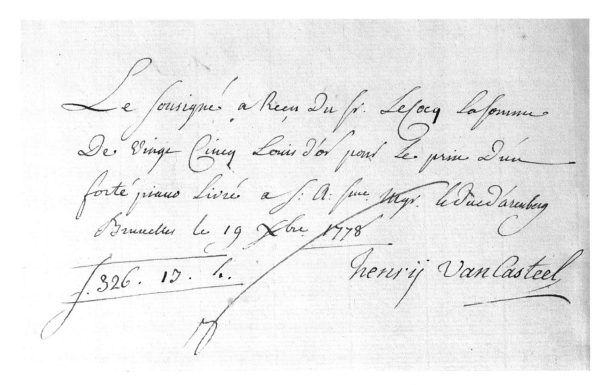

146.   Receipt of H.-J. Van Casteel. Brussels, State Archives of Belgium, Arenberg Collection, LA 10361.

(1755-1801), who also played Sophie in *Die Bergknappen* and Constanze in Mozart's *Die Entführung aus dem Serail*, given in 1782. During the Duke's Viennese sojourn of 1779 Mozart was still in the service of Prince-Archbishop Colloredo in Salzburg. Two years later, having moved to Vienna, he was to discover the freedom of working as a freelance musician.

It was no doubt from Vienna that the blind Duke brought back two manuscript scores, copied in the same hand, containing two extracts of Umlauf's two-act singspiel *Die schöne Schusterinn oder Die Pücefarbenen Schuhe*, whose première he probably attended on 22 June 1779 at the Burgtheater. 'Soll ein Schuh nicht drücken' is the fourth aria in act I of the work, while the duet 'Wie lieb ich dich mein Weibchen' appears as the fifth aria of the second act.[731]

Back in Brussels, Louis-Engelbert d'Arenberg took on a new manservant: the painter, harpist, and composer Ernst Johann Benedikt Lang (1749-1785), who at the time was living in Nürnberg.[732] In the autumn of 1779 Lang accompanied the Duke to the Théâtre de la Monnaie, as well as to the medicinal waters of Spa.[733] He stayed only a short time in the ducal family's employ, for on 30 April of the following year he received the sum of 200 florins 'pour retourner dans son pays'.[734] He left behind in the music library an autograph page dated '1780', which is the draft copy of an unidentified accompaniment (presumably for harp); it is bound (with a cord) together with twelve separate manuscript parts containing a duet and an air from Monsigny's *Le Déserteur*.[735]

The deaths of Charles of Lorraine on 4 July 1780, and of Empress Maria Theresa on 24 November of the same year, marked not only a turning point in the history of the Austrian Netherlands but also in the Arenberg family's involvement in politics. Previously close and sustained contacts now became

147. Louis-Engelbert d'Arenberg with his wife and his mother by Antoon van Clevenbergh, c. 1788.
     Private collection.

things of the past: the Duke's relations with the new Emperor, Joseph II (whom he met in 1781) and with the new Governors, Maria Christina of Austria-Lorraine and her husband Albert Casimir of Saxony, were much cooler.

In November 1781 the organist, harpsichordist, and composer from Brussels Laurent-François Boutmy (1756-1838) entered the service of the ducal family, just as his father Josse Boutmy had done fifty years earlier (serving Duke Léopold-Philippe d'Arenberg). He became harpsichord teacher to Pauline,[736] the Duke's only daughter, who was then aged seven. The young Princess had already received several harpsichord lessons the previous year in Enghien from an unidentified teacher;[737] she had also been introduced to music by Paul Mechtler's son, François, who was a violinist, like his father.[738] The child also began dancing lessons[739] with a teacher from Bordeaux, Jean-Baptiste Pitrot (1729-1809), who had been ballet master at the Théâtre de la Monnaie in 1771.[740]

As his father and grandfather had done, the blind Duke hosted numerous balls and concerts at his various residences. Several times during 1781 he called on the Brussels violinist François Gehot, who had just started in the orchestra of the Monnaie, which was once again being directed by his father-in-law Ignaz Vitzthumb.[741] During that year Gehot oversaw in Brussel the organization of eight balls, six of which were held during the carnival period.[742] Musicians (who have not been identified) performed at Heverlee on 17, 18, and 19 September.[743]

Travels of a listening Duke

At the beginning of April 1782 Louis-Engelbert arrived in England with his wife, some friends, and his mother, the Dowager Duchess Louise-Marguerite, who was then fifty-one years of age. During this visit, which lasted two months, the Duke was granted an audience with the King (since 1760) of Great Britain and Ireland, George III. The journal that the blind Duke kept during this sojourn (his words taken down by his secretary) contains a few interesting details regarding music.[744]

On 11 April a soirée held at the King's Theatre in London gave the Duke the opportunity to hear the Venetian soprano Maddalena Allegranti (1754-1801). Having earlier appearing at Venice, Florence, and the court at Mannheim, Allegranti had made her London début in *I viaggiatori felici* by the Italian composer Pasquale Anfossi (1727-1797), a 'dramma giocoso' previously premiered in Venice during the autumn of 1780.[745] The Duke emphasizes 'l'expression délicieuse de son chant'.[746] Even if he could not admire the choreography of the performance, the name of the Parisian choreographer Jean-Georges Noverre (1727-1810) is noted in the journal, as well as those of the dancers Louis-Marie Nivelon (1760-1837) and Pierre-Gabriel Gardel (1758-1840), and of Mlle Théodore (wife of Jean Bercher, or 'Dauberval') and Giovanna Baccelli. The latter made her début in London in the same year, 1782, and a portrait of her was made by the English painter Thomas Gainsborough. With regard to the orchestra, Louis-Engelbert considered it 'meilleur que celui de Paris' (better than the one in Paris), but he concluded all the same that 'l'ensemble de l'opéra de Londres ne peut être comparé à celui des Français'.[747]

In the London theatre of Drury Lane, on 22 April, the visiting gentlemen saw Shakespeare's

148. Giovanna Baccelli by J. Reynolds. Royal Library of
Belgium, Prints and Drawings Division, S III 51274.

tragedy *Romeo and Juliet*, followed by two pantomimes 'mêlées de chant' (interspersed with song).[748] The following day, while Duchess Louise-Pauline and her mother-in-law were being entertained in the drawing room of Lady Harcourt, the Duke chose to go to a concert at the home of a certain gentleman named Gor, where he heard the Italian violonist Felice Giardini (1716-1796), 'le meilleur violon qui existe peut-être', accompanied by 'un violoncelle supérieur à tout ce que j'avais entendu jusques là'[749] – this was probably the English cellist John Crosdill (c. 1751-1825). Giardini, who had made his London début in 1751, had taken part in the Bach-Abel concerts (which ceased on the death of Johann Christian Bach on 1 January 1782). In that year, 1782, Giardini became music master to the Prince of Wales, the future King George IV of England, whose cello teacher was Crosdill.[750] During the same evening Louis-Engelbert d'Arenberg listened to several young English female amateur singers, one accompanying herself on the harp.[751]

In May, he went to the opera on several occasions and relates in his journal the true story of the flight of the Italian composer Antonio Sacchini (1730-1786) from the British capital, where he had been living since 1772, and where his operas were particularly popular. Debt-ridden, the musician left England at this time for Paris.[752] The Duke had the following lines written in his journal:

> […] Sacchini ayant eu vent qu'on devait l'arrêter pour dettes, et que ses créanciers l'avaient désigné aux suppots de la justice, comme celui qui touchait le Clavecin dans l'Orchestre, sortit adroitement se faisant substituer par un autre musicien; Celui-ci, malgré ses réclamations ne manqua pas d'être arrêté et conduit en prison, où il ne fut que cinq heures, par bonheur pour sa bourse, puisqu'on le fit payer par les captureurs à raison de cinq guinées par heure de détention pour s'être mépris dans les fonctions de leur employ. C'est un usage bien sagement établi, à

149. F. Giardini by Lambert. Enghien, Arenberg Archives and Cultural Centre, Biographies of musicians, 9/1.

150. Antonio Sacchini by L. Jay. Royal Library of Belgium, Prints and Drawings Division, S II 87978.

fin que ces Messieurs soient attentifs à ne pas troubler la liberté publique, en s'emparant par etourderie de l'innocent au lieu du coupable. Le pauvre diable ne fut pas faché, comme on peut le croire de l'avanture, et Sacchini en profita pour se sauver.[753]

[[...] Sacchini, having got wind that he was going to be arrested for debt, and that his creditors had brought his name to the attention of the legal authorities, cleverly abandoned his duties as harpsichordist in the opera and had himself replaced by another musician. The latter, despite protesting, was duly arrested and taken to prison, where he remained for only five hours, luckily for his purse, since his captors had to pay him five guineas for every hour of detention on account of having committed an error while carrying out their duties. This is an established principle with the wise aim of making these gentlemen careful not to disturb public liberty by inadvertently seizing the innocent instead of the guilty. The poor devil was reportedly not angered, and Sacchini took advantage of the episode to escape.]

Before returning to the Austrian Netherlands the Duke bought from an unidentified London merchant two Cremonese violins, as well as two bows and a mahogany case, for the sum of 137 florins; but the transaction stipulated that payment would be made only after a trial period during which the quality of the instruments could be ascertained as being of the calibre sought.[754] These violins were probably intended to be played by the family in private during chamber music sessions. Manuscript scores of the duet 'Parla mio dolce amore' for two sopranos and orchestra from Sacchini's opera *Eumene*, two arias for soprano and orchestra by the same composer,[755] and the canzonetta *La biondina in gondoletta* by the Italian castrato Giuseppe Millico (1727-1802),[756] active in London in 1772, may have been among the Duke's London purchases, together with a series of musical prints.

151. G. Millico, *La biondina in gondoletta*, title page. Enghien, Arenberg Archives and Cultural Centre, Ms 414.

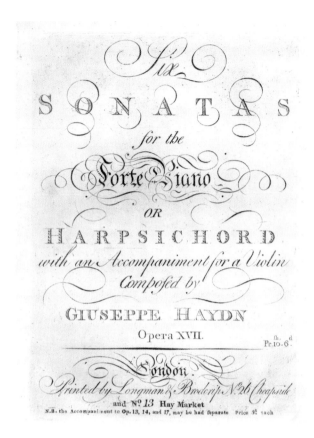

152. J. Haydn, *Six sonatas*, London, Longman & Broderip. Enghien, Arenberg Archives and Cultural Centre, I 762.

153. Masquerade costume from the 1780s. University of Leuven, Kunstpatrimonium, Arenbergverzameling (Artistic and Cultural Heritage).

The publications likely to have been acquired during this trip of 1782 constitute separate parts for instrumental pieces and the scores of works for voice with keyboard accompaniment. The Longman and Broderip print of the *Six sonatas for the forte piano or harpsichord with an accompaniment for a violin* Op. 17 by Joseph Haydn (1732-1809) appeared in 1781,[757] and that of *The Jessamine. A Collection of songs for the voice and harpsichord with the compass of the german flute, book the 3d*[758] by Thomas Curtis (active during the second half of the eighteenth century) was published around 1770.[759] The symphonic and chamber music of Joseph Haydn, who had been attached to the Hungarian Esterházy family at their residences of Eszterháza and Eisenstadt since the 1760s, were becoming disseminated ever more widely across Europe, thanks to the numerous editions published in Paris, London, and finally Vienna. The ducal family would soon show a keen interest in the work of this great composer, and other musical publications would swiftly be added to the library.

From the London publisher John Welcker the Duke procured *Six songs with an accompanyment for the great or small harp forte piano or harpsichord, dedicated to Mrs Hobard*[760] by Giuseppe Millico and *A third sett of six concertos for the harpsichord or piano forte* Op. 13 by Johann Christian Bach.[761] The *Three sonatas for the harpsichord or forte piano with accompanyments for a violin and bass ad libitum* Op. 3 by Ernst Eichner (1740-1777) were published by Robert Bremner around 1775,[762] while the Opp. 2, 3, and 4 of Johann Samuel Schroeter (1753-1788) were issued by William Napier.[763] Finally, *Sestini's favorite rondo in Il barone di Torre Forte* (*Tell me charming creature*), *adapted for the harpsichord piano forte or harp* by Tommaso Giordani (c. 1730-1806), a Neapolitan living in London from 1768 to 1783, was printed by Babb,[764] while *A fifth set of six sonatas for the harpsichord piano forte and organ with accompanyments for two violins and a violoncello, dedicated to Miss Stowe* Op. 7 by John Garth (c. 1722-c. 1810)[765] was published by the composer himself, becoming available that year (1782).[766] One further reason to believe that the ten London prints cited above were added to the ducal library after the Duke's stay in England is the fact that today they represent the sole examples listed for Belgium.

On his return to his Brussels residence the Duke held a *Grande mascarade des Amazones*,[767] and balls were once again given, such as on 27 December, with the participation of the musician Gehot.[768] The costumes made especially for the occasion, notably the Duchess's, are described in an inventory dated 3 January 1783. The wardrobe intended for these performances was particularly imposing: another record 'des habits de mascarades' drawn up in March 1787 details over 450 theatrical costumes and accessories.[769] Concerts in private were also arranged in Brussels by Paul Mechtler on 13 February and 15 March 1783,[770] and again on 19 November 1783 and 9 January 1784; during these final two concerts the musician himself played in a quartet, accompanied by three colleagues he had known since 1779 in the Théâtre de la Monnaie orchestra: Guillaume (1727-1797) and Jean-Baptiste (1737 - after 1799) van Maldere, brothers of the late violinist,[771] and the cellist Philippe-Jean Doudelet.[772]

With the blind Duke's support, on 21 November 1783 Jean-Pierre Minckelers, a professor at the University of Louvain, launched from the park at Heverlee the first balloon propelled by coal gas; several other launches would follow from Heverlee, as well as from Brussels and Enghien.

The season at the Théâtre de la Monnaie beginning on 21 April 1783 was marked by a new directorship: that of Alexandre Bultos and his younger brother Herman (1752-1801). This time the Duke took up the box situated in the third tier of the left-hand balcony, which was 'la loge de Madame Deveau', namely Marie-Élisabeth de Tassilon, wife of Louis-Marie Devaux,[773] and so abandoned his former *basse loge*, number 16.[774] The Duchess still held box number 17 in the second tier.[775] At New Year the ducal couple rewarded several employees at the opera house, such as the doorman, guard, ushers, and carpenters.[776] Gifts were also given to the Concert Bourgeois and the Concert Noble.[777]

The Concert Bourgeois had ceased its activities in 1778 and a new director, the wine merchant Pierre De Busscher, had tried to revive the association in 1781, declaring that 'à la demande du Duc d'Arenberg et du Prince de Ligne on alloit recommencer à donner des Concerts incessamment'. He even added 'que ces Seigneurs [...] auroient l'aveu de leurs Altesses R.les à cet égard', aiming to stress that the Governors Maria Christina of Austria-Lorraine and Albert Casimir of Saxony were also in favour of the society's revival.[778] Deprived of the Petite Boucherie concert room, several members of the Concert Bourgeois – among them the wealthy coachbuilder Jean Simons, future husband of the singer and composer Amélie-Julie Candeille[779] – had finally decided to hold their concerts in a building in the former Jesuit school. The money allocated by the Duke in January 1784 therefore relates to the sessions organized in this new venue, which would be used until December 1785. During this period the Concert Noble was flourishing, especially when, in 1779, it was furnished with a concert room of its own, located on the corner of the rue Ducale and the Place de Louvain and designed by the architect Laurent-Benoît Dewez.[780] Louis-Engelbert d'Arenberg had been a member of the association

154. [J.-R. P. de Walckiers], *Six romances*, Brussels, 1789. Enghien, Arenberg
      Archives and Cultural Centre, I 911/3.

since 1779; he appears in an initial list of members dating from that year that included more than 100 names, and again in the records for 1781 and 1783.[781]

In 1784 a Parisian print was dedicated to Duchess Louise-Pauline d'Arenberg: the *Trois sonates pour le clavecin ou le forte piano, avec accompagnement de violon* by the French writer and composer Caroline Wuiet (1766-1835), Baroness d'Auffdiener.[782] The author would surely have offered her patron a copy of this publication, but it no longer appears in the AACC Collection. The same year, another woman composer attracted the attention of the Duchess: Joséphine-Rosalie Pauline de Walckiers (1765-1836), daughter of Adrien-Ange de Walckiers and Dieudonnée Louise de Nettine, and also sister of Édouard de Walckiers, Receiver General and Adviser to the Austrian Netherlands Ministry of Finance. De Walckiers's opera in three acts *Zéphire et Flore* was staged at the Théâtre de la Monnaie on 5, 8, 12, and 15 March 1784. Not only did the Duchess attend the first performance on 8 March:[783] she also acquired a manuscript collection containing the airs 'Charmant objet de ma secrète flamme', 'À chaque belle à son tour', and 'On n'aime point dans nos forêts', plus the duet 'Son jeune cœur n'aime encore que sa beauté' and the trio 'Ma trop jalouse erreur'.[784] Another number, 'Quand laissant la

155. List by P. Mechtler dated 29 December 1784, page 1. Brussels, State Archives
of Belgium, Arenberg Collection, MG 3701.

cité voisine', appeared in June 1784 in the *Neuvième recueil de 36 ariettes d'opéra* published by Van Ypen and Mechtler.[785] Five years later a Brussels publication that can be reasonably attributed to the same composer was added to the ducal library: the *Six romances avec accompagnement de forte piano dédiées à ma sœur* – a print that today is among the *unica* of the AACC Collection.[786]

The works played at the concerts organized by Paul Mechtler were certainly those which Mechtler suggested to the Duke he acquire. A list drawn up by Mechtler on 29 December 1784 of the scores that were provided[787] shows that among the works acquired were symphonies by Haydn, Hoffmeister, Jadin, Kaa, Saint-Georges, and Vanhal; quartets by Jadin and 'Vanhoff fils'; and the overtures from

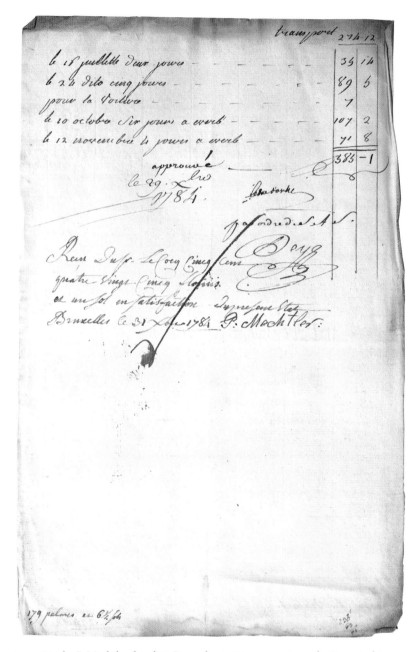

156. List by P. Mechtler dated 29 December 1784, page 2. Brussels, State Archives
of Belgium, Arenberg Collection, MG 3701.

La frascatana by Paisiello and *L'amour soldat* by Sacchini. The *Six quartetto pour deux violons, alto et violoncelle dont le deuxième, quatrième et sixième sont pour flutte ou violon* Op. 1 and the *Six simphonies à grand orchestre qui peuvent s'exécuter à quatre parties* Op. 4 by Jean-Baptiste Jadin (b. 1744) from Namur were published by the Van Ypen brothers,[788] as were the *Trois simphonies pour deux violons, alto, basso, deux fluttes et deux cors* by the German composer Franz Ignaz Kaa,[789] and the *Trois quatuor concertants pour deux violons, alto et basse* by Jean-Baptiste van Hoof (b. 1755), a composer originally from Lier working in Antwerp.[790] As an associate of the Brussels publishers, Mechtler was of course well placed to deal in these publications.[791] As for the other works, these were probably prints bought through the intermediary François Godefroy de la Rivière, a Brussels-based agent for several Paris publishing houses from the middle of the 1770s.[792] Rivière's name appears most notably on the title page of the edition by Jean-Georges Sieber dated 1774, probably the one indicated here, of Haydn's *Trois simphonies à deux violons, alto et basse, cor et hautbois* Op. 25,[793] corresponding to the symphonies Hoboken I 43 ('Mercury'), I 52, and I 47.[794] The other Haydn symphonies, mentioned without any identifying details in the list, are perhaps the three Parisian publications by Sieber and Imbault, dating from between 1782 and 1784, of the *Simphonies périodiques* numbers 6, 11, and 15, corresponding to Hoboken I 63 ('La Roxelane'), 65, and 73 ('La chasse') – volumes that are still in the AACC Collection today.[795] Although absent from Mechtler's list, the 1784 Schott edition containing separate parts of the *Grand concert pour le clavecin N° 7 copié d'après le journal de pieces de clavecin de Mr Boyer* (Hoboken XVIII: 11) must have been added to the Duke's collection during the same period.[796]

Another work cited in the list is probably a Parisian print published by Antoine Bailleux that was sold in Brussels containing *Deux simphonies concertantes pour deux violons principaux, deux violons ripieno, deux hautbois obligés, deux cors ad libitum, alto et basse, avec un violoncello obligé en suprimant le second violon principal* Op. 6 by Joseph Boulogne, Chevalier de Saint-Georges (1745-1799).[797]

Among the scores that Mechtler sold to the Duke in the autumn of 1785[798] we can identify the Parisian print by Sieber, sold through Godefroy, of Haydn's *Simphonies à deux violons, alto et basse, cor et hautbois* Op. 35 (Hoboken Ia 13, 6, 10, 5, 1, and 2),[799] plus the Brussels Van Ypen prints of Jadin's *Six trio pour deux violons et violoncelle* Op. 5,[800] the *Six sonates à deux violons* Opp. 2 and 3 by Jean-François Redein (1748-1802) from Antwerp,[801] and the *Ouverture de Zémire et Azor* in its arrangement

157.   J. Haydn, *Il maestro e lo scolare*, Amsterdam, Schmitt. Enghien, Arenberg Archives and Cultural Centre, I 895/11.

158.   L.-F. Boutmy, *Romance*. Enghien, Arenberg Archives and Cultural Centre, Ms 63.

for keyboard by Ferdinand Staes.[802] Gossec's name similarly appears on the list, indicating the acquisition of unspecified symphonies and a motet. Curiously, these scores, like most of those cited in the two lists, no longer exist in the AACC Collection. Could it be that they departed with Mechtler when he left the Arenbergs' service?

Laurent-François Boutmy continued to teach the harpsichord to Princess Pauline at both the Brussels and Heverlee residences,[803] the latter possessing 'deux Clavessins et un forté piano'.[804] It was doubtless he who suggested that the family purchase the Amsterdam print of Haydn's keyboard piece for four hands, *Il maestro e lo scolare* (Hoboken XVIIa: 1), which appeared from Schmitt in 1783: a piece that enables teacher and pupil to play together.[805] Boutmy also arranged for a copy to be made of a keyboard arrangement of the overture of the opera *Le Seigneur bienfaisant* by the French composer Étienne-Joseph Floquet (1748-1785),[806] first staged in Paris in September 1780.[807] This newly created manuscript was explicitly intended for the Duchess of Arenberg[808] and joined a Paris print of *Airs détachés du Seigneur bienfaisant* already in the library.[809] Boutmy celebrated the birth of Prince Prosper-Louis, born on 28 April 1785 at Enghien,[810] by writing a *Romance composée pour Madame la Duchesse D'Arenberg le 11 mai 1785 à l'occasion de la naissance de son Altesse le Prince Prosper* for soprano and keyboard, the two-page autograph manuscript of which is still held today by the AACC Collection.[811]

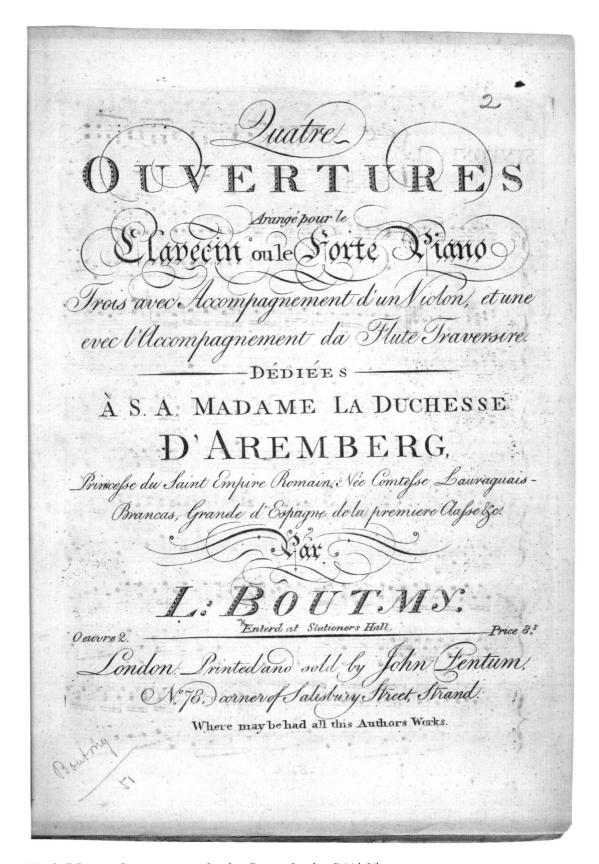

159.   L.-F. Boutmy, *Quatre ouvertures*, London, Fentum. London, British Library.

Three further autograph manuscripts were left by Boutmy in the music library,[812] among them that of his keyboard arrangement of the overture from the *Scipione* of Giuseppe Sarti (1729-1802), a 'dramma per musica' first performed in Venice in 1778.[813] There is no trace, however, of the print that Boutmy published in London of his *Quatre ouvertures arangé pour le clavecin ou le forte piano, trois avec accompagnement d'un violon, et une evec [sic] l'accompagnement da [sic] flute traversire [sic] Op. 2*, which he dedicated (as stated on the title page) to the Duchess of Arenberg; a copy of this print is held by the British Library in London.[814] It is likely that Boutmy arranged for this work to be published during the trip he made to England (and London in particular) between June 1785 and early 1786, taking with him a pianoforte made by Van Casteel;[815] indeed, John Fentum in London, who published the work, was active in the British capital from 1784 onwards. Was Boutmy the actual owner of the instrument, or was it on loan from the ducal family? We do know, however, that Van Casteel was in regular touch with the Arenberg family, since he appears in the accounts for the tuning of his instrument.[816] During Boutmy's absence Borremans stepped in to give Princess Pauline harpsichord lessons;[817] the Princess was also receiving dancing lessons from someone called Perolle, a dancer at the Théâtre de la Monnaie since 1781.[818] When Boutmy returned, he soon began to teach the rudiments of composition to his young pupil,[819] who was now having singing lessons as well.[820] In a letter to Prosper-Louis d'Arenberg in 1828 Boutmy speaks of the opportunities he has had, thanks to the blind Duke, to meet in the family home various well-known figures from the musical world, including the Italian castrato Giusto Ferdinando Tenducci, known as 'il Senesino' (c. 1735-1790), and Amantini, a soprano in the service of the Queen of France around 1783.[821] We do not know whether these meetings with other artists took place in Brussels or in Paris. At all events, the name 'Tenducci' appears in the music library – on the incomplete manuscript score for voice and keyboard of the air 'Water parted from the sea', 'sung by Mr Tenducci in Artaxerxes', *Artaxerxes* being the opera by Thomas Augustine Arne (1710-1788), who first staged the work at London's Covent Garden on 2 February 1762, with the castrato Tenducci in the role of Arbace.[822] Appearing in the third act, the air in question reveals the imaginative talent of this composer, who evokes through his beautifully melodic lines the flowing of a river.

On several occasions Duchess Louise-Pauline d'Arenberg, with her zest for discovering new music, arranged for scores to be sent to her directly from the French capital. Accordingly, after the birth of her son Prosper[823] the Leduc print of the *Airs variés à quatre mains pour le clavecin ou forte piano* Op. 14 by the French composer and organist Jean-Jacques Beauvarlet-Charpentier (1734-1794) was delivered to Brussels.[824] Louise-Pauline also purchased a 'caisse de musique', its contents not specified, which was supplied by the Marquis Paul Arconati (1754-1821) – this Arconati being the third son of the Milanese Marquis Giangaleazzo Arconati Visconti who had been chamberlain to Empress Maria Theresa.[825] All these musical publications were added to the shelves of the library, which was becoming enriched by a multitude of works covering many subjects, these having been procured in particular from the Brussels booksellers Louvois, Flon, and Dujardin,[826] as well as at public sales.[827] In the town of Enghien the Duchess followed her husband's example by joining the local musical society, about whose activities, however, we know very little.[828]

In 1785 Louis-Engelbert d'Arenberg collaborated with Ferdinand Pierre Rapédius de Berg (1740-1800), the *Amman* of Brussels,[829] and the Brussels writer Marie-Caroline Murray (1741-1831),[830] to

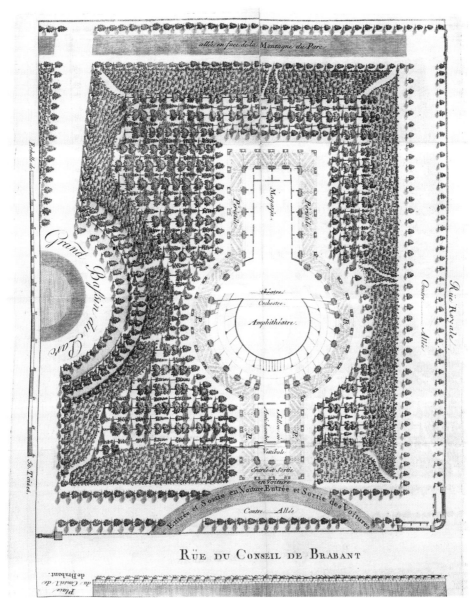

160. Plan for the *Projet de construction d'une salle de spectacle pour Bruxelles*, Brussels, Dujardin.
Royal Library of Belgium, Rare Books Division, IV 48.695 A.

publish anonymously with the bookseller Dujardin a *Projet de construction d'une salle de spectacle pour Bruxelles*.[831] The authors, aware of the increasing dilapidation and structural frailty of the Théâtre de la Monnaie, proposed that a new theatre be built in Brussels Park. The idea, which never came to fruition, was to choose a different site in the Park from the one occupied since 1783 by the round theatre, which had been built by the Bultos brothers to host the evening entertainments (*vauxhalls*) accompanied by an orchestra that had been held there since 1781.[832] Marie-Caroline Murray, daughter of the lawyer Jean-Baptiste Murray and Anne-Catherine Savage, was a friend not only of Cobenzl and the Prince de Ligne but also of Louis-Engelbert d'Arenberg, whom she had served as literary assistant since 1779. The Duke did not hesitate to lend Marie-Caroline his box at the Monnaie, as he did on

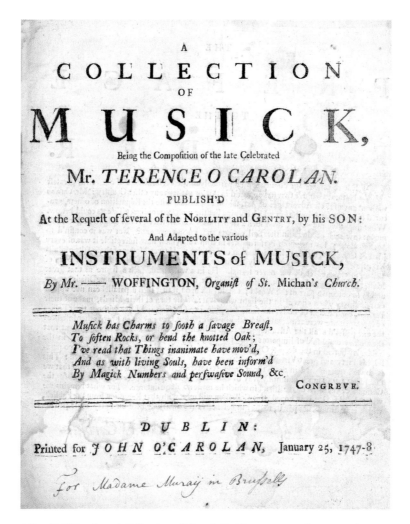

161.   T. O'Carolan, *A Collection of Musick*, Dublin, 1748. Enghien, Arenberg
       Archives and Cultural Centre, I 579.

23 December 1785,[833] two days after attending a performance of Paisiello's *Le Barbier de Séville* there
himself.[834] Marie-Caroline Murray deposited in the ducal library two manuscripts that had belonged
to her, as well as an Irish print dated 1747-1748 and called *A Collection of Musick*, in which John
O'Carolan – son of the blind Irish harpist, singer, and composer Turlough O'Carolan (1670-1738) –
presents a selection of pieces by his father in a version 'adapted to the various instruments of musick'
by John Woffington, organist at St Michan's Church in Dublin. With the note 'For Madame Muraÿ
in Brussels' written at the bottom of the title page, this copy in the AACC Collection is unique, since
up to this day only an incomplete volume has been recorded, at the National Library of Ireland.[835]
Characterized by a style both derived from popular Irish folklore and showing the influence of such
Italian composers as Vivaldi, Corelli, and Geminiani, the music of O'Carolan, who wrote over two
hundred airs, has traversed the centuries and is still played today; perhaps it held a certain resonance
for Marie-Caroline Murray because its creator was, like the Duke, afflicted by blindness.

Manuscript collection Ms 10 bears the traces of its successive owners Anne-Catherine Savage and
her daughter Marie-Caroline.[836] It brings together French vocal pieces, all of which are anonymous

except one, which is attributed to the French composer Toussaint Bertin de La Doué (c. 1680-1743) – the drinking song 'Qu'entends-je! Quel bruit me réveille', which was published in Paris in 1709 in the annual *Recueil d'airs sérieux et à boire*. It contains, too, an anonymous, incomplete aria, 'Sento da ignota face', identified as one sung by the character Laodicea in act I scene 6 of Porpora's *La verità nell'inganno*, a 'dramma per musica' first staged in Milan in 1726. Another manuscript collection, including the detail 'Muray', includes twenty *ariettes* or romances that come from Monsigny's *Le Roi et le fermier*, as well as from Philidor's *Le Maréchal ferrant* and *Le Bûcheron*.[837]

The concerts held in Brussels were regularly attended by the blind Duke. At the start of 1786, he would go to hear the singer Colette-Marie-Françoise Cifolelli, born in Ghent in 1764,[838] paying the exorbitant subscription of 480 florins.[839] The artist was in fact the elder daughter of Giovanni Cifolelli, who had collaborated with Vitzthumb in 1777 on the composition of the opera *Céphalide ou les Autres mariages samnites*.

On 28 October of that same year, 1786, the new château at Enghien – built to plans provided by the architect Louis-Joseph Montoyer – was destroyed by fire, only shortly after renovations (begun in 1783) had been completed. This new misfortune would unfortunately not be the last the blind Duke would have to endure.

Louis-Engelbert continued to subscribe to the Concert Noble, at the same time attending, with a group of around twenty people, a concert held by the Concert Bourgeois on 13 March 1787 to mark the return of the association to the concert room at the Place de Bavière. That same day, the Abbé André-Étienne Lepreux, music master at the Sainte-Chapelle in Paris and a Freemason since 1786 at the Parisian Lodge *L'Olympique de la Parfaite Estime*, offered a programme that was essentially religious in spirit, including a motet and an oratorio, plus his choral anthem *Caelo quos eadem*. Like the Concert Spirituel in Paris, where Lepreux had just been applauded for his *Te Deum*, this Brussels concert society played a part in the secularization of sacred music. The performers in Brussels were all artists connected with the Théâtre de la Monnaie, for in addition to Colette Cifolelli – who had been married to French *haute-contre* Jacques-Charles Ricquier (1752-1831) since 24 April 1786 – the Duke and his guests heard the *haute-contre* Charles-François-Honoré Lanctin, known as Duquesnoy (1758-1822) and the baritone Henri Mees (1757-1820).[840] It was likewise in 1787 that the Duke took an interest in a musical instrument with an unusual sound: the glass harmonica. Invented by Benjamin Franklin in 1761, this had become all the rage during the 1780s. The Duke bought one of these instruments from a certain Joseph Gorner for the sum of 113 florins 8 sols. For Louis-Engelbert, this acquisition probably arose more out of curiosity than from a genuine desire to play the instrument. At all events, no music for the instrument indicating that it had actually been played in a serious way has been found.[841]

A Duke in revolt

On 20 December 1787 Emperor Joseph II forced Louis-Engelbert d'Arenberg to resign as High Bailiff of Hainaut, giving the Duke's blindness as the reason for this decision. Exasperated, the Duke left Brussels on 18 February 1788 for a two-month tour of the south of France, which took him to Lyon and

162.   Joseph II by A. Cardon. Royal Library of Belgium, Prints and
       Drawings Division, F. 38011.

Marseille. His account, taken down by his secretary in the form of letters to the Duchess (who remained at home, having given birth on 10 January to Prince Paul), contains a few interesting reflections about the performances he attended.[842] He thought the opera company of Lyon to be superior to that of Marseille but states nonetheless that 'elle ne vaut cependant pas celle de Bruxelles'.[843] In Marseille he admired Mme Ponteuil, the wife of Jean-Baptiste Triboulet, known as Ponteuil, whom he preferred to Colette Cifolelli, having heard the latter not long before in the Austrian Netherlands capital.[844] In his letter of 20 March he describes a 'concert d'amateurs aussi bon au moins que tous ceux que nous avons à Bruxelles', noting that only the women were singing and that they had an annoying tendency to mispronounce the Italian language when doing so, adding that it 'est étonnant combien cela nuit à la musique' (it is striking how much this blights the music). He concludes, with reference to them, that 'sans goût et sans maitre, il est impossible qu'elles se perfectionnent' (having neither taste nor a master, it is impossible for them to improve).[845] On his return the Duke stopped again in Lyon and noted that he had 'observé avec attention ce qui pourrait être utile à la troupe de Bruxelles, puisque c'est la ville de province où il y a le plus de bons acteurs pour l'opéra comique' (observed closely something that could be useful to the company in Brussels, for this provincial city has a wealth of good actors for the 'opéra-comique'). He mentions the female singers D'Arbouville, Guirardin, and Crêtu,[846] as well as

concert chez sa belle soeur, Mad.ᵉ Groslay,
nous n'avions qu'a les aller chercher pour
nous y rendre. Effectivement, nous trou=
=vames un concert d'amateurs aussi bon
au moins que tous ceux que nous
avons à Bruxelles, mais pas un home
qui chantat. Ce furent quatre femmes
qui soutinrent ce Concert: Elles sont
excellentes musiciennes puisqu'elles s'ac=
=compagnent du Clavecin. Elles écorchent
l'Italien, parcequ'elles n'ont point de
goût et qu'elles sont écrasées par le
talent de Mad.ᵉ Tessier qui a été cinq
ans à Naples, et qui est parfaite
sans avoir une voix bien agréable. Leur
accent est choquant en francais, et
il est étonnant combien cela nuit à
la Musique. Leur voix sont fraiches,
jolies; l'une entr'autres a les sons
fort arrondis; Mais sans goût et
sans Maitre, il est impossible qu'elles

163. *Voyage dans les Provinces méridionales de la France.* Enghien, Arenberg
      Archives and Cultural Centre, Biography Louis-Engelbert d'Arenberg, box
      43/2.

the male singers Saint-Aubain and Desforges, adding that the others, 'plus médiocres, ne valent pas la peine d'être nommés, puisque je ne les ai pas remarqués' ([who are] more mediocre, are not worth mentioning, for they did not capture my attention).[847]

In May 1788 Louis-Engelbert was back in Paris, where, with his family, he attended the wedding of his younger brother, Louis-Marie. The Duke then spent the remainder of the year at Heverlee, where the harpsichord and piano were tuned by a certain F. M. J. De Prins.[848] From February to October 1789 he went away again: first to France for a second time, and then to Switzerland and Germany.[849] Revolutionary tensions in Brussels caused the musician Laurent-François Boutmy to flee the city, and as a result a new harpsichord teacher, Eugène Godecharle (1742-1798), was appointed to instruct the Princess Pauline.[850] Boutmy left two prints of his own compositions in the music library: one a Parisian edition, the *Trois sonates pour le piano forté dialoguées avec l'accompagnement d'un violon obligé*; the other, a London edition, the *Three sonatas for the piano forte or harpsichord with an accompanyment for the violin dedicated to Miss Luisia Byng*, about which a reviewer in the London periodical *The Analytical Review* of 1788 wrote: 'For the advantage of the pupil, as well as the pleasure of the *amateur*, we can strongly recommend this little publication'.[851]

The end of the year 1789 was made turbulent by the Brabant Revolution, a rebellion against the rationing measures imposed by Emperor Joseph II. The blind Duke and his brother Auguste, Count de La Marck, and his brother-in-law, Guillaume d'Ursel, rallied to the side of Joseph II's opponents, thereby joining the Democratic camp led by the lawyer Jean-François Vonck (1743-1792). The Duke's sister, Marie-Flore, likewise a Democrat, had been detained at her Brussels house shortly before 1789. Some revolutionary songs make reference to Louis-Engelbert's involvement.[852] In January 1790 the Republic of the United States of Belgium was established, but it proved short-lived, for in December of the same year the Treaty of The Hague restored the *Ancien Régime*. Emperor Leopold II succeeded his brother Joseph II, who had died on 20 February 1790, and the Governors General Maria Christina and Albert Casimir returned to the Austrian Netherlands.

From June 1790 to January 1791 the Duke and his family were in Paris. The Duke embarked on a new tour that took him to several Italian cities, notably Rome, where he would meet such artists as the painters Angelica Kauffmann and Élisabeth-Louise Vigée-Lebrun – who had fled from a France at boiling point – and also the sculptor Antonio Canova and the mosaic artist Giacomo Raffaelli. On this tour he dictated his journal to one of his travelling companions, Guillaume Bosschaert;[853] this account, even more than the others discussed above, bears witness to the Duke's fervent interest in music, in particular singing.[854] In Genoa, at the Teatro San Agostino, the party saw the 'commedia per musica' *L'inganno amoroso* by Pietro Alessandro Guglielmi, a work that had been first performed in Naples on 12 June 1786. But the Duke observes that he could not really enjoy the performance because 'le bruit que l'on y fait empêche qu'un étranger puisse profiter du chant ou de la musique' (the commotion in the audience prevents a foreigner from enjoying the singing and the music).[855] In Genoa he also attended the Teatro del Falcone, owned by the Durazzo family,[856] while in Siena the city's opera house was hosting another Neapolitan work by Guglielmi, *La pastorella nobile*, and the visitors admired both the company and the orchestra.[857] Once in Rome at the beginning of March, the Duke's party discovered the Teatro Argentina and the Teatro Valle, a smaller-scale theatre used for

VONCK, de la Liberté courageux defenseur,
A du s'expatrier pour prix de son ardeur:
Mais Vainqueur de l'envie, au temple de memoire
Son nom sera gravé par les mains de la gloire.

164.   Jean-François Vonck by J.-J. Durig. Royal Library of
Belgium, Prints and Drawings Division, S II 47176.

the comic repertoire.[858] In the chapel of Casa Nuova the Duke was taken with Paisiello's oratorio *La passione di Gesù Cristo*.[859] He also attended private concerts, such as one on 3 April at the residence of Sig.a Flaviani, who had been hosting regular concerts since the late 1780s.[860] In the home of other dignitaries he heard the violonist Ferdinand Fränzl (1767-1833), originally from Mannheim, as well as a family of musicians, the Tayllers, who were accompanied by the Italian composer Giovanni Cavi (c. 1750-1821). The Duke admired this instrumentalist's performance, but added: 'comme il n'y avait point de voix chantante, cela fut monotone'.[861] On 10 April, at the home of Sig.a Flaviani, Louis-Engelbert heard the *Miserere* by Giuseppe Sarti performed by his host and a 'demoiselle de 16 ans et une basse-taille de la chapelle du pape' (a young lady of 16 and a *basse-taille* from the Papal Chapel), while on 21 April (Holy Thursday) he heard the famous *Miserere* by Gregorio Allegri (1582-1652) at the Sistine Chapel, sung by two choirs, discovering there 'une chose unique en Europe, l'harmonie et la mélodie d'un chœur de voix d'homme et de soprano qui font l'effet le plus onctueux'. On Holy Friday he returned to hear again Allegri's work – which the young Mozart had written down from memory when he came to Rome in 1770 – and noted that though the melody was sung *a cappella*, 'on jurerait un instant qu'il y a un orgue'.[862] On 17 April he was able to meet the composer Paisiello in

165.   Musical Feast at the Teatro Argentina in Rome by G. P. Panini. Paris, Louvre.

person during a concert at which the young Anna Maria Pellegrini Celoni (c. 1780-1835) was singing. The Duke declared of Pellegrini's voice: 'c'est la plus grande, la plus belle et la plus douce, les difficultés et les bravoures sont pour elle des jeux, qui la rendent encore plus supérieure, et je doute qu'on puisse entendre mieux en Italie'.[863] At the Palazzo Colonna, on 22 April, he was in the audience for the first performance of Guglielmi's sacred tragedy *La morte di Oloferne*, in which the Italian soprano Brigida Giorgi Banti (1755-1806) sang the role of Judith;[864] the blind Duke noted that the concert programme was distributed at the entrance and that he liked the singer's voice and manner of singing.[865]

On 10 and 11 September 1791, as Louis-Engelbert was passing through Bergamo, he attended two performances of the pasticcio *Didone*, inspired by Piccinni's *Didone abbandonata*. The work was presented at the Teatro Riccardi, a concert hall that had just reopened its doors on the previous 24 August,[866] with the Portuguese mezzo-soprano Luísa Todi (1753-1833) in the main role;[867] regarding this singer, the Duke affirmed: 'cette actrice mérite toute sa réputation, on ne peut s'imaginer une voix ni plus fournie, ni plus variée, ni plus harmonieuse. Musicienne accomplie, elle joint à ce talent, de l'âme et de l'expression, qualités que l'on ne trouve point dans les opéras d'Italie'.[868] In Turin he attended a performance of Paisiello's opera *Le gare generose*, noting: 'le drame est mauvais, les acteurs sont passables mais la musique est excellente'.[869]

166. Giovanni Paisiello by É.-L. Vigée-Lebrun. Versailles,
    Musée national des châteaux de Versailles et de Trianon.

A number of musical manuscripts appear to have been acquired during this tour to Italy, or, at the very least, soon afterwards. Seven of them offer movements from works by Pietro Alessandro Guglielmi taken from the oratorio *Debora e Sisara* as well as the operas *Enea e Lavinia* and *La pastorella nobile*, a work he heard in Siena.[870] Giovanni Paisiello, whom he met in Rome,[871] was certainly among the Duke's favourite composers, since thirty or so manuscripts of his works are owned by the family library, either in separate parts or as scores; these contain extracts from *Socrate immaginario* (first staged in 1775), *La serva padrona* (1781), *Il re Teodoro in Venezia* (1784), *La grotta di Trofonio* (1785), *Pirro* (1787), *Fedra* (1788), *L'amor contrastato* (1788), *Catone in Utica* (1789), *Nina, o sia La pazza per amore* (1789), and *I zingari in fiera* (1789).[872] We may assume that the composer himself gave the Duke some of these manuscript copies. One of these, that of the duetto 'Nel cor più non mi sento', from Paisiello's 'commedia per musica' *L'amor contrastato*, which was first staged at the Teatro dei Fiorentini in the autumn of 1788, is particularly eye-catching;[873] the AACC's copy of the manuscript score has a soft binding with a title page on which one sees an engraved frame trimmed with ribbon, the latter exhibiting watercolour brush-marks of gold, green, and soft pink. It was created by the Venetian master-engravers Innocente Alessandri and Pietro Scattaglia. These artists were at this time engraving in Venice not only musical

167. G. Paisiello, 'Nel cor più non mi sento' [*L'amor contrastato*]. Enghien, Arenberg Archives and Cultural Centre, Ms 92.

works but also ready-made title pages such as this one, on which the copyists would then transcribe, inside the printed frame, the title of the piece given within the body of the manuscript. As is the case for the manuscript in question, the Venetian address engraved on the title page is generally worded as follows: 'Si vendono in Venezia da Alessandri e Scataglia all'Insegna della B.V. della Pace sul Ponte di Rialto, presso de quali si trova ogni sorta di Musica Vocale e Instrum.le'.[874] In this example, the title of the duetto and the composer's name have been inscribed subsequently in blue and red ink. Another manuscript score preserved in the collection transmits the duetto 'Giusto ciel', sung by the characters Cesare and Bruto in the 'opera seria' *La morte di Giulio Cesare* by Gaetano Andreozzi (1755-1826), who was a pupil and nephew of the composer Niccolò Jommelli; this work was first staged at the Teatro Argentina in Rome during the carnival season of 1790.[875] A rival of Paisiello, Domenico Cimarosa (1749-1801), is also among the composers admitted to the ducal library, being represented by nine manuscript scores of arias from his operas *Le donne rivali* (1780), *Artaserse* (1784), and *Il credulo* (1786) – all of them works from that composer's Italian period. Cimarosa would subsequently travel to St Petersburg, and in 1792 to the court of Vienna, where his opera *Il matrimonio segreto* would be encored at Emperor Joseph II's request. Another manuscript that stands out in the AACC Collection, consisting of two oblong volumes with an identical hard-cover binding, is a complete score of one of

168.   D. Cimarosa by C. Deblois, 1867. Royal Library of Belgium, Music
        Division, Fétis 4749 A Mus.

Cimarosa's sacred works: the oratorio *Assalonne*, which was presented in Florence in 1779 and again in Venice in 1782.[876] During this period Cimarosa would pen two further oratorios: *La Giuditta* and *Il sacrificio d'Abramo*. The two volumes offer not the original Latin version but the two acts comprising the Italian version. On the cover page of the first volume, corresponding to the first act, the names of the four characters in the work have been inscribed: David, Absalom, Abigail, and Joab; these are sung, respectively, by two sopranos and two altos. The story tells of Absalom's rebellion against his father David; Joab, allied with David, will eventually slay the unfaithful son.

Back in the Austrian Netherlands in October 1791, the blind Duke decided to move a quantity of paintings, books, and various *objets d'art* to his duchy of Arenberg in the Eifel for safe-keeping during this troubled period; over seventy boxes were transported there.[877] On the death of Emperor Leopold II in 1792 his son Francis II succeeded him; the Archduke Charles, Francis's brother, was appointed Governor General, but only for a short time, since in June 1794 the Austrian Netherlands were occupied by the French army before becoming officially annexed in 1795. By October 1794 the Duke had definitively lost his duchy of Arenberg – but in June of that year he had already removed to his house in the Viennese suburb of Gumpendorf, taking all his possessions with him – all this occurring just after the marriage of his daughter Pauline to Prince Joseph of Schwarzenberg (1769-1833)

169.   D. Cimarosa, *Assalonne*. Enghien, Arenberg Archives and Cultural Centre, Ms 264.

on 25 May at Heverlee. The family had been plunged into mourning on the previous 6 February, the day on which Élisabeth Pauline de Gand-Vilain de Mérode, Duchess Louise-Pauline's mother, had been executed in the Place de la Révolution (the present-day Place de la Concorde) during the Terror. In order to be erased from the list of émigrés and thereby avoid acts of confiscation, the mother and wife of the blind Duke returned to Brussels in December 1795 with Princes Pierre and Philippe, while Louis-Engelbert continued his exile with his eldest sons Prosper-Louis and Paul. During this fraught period the greater part of the ducal library remained in Brussels, but obviously no further acquisitions were made at this time. The library would come back to life after the return of the blind Duke to the capital, which occurred in September 1803.

During his exile in Vienna Louis-Engelbert noticed with pleasure and pride how musical his son Paul was. He had a letter written to Count Rudolph Taaffe in November 1801 in which he says that his son, then aged thirteen, had 'un gout decidé pour la musique' (a decided taste for music), and that he 'joue presqu'à la première vuë des pièces de clavecin que l'on lui présente lorsqu'elles ne sont pas trop difficiles' (plays almost at first sight harpsichord pieces that are presented to him, whenever they are not too difficult).[878]

170. Pauline d'Arenberg by D. Oelenheinz. Private collection.

171. J. Haydn by Darcis, after Guérin. Royal Library of Belgium, Music Division, Mus. 21.736 C 1.

This enforced period spent in the Austrian capital allowed Louis-Engelbert d'Arenberg regularly to meet his beloved daughter Pauline and his son-in-law Prince Joseph of Schwarzenberg, who also had a keen interest in music. Together they often frequented the *Gesellschaft der Associerten*, an organization of nobles headed by Baron Gottfried van Swieten, son of the Gerard van Swieten already mentioned, who is notable for having commissioned from Mozart an adaptation of Handel's *Messiah*. It was in this context that the blind Duke in 1798 had the chance to attend, at the Schwarzenberg Palace, the first performances of Joseph Haydn's oratorio *Die Schöpfung* (*The Creation*), as his letter dictated to Taaffe three years later shows: 'Le compositeur Haydn a deployé dans sa musique tous ses moïens harmoniques et mélodiques, et il s'y trouve des effets sublimes en force et delicieux en charmes [...] J'ai assisté à 4 de ces concerts, et quoique cela dure plus de 3 heures, j'y ai trouvé chaque fois de nouvelles beautés. La *Schöpfung* peut avoir plus de genie, mais certainement ce dernier œuvre montre l'art et le talent jusqu'à la sublimité, car dans tous les actes il se trouve à chaque instant des morceaux qui étonnent et ravissent'.[879]

From his time in London in 1791 Joseph Haydn had brought back to Vienna an English libretto based on Milton's *Paradise Lost* that Baron van Swieten hastened to translate into German. With the libretto completed in 1796, the composer then worked on the music (commissioned by the *Gesellschaft der Associerten*) up to the end of 1797. The first performances of *Die Schöpfung*, which were by invitation only, took place at the Prince of Schwarzenberg's residence on 29 and 30 April 1798,

172. Joseph of Schwarzenberg by D. Oelenheinz. Private collection.

with Haydn conducting the orchestra and Antonio Salieri (1750-1825) at the harpsichord. The work created such a stir that crowds gathered around the palace, and there were some scuffles. Two further private performances took place there on the following 7 and 10 May, before the public première finally materialized on 19 March 1799 at the Burgtheater. This eagerly awaited concert attracted a full house; the work subsequently played to packed audiences in most of the European capitals, not least London and Paris. In attendance at the four private performances, the blind Duke thus had the privilege of hearing the work under the direction of the composer Haydn himself. Although no document has come down to us to confirm this, he probably also attended the private première of Haydn's oratorio *Die Jahreszeiten* (*The Seasons*) at the Schwarzenberg Palace on 24 April 1801.

The presence in the AACC Collection of a manuscript copy of a work by Salieri, as well as eleven Haydn prints, published in Mainz, Amsterdam, London, Paris, and Offenbach, may surely be explained in part by the privileged contacts established in Vienna with these musicians during that period. An oblong volume with a hardback cover, which today has the classmark Ms 11, was acquired from the workshop of the famous Viennese copyist Wenzel Sukowaty (1746-1810). This contains the score of the first act of the 'dramma giocoso' in two acts *La scuola de' gelosi*, by Antonio Salieri, a work first performed at the Teatro San Moisè in Venice on 28 December 1778 during carnival, and revived at Vienna's Burgtheater in a second version with a libretto by Lorenzo Da Ponte on 22 April

173.   A. Salieri, *La scuola de' gelosi*. Enghien, Arenberg Archives and Cultural Centre, Ms 11.

1783.[880] Resident in Vienna since 1766, the Italian composer was at that time one of the best-known personalities of Viennese musical life, occupying the post of Court Composer and Director of the Italian Opera from 1774. He also became kapellmeister of Emperor Joseph II in 1788. The volume in the ducal library has a unique status, for it is in fact the only manuscript in the collection to contain not an individual aria but an entire operatic act, without this being a copy of a print (as is the case for some older manuscript volumes of Lully's operas). The complementary volume, containing the second act, may have formed part of the collection before disappearing. Since 1778 Wenzel Sukowaty's workshop, where several copyists were employed, had been producing most of the copies of works intended for the Viennese stage and in particular the Burgtheater. A few of these have come down to us, principally at the Österreichische Nationalbibliothek in Vienna, which holds copies of the scores of the Mozart operas *Die Entführung aus dem Serail* (1782), *Le nozze di Figaro* (1786), and *Così fan tutte* (1790).

Regarding the Haydn publications in the collection, it is possible in chronological terms that while in Vienna the blind Duke (via a dealer in the Austrian capital) came by two editions published in 1795 in Mainz by J. André, including the two series of three trios for keyboard, violin, and cello (Hoboken XV: 18-20 and 21-23).[881]

Ludwig van Beethoven (1770-1827), a pupil of Haydn who had been living in Vienna since 1792, was also among the protégés of van Swieten and the Prince of Schwarzenberg, and would in turn

174. L. van Beethoven in Vienna, 1801. Royal
     Library of Belgium, Music Division, Fétis
     4749 A Mus.

175. L. van Beethoven, *Sonata* Op. 27/2 ['Moonlight sonata'], Vienna, Cappi. Enghien, Arenberg
     Archives and Cultural Centre, I 939/8.

176. Louis-Engelbert d'Arenberg, c. 1815, portrait medallion. Private collection.

impress the ducal family not only with his talent as a pianist but also as a composer. In 1803 the blind Duke probably brought back to Brussels several original Viennese prints by Beethoven, which are still held by the AACC Collection today. For the piano he acquired the *Sonate* no. 14 in C sharp minor Op. 27 no. 2 (the 'Moonlight Sonata'), composed in 1801 and published by Giovanni Cappi in March of the following year with a dedication to the Countess Giulietta Guicciardi (1784-1856), one of Beethoven's pupils in Vienna around 1800.[882] From the publisher of the 'Bureau d'arts et d'industrie' the Duke acquired the *Grande sonate pour le pianoforte* Op. 28, which came out in August 1802, and the *Bagatelles* Op. 33, published in May 1803.[883] From the same publisher, for the benefit of the chamber music repertoire, the *Trois sonates pour le pianoforte avec l'accompagnement d'un violon* Op. 30 were purchased; these were published in May and June 1803.[884] The music library was later to be augmented by five further Beethoven prints, which became the joy of the musician of the family, Prince Paul d'Arenberg.

Two Mozart prints, published in Vienna before 1803, were also very likely procured by the Duke during his period in the Austrian capital. These were the *Ouvertura per il clavicembalo ricavata dall'opera La clemenza di Tito*, an anonymous keyboard arrangement published by Artaria,[885] and the *Quartetto pour le clavecin ou pianoforte avec violon, viole et violoncelle* published under the opus number 100 by Tranquillo Mollo, whose firm of 'T. Mollo et Comp.' was established in 1798.[886] This publication is in fact an arrangement of the famous Quintet for Clarinet and Strings KV 581. To these two editions, which today constitute the only examples recorded for Belgium, would subsequently be added ten others, which are likewise unique in Belgian libraries.

When the Duke eventually returned to Brussels, he became a French citizen. Under the Empire the Arenberg family were soon obliged to become a part of Napoleon's inner circle, when, on 1

177. W. A. Mozart by C. Mayer. Royal Library of
Belgium, Music Division, Fétis 3149 A Mus.

178. W. A. Mozart, *Ouvertura per il clavicembalo*, Vienna, Artaria, title page. Enghien, Arenberg Archives
and Cultural Centre, I 939/3.

February 1808, the eldest son of the blind Duke, Prosper-Louis, made a politically expedient marriage to Stéphanie Tascher de la Pagerie (1788-1832), niece of Empress Joséphine. As if the blind Duke's life had not already had more than its share of tragedy, on 1 July 1810 his only daughter Pauline (sister-in-law of the Austrian ambassador Charles Philip of Schwarzenberg) perished when fire ravaged the Austrian embassy in Paris, where a ball was being held. Two years later, on 12 August, Louis-Engelbert lost his dearly loved wife, Louise-Pauline. During these last years of his life he nonetheless continued to remain active, taking an interest in industrial and technical discoveries. Thus in 1817 he allowed Carl Senefelder to set up his lithography workshop in the ducal palace in Brussels, lithography being a printing procedure invented by his brother Aloys Senefelder that would soon sweep the whole of Europe, not least in the sphere of music publishing.

Following in the footsteps of his Italophile grandfather and the great patron that was his father, the blind Duke continued to allow the family library to expand through the acquisition of new scores,

179. C. de Lasteyrie, *À la mémoire du duc d'Aremberg.*
      Royal Library of Belgium, Prints and Drawings Division,
      S II 51431.

some of these purchases being made in Brussels, but many in the course of his prolonged visits to Paris and Vienna or during his sojourns in England and Italy. With this generation the music collection gained essentially in the area of instrumental music for chamber and symphonic ensembles emerging from the presses of the principal European publishing centres in Europe: Paris, Vienna, London, and Leipzig. As the centre of European musical life gradually shifted from Paris to Vienna – the city that established the careers of Mozart, Haydn, and then Beethoven – the ducal family, curious about everything, followed this trend by acquiring musical publications that were at that time rarely available in other libraries of the future state of Belgium. This ensured that the AACC Music Collection remains today a significant repository of prints, often the only copies in the country. Even though he lived until 1820, the blind Duke no longer played a significant role in the growth of the Music Collection after the troubled period of his Viennese exile, this mission devolving from that time onwards to his musician son Paul.

EPILOGUE

In a French, Dutch, and finally independent Belgium, the Arenberg Music Collection, along with the library as a whole, would continue to grow. It was the blind Duke's second son, Prince Paul (b. Brussels 10 January 1788, d. Rome 22 January 1844), who during the first half of the nineteenth century was without question the member of the lineage with the greatest interest in music. Many manuscript and printed works exhibit one or more annotations written in the Prince's hand which establish that they belonged to him.

Prince Paul was certainly musical, having learnt the harpsichord and the piano, but certain congenital conditions such as his small stature nonetheless put him at a disadvantage. He entered the clergy, became an Honorary Canon of the Chapter of Saint-Aubin Cathedral in Namur, and a

180.   Prince Paul d'Arenberg by A. Lemonnier. Royal Library of Belgium, Prints and Drawings Division, S II 111931.

181.   Paul d'Arenberg, *Missa brevis*. Enghien, Arenberg Archives and Cultural Centre, Ms 25.

182. Paul d'Arenberg, *Sonatine*, Brussels, Weissenbruch, title page. Enghien, Arenberg
      Archives and Cultural Centre, I 922.

Knight of the Order of Christ. But music remained his passion.[887] He suggested to his father, and then
to his elder brother Prosper-Louis, who became Duke in 1820, that they acquire a large repertoire
of chamber music. He also composed some music and left behind in the AACC Collection thirty or
so unpublished autograph manuscripts, including a *Missa brevis* in G,[888] as well as various works for
piano including *contredanses*, nocturnes, polonaises, and walzes, which were inspired particularly by
his discovery of the keyboard music of the virtuosos Johann Baptist Cramer (1771-1858) and Muzio
Clementi (1752-1832). Other manuscripts by the Prince are preserved both in the Arenberg Collection
of the University Archives of Katholieke Universiteit Leuven and in the music library of Saint-Aubin
Cathedral in Namur, deposited today at the Institut Supérieur de Musique et de Pédagogie in Namur.
Paul would even publish an Op. 1: a *Sonatine pour le forte-piano avec accompagnement de violon*

183.   W. A. Mozart, *Andante avec variations*, Offenbach, J. André. Enghien,
Arenberg Archives and Cultural Centre, I 791.

issued both in Paris by the publisher Leduc and in Brussels by Weissenbruch, dedicating it to his uncle Prince Auguste d'Arenberg.[889] Certain works in manuscript by Belgian composers were also dedicated to him, such as the Op. 1, *Ma Normandie, air varié pour flûte avec accompagnement de piano*, of Égide Aerts (1822-1853)[890] and the donated *Premier concerto pour flûte* Op. 9 of Jean-François-Joseph Lahou (1798-1847), first flute at the Théâtre Royal de la Monnaie.[891]

Among the prints acquired by Paul the repertoire for piano holds sway, most often in combination with one or several other instruments. A number of chamber compositions by Mozart, Haydn, and Beethoven were added to the publications acquired previously. Among works by Mozart, Paul acquired the *Quatuor pour le clavecin ou piano-forte, violon, alto-viola, violoncelle* (Piano Quartet in G minor) KV 478, which was Mozart's very first composition of this kind, in the Schott edition (Mainz).[892] The

184.   L. van Beethoven, *Notturno*, Leipzig, Hoffmeister. Enghien, Arenberg Archives and Cultural Centre, I 939/10.

only trio is an arrangement of the ouverture to the opera *La clemenza di Tito* kv 621, which appeared in the *Etrennes pour les Dames*, a periodical publication edited by Johann André in Offenbach.[893] There are six prints containing duets for keyboard and violin; these are the sonatas kv 284, 333, 284, 296, 376, 377, 378, 379, 380, and 454, which appeared from the publishing houses of Longman and Broderip in London, Breitkopf & Härtel in Leipzig, and Schott in Mainz.[894] Another item is a print by Johann M. Goetz in Mannheim of the *Ouverture aus der Zauberflöte für das Clavier mit Begleitung einer Violine* kv 620.[895] As for pieces for solo piano, these comprise, first, an arrangement of the Masonic opera *Die Zauberflöte* by Friedrich Eunike, published by Nikolaus Simrock in Bonn[896] and, second, the *Andante avec variations pour le piano forte* Op. 63 kv Anh. 286, published by André, of which one part is by the German pianist August Eberhard Müller (1767-1817).[897]

Haydn's *Dernière sonate pour le piano avec accompagnement de violon, composée expressement pour Madame la Maréchale Moreau* (Hoboken XV: 31) appears in a Paris print by Nadermann which dates to around 1820.[898] The three trios for keyboard, violin, and cello (Hoboken XV: 3-5) come to complete the collection, in Hummel's Amsterdam edition (after 1819), under the title *Trois sonates pour le clavecin avec l'accompagnement d'un violon et violoncello*.[899] The Hoboken sonatas XV: 6-8, written for the same instruments, are taken from the *Collection complette des sonates de piano* published by Pleyel, which also contained the sonatas for piano and violin Hoboken XVI: 44-46.[900]

Four original Beethoven prints complete the collection: the *Notturno pour fortepiano et alto*

(Nocturne in D major for Piano and Viola) Op. 42 appeared in Leipzig from Hoffmeister in January 1804.[901] As regards the piano pieces entitled *Trois grandes marches* for four hands (Op. 45), these were published in Vienna by the 'Bureau d'arts et d'industrie' two months later.[902] Purchases were made of further works for solo piano: namely, two Breitkopf & Härtel (Leipzig) prints comprising, first, the *VI variations* Op. 34, published in April 1803,[903] and, second, the fifteen *Variations* Op. 35, on sale from August of that same year.[904] A final edition was also added: that of the *XIII variations sur l'air Es war einmal ein alter Mann* WoO 66 (from the singspiel *Das rote Käppchen* by Carl Ditters von Dittersdorf), published by Giovanni Cappi in Vienna in 1803, ten years after the publication of the original Simrock edition (Bonn).[905]

In addition to Daniel Steibelt (1765-1823) and Ignace Pleyel (1757-1831), we discover the name of Henri Messemaeckers (1778-1864), a piano teacher and composer from Brussels – in connection with not only his own compositions but also a large number of scores that he published in Brussels from approximately 1808 to 1848.

During the same period Prince Paul collected several engraved portraits in profile of musicians, created by the Frenchman Edmé Quenedey (1756-1830), who used the 'physiognotrace' procedure invented in 1786 by his associate, the cellist Gilles-Louis Chrétien (1754-1811).[906] To the engravings dating from 1808 (Grétry, Méhul), 1809 (Cherubini, Monsigny, Paër), and 1813 (Gossec), as well as other, non-dated ones (H. Berton, Dalayrac, Gluck, Haydn), the Prince added matching biographies in manuscript.[907]

After Prince Paul the music library did not grow significantly, even though a few manuscript and printed works from the second half of the nineteenth century and the first years of the twentieth merit a mention on account of their historical interest, such as a series of publications typical of a certain kind of salon music that were variously dedicated to the ninth Duke of Arenberg, Engelbert-Marie (1872-1949) and to his mother Éléonore-Ursule (1845-1919), Princess and Duchess of Arenberg.

NOTES

1 *Le théâtre de la Monnaie au XVIIIe siècle*, ed. by M. Couvreur (Brussels, 1996).

2 The archives of the Serene House of Arenberg had been entrusted to the Capuchin Friars in 1964. Once the renovations of a house at the rear of the friary itself in Enghien at 8, rue de l'Yser, had been completed, Father August Roeykens set to work classifying a first consignment of 162 boxes in 1967 (Y. Delannoy, 'In memoriam Jean-Pierre Tytgat', *Annales du Cercle archéologique d'Enghien*, 39 (2005), pp. 177-183).

3 M. Cornaz, 'La Monnaie et le commerce des ouvrages lyriques à Bruxelles', in *Le théâtre de la Monnaie*, pp. 275-297.

4 The doctoral thesis, *L'édition et la diffusion de la musique à Bruxelles au XVIIIe siècle*, was successfully defended in December 1996. A revised version was later awarded a prize by the Royal Academy of Belgium, which selected it for publication under the same title in 2001.

5 From 1993 to 1998, on behalf of the Université Libre de Bruxelles, I took part in this project of the *Répertoire International des Sources Musicales*, focusing on manuscripts of polyphonic music c. 1600-1850 (RISM series A/II), which had been funded by the Belgian State's *Services fédéraux des affaires scientifiques et culturelles*.

6 Delannoy, 'In memoriam Jean-Pierre Tytgat', p. 177.

7 M. Cornaz, 'Le fonds musical des archives privées de la famille d'Arenberg à Enghien', *Revue Belge de Musicologie*, 49 (1995), pp. 129-210.

8 A notable revelation was the uniqueness of the example of the *Second livre de pièces de clavecin* by Pierre Février: see P. Février, *Second livre de pièces de clavecin*, introduction to the facsimile by M. Cornaz (Brussels, 'Musica Bruxellensis' series, I, 2000).

9 M. Cornaz, *Les Princes de Chimay et la musique*, PhD thesis for the 'agrégation de l'Enseignement Supérieur', Université Libre de Bruxelles, March 2001; an extensively revised version was published in 2002.

10 Delannoy, 'In memoriam Jean-Pierre Tytgat', p. 178.

11 *Ibid.*, p. 201.

12 RISM's *Online Catalogue of Musical Sources* is available online at <www.rism.info>.

13 M. Cornaz, 'Inventaire complet du fonds musical des archives privées de la famille d'Arenberg à Enghien', *Revue Belge de Musicologie*, 58 (2004), pp. 81-202.

14 M. Cornaz, 'Monteverdi de Mantoue à Bruxelles: Les voyages de l'archiduc Albert en Italie (1598) et de Vincenzo Gonzaga dans les anciens Pays-Bas (1599)', *Orfeo io sono*, 2008, pp. 60-72. A paper arising from this article was given at the conference *Orfeo* organized by the Musical Instruments Museum (Brussels, 25 and 26 October 2007).

15 The study *Les ducs d'Arenberg et la musique au XVIIIe siècle* was awarded a prize by the Royal Academy of Belgium on 22 November 2008.

16 Following the publication of my book *Les ducs d'Arenberg et la musique au XVIIIe siècle* (Turnhout, 2010), I was invited to view several manuscript sources housed at the Montagu Music Collection (Northants, England); see M. Cornaz, 'Unknown sources of Italian baroque music and new Vivaldi operatic discoveries in the Montagu Music Collection (Boughton House, UK)', *Revue Belge de Musicologie*, 66 (2012), pp. 249-268.

17 The various holders of the title were sovereign Dukes of Arenberg in the Eifel region, to the west of Koblenz, but resided virtually permanently in the Netherlands, where a large part of their possessions were located. Duke Louis-Engelbert would be the last reigning Duke in the old territories of the Eifel (see below).

18 Full references for the account books consulted are given in the Bibliography.

19 C. de Moreau de Gerbehaye, M. Derez, and A Mertens, 'Het archief', in *Arenberg in de Lage Landen*, ed. by J. Roegiers (Leuven, 2002), pp. 378-383.

20 Xavier Duquenne's handwritten descriptions were entered into a database created in 1996.

21 J.-P. Tytgat, 'Nota over het archief van Arenberg', internal note preserved in a file at the AACC.

22 Documents relating to houses and estates abroad (Germany, France, Holland, and Italy) are likewise held by the AACC.

23 There are over thirty-nine metres of correspondence relating to the period 1550 to 1904.

24 For a detailed history of the Arenberg family, I would draw the reader's attention to the collective volume *La Maison d'Arenberg en Wallonie, à Bruxelles et au G.-D. de Luxembourg depuis le XIVe siècle. Contribution à l'histoire d'une famille princière*, ed. by J.-M. Duvosquel and D. Morsa (Enghien, 2011).

25 J. Roegiers, 'De bibliotheek', in *Arenberg in de Lage Landen*, pp. 358-369. The inventory is transcribed in full by J. Bosmans in *Annales du Cercle archéologique d'Enghien*, 1 (1880), pp. 462-463.

26 State Archives of Belgium (hereafter, SAB), Arenberg Collection, LA 725.

27 '[...] pour avoir eu l'honneur d'avoir servy & enseigné l'art de toucher les Instrume[n]ts à Mons[eigneur]. Son Excell[ence]. vostre frere feu Ducq d'Arschot & de Croÿ lorsqu'il estoit encore Estudiant aux bo[n]nes lettres en Université de Louvain'. G. Huybens, 'Leonardus Nervius, *Cantiones sacrae* [...]', in *Antwerpse Muziekdrukken: Vocale en instrumentale polyfonie (16de-18de eeuw)*, exhibition catalogue (Antwerp, 1996), pp. 77-78.

28 Baron de Reiffenberg, *Une existence de grand seigneur au seizième siècle: Mémoires autographes du duc Charles de Croy* (Brussels, 1845).

29 G. Birkner, 'La tablature de luth de Charles, duc de Croÿ et d'Arschot (1560-1612)', *Revue de Musicologie*, 49/1 (1963), pp. 18-46.

30 G. E. Van Even, 'Notice sur la bibliothèque de Charles de Croÿ, duc d'Aerschot (1614)', *Bulletin du Bibliophile Belge*, 9 (1852). See Cornaz, *Les Princes de Chimay et la musique* (Brussels, 2002), pp. 23-27, and Cornaz, 'Monteverdi de Mantoue à Bruxelles'.

31 Roegiers, 'De bibliotheek', p. 358.

32 SAB, Arenberg Collection, LA 6746, accounts of Charles de Ligne, Prince of Arenberg, for the year 1598: receipt signed 'A. Francisque', for lessons given between 22 January and 22 February 1598.

33 P. Vendrix, 'Francisque, Antoine', in *Dictionnaire de la musique en France aux XVIIe et XVIIIe siècles*, ed. by M. Benoit (Paris, 1992), p. 303.

34 AACC, Annual accounts of the trésoriers généraux (treasurers-general), 63/15, register of 1602 (general account of Anne de Croÿ).

35 'Le genereux Alidor, aussi vaillant que sage, est aymé des Dames, redouté des hommes, & admiré de tous ensemble. La grandeur de son merite, a du rapport avec celle de sa naissance, ayant acquis autant de gloire par ses actions, que la nature luy a donné dans le berceau'; J. Puget de la Serre, *Le Roman de la cour de Bruxelles, ou les advantures des plus braves cavaliers qui furent jamais, et des plus belles dames du monde*, Spa, Keulen [Liège], 1628, p. 19. This key work, in which ladies and gentlemen of the court are represented as fictional characters, describes (without assigning dates) balls and parties where violins are mentioned, but gives no further details.

36 SAB, Arenberg Collection, MG 3558, expenses memorandum of Gaspar Dandeleu, adviser to the family. I became aware of this exceptional document thanks to Xavier Duquenne, whom I would like to thank here.

37 Cornaz, 'Monteverdi de Mantoue à Bruxelles'.

38 SAB, I 002, Chambre des comptes, 1837, f. 126v: this note appears in the *Libros de la Razon* from 1612 to 1618, after another that is dated May 1613; see S. Thieffry, 'La chapelle royale de Bruxelles de 1612 to 1618 d'après les *Libros de la Razon* de l'archiduc Albert', *Revue Belge de Musicologie*, 55 (2001), p. 116.

39 A detail given in the copy of the expenses memorandum; this copy, attached to the memorandum, is likewise dated 15 September 1624 (SAB, Arenberg Collection, MG 3558).

40 F. Lesure, 'La facture instrumentale à Paris au seizième siècle', *The Galpin Society Journal*, 7 (1954), p. 51.

41 '[…] plusieurs fois racommodé les orgues'. P. Roose, 'Langhedul', in *Dictionnaire des facteurs d'instruments de musique en Wallonie et à Bruxelles du 9e siècle à nos jours*, ed. by M. Haine and N. Meeùs (Liège, 1986), pp. 242-243.

42 *RISM, Einzeldrucke vor 1800* (Kassel, 1971-1999) [hereafter, RISM], M 3737.

43 This is confirmed by the copy of the memorandum, which lists 'les livres de musicqs de Mortaro a 12 voc.' (music books by Mortaro for 12 voices).

44 J. Roche and T. Carter, 'Mortaro, Antonio', in *Grove Music Online. Oxford Music Online* (consulted 12 March 2015), article 19172.

45 'Phalesius selon son billet' (Phalesius according to his invoice). RISM mentions a single Phalèse print earlier than 1624 containing works by a composer with the surname Praetorius, which is dated 1622: the *Cantiones sacrae de praecipuis festis totius anni octonis vocibus, cum basso ad organum* by Hieronymus Praetorius (RISM P 5340); S. Bain and H. Vanhulst, 'Phalèse', in *Grove Music Online. Oxford Music Online* (consulted 12 March 2015), article 21541.

46 Roegiers, 'De bibliotheek', p. 360.

47 These globes can be seen today in the entrance halls of the Royal Library of Belgium.

48 AACC, Manuscripts, 29/10 (Catalogue of books held by the library of his HSH Monseigneur the Duke of Arenberg).

49 AACC, Manuscripts, 29/12 (Catalogue of books held in Brussels and at Enghien in the cabinets of HSH the Duchess of Arenberg. Grand operas, 'opéras bouffons' with their scores, music, and detached airs, detached pieces and dramatic works, historical, legal, political, and literary books etc).

50 AACC, Manuscripts, 29/13.

51 AACC, Manuscripts, 29/10; second copy in AACC, Manuscripts, 29/11.

52 Paquot was Librarian at the University of Louvain from 1769 to 1772; see J. Roegiers, 'De bibliothek. Boeken om te lezen', in *De blinde hertog. Louis Engelbert & zijn tijd. 1750-1820* (Leuven, 1996), p. 175.

53 A work appearing in 18 volumes between 1763 and 1770 (Memoirs serving towards the literary history of the seventeen provinces of the Netherlands, the principality of Liège, and a number of neighbouring lands).

54 Roegiers, 'De bibliotheek', pp. 360-361.

55 It has not been possible to ascertain who compiled the 1769 catalogue.

56 Roegiers, 'De bibliotheek', p. 360.

57 *Ibid.*, p. 361.

58 Voncken would in fact occupy the position until 1838; see Roegiers, 'De bibliotheek', p. 362.

59 J. Coppieters, *Brieven in tijden van verandering. De correspondentie van Louise Margareta van der Marck (1730-1820), douairière van Arenberg*, unpublished undergraduate dissertation, Katholieke Universiteit Leuven, 2005, p. 90.

60 AACC, Biography Louise-Marguerite de La Marck, 80 (box 36-38): 'Liste des livres de theatre, Musique et Journeaux appartenant a S.A Madame la Duchesse, Venant de son hotel, porte de hal En mars 1818' (List of dramatic works, music, and journals belonging to HSH the Duchess, from her private residence, Porte de Hal, in March 1818).

61 AACC, Manuscripts, 29/23: Sixteen-page inventory, untitled.

62 AACC, Manuscripts, 29/23.

63 The inventory lists in particular the Viennese print of *Caroussel Musik*, mentioning the year 1814 (see AACC, Music Collection, I, 916/3).

64 C. Lemaire, 'La bibliothèque des ducs d'Arenberg, une première approche', in *Liber Amicorum Herman Liebaers* (Brussels, 1984), pp. 81-106. See SAB, Arenberg Collection, SA 1598 I-8 (1822-1825).

65 Roegiers, 'De bibliotheek', p. 361; W. d'Hoore, *Le Palais d'Egmont-Arenberg à Bruxelles* (Louvain-la-Neuve, 1991), p. 73.

66 d'Hoore, *Le Palais d'Egmont-Arenberg à Bruxelles*, pp. 73-76. See also the documents assembled on the subject by the archivist Édouard Laloire: AACC, 60/10, file 19. Only four allegories survive: law, geometry, medicine, and geography.

67 AACC, Manuscripts, 29.

68 d'Hoore, *Le Palais d'Egmont-Arenberg à Bruxelles*, pp. 83-84.

69 Roegiers, 'De bibliotheek', p. 363.

70 Lemaire, 'La bibliothèque des ducs d'Arenberg', p. 83.

71 Roegiers, 'De bibliotheek', p. 365.

72 *Ibid.*, p. 366.

73 It would later be ceded to the Belgian State.

74 Lemaire, 'La bibliothèque des ducs d'Arenberg', p. 89.

75 Roegiers, 'De bibliotheek', pp. 367-368.

76 *Ibid.*, pp. 368-369.

77 On Léopold-Philippe, see P. Neu, *Die Arenberger und das Arenberger Land* (Koblenz, 1995), II, pp. 168-209; J. Descheemaeker, *Histoire de la Maison d'Arenberg d'après les archives françaises* (Neuilly-sur-Seine, 1969), pp. 177-201; É. Laloire, *Généalogie de la maison princière et ducale d'Arenberg (1547-1940)* (Brussels, 1940), p. 23.

78 On Duke Philippe-Charles d'Arenberg, see Neu, *Die Arenberger und das Arenberger Land*, pp. 119-124; Descheemaeker, *Histoire de la Maison d'Arenberg*, pp. 169-170; Laloire, *Généalogie*, p. 22.

79 The couple were married on 12 February 1684.

80 Marie-Anne would marry François-Egon de la Tour d'Auvergne, Duke of Bouillon (1671-1710), in Brussels on 20 November 1707; see Neu, *Die Arenberger und das Arenberger Land*, p. 122.

81 These lessons must have commenced before 23 June 1681, the date when Philippe-Charles became third Duke of Arenberg. Indeed, the *Livre de raison* by La Grené (SAB, Manuscrits divers, 2663), which records the dancing master's activities up to 1687, makes mention of lessons given to the 'prince d'Arenberg'. See J.-P. Van Aelbrouck, *Dictionnaire des danseurs à Bruxelles de 1600 à 1830* (Liège, 1994), p. 155.

82 Maria Theresia von Herberstein died in 1682, and the Genoese Enrico del Carretto in 1685.

83 P. Neu, 'Marie Henriette Félicité del Carretto / d'Alcaretto, Marquise de Savona y Grana (1671-1744)', in *Arenberger Frauen*, ed. by P. Neu (Koblenz, 2006), p. 165. As an adult, Léopold-Philippe would take legal action against his mother, whom he accused of having mismanaged their fortune.

84 These works may obviously have been added to the family library later on during the course of the eighteenth century, but this seems less likely, for at this time works were generally acquired shortly after their publication.

85 In the section 'Beaux-Arts' of the catalogue of 1777, the heading 'Musique' describes the presence of the work in the following way: 'Hirschen, Kircherus Germaniae redonatus, seu Artis magnae de Consono & Dissono Ars minor. Halle de Suabe, en Allemand, 1662, in 12-'. Copies of this translation are preserved in various libraries, including the Fétis collection at the Royal Library of Belgium (classmark Fétis 5.351 A).

86 C. M. Chierotti, 'La *Musurgia Universalis* di Athanasius Kircher' (online publication) <http://www.chierotti.net/kircher/articolo1> (consulted 25 February 2015).

87 Under the heading 'Liturgie' in the library catalogue of 1768, the following reference appears: 'Paraphrase des Pseaumes de David par Godeau, en vers francais et en musique, corrigé par Gobert, Paris, 1676 in 12- 2 volumes'. The work is cited also in the catalogues of 1777 and 1778.

88 B. Gagnepain, 'Gobert, Thomas', in *Dictionnaire de la musique en France aux XVIIᵉ et XVIIIᵉ siècles*, p. 322.

89 Cornaz, 'Inventaire complet du fonds musical des archives privées de la famille d'Arenberg à Enghien', p. 172, classmark I 1035; RISM L/LL 2992.

90 AACC, Music Collection, I 1039 (RISM L/LL 2944). This print includes an inked annotation: 'Ce livre apartient a Mlle Choiseau' (This book belongs to Mlle Choiseau). An actress known as Choiseau is cited as a member of the company at La Monnaie in 1705 in a work by Quesnot de La Chênée entitled *Parnasse Belgique* (Cologne, 1706).

91 AACC, Music Collection, I 1062 (RISM C/CC 3391).

92 *Ibid.*, I 1014 (RISM D/DD 1767).

93 *Ibid.*, I 1020 (RISM M/MM 381).

94 *Ibid.*, I 1009 (RISM C/CC 751).

95 *Ibid.*, I 1012 (RISM C/CC 712).

96 *Ibid.*, I 1001.

97 B. Nestola, 'Spoglio dei volumi di "Meilleurs airs italiens" pubblicati da Christophe Ballard (1699-1708)', 'Cahiers Philidor 26' (Versailles, 2004), 9 pp., online publication at <http://www.cmbv.fr>. M. Cornaz, 'La cantate italienne et française au sein de la collection musicale des archives d'Arenberg: nouvelles perspectives', in *Music and Musicians in Europe from the late Middle Ages to Modernism. Essays in Memory of Frank Dobbins*, ed. by M.-A. Colin (Turnhout, 2015, forthcoming); the piece identified in the collection, *La farfalla corre al lume*, is in fact the second line of the second aria 'Se per brama di gioire' from the cantata *Sconsigliato consiglio*.

98 AACC, Music Collection, Ms. 6. The AACC Music Collection also houses the 1708 Ballard edition of *Alceste* (classmark I 1042; RISM L/LL 2935).

99 *Ibid.*, Ms 7.

100 *Ibid.*, Ms. 13.

101 *Ibid.*, Ms. 12.

102 *Ibid.*, Ms. 8.

103 *Ibid.*, Ms. 32.

104 *Ibid.*, Ms. 9.

105 *Relations véritables*, edition of 25 January 1695.

106 *Ibid.*, 13 November 1696.

107 *Ibid.*, 31 December 1697.

108 Neu, *Die Arenberger und das Arenberger Land*, p. 169; H. de Mérode-Westerloo, *Mémoires du Feld-Maréchal Comte (Johann Philipp Eugen) de Mérode-Westerloo, Capitaine des Trabans de l'Empereur Charles VI* (Brussels, 1840), I, p. 74.

109 The Governor of the Spanish Netherlands who succeeded del Carretto and preceded Maximilian Emanuel of Bavaria was Francisco Antonio de Agurto, Marquis of Gastañaga.

110 Regarding Pietro Torri, see: M. Couvreur, 'Joseph-Clément de Bavière, Pietro Torri et le développement de l'oratorio dramatique en France (1707-1714)', in *Noter, annoter, éditer la musique. Mélanges offerts à Catherine Massip*, ed. by C. Reynaud and H. Schneider (Geneva, 2012), pp. 73-90; I. M. Groote, *Pietro Torri. Un musicista veronese alla corte di Baviera* (Verona, 2003).

111 Pietro Torri's name does not appear in the accounts and receipts preserved in the Arenberg Archives.

112 In his doctoral thesis Sebastian Biesold (University of Bonn) brings to light certain archival documents signed by Torri that allow us, Biesold argues, to authenticate the Munich manuscripts. I would like to thank Sebastian Biesold for sharing his research findings with me.

113 The Italian word 'Trastulli' (plural of 'trastullo') literally means 'amusements'.

114 D-Mbs, Mus. Ms. 178 (RISM ID no. 456010822). The entire *Trastulli* collection is digitized at the site <http://daten. digitale-sammlungen.de>.

115 GB-Lbl. We refer here to manuscripts Add. 22099 (see RISM ID no. 806436349) and Harley 1272 (see RISM ID no. 800260576). The Harley manuscript 1272 is headed by the name 'Sig.r Tossi'. This may likewise be an error of transcription by the copyist, who misread Torri's name. In *A catalogue of the Harleian manuscripts, in the British Museum* (London, 1808), p. 643, it is stated that the aria 'Vezzose pupille' is also attributed to Bononcini.

116 Cornaz, 'La cantate italienne et française au sein de la collection musicale des archives d'Arenberg'. These details regarding the pieces by Torri did not appear in M. Cornaz, *Les ducs d'Arenberg et la musique au XVIIIe siècle. Histoire d'une collection musicale.*

117 C. Stellfeld, *Les Fiocco, une famille de musiciens belges aux XVIIe et XVIIIe siècles* (Brussels, 1941).

118 AACC, Music Collection, Ms 27.

119 This motet is also found (in separate manuscript parts) in the section of the music collection of Sainte-Gudule housed at the library of the Royal Conservatory in Brussels. The final page of manuscript Ms 27 is torn, and so the final notes are missing. Identifying Fiocco has been made possible through using the RISM database.

120 J.-E. d'Arenberg, 'De heren, graven, prins-graven en hertogen van Arenberg', in *Arenberg in de Lage Landen*, p. 38.

121 Stellfeld, *Les Fiocco,* p. 16. We may note that Pietro Torri would subsequently follow his employer on his various peregrinations, returning to Munich with him in 1701, and then going back with him to Brussels in 1705, on to Mons in 1706, and then to Namur in 1711, before returning for good in 1715 to Munich, the city where Torri died in 1737.

122 M. Couvreur, 'Pietro Antonio Fiocco, un musicien vénitien à Bruxelles (1682-1714)', *Revue Belge de Musicologie*, 55 (2001), p. 151. Torri would also work for the younger brother of Maximilian Emanuel of Bavaria, Joseph Clemens, Elector of Cologne when the latter stayed at Valenciennes and at the Château de Raismes, the property of Charles-Joseph Le Danois, Marquis de Cernay (1677-1734); see J. Loridan, 'L'Électeur de Cologne à Valenciennes (1708-1714)',

Revue de Lille, 18th year, 3rd series, I (May 1907), pp. 570-595. Located to the north of Valenciennes, this summer residence witnessed entertainments that included music, most notably on a stage raised up on pilotis. Although a part of the Raismes forest had belonged to the Arenberg family since the seventeenth century, it was only in 1774, upon the marriage of the Prince and Duke Auguste d'Arenberg (1753-1833) to Marie Le Danois, Marquise de Cernay (see below), that the entire property came into the Arenbergs' possession.

123   AACC, Accounts of the caissiers trésoriers généraux, 64/28/II (accounts and receipts of Domis, 1703-1705). The pistole is a gold coin. If we know that the daily wage of a *compagnon imprimeur* (a former apprentice continuing to work under a master) amounted to about 1 florin in the middle of the eighteenth century (see M. Cornaz, *L'édition et la diffusion de la musique à Bruxelles au XVIIIᵉ siècle* (Brussels, 2001), p. 29), we can appreciate better what 168 florins meant at that time.

124   Couvreur, 'Pietro Antonio Fiocco', p. 160; A. Herneupont, 'Musicisti italiani nel Belgio nel secolo XVIII: Pietro-Antonio, Giovanni Giuseppe e Giuseppe Ettore Fiocco', *Rivista Musicale Italiana*, 47 (1943), fasc. I-II, p. 8.

125   N. Meeùs, 'Mahieu, Jérôme', in *Dictionnaire des facteurs d'instruments de musique*, p. 274.

126   M. Couvreur, 'Le séjour de Desmarest à Bruxelles. Aperçu de la vie artistique dans la capitale des anciens Pays-Bas espagnols à la fin du XVIIᵉ siècle', in *Henry Desmarest (1661-1741): exils d'un musicien dans l'Europe du Grand Siècle*, ed. by J. Duron and Y. Ferraton (Liège, 2005).

127   R. Fagon, 'Matho, Jean-Baptiste', in *Grove Music Online. Oxford Music Online* (consulted 12 March 2015), article 18069; C. Wood, 'Desmarest, Henry', in *Grove Music Online. Oxford Music Online* (consulted 12 March 2015), article 07630.

128   This rehearsal is mentioned in the 19 October 1700 issue of the newspaper *Relations véritables*.

129   AACC, Music Collection, I 1038 (RISM L/LL 3015).

130   *Ibid.*, I 1007 (RISM C/CC 731).

131   *Ibid.*, I 1010 (RISM C/CC 745).

132   *Ibid.*, I 1017 (RISM L 160).

133   These works are still held today (unclassified) by the AACC. The first volume, notably, includes Lully's operas *Cadmus et Hermione, Alceste, Thésée,* and *Atys*.

134   L. Renieu, *Histoire des théâtres de Bruxelles depuis leur origine jusqu'à ce jour*, 2 vols (Paris, 1928), II, p. 675.

135   AACC, Accounts of the caissiers trésoriers généraux, 64/25 (accounts of Albert Ignace Delaunoy, 1706- 1709).

136   *Relations véritables*, issue of 21 January 1707.

137   E. Selfridge-Field, *The Calendar of Venetian Opera. A New Chronology of Venetian Opera and Related Genres, 1660-1760* (Stanford, 2007), p. 195.

138   *Ibid.*, p. 196.

139   I would like to thank Louise K. Stein for sharing with me her research findings, which were presented especially in her paper 'Alessandro Scarlatti's First Opera for Naples, *La Psiche*: Arias and Production in 1683-4' at the 15th Biennial International Conference on Baroque Music (Southampton, UK) in July 2012.

140   C. Sartori, *I libretti italiani a stampa dalle origini al 1800*, 7 vols (Cuneo, 1991) [hereafter, Sartori], 19283.

141   Neu, *Die Arenberger und das Arenberger Land*, p. 171. The collar of the Order of the Golden Fleece was conferred on him in April 1700 by the Elector Maximilian Emanuel of Bavaria, Governor of the Low Countries.

142   Laloire, *Histoire des deux hôtels d'Egmont*, pp. 69-70; cited in d'Hoore, *Le Palais d'Egmont-Arenberg à Bruxelles*, p. 44.

143   AACC, Annual accounts of the trésoriers généraux, 63/22-28 (account of Albert Ignace Delaunoy, January to June 1709): the *maître d'hôtel* (butler) La Chapelle paid 4 pistoles 'à un joueur de lut et de violon'.

144   Couvreur, 'Pietro Antonio Fiocco', p. 152.

145   Neu, *Die Arenberger und das Arenberger Land*, p. 173.

146   *Philandre, Pastorale présentée à Son Altesse Monseigneur Léopold Joseph, par la grâce de Dieu, duc d'Arembert [...] chevalier de l'ordre de la Toison d'Or, conseiller d'état dans les Païs-Bas, gentil-homme de la chambre du Roy, grand bailli du Hainaut.* 'Par le collége de la Compagnie de Jesus à Mons, le 19 janvier 1710' (Mons, Laurent Preud'homme, 1710): cited in F. Faber, *Histoire du théâtre français en Belgique depuis son origine jusqu'à nos jours*, 5 vols (Brussels and Paris, 1880), IV, p. 341.

147   M. Couvreur and J.-P. Van Aelbrouck, 'Gio Paolo Bombarda et la création du Grand Théâtre de Bruxelles', in *Le théâtre de la Monnaie*, p. 14; SAB, Notariat du Brabant, 1617, minutes of the notary Delvaille.

148   In his memoirs Jean André Mabille, a contemporary of the Duke and his wife, emphasized this enjoyment of music: see J. A. Mabille, *Mémoires touchant mes voyages, négociations, entremises pour la très illustre maison d'Egmont* (Paris, 1909); cited in Neu, *Die Arenberger und das Arenberger Land*, p. 190.

149   The identification was made possible through consultation of the RISM database. A. Romagnoli, 'Mancini, Francesco', in *Grove Music Online. Oxford Music Online* (consulted 12 March 2015), article 17594.

150   Regarding Belgian libraries, the RISM lists numerous manuscripts containing cantatas and sacred works by Mancini, but not his 'dramma per musica' *Gli amanti generosi*.

151   AACC, Annual accounts of the trésoriers généraux, 63/22-28 (account of Jean-Baptiste Deschamps, 1713): payment of the considerable sum of 1000 florins to the t'Serstevens brothers (f. 29r). In 1714 the Duke paid the brothers 1470 florins

12 sols 'pour livrance de livres' (AACC, Annual accounts of the trésoriers généraux, 63/22-28 (account of Jean-Baptiste Deschamps, 1714), f. 22r).

152 AACC, Annual accounts of the trésoriers généraux, 63/22-28 (account of Jean-Baptiste Deschamps, 1713), f. 29r.

153 AACC, Music Collection, I 1013 (RISM B/BB 3817).

154 In 1722 Bourgeois would briefly become director of the Théâtre de la Monnaie.

155 AACC, Music Collection, I 1015 (RISM D/DD 1840).

156 See the website *CESAR* (*Calendrier électronique des spectacles sous l'ancien régime et sous la révolution*; <http://www. cesar.org.uk/cesar2>), entry 'Monnaie'.

157 Neu, *Die Arenberger und das Arenberger Land*, p. 177.

158 G.-J. de Boussu, *Histoire de la ville de Mons ancienne et nouvelle* (Mons, 1725), p. 330. On Boussu, see in particular S. Dangreau, *Gilles-Joseph de Boussu, dramaturge (1681-1755)*, unpublished undergraduate dissertation, Université Libre de Bruxelles, academic year 2005-2006.

159 de Boussu, *Le Retour des plaisirs* (Mons, 'N. Varret et la veuve Preud'homme', 1719). Mons University Library holds a copy of this print (classmark 1601/71).

160 This manuscript is kept under the classmark Mus. Ms. 4448. It was formerly the property of Claude Houzeau de Lehaie, a descendant of Gilles-Joseph de Boussu.

161 M. Cornaz, 'Un opéra retrouvé d'André Vaillant: *Le Retour des plaisirs*', in *Hainaut terre musicale*, ed. by F. Thoraval and B. Van Wymeersch (Turnhout, 2015, forthcoming). The printed libretto of *Hedwige, reine de Pologne* is preserved at Mons University Library (classmark 1601/70) and at the Royal Library of Belgium (classmark II 55.930 A (RP)).

162 See J-P. Huys, 'Princes en exil, organisateurs de spectacles. Sur le séjour en France des électeurs Maximilien II Emmanuel de Bavière et Joseph-Clément de Cologne', in *Spectacles et pouvoirs dans l'Europe de l'Ancien Régime (XVIᵉ-XVIIIᵉ siècle)*, ed. by M.-B. Dufourcet, C. Mazouer, and A. Surgers (Tübingen, 2011), p. 138. Foucquier, author of *L'Immaculée conception*, *Les Plaisirs de Mariemont*, and *Le Gouvernement de Valenciennes*, could be a certain Marie Marguerite Bernardine Foucquier, author of the libretto *Le Génie de Panthemont, ou les Festes de Flore et des plaisirs célébrées en l'honneur de Mme Charlotte Colbert de Croissi, abesse de l'abbaye royale de Panthemont à Paris, le jour de sa réception, au mois d'avril 1716* (Paris, [1716]).

163 AACC, Annual accounts of the trésoriers généraux, 63/22-28 (account of Théodore Frantzen): payment of 15 florins 16 patars 2 deniers on 18 December 1715. Cornaz, 'Un opéra retrouvé d'André Vaillant: *Le Retour des plaisirs*'. These details did not appear in Cornaz, *Les ducs d'Arenberg et la musique au XVIIIᵉ siècle. Histoire d'une collection musicale*.

164 On the basis of a transcription made in 2014 by Kris De Baerdemacker (Royal Library of Belgium), *Le Retour des plaisirs* was re-enacted in December 2015 as part of an educational and musicological project organized jointly by the Conservatoire of Mons and the Royal Library of Belgium.

165 *Daphnis, pastorale, présentée à Son Altesse [...] duc d'Aremberg*, 'Par le collége de la Compagnie de Jesus en cette ville' (Mons, 'Jean-Nicolas Varret et la veuve Preud'homme', 1719); see Faber, *Histoire du théâtre français en Belgique*, IV, p. 341.

166 AACC, Accounts of the caissiers trésoriers généraux, 64/27/II. 1 florin is worth 20 sols (see Cornaz, *L'édition et la diffusion de la musique*, p. 29).

167 RISM C 3658, C 3693, C 3730 and C 3762.

168 RISM P 1686 and P 1687.

169 At the same time, it should be borne in mind that the catalogues of the second half of the eighteenth century do not offer a comprehensive picture of the contents of the music library.

170 AACC, Accounts of the caissiers trésoriers généraux, 64/27: the receipt signed 'J. Mahieu' in Brussels on 14 May 1720 concerns a double manual harpsichord delivered to the Duke in Paris; 25 pistoles corresponds to 262 florins 10 sols. Meeùs, 'Mahieu, Jérôme', p. 274.

171 AACC, Annual accounts of the trésoriers généraux, 63/22-28 (account of Théodore Frantzen, 1720), f. 90v.

172 See Stellfeld, *Les Fiocco*.

173 F.-M. Arouet (Voltaire), epistle VII 'A Monsieur le duc d'Aremberg'.

174 AACC, Annual accounts of the trésoriers généraux, 63/22-28 (account of André Bureau de St André, January 1722 to 31 May 1723), f. 31v.

175 AACC, Annual accounts of the trésoriers généraux, 63/22-28 (account of André Bureau de St André, 1 June 1723 to 31 December 1724), f. 148v.

176 AACC, Accounts of the caissiers trésoriers généraux, 64/27/II.

177 AACC, Annual accounts of the trésoriers généraux, 63/22-28 (account of André Bureau de St André, 1 June 1723 to 31 December 1724), f. 149r.

178 *Ibid.*, f. 150r.

179 See entry 'Dulondel', *CESAR*.

180 AACC, Annual accounts of the trésoriers généraux, 63/22-28 (account of André Bureau de St André, 1 June 1723 to

31 December 1724), f. 150r: 'Payé a f: Hanot maitre a danser a Mons la somme de quatre vingt quinze florins quatre sols par ordre de S. alt: Madame en suivant quitt.ce du 4: mars 1724'. François Hanot was also working in Tournai: see M. Cornaz, 'L'édition musicale à Tournai aux xviiᵉ et xviiiᵉ siècles', *Le livre et l'estampe*, 53 (2007), p. 73.

181   M. Cornaz, 'Spectacles privés chez les ducs d'Arenberg', *Études sur le 18ᵉ siècle* (2005), pp. 87-98.

182   AACC, Annual accounts of the trésoriers généraux, 63/22-28 (account of André Bureau de St André, 1725), f. 142v. This is therefore not the cantata *Le Triomphe de la Paix* by Pietro Torri, as I suggested in my article 'Spectacles privés chez les ducs d'Arenberg', p. 89.

183   The precise description is: 'La Fête d'Enghien, ou le Triomphe de la Paix. Divertissement mis en Musique par Fiocco. Avec un Prologue. MSS.'. The manuscript vanishes in the library's later catalogues.

184   AACC, Annual accounts of the trésoriers généraux, 63/22-28 (account of André Bureau de St André, 1725), f. 116r; Cornaz, *L'édition et la diffusion de la musique*, p. 143. The print acquired by the Duke was perhaps the one published by Brunel in Paris that same year (1725) under the title of *Les Œuvres de Monsieur de Molière, nouvelle édition [...] augmentée d'une nouvelle vie de l'auteur et de la Princesse d'Elide, Enrichie de figures en taille-douce*.

185   AACC, Annual accounts of the trésoriers généraux, 63/22-28 (account of André Bureau de St André, 1725), f. 140v.

186   AACC, Annual accounts of the trésoriers généraux, 63/22-28 (account of André Bureau de St André, 1726), f. 133v; payment mentioned for the date of 16 March 1726.

187   Marie-Victoire was born in Brussels on 26 October 1714.

188   M. Galand, 'Relations et liens financiers entre le gouvernement et le théâtre de la Monnaie sous le régime autrichien', in *Le théâtre de la Monnaie*, p. 118.

189   M. Talbot, *The Vivaldi Compendium* (Woodbridge, 2011), p. 45. The meeting at Lipica (in present-day Slovenia) is brought to light in J. Ágústsson, 'Zu *Lippiza* den *venetian*: Ersten *Musico* eine *Medalie*': Vivaldi meets Emperor Charles VI, 9 September 1728', *Studi vivaldiani*, 14 (2014), pp. 27-38.

190   This hypothesis is advanced in Renieu, *Histoire des théâtres de Bruxelles*, II, p. 679.

191   On the Denzios and Peruzzis, see M. Jonášová, 'I Denzio: tre generazioni di musicisti a Venezia e a Praga', *Hudební věda*, 45 (2008), pp. 57-114. The author presents here several previously unpublished biographical details.

192   I thank Louis Delpech for communicating these unpublished details regarding Antonio Maria Peruzzi and his wife in Dresden. See L. Delpech, 'Le Hainaut 'au centre des affaires'. Circulation des troupes et mobilité des musiciens entre la France et la Saxe (1700-1710)', *Hainaut terre musicale*; Faber (*Histoire du théâtre français en Belgique*, I, p. 106) states that the first name of Antonio Maria Peruzzi's wife was Anna Maria; it is probable that the soprano Anna Maria Peruzzi (known as 'La Parrucchiera'), who made her début in Bologna in 1728 (see D. Libby and J. Rosselli, 'Peruzzi, Anna', in *The New Grove Dictionary of Opera. Grove Music Online. Oxford Music Online* (consulted 12 March 2015), article O007438), was not Anna Henriette, who in 1728 would have been aged over 30.

193   Jonášová, 'I Denzio', p. 88.

194   The Royal Library of Belgium holds a copy of this libretto, whose publisher is unknown (classmark VB 6.464/24 A), as does the library of the Royal Conservatory of Brussels (classmark 22.250).

195   S. Hansell and D. E. Freeman, 'Bioni, Antonio', in *Grove Music Online. Oxford Music Online* (consulted 12 March 2015), article 03111. We recall that the second version of Vivaldi's *Orlando* was not staged at Venice's Teatro Sant'Angelo until 27 November 1727. B. Forment ('Italian Opera "Under the Belgian Climate": the 1727-30 Seasons at the Monnaie', *Journal of the Alamire Foundation*, 4 (2012), pp. 259-280), working from preserved Brussels librettos, attempts to reconstruct the musical structure of the Italian operas staged at the Théâtre de la Monnaie by the Peruzzi and Landi troupes.

196   This overture (classmark 34.108) is also found in a British source (GB-Ob, Mus. ms. E.36), but without any mention of the composer's name. These details emerge from research carried out by Michael Talbot that has been communicated to RISM. Talbot has also identified in the Sainte-Gudule collection several overtures which appear to be connected with the Italian operas given on the Brussels stage.

197   M. Cornaz, 'Un Belge à la rencontre d'Antonio Vivaldi: le voyage musical de Corneille van den Branden de Reeth en France et en Italie', *Studi vivaldiani*, 13 (2013), pp. 59-60.

198   Forment, 'Italian Opera', p. 277.

199   The library of the Royal Conservatory of Brussels holds copies of these librettos; see J.-P. Van Aelbrouck, *Livrets de ballets, opéras et pièces de théâtre imprimés ou représentés à Bruxelles (1600-1800)* (Brussels, 1993), unpublished.

200   AACC, Annual accounts of the trésoriers généraux, 63/22-28 (account of André Bureau de St André, 1727), f. 144r: 'Payé le 14: dudit [October] a la D.lle Perouz la somme de deux cents dix florins pour le premier payement de la loge de l'opera'.

201   AACC, Music Collection, Ms 99 and Ms 491. Ms 99 includes the first aria of the cantata ('La viola che languiva'), while Ms 491 contains the recitative that follows ('Già le sue frondi d'oro') and the final aria ('Per quelle sponde'). In Cornaz, *Les ducs d'Arenberg et la musique au xviiiᵉ siècle. Histoire d'une collection musicale*, 'Già le sue frondi d'oro' and 'Per quelle sponde' were not identified as belonging to the cantata *La viola che languiva*. E. L. Sutton, *The Solo Vocal Works of Nicola Porpora: An Annotated Thematic Catalogue*, PhD dissertation, University of Minneapolis, 1974: this cantata is referenced here under number 55. Regarding this cantata, see also *Clori. Archivio della Cantata italiana* at <http://cantataitaliana.it> (consulted 6 January 2015).

202 AACC, Music Collection, Ms 342.

203 W. Dean, 'Dotti, Anna Vincenza', in *Grove Music Online. Oxford Music Online* (consulted 12 March 2015), article 08055.

204 W. Dean, 'Antinori, Luigi', in *Grove Music Online. Oxford Music Online* (consulted 12 March 2015), article 01021.

205 Renieu, *Histoire des théâtres de Bruxelles*, II, p. 679; Jonášová, 'I Denzio', p. 88.

206 Forment, 'Italian Opera', p. 270. In Madrid he composed the 'capriccio' *L'interesse schernito dal proprio inganno*, the libretto of which was published in 1722 (see Sartori 13376).

207 Faber, *Histoire du théâtre français en Belgique*, I, p. 107.

208 Renieu, *Histoire des théâtres de Bruxelles*, II, p. 680. In that spring of 1728 Corradini had already composed three operatic works performed in Naples.

209 AACC, Annual accounts of the trésoriers généraux, 63/22-28 (account of Tamineau 1727-1729), f. unpaginated: 'Payé le 2 Avril 1728 au joüeur de viollont italiens la somme de treises florins un sol pour avoir joüé pendant le consert par ordre de S.A'.

210 Library of the Royal Conservatory of Brussels, classmarks 22.255 and 22.257.

211 AACC, Music Collection, Ms 303. Identification was made possible through consultation of the RISM database.

212 D. Libby, 'Paita, Giovanni', in *The New Grove Dictionary of Opera. Grove Music Online. Oxford Music Online* (consulted 12 March 2015), article O008210.

213 K. S. Markstrom, *The Operas of Leonardo Vinci* (New York, 2007), p. 249.

214 A libretto of *Griselda* was printed in Brussels by an unknown publisher (library of the Royal Conservatory of Brussels, classmark 22.258). J. W. Hill and F. Giuntini, 'Orlandini, Giuseppe Maria', in *Grove Music Online. Oxford Music Online* (consulted 12 March 2015), article 20473.

215 Seltridge-Field, *The Calendar of Venetian Opera*, p. 353.

216 The libretto published in Brussels (publisher not stated) specifies that these 'intermezzi comici musicali' were to 'representarsi in Brusselle nel dì della nascita della Imperatrice regnante' (library of the Royal Conservatory of Brussels, classmark 22.259).

217 C. Timms, 'Ungarelli, Rosa', in *Grove Music Online. Oxford Music Online* (consulted 12 March 2015), article 40864. Having made her début in productions of 'opere serie' in Florence, Rosa Ungarelli subsequently sang in comic intermezzi.

218 C. Timms, 'Ristorini, Antonio Maria', in *Grove Music Online. Oxford Music Online* (consulted 12 March 2015), article 40863. Ristorini made his début as a singer of 'opera seria'. In Venice in 1719 with his wife, he sang in the first performance of the revised version of *Il marito giocatore e la moglie bacchettona*, entitled *Serpilla e Baiocco*.

219 A bilingual libretto was printed in Brussels for the performance (library of the Royal Conservatory of Brussels, classmark 22.262).

220 Forment, 'Italian Opera', p. 272.

221 These attributions did not appear in Cornaz, *Les ducs d'Arenberg et la musique au XVIIIᵉ siècle. Histoire d'une collection musicale*.

222 AACC, Music Collection, Ms 409. This identification was made possible through consultation of the RISM database, which records a manuscript preserved at Sondershausen with the same music and including the names of Orlandini and the Venetian theatre, but which does not specify the opera's title (see RISM ID no. 250004602). I was able to find the aria in question by consulting the *Ifigenia* libretto (see Sartori 12748) available online at <http://daten.digitale-sammlungen.de>.

223 AACC, Music Collection, Ms 535.

224 As stated in the Venetian libretto of 1720: see Sartori 1774; this libretto is available online at <http://daten.digitale-sammlungen.de>.

225 AACC, Music Collection, Ms 461. The manuscript states that this is a 'Cantata a voce sola per cembalo'. J. L. Jackman and P. G. Maione, 'Falco, Michele', in *Grove Music Online. Oxford Music Online* (consulted 12 March 2015), article 09254. Cornaz, 'La cantate italienne et française'.

226 RISM ID no. 850009902. This source is available online at <www.internetculturale.it> (consulted 12 February 2015).

227 Faber, *Histoire du théâtre français en Belgique*, I, p. 107. D. Libby, 'Pasi, Antonio', in *The New Grove Dictionary of Opera. Grove Music Online. Oxford Music Online* (consulted 12 March 2015), article O007396. Pasi would close his career in Venice in 1730 and in Florence in 1732.

228 This identification was absent in Cornaz, *Les ducs d'Arenberg et la musique au XVIIIᵉ siècle. Histoire d'une collection musicale*.

229 The verso side of the second folio gives only the first bars of this aria, in which the vocal part has not yet started.

230 Identification of the provenance of this aria was made possible thanks to consultation of the following volume: A. L. Bellina, B. Brizi, and M. G. Pensa, *I libretti vivaldiani. Recensione e collazione dei testimoni a stampa* (Florence, 1982), p. 58. Note that the attribution to *Farnace* was not mentioned in my inventory of 2004: see 'Inventaire complet du fonds musical', p. 133. See M. Cornaz, 'Deux arias de l'opéra perdu *L'inganno trionfante in amore* RV 721 et autres découvertes vivaldiennes dans les archives privées de la famille d'Arenberg à Enghien', in '*La la la… Maistre Henri*' *mélanges de musicologie offerts à Henri Vanhulst*, ed. by C. Ballman and V. Dufour (Turnhout, 2010), pp. 341-346.

231 See entry 'La costanza combattuta in amore', *CESAR*.

232 See entry 'Monnaie', *CESAR*.

233 Library of the Royal Conservatory of Brussels, classmark 22.260.

234 This libretto is recorded in the family library catalogues of 1768, 1777, and 1778. In the catalogue of 1768, in the section 'Belles Lettres Poëtes Italiens, Anglois et Allemands', we read: 'Lucio Papirio Dramma per Musica, per Solemnisare il nome di Carolo VI, Bruse: 1728 in 4to.'.

235 Forment ('Italian Opera', pp. 272-276) brings this source to light and presents a transcription of the overture; the source from the library of the Royal Conservatory of Brussels (classmark 33.877) is described in the RISM database (see RISM ID no. 703000479).

236 M. Talbot, 'Girò [Tessieri], Anna', in *Grove Music Online. Oxford Music Online* (consulted 12 March 2015), article 40662; Talbot, *The Vivaldi Compendium*, pp. 88-89.

237 M. Talbot and M. White, 'A Lawsuit and a Libretto: New Facts Concerning the Pasticcio *La ninfa infelice e fortunata*', *Studi vivaldiani*, 14 (2014), pp. 69-81.

238 R. Strohm, *The Operas of Antonio Vivaldi*, 2 vols (Florence, 2008), II, pp. 393-394.

239 The presence of the watermark with the letters 'PIB' on the folios of Ms 469 leads us to believe that this is a paper manufactured in the Austrian Netherlands: see Cornaz, *L'édition et la diffusion de la musique*, pp. 42-43.

240 See entry 'Monnaie', *CESAR*, with a list of performances. The bilingual libretto published in Brussels gives the additional details 'da rappresentarsi nel teatro di Brusselles nel carnovale dell' anno 1729' (library of the Royal Conservatory of Brussels, classmark 22.264).

241 Bellina, Brizi, and Pensa, *I libretti vivaldiani*, p. 77.

242 Strohm, *The Operas of Antonio Vivaldi*, II, p. 347.

243 Please note that the attribution of these two arias to *L'inganno trionfante in amore* was not mentioned in my inventory of 2004: see 'Inventaire complet du fonds musical', p. 119.

244 Strohm, *The Operas of Antonio Vivaldi*, II, p. 352.

245 Strohm, *The Operas of Antonio Vivaldi*, I, pp. 5-6.

246 RISM ID no. 701001543; the score of 'Langue il fior' appears on pp. 12-22 in the manuscript collection 'X. Arie de diversi Maestri. Dresden 1740' (classmark 15.179/2).

247 The CD *New Discoveries II* (Naïve, 2012) presents recordings of the arias 'S'odo quel rio che mormora' and 'Langue il fior', together with those of the two other arias preserved in Berlin ('Palpita il core e freme' and 'Sono nel mar d'aspri tormenti').

248 S. Mamy, *La musique à Venise et l'imaginaire français des Lumières* (Paris, 1996), pp. 98-104.

249 F. M. Sardelli, *Catalogo delle concordanze musicali vivaldiane* (Florence, 2012), pp. 210-211.

250 AACC, Music Collection, Ms 329. O. Termini, 'Pollarolo, Antonio', in *Grove Music Online. Oxford Music Online* (consulted 12 March 2015), article 22024.

251 The libretto published in Venice in 1726 (Sartori 24124) has been digitized and appears on the website <http://daten.digitale-sammlungen.de> (consulted on 25 February 2015).

252 The librettos of all these works were printed in Brussels (see Van Aelbrouck, *Livrets de ballets*). We may note that Torri's opera was performed at the Munich court on 12 October 1719.

253 Renieu, *Histoire des théâtres de Bruxelles*, II, p. 681.

254 Librettos of these works were also printed in Brussels. See Van Aelbrouck, *Livrets de ballets*.

255 Forment, 'Italian Opera', p. 279.

256 D. E. Freeman, *The Opera Theater of Count Franz Anton von Sporck in Prague* (New York, 1992), pp. 158-159, states that the name of the singer's husband was Antonio rather than Luigi, contrary to what is stated in the various editions of the *New Grove Dictionary*.

257 As shown in the printed libretto: Bellina, Brizi, and Pensa, *I libretti vivaldiani*, p. 88.

258 AACC, Music Collection, Ms 459.

259 The copy of this edition consulted (RISM M 118) was the one held by the Music Department at the Bibliothèque Nationale de France (classmark Vm^7 780).

260 Freeman, *The Opera Theater of Count Franz Anton von Sporck in Prague*.

261 J. Isnardon, *Le théâtre de la Monnaie depuis sa fondation jusqu'à nos jours* (Brussels, 1890), p. 20.

262 AACC, Annual accounts of the caissiers, 63/29-35 (account of Pascal Henrion, 1731), II, f. 157v. An English gold coin often used by travelling artists, the guinea was accepted as legal tender in the Austrian Netherlands. Since he was often travelling, Landi probably asked the Duke to be paid in guineas – the value of which, unlike that of local coins, he knew. Warm thanks are due to Raf Van Laere (Royal Numismatic Society of Belgium) for this information.

263 AACC, Annual accounts of the caissiers, 63/19-35 (account of Pascal Henrion, 1732), I, f. 150r.

264 SAB, Conseil privé, 1090 (Comédies et Théâtres); this document is reproduced in Faber, *Histoire du théâtre français en Belgique*, IV, pp. 23-24.

265 The anonymous arias are 'Una volta mi rideva' and 'Putti, un conseggio' (the second aria, in dialect, means 'Boys, [I need] some advice'). Some attributions were absent in Cornaz, *Les ducs d'Arenberg et la musique au XVIIIᵉ siècle. Histoire d'une collection musicale*.

266 Selfridge-Field, *The Calendar of Venetian Opera*, p. 428.

267 The collection Ms 491 gives neither Handel's name nor the title *Il pastor fido*. These attributions were made possible through consultation of the RISM database. We may note that this aria was not listed in my inventory of 2004.

268 The libretto published in Venice in 1730 (Sartori 7052) is digitized at <http://daten.digitale-sammlungen.de>. Selfridge-Field, *The Calendar of Venetian Opera*, pp. 418-419; see the RISM database.

269 Selfridge-Field, *The Calendar of Venetian Opera*, p. 431.

270 The libretto (Sartori 9418) may be consulted online at <http://daten.digitale-sammlungen.de>. On page 42 of the libretto we indeed read (under the note 'Fine del Dramma') the instruction: 'Alla Pagina 17. In vece dell'Aria che dice Torna ec.', followed by the text of the replacement aria: 'Non mi chiamar crudele'.

271 AACC, Music Collection, Ms 82 and Ms 81.

272 Selfridge-Field, *The Calendar of Venetian Opera*, p. 404.

273 RISM ID no. 701002230.

274 Mamy, *La musique à Venise*, p. 388.

275 The aria was identified as belonging to this opera through consultation of the RISM database. See J. W. Hill, 'Pescetti, Giovanni Battista', in *Grove Music Online. Oxford Music Online* (consulted 12 March 2015), article 21408.

276 AACC, Music Collection, Ms 384. J. W. Hill, 'Veracini, Francesco Maria', in *Grove Music Online. Oxford Music Online* (consulted 12 March 2015), article 29178.

277 This engraved portrait still forms part of the archives of the AACC today (Biographies of musicians, 9/1). On the portrait we read: 'Amiconi Pin[xit]:' and '1735 Appo Wagner Venezia C.P.E.S.'. Amigoni was working in London from 1730 to 1739 and met the famous castrato on several occasions. See D. Heartz, 'Farinelli revisited', *Early Music*, 18/3 (1990), pp. 430-443.

278 Neu, *Die Arenberger und das Arenberger Land*, p. 202.

279 Bellina, Brizi, and Pensa, *I libretti vivaldiani*, p. 57. Please note that my inventory of 2004 did not suggest any attribution for this work. The identification of the composer and opera was achieved through an examination of the textual incipit and consultation of the RISM database.

280 RISM ID no. 451002144.

281 D. Libby, 'Fontana, Giacinto', in *The New Grove Dictionary of Opera. Grove Music Online. Oxford Music Online* (consulted 12 March 2015), article O003247.

282 Please note that this aria was not included in my inventory of 2004. Identification of the composer and the opera was made possible through consultation of the RISM database.

283 Cornaz, 'Inventaire complet du fonds musical', p. 119. Contrary to what I earlier indicated, Ms 306 contains not two arias but only one, 'Per quell'affetto', preceded by the recitative 'Queste pupille'.

284 In the upper left-hand corner of the first page we read: 'S. Gio. Gri.mo'. Two separate parts (vl 1, ob) of the aria 'Pietoso ciel difendimi' are also preserved in the music collection of AACC under the classmark Ms 386.

285 This is the aria 'La speranza, la costanza vincerà'.

286 *Didone abbandonata: Leonardo Vinci*, ed. H. M. Brown (New York and London, 1977).

287 Strohm, *The Operas of Antonio Vivaldi*, II, p. 583.

288 Library of the Royal Conservatory of Brussels (classmark 4.958/1) (RISM ID no. 706001017).

289 AACC, Music Collection, Ms 412. See S. Hansell and O. Termini, 'Bigaglia, Diogenio', in *Grove Music Online. Oxford Music Online* (consulted 12 March 2015), article 03066.

290 The legend 'cassinense' recalls the fact that it was at Monte Cassino that Saint Benedict completed the drafting of the Benedictine rule. Today the former Benedictine Abbey of San Giorgio Maggiore houses the Giorgio Cini Foundation.

291 The manuscript 15.155 at the library of the Royal Conservatory of Brussels includes the cantata *Se in cielo il dì* with the note 'del P. D. Diogenio Bigaglia Monaco Cassi:ne' (RISM ID no. 703002583). As regards the manuscript volume with classmark Ms II 3952 Mus. (Fétis 2431) at the Royal Library of Belgium, this contains the cantata *Deh, vanne al mar più lento* with the heading 'del P: d: Diogenio Bigaglia mon.co Cassinense' (RISM ID no. 700006605).

292 RISM B 2636.

293 Jean-Benjamin de La Borde, *Essai sur la musique ancienne et moderne*, 4 vols (Paris, 1780), III, p. 170.

294 Cornaz, 'La cantate italienne et française'.

295 AACC, Annual accounts of the trésoriers généraux, 63/22-28 (account of André Bureau de St André, 1727), f. 144v: payment to Boutmy of 346 florins 10 sols.

296 M. Cornaz, 'Josse Boutmy', in *Nouvelle Biographie Nationale* (Brussels, 2007), IX, pp. 62-65.

297 This work is cited in the third section ('Differente Musique et Airs detachés') of the catalogue of 1769; it disappears from later catalogues and no longer exists in the AACC Collection today.

298 B. François-Sappey, 'Principes de l'accompagnement du clavecin', in *Dictionnaire de la musique en France aux XVIIe et XVIIIe siècles*, p. 574.

299 AACC, Music Collection, I 691. This previously unknown print has not yet been listed by RISM.

300 RISM B 3941.

301 AACC, Music Collection, I 867 and I 1072.

302 In the third section of the Duchess of Arenberg's library catalogue of 1769 ('Differente Musique et Airs detachés') we find: 'Pièces de clavecin par Boutmy 1er & 3.me livre 2 vol.'.

303 Cornaz, *L'édition et la diffusion de la musique*, pp. 68-69; see B4 in M. Cornaz, *Les éditions musicales publiées à Bruxelles au XVIIIe siècle (1706-1794). Catalogue descriptif et illustré* (Brussels, 2008), pp. 32-37. This publication does not list the Antwerp Conservatory library's example of Op. 3, which has only recently come to scholarly attention (example not cited by RISM).

304 As may be heard on the CD *Josse Boutmy, Troisième livre de pièces de clavecin*, Isabelle Sauveur (harpsichord), project dir. by M. Cornaz (CD 'Musique en Wallonie' MEW 0524, 2005).

305 In the third section of the Duchess of Arenberg's library catalogue of 1769 ('Differente Musique et Airs detachés') appears the 'Traité de l'Harmonie reduitte à ses principes naturels, divisé en 4 livres Paris 1722 par Rameau'. This work no longer forms part of the AACC Collection.

306 H. Schneider, 'Traité de l'harmonie réduite à ses principes naturels', in *Dictionnaire de la musique en France aux XVIIe et XVIIIe siècles*, p. 687.

307 Van Aelbrouck, *Dictionnaire des danseurs*, pp. 104-105. See AACC, Annual accounts of the trésoriers généraux, 62/22-28 (account of Tamiseau, 1727-29), unpaginated folio ('51e chapitre de mise consernant le S.r Deschars'): 'Payé le 30. juillet 1728 au S. deschars la somme de quarante deux florins pour avoir montré a dancer au prince et la princesse'.

308 AACC, Annual accounts of the caissiers, 63/22-28 (account of Pascal Henrion, January to June 1730), f. 132r; AACC, Annual accounts of the caissiers, 63/22-28 (account of Pascal Henrion, July to December 1730), f. 235r; AACC, Annual accounts of the caissiers, 63/29-35 (account of Pascal Henrion, 1731), f. 178v; AACC, Annual accounts of the caissiers, 63/29-35 (account of Pascal Henrion, May to August 1733), f. 66v; AACC, Accounts and *renseignements* of Philippe Vandermale for 1734: payment of 21 florins on 15 February 'que S.A. lui a accordé de pension chaque mois' (which HSH granted him in salary each month).

309 d'Hoore, *Le Palais d'Egmont-Arenberg à Bruxelles*, p. 44.

310 This print is no longer in the AACC Music Collection. E. Vander Straeten, in his book *La musique aux Pays-Bas avant le XIXe siècle* (Brussels, 1867-1888), II, pp. 95-103, states that he possessed a copy of this print which in the nineteenth century had belonged to the organist Lados, music teacher to the ducal family (see J.-H. Fiocco, *Pièces de clavecin opus 1*, introduction to the facsimile by H. Vanhulst (Brussels, 'Musica Bruxellensis' series, IV, 2009)).

311 Cornaz, *L'édition et la diffusion de la musique*, pp. 39-46. RISM F 860; examples are held by, principally, the Bibliothèque Nationale de France and the British Library.

312 Herneupont, 'Musicisti italiani nel Belgio nel secolo XVIII', p. 18.

313 Cornaz, *L'édition et la diffusion de la musique*, p. 59.

314 AACC, Music Collection, I 859.

315 Cornaz, *L'édition et la diffusion de la musique*, p. 49.

316 S. Clercx, 'Les clavecinistes belges et leurs emprunts à l'art de François Couperin et de J. Ph. Rameau', *La Revue musicale*, 192 (1939), pp. 11-22.

317 In the third section ('Differente Musique et Airs detachés') in the Duchess of Arenberg's library catalogue of 1769 appears: 'Sonates mêlées pour la Flute traversiére par M. Blavet Paris 1732'.

318 AACC, Music Collection, I 761. This print had until now not been identified and therefore does not appear in the RISM printed volumes. It is cited in the Duchess of Arenberg's library catalogue of 1769 under 'Differente Musique et Airs detachés'.

319 Renieu, *Histoire des théâtres de Bruxelles*, II, p. 682.

320 AACC, Annual accounts of the caissiers, 63/29-35 (account of Pascal Henrion, 1731), I, f. 206r; AACC, Annual accounts of the caissiers, 63/29-35 (account of Pascal Henrion, 1731), II, f. 156v: 'au sieur Bruseau Entrepreneur des Spectacles ou Comedies trente pistoles pour la moitié de l'abonnement de la loge que S. A. M.gr occupe au grand theatre'; AACC, Annual accounts of the caissiers, 63/29-35 (account of Pascal Henrion, 1732), I, f. 150r (12 February): payment of half of the subscription for the box, that is, 315 florins; AACC, Annual accounts of the caissiers, 63/29-35 (account of Pascal Henrion, January to April 1733), f. 86r (4 March): payment of the remainder of the subscription. Bruseau directed La Monnaie from 1731 to 1733.

321 AACC, Annual accounts of the caissiers, 63/29-35 (account of Pascal Henrion, 1731), II, f. 155r: payment of 20 escalins gave the Duke the use of a box.

322 Renieu, *Histoire des théâtres de Bruxelles*, I, pp. 293-298; M. Cornaz, *La vie musicale à Bruxelles et dans les villes des Pays-Bas autrichiens vue par le biais de la* Gazette de Bruxelles *et de la* Gazette des Pays-Bas (unpublished undergraduate dissertation, awarded a prize by the Belgian Royal Academy on 9 November 1993), p. 39.

323 For a complete list of works performed at the Théâtre de la Monnaie between 1730 and 1733, see entry 'Monnaie', *CESAR*.

324 A. de Place, 'Quinault, Jean-Baptiste Maurice', in *Dictionnaire de la musique en France aux XVIIe et XVIIIe siècles*, p. 585.

325 AACC, Music Collection, I 838 (RISM Q/QQ 106). *Le Triomphe du temps* is a comedy by Marc-Antoine Legrand for which Quinault wrote the music.

326 J. Duron, 'Moreau, Jean-Baptiste', in *Dictionnaire de la musique en France aux XVIIe et XVIIIe siècles*, p. 477.

327 Cornaz, 'Spectacles privés', p. 90.

328 AACC, Annual accounts of the caissiers, 63/29-35 (account of Pascal Henrion, 1732), I, f. 102r (1 March), 4 escalins 'pour des couleurs pour le theatre'; f. 102v (7 March), 4 florins 10 sols paid to the cabinet-maker Mouhat 'pour deux journées de travail qu'il a emploiée a faire des bobeches pour le theatre' (for two days of work which he employed in making candle-rings for the theatre).

329 AACC, Annual accounts of the caissiers, 63/29-35 (account of Pascal Henrion, 1732), I, f. 104r.

330 *Ibid.*, f. 136r (26 May 1731), 6 florins to the painter Mesurolles 'pour six journées qu'il a emploiées a peindre les decorations du theatre d'Enghien' (for six days he spent on the decorative painting of the Enghien theatre); f. 136v (31 May 1732): 'au S.r Mouhat Ebeniste vingt florins Cinq Sols pour neuf journées qu'il a emploiée a travailler au theatre d'Enghien dans le tems que S. A. Monseig.r y a donné une fête' (to M. Mouhat cabinet-maker twenty florins five sols for nine days spent working on the Enghien theatre during the time when His Lordship held a fête); f. 105v (10 June 1732): 'au sieur Vandermael Cent trente deux florins quatre sols six deniers qu'il avoit païé pour changement et embellissement du Theatre lors que S.A. Mgr a donné une feste a Enghien' (to M. Vandermael one hundred and thirty-two florins four sols six deniers as payment for updating and embellishing the theatre when His Lordship gave a fête at Enghien); II, f. 74r (3 July 1732), 22 florins 12 sols to a certain Pilloy for painting; f. 74r (12 July): 'Le 12. d.o au sieur Rosenberg peintre vingt deux florins huit sols a compte de ses ouvrages au theatre d'Enghien' (the 12th *do.* to M. Rosenberg painter twenty-two florins eight sols for his work on the Enghien theatre); the painter Rosenberg was already in the Duke's service in 1730 and 1731 and in still mentioned in the accounts of 1734 for having carried out 'ouvrages faits au theatre du Château d'Enghien' (works carried out on the Château d'Enghien theatre) 'pour un montant de 33 florins' (for the sum of 33 florins) (AACC, Accounts and *renseignements* of Philippe Vandermale, 1734, 64/31/I). Note, too, that a pulley was delivered for the theatre on 1 May 1733 (AACC, Accounts and *renseignements* of Philippe Vandermale, 1734, 64/31/I).

331 AACC, Annual accounts of the caissiers, 63/29-35 (account of Pascal Henrion, 1732), II, f. 97r (11 August 1732): 'a la veuve Vincx deux florins deux sols pour avoir logé les musiciens qui ont joués a la fête que S.A. à donné a Enghien' (to widow Vincx two florins two sols for lodging the musicians who played at the fête His Lordship held at Enghien).

332 Faber, *Histoire du théâtre français en Belgique*, III, p. 345; E. Mathieu, *Histoire de la ville d'Enghien* (s.l., 1876), pp. 697-698.

333 d'Hoore, *Le Palais d'Egmont-Arenberg à Bruxelles*, p. 44.

334 AACC, Annual accounts of the caissiers, 63/29-35 (account of Pascal Henrion, May to August 1733), f. 68v; The Duke paid four *escalins* (an old silver coin of the Low Countries) for these two instruments.

335 Van Aelbrouck, *Dictionnaire des danseurs*, p. 193.

336 AACC, Annual accounts of the caissiers, 63/29-35 (account of Pascal Henrion, May to August 1733), f. 85v: 14 florins 3 sols for the dancing master's travel expenses to Enghien 'pour la Commedie'.

337 AACC, Annual accounts of the caissiers, 63/29-35 (account of Pascal Henrion, May to August 1733), f. 85v: 'Le 27 juin susdit sieur Peres maitre des dances quatre mirlitons qui joins avec les sept que Mons.r Barret luy a donné et celuy qu'il a eu pour son prevost font douze et cela pour deux voiages qu'il a fait a Enghien ou il a joué par ordre et suivant quittance'.

338 Neu, *Die Arenberger und das Arenberger Land*, p. 122.

339 *Ibid.*, p. 201.

340 d'Hoore, *Le Palais d'Egmont-Arenberg à Bruxelles*, p. 46.

341 AACC, Annual accounts of the caissiers, 63/29-35 (account of Philippe Vandermale, 1 May 1736 to 30 June 1737), f. 51r: for 42 florins 'L. Bizant' repaired 'les grand et petit clavecins de la Maison'. By 1753 Louis Bizant would be among the staff at the court of Charles of Lorraine in Brussels (see M. Awouters, in *Dictionnaire des facteurs d'instruments de musique*, p. 55).

342 Cornaz, *l'édition et la diffusion de la musique*, p. 75.

343 AACC, Annual accounts of the caissiers, 63/29-35 (account of Philippe Vandermale, 1 May 1736 to 30 June 1737), f. 69v: Godecharle was paid 14 florins for this work on presenting an invoice dated 20 March 1737.

344 This performance is mentioned in the Brussels newspaper *Relations véritables* of 12 October 1734.

345 This performance is mentioned in the Brussels newspaper *Relations véritables* of 16 November 1734.

346 AACC, Music Collection, Ms 7.

347 Under the section heading 'Poëtes Dramatiques et Lyriques ou Differens Théâtres' of the 1768 catalogue we find mention of this work with the further detail 'Amsterdam, 1734, 2 vols'. The date '1734' can probably be explained by the fact that the printing rights (reproduced in the edition) were granted that year, even though the first volume to emerge was dated 1735. These volumes no longer appear in the AACC Collection. See E. Kocevar, 'Parfaict', in *Dictionnaire de la musique en France aux XVIIe et XVIIIe siècles*, p. 526.

348 For the precise dates of all the performances, see entry 'Monnaie', *CESAR*. A libretto of *L'Enfant prodigue* was published in Brussels by Nicolas Stryckwant for the performance 'sur le grand théatre de la Monnoye le 18 janvier 1738' (see Van Aelbrouck, *Livrets de ballets*).

349 C. Maroy, 'Les séjours de Voltaire à Bruxelles', *Annales de la Société d'archéologie de Bruxelles*, 19/3-4, 1905, pp. 11-12.

350 F.-M. Arouet, known as Voltaire, *Correspondance*, ed. by T. Besterman (Oxford, 1968-1977), D2040. We note, too, that three letters also bear witness to a correspondence between Voltaire and Duke Léopold-Philippe d'Arenberg.

351 Under the subject heading 'Poëtes Dramatiques et Lyriques ou Differens Théatres' of the 1768 catalogue it is mentioned that the library at that time contained eight volumes of the Amsterdam edition of Voltaire's *Œuvres*.

352 R. Pomeau, *Voltaire et son temps* (Paris and Oxford, 1995), I, p. 374. Cornaz, *Les Princes de Chimay et la musique*, pp. 31-32.

353 See above.

354 The comedy *Le Misanthrope* was first staged in Brussels on 16 January 1735, while *La Princesse d'Élide*, with music by Lully, was performed on 11 February 1736 (see entry 'Monnaie, *CESAR*).

355 The two prints are mentioned in the Duchess of Arenberg's 1769 catalogue, under the subject heading 'Grand operas françois en partition'.

356 AACC, Music Collection, I 1005 (RISM F/FF 1793).

357 *Ibid.*, I 1044 (RISM R/RR 2993).

358 See entry 'Monnaie', *CESAR*.

359 AACC, Annual accounts of the caissiers, 63/29-35 (account of Jacques Gaillard, 2 June 1742 to 30 November 1742); AACC, Annual accounts of the caissiers, 63/29-35 (account of Philippe Vandermale, 1 January to 31 December 1743), f. 52v: disbursement made on 31 March of 183 florins 16 sols 3 deniers for the payment of wages to 'S.r Tabary Maitre des Dances'.

360 See entry 'Tabari', *CESAR*.

361 Neu, *Die Arenberger und das Arenberger Land*, p. 122.

362 O. Roux, 'Vaucanson, Jacques de', in *Dictionnaire de la musique en France aux xviie et xviiie siècles*, p. 699.

363 Supplement to the *Gazette de Bruxelles*, 13 March 1744. Cited in Cornaz, *La vie musicale à Bruxelles*, p. V.

364 The Vaucanson print is mentioned in the library catalogue of 1768 under the subject heading 'Arts Métiers et Manufactures', with the description: 'Paris 1738 in 4to de 11 pages'. However, the pamphlet does not seem to have remained in the Arenbergs' possession.

365 Supplement to the *Gazette de Bruxelles*, 13 March 1744.

366 Supplement to the *Gazette de Bruxelles*, 7 April 1744.

367 d'Arenberg, 'De heren, graven, prins-graven en hertogen van Arenberg', p. 38.

368 Faber, *Histoire du théâtre français en Belgique*, II, p. 163.

369 AACC, Music Collection, Ms 454; in the upper right-hand corner of the page we read: 'le 7 juillet 1748'.

370 The air 'Habitants de ce doux empire' appears first among the engraved airs of the publication and bears the number '201', a number mentioned in Ms 454.

371 Cornaz, *L'édition et la diffusion*, pp. 70-71; Van Aelbrouck, *Livrets de ballets*.

372 Neu, *Die Arenberger und das Arenberger Land*, p. 208.

373 AACC, Accounts of the caissiers trésoriers généraux, 64/34/I (accounts and receipts of Philippe Vandermale, 1748-49): receipt of J. de Beer from 21 February 1749 stating that the latter received 7 florins 14 sols for having spent five and a half days 'a Ecrire le Catalogue de Livres de Monseig.r le Duc d'Arenberg, ainsy que les avoir numerotés'; receipt of J. Moris dated 1 March 1749 stating that, for 3 écus, Moris had worked for five days on 'l'amenagement de la Bibliotecque de Son Altesse Monseigneur le Duc d'Arenbergh'.

374 AACC, Annual accounts of the caissiers, 63/29-35 (account of Philippe Vandermale, 1749), I, f. 66r: payment on 3 March to Louis Bizant of 7 florins; the receipt is preserved: AACC, Accounts of the caissiers trésoriers généraux, 64/34 (accounts and receipts of Philippe Vandermale, 1748-49).

375 AACC, Annual accounts of the caissiers, 63/29-35 (account of Philippe Vandermale, 1749), I, f. 57v: payment of 315 florins on 22 February 1749; f. 67r: payment of 84 florins on 11 June (the receipt of the latter payment is preserved: AACC, Accounts of the caissiers trésoriers généraux, 64/34/I (accounts and receipts of Philippe Vandermale, 1748-49)).

376 We may recall that the Parisian Joseph Bruseau de La Roche had been director of the Monnaie from 1731 to 1733.

377 This is a libretto without music (see Cornaz, 'La Monnaie et le commerce des ouvrages lyriques', p. 279).

378 Cornaz, *L'édition et la diffusion de la musique*, p. 156.

379 Cornaz, *L'édition et la diffusion de la musique*, p. 158; N. Zaslaw, 'Some notes on Jean-Benoît Leclair', *Revue Belge de Musicologie*, 19 (1965), pp. 97-101; also N. Zaslaw, 'Postscript on Jean-Benoît Leclair', *Revue Belge de Musicologie*, 21 (1967), pp. 124-125.

380 A copy of the licence agreement is preserved at Enghien: AACC, Biography Léopold-Philippe, 35/28 (23 Personalia), file 'Octroi d'un théâtre à Bruxelles 1749'.

381 The licence of 21 June 1749 is kept at the SAB, Conseil privé, 1090 (Comédies et Théâtres). It is reproduced in Faber, *Histoire du théâtre français en Belgique*, IV, pp. 42-43.

382 AACC, Music Collection, I 766 (RISM V 969).

383 Cornaz, *L'édition et la diffusion de la musique*, p. 57; M. Cornaz, 'Charles de Lorraine et l'édition musicale bruxelloise', *Bulletin de Dexia Banque* (special issue ed. by C. Sorgeloos: *Autour de Charles de Lorraine, gouverneur général des Pays-Bas autrichiens, 1744-1780 Culture et Société*), 54th year, no. 212 (2000/2), pp. 71-78.

384 S. Willaert, 'Crosa, Giovanni Francesco', in *Grove Music Online. Oxford Music Online* (consulted 12 March 2015), article 51571.

385 Renieu, *Histoire des théâtres de Bruxelles*, II, p. 687.

386 R. Wangermée, 'Du divertissement de cour à l'opéra-comique', in *Le théâtre de la Monnaie*, p. x; R. G. King, F. Piperno, and S. Willaert, 'Laschi, Filippo', in *The New Grove Dictionary of Opera. Grove Music Online. Oxford Music Online* (consulted 12 March 2015), article O902804.

387 *Gazette de Bruxelles*, supplement of Tuesday 5 August 1749 (cited in Cornaz, *La vie musicale à Bruxelles*, p. XII). The issue of 8 August adds that on 5 August H.R.H. Charles of Lorraine 'se rendit au Grand Théatre où Elle vit la prémiére Réprésentation de l'Opera Comique Italien; il y eut un grand concours de monde, & les Acteurs s'attirèrent l'aprobation des tous les Spectateurs par la beauté des airs nouveaux' (attended the Grand Theatre, where he saw the first performance by the Italian Opéra-Comique; there was a large audience, who were all won over by the actors' performances and the beauty of the new arias).

388 As the catalogue of 1777 attests. In the section 'Theatre des Grecs, des Latins, des Italiens, &c' we in fact read: 'Li tre Cicisbei Ridicoli, Drammajocoso per Musica [Italien-Français] Bruxelles, 1749, in-12'. Copies of this bilingual libretto are held by the Royal Library of Belgium and the Royal Conservatory of Brussels (see Van Aelbrouck, *Livrets de ballets*).

389 M. F. Robinson and D. E. Monson, 'Latilla, Gaetano', in *Grove Music Online. Oxford Music Online* (consulted 12 March 2015), article 16071.

390 F. Walker, '"Tre giorni son che Nina": An Old Controversy Reopened', *The Musical Times*, 90, no. 1282 (1949), pp. 432-435.

391 D. E. Monson, 'Galuppi, Baldassare', in *Grove Music Online. Oxford Music Online* (consulted 12 March 2015), article 50020.

392 Is the legend 'atto 2:a scena 3.a Sigismondo' likewise found in Ms 72 the result of an error? The role of 'Sigismondo', absent from *La forza d'amore*, indeed appears in *L'Arminio* by Galuppi, staged not in 1745 but in 1747.

393 A copy of this libretto is preserved in the library of the Royal Conservatory of Brussels (classmark 22.247) (see Van Aelbrouck, *Livrets de ballets*).

394 *Gazette de Bruxelles*, supplement of Tuesday 23 September (cited in Cornaz, *La vie musicale à Bruxelles*, p. XIII).

395 P. Howard, *The Modern Castrato: Gaetano Guadagni and the Coming of a New Operatic Age* (New York, 2014), p. 43.

396 R. Rasch, 'Italian Opera in Amsterdam 1750-1756: The Troupes of Crosa, Giordani, Lapis, and Ferrari', in *Opera in Central Europe, I: Institutions and Ceremonies*, ed. by M. Bucciarelli, N. Dubowy, and R. Strohm (Berlin, 2006), pp. 118-119.

397 *Gazette de Bruxelles*, Tuesday 7 October; M. Cornaz, 'Lieux de concerts publics et privés à Bruxelles au XVIIIᵉ siècle', *Études sur le 18ᵉ siècle* (2007), p. 99.

398 Van Aelbrouck, entry 'Hus', *CESAR*.

399 Renieu, *Histoire des théâtres de Bruxelles*, II, p. 687.

400 *Almanach historique et chronologique de la comedie françoise etablie à Bruxelles*, 1754, ff. 23-24.

401 *Gazette de Bruxelles*, supplement of 7 November 1749 (cited in Cornaz, *La vie musicale à Bruxelles*, p. XIV).

402 The Royal Library of Belgium holds a copy of this libretto (classmark II 15.107 A 77/3).

403 AACC, Music Collection, I 804 (RISM P 1348/PP 1348).

404 AACC, Annual accounts of the caissiers, 63/29-35 (account of Jacques Gaillard, 1750), f. 149r et seq.

405 AACC, Annual accounts of the caissiers, 63/29-35 (account of Jacques Gaillard, 1751), f. 156r: payment on 9 March of 35 florins 14 sols 3 deniers for costumes ordered from Paris.

406 *Ibid.*, f. 158r: payment on 22 May of 17 florins to 'M.r du Ransi' for a 'caisse d'habits de Comedie'.

407 The actor Pierre Paran signed a new contract on 19 August 1751 for a season in Brussels, an agreement in which his wife Louise was also contracted 'pour figurer dans les ballets' (see Van Aelbrouck, *Dictionnaire des danseurs*, p. 191).

408 AACC, Annual accounts of the caissiers, 64/1-7 (account of Jacques Gaillard, 1752), f. 163v: payment on 25 March of 100 French écus 'au S.r le mair Comedien pour une gratification'; Van Aelbrouck, *Dictionnaire des danseurs*, p. 166.

409 AACC, Annual accounts of the caissiers, 64/1-7 (account of Jacques Gaillard, 1752), f. 161v: payment on 6 February to Dubois of 157 florins 10 sols 'pour un Rideau qu'il a peint pour la Comedie'. P. de Zuttere ('Notes sur quelques décorateurs', in *Le théâtre de la Monnaie*, p. 256) cites the account book of 1754 but not that of 1752. Dubois also painted in 1753 the great drawing room at the Duke's Brussels residence.

410 This advertisement is quoted in the chapter 'La comédie de salon et de cour au temps de Charles de Lorraine' in H. Liebrecht, *Histoire du théâtre français à Bruxelles au XVIIe et au XVIIIe siècle* (Paris, 1923), p. 300.

411 A. Verbrugge, 'La garde-robe', in *La Maison d'Arenberg*, p. 425.

412 *Gazette de Bruxelles*, supplement of 8 February 1752.

413 d'Hoore, *Le Palais d'Egmont-Arenberg à Bruxelles*, p. 53: the sale nevertheless took effect only two years later at the instigation of the Egmont and Arenberg heirs.

414 P. De Zuttere, 'Notes sur quelques décorateurs', in *Le théâtre de la Monnaie*, pp. 261-262.

415 Renieu, *Histoire des théâtres de Bruxelles*, II, p. 688.

416 AACC, Annual accounts of the caissiers, 64/1-7 (account of Jacques Gaillard, 1753), f. 169r: payment of 30 June of 283 florins 10 sols to Madame Durancy 'pour la lorgnette de S: A: Mgr a la Comedie' for 1752 and 1753.

417 Cornaz, 'Spectacles privés chez les ducs d'Arenberg', pp. 92-93.

418 *Gazette de Bruxelles*, 7 November 1752. The five-act prose comédie *L'Important de cour* is the work of David-Augustin de Brueys.

419 The libretto of this new version, which was published for the occasion by Jean-Joseph Boucherie in Brussels, specifies: 'Réprésenté à Bruxelles le 28 février 1753 par les comediens françois sous les ordres de Son Altesse Royale' (Performed in Brussels on 28 February 1753 by the French actors by order of His Royal Highness) (Royal Library of Belgium, classmark II 15.107 A 70/3). The performance is reported in the *Gazette de Bruxelles* of 2 March 1753: 'On y admira la Beauté des Décorations, & les Acteurs s'acquitterent de leurs Rôles d'une façon à mériter les louanges & l'approbation de S.A.R. & de tous les assistans dont le nombre étoit extraordinaire' (The decoration was very handsome, and the actors played their roles in such a way as to merit the praise and approbation of H.R.H. and all the extraordinarily large throng of spectators).

420 The libretto, published by Jean-Joseph Boucherie, has the legend: 'Représenté pour la premiere fois à Bruxelles le 24 mai 1753 par les comédiens français sous les ordres de Son Altesse Royale' (Royal Library of Belgium, classmark Faber 2047 A I/3).

421 In the 'Mathématiques' section of the 1768 library catalogue appears the subject heading 'Musique' which mentions the following: 'Lettre sur la Musique françoise par J. J. Rousseau 1753'. The *Lettre* is also given in the catalogues of 1777 and 1778. It is no longer held by the AACC Collection.

422 A. Vanderhagen, whose first name is not known, was the uncle of the clarinettist Armand-Jean-François-Joseph Vanderhagen (1753-1802), who came from Antwerp.

423 AACC, Annual accounts of the caissiers, 64/1-7 (account of Jacques Gaillard, 1753), f. 167v: payment on 10 March of ten écus (196 florins) 'pour la Simphonie de huit representations a l'hotel de S: A:'.

424 SAB, Arenberg Collection, SA II 13307: with planned works costing an estimated 60200 florins (!): 'il conviendroit de faire 4 murs de 8 pieds de longueur visavis lun de lautre au comencement du theatre et deux à la fin du même a l'autre bout. Lon couvriroit ces deux Murs de dalles de pierre et lon feroit (a la hauteur a regler lorsque lon construira le theatre) deux trous de la grandeur necessaire pour y faire passer des poutres […]'.

425 AACC, Annual accounts of the caissiers, 64/1-7 (account of Jacques Gaillard, 1754), f. 100v. Further research would perhaps allow more light to be shed on the history of the Château in Heverlee and the existence of a private theatre there before 1754.

426 Liebrecht, 'La comédie de salon', p. 300.

427 P. Claeys, *Histoire du théâtre à Gand*, 3 vols (Ghent, 1892), II, p. 8.

428 Renieu, *Histoire des théâtres de Bruxelles*, II, p. 688.

429 AACC, Music Collection, Ms 73.

430 *Ibid.*, Ms 74.

431 I 1061 (RISM D/DD 1097). This print is listed in the Duchess of Arenberg's library catalogue of 1769, under the subject heading: 'Opera Bouffons en Partitions'.

432 Laloire, *Généalogie de la maison princière et ducale d'Arenberg (1547-1940)*, p. 23.

433 See previous chapter; between 1728 and 1734, the ducal children had dancing lessons from Pierre Deschars.

434 d'Arenberg, 'De heren, graven, prins-graven en hertogen van Arenberg', p. 38.

435 Neu, *Die Arenberger und das Arenberger Land*, pp. 215-216.

436 Louise-Marguerite was born in Paris on 18 August 1730.

437 J. Coppieters, 'Louise Margareta van der Marck (1730-1820)', in *Arenberger Frauen*, pp. 221-222.

438 Laloire, *Généalogie de la maison princière et ducale d'Arenberg (1547-1940)*, p. 23; Neu, *Die Arenberger und das Arenberger Land*, p. 218; J. de Chestret de Haneffe, *Histoire de la Maison De La Marck y compris les Clèves de la seconde race* (Liège, 1898), pp. 238-240.

439 N. Zaslaw, 'Leclair's "Scylla et Glaucus"', *The Musical Times*, 120, n° 1641 (1979), pp. 900-904.

440 RISM F 692.

441 Février published his first book in 1734; the second is cited in a catalogue of 1737: see P. Février, *Second livre de pièces de clavecin*, introduction to the facsimile by M. Cornaz.

442 AACC, Music Collection, I 861.

443 *Ibid.*, I 988 (RISM B 3801). This copy is the only one recorded in Belgium today. The print was listed in the library catalogue of the Duchess of Arenberg of 1769 under the section heading 'Differente Musique et Airs detachés'.

444 J.-C. Maillard, 'vielle à roue (répertoire)', in *Dictionnaire de la musique en France aux xviie et xviiie siècles*, pp. 712-713.

445 Neu, p. 208.

446 AACC, Annual accounts of the caissiers, 64/1-7 (account of Jacques Gaillard, 1754), f. 154r. A 'lorgnette' is a box located in the rounded angle where the balcony begins, and therefore the closest to the stage.

447 He was probably the nephew of the architect Giovanni Niccolò Servandoni.

448 AACC, Annual accounts of the caissiers, 64/1-7 (account of Jacques Gaillard, 1755), f. 130r: payment on 1 July of 378 florins for a six month subscription to three boxes; f. 128v: payment on 1 April of 315 florins to Dubois for 'l'Embellissement du Grand Theatre'. For the record, Duke Léopold-Philippe had also paid Dubois.

449 This performance is mentioned in the supplement of the *Gazette de Bruxelles* of Friday 25 October 1754; the work aroused 'beaucoup d'applaudissemens' (cited in Cornaz, *La vie musicale à Bruxelles*, p. XX). Jean-Joseph Boucherie published a libretto for the occasion (see Van Aelbrouck, *Livrets de ballets*). *Titon et l'Aurore* had been first staged on 9 January 1753.

450 This performance is cited in *Le Littérateur Belgique* of 24 April 1755 (see entry 'Monnaie', CESAR).

451 The 1777 library catalogue mentions, under the section 'Operas, Ballets, &c', 'Deux Pieces des Indes Galantes. In-12'. This publication no longer forms part of the AACC Collection.

452 Van Aelbrouck, *Dictionnaire des danseurs*, pp. 107-108.

453 AACC, Annual accounts of the caissiers, 64/1-7 (account of Jacques Gaillard, 1756), f. 137r: reimbursement of Rozière on 17 February of the 124 florins 10 sols he had given to Devisse at the Duke's request.

454 The 1768 library catalogue mentions, under 'Poëtes Dramatiques et Lyriques ou Differens Théatres', the three-volume Parisian print of 1750.

455 d'Hoore, *Le Palais d'Egmont-Arenberg à Bruxelles*, p. 55. The works projected by the architect Servandoni could finally be executed.

456 AACC, Annual accounts of the caissiers, 64/1-7 (account of Jacques Gaillard, 1756), f. 137v: payment on 6 March of 59 florins 10 sols to the musicians who 'ont joués a l'hotel de S: A: S:'.

457 d'Arenberg, 'De heren, graven, prins-graven en hertogen van Arenberg', p. 41.

458 C.-J. de Ligne, *Fragments de l'histoire de ma vie* (Paris, 2000), I, p. 43.

459 AACC, Annual accounts of the caissiers, 64/1-7 (account of Jacques Gaillard, 1757), f. 118r, payment of 5 florins 19 sols to musicians 'par ordre de Sad.e altesse'; f. 129v, payment on 4 December of 7 florins 'aux joueurs pour le divertisse.mt que S: A: Mad.e a donné a ses Gens'.

460 *Ibid.*, f. 129r, payment of 252 florins for a half-year subscription for two boxes instead of three.

461 AACC, Annual accounts of the caissiers, 64/1-7 (account of Jacques Gaillard, 1758), f. 106r: payment on 9 January of 15 florins 15 sols to the Brussels bookseller François t'Serstevens 'pour les Mercures de France'; f. 126v: payment on 9 January of 18 florins 18 sols for the Brussels gazettes; f. 128r: payment on 10 March of 20 florins 17 sols for the Utrecht gazettes that were sent to the Duke on campaign ('qui ont été adressées a S: A: Mgr à l'armée').

462 M. Cornaz, 'Le Concert Bourgeois: une société de concerts publics à Bruxelles durant la seconde moitié du xviiie siècle', *Revue Belge de Musicologie*, 53 (1999), pp. 113-136.

463 Cornaz, 'Lieux de concerts publics et privés', p. 101.

464 *Gazette de Bruxelles*, supplement of Friday 22 March 1754.

465 His son, Louis-Engelbert d'Arenberg, would be involved in the Concert Noble in the 1780s; the first precise mention in the accounts dates from 1784 (see below).

466 The first mention of the Concert Bourgeois ('le Concert ordinaire formé par une Compagnie de Bourgeois de cette ville') is an account in the *Gazette de Bruxelles* of 19 March 1754, which also alludes to concerts that had taken place during the winter. The *Gazette de Bruxelles* of 21 November 1755 reports on a concert that had taken place two days earlier, while the *Gazette de Bruxelles* of 12 March 1756 mentions a concert on 10 March that was attended by the Governor and 'un grand nombre de Personnes de la premiere distinction'.

467 The Concert Bourgeois was nonetheless mentioned for the first time only in the Duke's accounts of 1759 (see below).

468 *Gazette de Bruxelles*, Friday 5 November 1756.

469 M. Cornaz, 'La circulation de la musique et des musiciens entre Bruxelles et Vienne durant le gouvernement de Charles de Lorraine', *Études sur le 18e siècle* (2004), p. 189. The music of this prologue has not come down to us.

470 *Ibid.*, p. 190.

471 *Gazette de Bruxelles*, Friday 1 July 1757. G. Salvetti and T. H. Keahey, 'Besozzi', in *Grove Music Online. Oxford Music Online* (consulted 12 March 2015), article 02957.

472 *Gazette de Bruxelles*, Wednesday 6 July 1757. Antonio and Carlo Besozzi would appear the following December at the Concert Spirituel in Paris.

473 M. Galand, *Charles de Lorraine, gouverneur général des Pays-Bas autrichiens (1744-1780)* (Brussels, 1993), p. 34.

474 AACC, Annual accounts of the caissiers, 64/1-7 (account of Jacques Gaillard, 1759), f. 108r.

475 AACC, Annual accounts of the caissiers, 64/1-7 (account of Jacques Gaillard, 1760), f. 112r: payment of 23 February 'pour les fraix du Concert Bourgeois'; AACC, Annual accounts of the caissiers, 64/1-7 (account of Jacques Gaillard, 1762), f. 138r; AACC, Annual accounts of the caissiers, 64/1-7 (account of Jacques Gaillard, 1763), f. 121v; AACC, Annual accounts of the caissiers (account of Jacques Gaillard, 1764), f. 77r. A gold coin, the double sovereign was worth 17 florins 17 sols (see Cornaz, *L'édition et la diffusion*, p. 29).

476 Tytgat, 'Een blinde hertog', in *De blinde hertog*, p. 11.

477 SAB, Arenberg Collection, LA 8464, folder regarding the expenses in Paris: a man called Turiet was paid 48 pounds in August 1759 for one month of 'Leçons de Musique et Clavecin'; he was replaced in October by a musician named Chauvin.

478 *Ibid.*, statement of expenses 'faites pour Monsieur le Prince d'Arenberg, depuis son arrivée à Paris': on 31 December 1759, payment of 48 pounds for two months of lessons given by the 'S.r Beate maitre a danser'. See entry 'Jean-François Béate', *CESAR*.

479 AACC, Annual accounts of the caissiers, 64/1-7 (account of Jacques Gaillard, 1760), f. 93r: payment on 14 April to Bigot of 52 florins 10 sols 'pour avoir montré a danser pendant cinq mois au prince auguste'. We meet Bigot again in the account books of 1761, 1762, 1763, and 1764 with regard to lessons given 'aux princes'.

480 Van Aelbrouck, *Dictionnaire des danseurs*, pp. 76 and 214.

481 Royal Library of Belgium, classmark Ms II 2780 Mus. Gages perhaps received this volume from Duke Louis-Engelbert d'Arenberg during the 1770s, since the latter was a member of the Masonic Lodge *L'Heureuse rencontre*, while the former had been Provincial Grand Master of the Austrian Netherlands since 1770 (see below).

482 G. Lernout, 'Notities over belangrijke gebeurtenissen tussen 1760 en 1786, opgesteld door Jérôme Debiefve, eerste secretaris van de hertog van Arenberg', *Het oude land van Edingen en omliggende*, XXXVII/1 (2009), p. 11.

483 *Ibid.*, p. 14; Neu, pp. 226-227.

484 *Gazette des Pays-Bas*, supplement of Thursday 4 June 1761.

485 Galand, *Charles de Lorraine*.

486 Cornaz, 'Le Concert Bourgeois', p. 121.

487 Cornaz, 'La circulation de la musique', p. 192; D. Dujardin, 'Vitzthumb, Ignaz', in *Grove Music Online. Oxford Music Online* (consulted 12 March 2015), article 29540; M. Cornaz, 'Ignace Vitzthumb et les opéras de Grétry', in *Grétry. Un musicien dans l'Europe des Lumières*, ed. by B. Demoulin, J. Duron, J.-P. Duchesne, C. Pirenne and F. Tilkin, *Art & fact*, 32 (2013), p. 124.

488 In 1767 he advanced for these the sum of 640 florins, relating to a year's subscription (AACC, Annual accounts of the caissiers, 64/1-7 (account of Jacques Gaillard, 1767), f. 98v).

489 The first references to 'abonnements suspendus' appear in the accounts of 1760. That year the family attended three 'abonnements suspendus', on 21 January, 11 April, and 8 October (AACC, Annual accounts of the caissiers, 64/1-7 (account of Jacques Gaillard, 1760), f. 111v, 112v, and 114r).

490 AACC, Annual accounts of the caissiers, 64/1-7 (account of Jacques Gaillard, 1761), f. 126v: payment on 10 June of 35 florins 14 sols 'aux Comediens a heverlé par ordre de son Altesse'; AACC, Annual accounts of the caissiers, 64/1-7 (account of Jacques Gaillard, 1763), f. 124r: payment of 19 florins 12 sols on 23 November for 'musiciens a heverlé'; AACC, Annual accounts of the caissiers, 64/1-7 (account of Jacques Gaillard, 1764), f. 75v: payment on 2 January of 39 florins 4 sols 'aux musiciens a heverlé'.

491 AACC, Annual accounts of the caissiers, 64/1-7 (account of Jacques Gaillard, 1762), f. 139v: payment on 18 May of 26 florins 2 sols 8 deniers 'a quatre musissiens pour le souper du 17'.

492 *Ibid.*, f. 141r: payment on 13 December of 52 florins 10 sols 'pour cincq representations a la Comedie flamende'.

493 Cornaz, *L'édition et la diffusion*, p. 293.

494 *Mozart en Belgique*, ed. by F. de Haas and I. Smets (Antwerp, 1990).

495 O. E. Deutsch, *Mozart: Die Dokumente seines Lebens* (Kassel, 1961), p. 110.

496 *Ignace Vitzthumb, Recueils d'ariettes (1775-1777)*, ed. by M. Cornaz (Brussels, 2011), I, p. 7. If we suppose that Leopold Mozart's reference 'Vicedom' alludes not to Vitzthumb but to the cellist at the court chapel, Jacques Vicedomini, it is improbable that the Mozart family did not meet Vitzthumb.

497 D. Black, 'The Mozart family gives a concert in Brussels', in *Mozart: New Documents*, ed. by D. Edge and D. Black, first published 5 November 2014, consulted 9 January 2015 (<https://sites.google.com/site/mozartdocuments/documents/1763-11-09>). I am very grateful to Patrizia Rebulla for communicating this information to me.

498 Cornaz, 'La circulation de la musique', p. 193.

499 M. Awouters, in *Dictionnaire des facteurs d'instruments de musique*, pp. 312-313.

500 AACC, Annual accounts of the caissiers, 64/1-7 (account of Jacques Gaillard, 1764), f. 59v: payment on 16 January of 29 florins 8 sols for the tuning. Numans appears in the ducal accounts up to 1769; in that last year he was remunerated for the tuning and maintenance of the harpsichord 'des princes' carried out in 1768.

501 AACC, Annual accounts of the caissiers, 64/1-7 (account of Jacques Gaillard, 1765), f. 65r: payment of 17 florins 17 sols 'a celui qui a mis en Etat un orgue et petit Clavessin pour le prince'.

502 AACC, Correspondence Charles-Marie-Raymond d'Arenberg, box 40/26, folder 41/7/I/3 ('Correspondances avec divers 1766-1778').

503 *Loc. cit.*

504 See entry 'Monnaie', *CESAR*. The performance on 3 August 1762 is cited in the *Gazette des Pays-Bas* (see Van Aelbrouck, *Représentations à Bruxelles 1695-1794* (unpublished)).

505 Lernout, 'Notities over belangrijke gebeurtenissen tussen 1760 en 1786, opgesteld door Jérôme Debiefve, eerste secretaris van de hertog van Arenberg', p. 16.

506 She died on 3 May 1766 in her Brussels residence in the Porte de Hal and was buried at Enghien.

507 Liebrecht, 'La comédie de salon', p. 302.

508 SAB, D'Ursel Collection, R 48, inventory of the château at Heverlee; this information was kindly shared with me by Xavier Duquenne.

509 AACC, Annual accounts of the caissiers, 64/1-7 (account of Jacques Gaillard, 1765), f. 66v: payment on 8 August of 20 florins 16 sols 6 deniers 'pour du Camelot rouge pour faire un habit de Comedie au prince'.

510 *Ibid.*, f. 81v: payment on 4 February of 19 florins 12 sols 'pour les chandelles et Lampions du Theatre de la monoye le jour de la repetition'.

511 *Ibid.*, f. 82r: payment on 22 February of 19 florins 12 sols 'pour les illuminations au Grand Theatre pour la repetition'.

512 See entry 'Le Roi et le fermier', *CESAR*.

513 AACC, Annual accounts of the caissiers, 64/1-7 (account of Jacques Gaillard, 1766), f. 64: payment on 9 January of 52 florins 5 sols 4 deniers 'au Sr Billionny pour un mois de Leçons de danse'; f. 65r: payment on 4 February of 39 florins 4 sols to Billioni, for a month of lessons; f. 65v: payment on 11 March to Billioni of the same amount. Van Aelbrouck, *Dictionnaire des danseurs*, pp. 77-78.

514 Van Aelbrouck, *Dictionnaire des danseurs*, pp. 217-219.

515 AACC, Annual accounts of the caissiers, 64/1-7 (account of Jacques Gaillard, 1767), f. 72v: payment on 28 January of 39 florins 4 sols to Saint-Léger. He was advanced the same amount again on 16 March (f. 74r) and then disappears from the accounts. Riddled with debt, Saint-Léger, too, would leave Brussels at the end of 1769.

516 Van Aelbrouck, *Dictionnaire des danseurs*, p. 187.

517 *Gazette des Pays-Bas*, supplement of Thursday 19 February 1767: this newspaper states that the reopening took place on Monday 16 February.

518 This booklet was printed in Brussels by François t'Serstevens.

519 Vitzthumb's name is mentioned in the *Gazette des Pays-Bas* of 19 February 1767.

520 Pierre van Maldere died in the night of 1-2 November 1768. Charles of Lorraine recorded (with his rather wayward spelling) in his *Journal secret*: 'La nuit, Vanmalder et tombé dans une espèce d'apoplexie et l'ont l'a trouvé le matin sens connaissance, dont il n'est pas revenus' (*Journal secret de Charles de Lorraine 1766-1779*, ed. by M. Galand (Brussels, 2000), p. 117).

521 AACC, Annual accounts of the caissiers, 64/1-7 (account of Jacques Gaillard, 1767), f. 98r.

522 Cornaz, 'Le Concert Bourgeois', pp. 123-124.

523 Cornaz, *L'édition et la diffusion*, p. 112.

524 AACC, Annual accounts of the caissiers, 64/1-7 (account of Jacques Gaillard, 1767), f. 74r: payment on 5 March of 27 florins 17 sols 8 deniers to Staes for a month of lessons. Staes's name appears through that year of 1767. In 1768, the harpsichord master also supplied 'de la musique' to the family (AACC, Annual accounts of the caissiers, 64/1-7 (account of Jacques Gaillard, 1768), f. 69r: payment on 30 January of 14 florins 16 sols 4 deniers 'pour de la musique').

525 *Ibid.*, (account of Jacques Gaillard, 1767), f. 79v: payment on 7 November of 10 florins 10 sols 'au S.r dodelet une pistolle pour un mois de leçon de musique'.

526 SAB, Conseil des Finances, 2074: document dated 18 August 1786, drafted during Henri-Jacques de Croes's succession to the post of musical director (see Cornaz, 'Le Concert Bourgeois', p. 126).

527 AACC, Annual accounts of the caissiers, 64/1-7 (account of Jacques Gaillard, 1767), f. 79v: payment on 24 November of 17 florins 17 sols 'au S.r Trappeniers maitre a danser'. Van Aelbrouck, *Dictionnaire des danseurs*, pp. 228-229.

528 *Journal secret*, p. 62.

529 *Loc. cit.*; these performances are cited in Liebrecht, 'La comédie de salon', p. 310.

530 Dujardin, 'La direction artistique d'Ignace Vitzthumb', in *Le théâtre de la Monnaie au XVIIIᵉ siècle*, pp. 160-161.

531 De Zuttere, 'Notes sur quelques décorateurs', p. 259.

532 Paul Mechtler was a friend of Vitzthumb; in 1761, he was present at the baptism of Paul, the composer's son. In 1779, he would become the official music engraver of the Van Ypen brothers' publishing house in Brussels (Cornaz, *L'édition et la diffusion*, pp. 81-88). He would work for the Arenberg family from 1771 (see below).

533 AACC, Annual accounts of the caissiers, 64/1-7 (account of Jacques Gaillard, 1768), f. 92v.

534 *Ibid.*, f. 94v: payment to Vitzthumb and Debatty on 23 November 'pour la Comedie flamende a heverlé 400 écus'.

535 R. Rasch, 'Opera in a Different Language. Opera Translations in the Dutch Republic in the Eighteenth Century', in *Music and the City*, ed. by S. Beghein, B. Blondé, and E. Schreurs (Leuven, 2013), p. 47.

536 De Zuttere, 'Notes sur quelques décorateurs'.

537 *Journal secret*, p. 127.

538 *Ibid.*, p. 133. This detail is cited in Liebrecht, 'La comédie de salon', p. 298.

539 *Description de toutes les fêtes [...] qui ont parus à l'occasion du Jubilé de vingt-cinq ans de Gouvernement de S.A.R. Charles-Alexandre Duc de Lorraine* (Brussels, H. Vleminckx, [1769]).

540 AACC, Annual accounts of the caissiers, 64/1-7 (account of Jacques Gaillard, 1769), f. 88r.

541 *Chanson nouvelle à l'occasion du jubilé de S. A. R. chanté au Concert Bourgeois le 31 Mars 1769* (Brussels, Josse Vanden Berghen, [1769]); regarding Pagès and Vitzthumb, see M. Cornaz, 'La collection musicale du château des princes de Ligne à Belœil', in *Hainaut terre musicale*.

542 AACC, Music Collection, Ms 237 (eight separate parts: A & B, vl 1, vl 2, vla, ob 1, ob 2, fag, cor 2); other manuscript sources are listed in the RISM database, in particular under number 800250833.

543 *Ibid.*, I 666 (RISM L 203/LL 203).

544 AACC, Annual accounts of the caissiers, 64/1-7 (account of Jacques Gaillard, 1769), f. 87r: payment on 11 February of 70 florins 'pour encourager les arts de l'Academie Roÿale dont son altesse mgr s'est déclaré protecteur'. Charles de Lorraine had in 1763 offered to support the Académie generously as a patron, and in 1768 a call went out to private individuals to secure the necessary funds to establish an academy of painting, sculpture, and architecture worthy of royal patronage. The Duke would continue to advance the annual sum of 70 florins until the end of his life.

545 AACC, Annual accounts of the caissiers, 64/1-7 (account of Jacques Gaillard, 1769), f. 88r: payment to Vitzthumb on 1 April of 340 florins 4 sols 'pour les Concerts pendant les Carnevalles' and 315 florins 'pour trois mois de clarinettes'; the mention of 5 clarinets occurs in the account book of 1776.

546 AACC, Annual accounts of the caissiers, 64/1-7 (account of Jacques Gaillard, 1769), f. 92r: payment on 19 December of 225 florins 8 sols for unspecified musical instruments. Awouters, 'Jean-Hyacinthe II-Joseph Rottenburgh', in *Dictionnaire des facteurs d'instruments de musique*, pp. 351-352. We find Rottenburgh again in the accounts of 1773 in connection with flutes supplied to Prince Charles d'Arenberg (see below).

547 AACC, f. 91r: payment on 29 September of 25 florins 4 sols 'pour un abonnement suspendu en faveur de M.r Belcour'. On this night the comedies *Les Femmes savantes* by Molière and *Le Somnambule* by Antoine de Fériol de Pont-de-Veyle were performed (see entry 'Monnaie', *CESAR*).

548 Galand, 'Relations et liens financiers entre le gouvernement', pp. 126-127.

549 AACC, Annual accounts of the caissiers, 64/1-7 (account of Jacques Gaillard, 1769), f. 91v: payment on 6 December of 178 florins 10 sols for an 'abonnement suspendu' in favour of 'amad. De foy Comedienne'.

550 See entry 'Le Déserteur', *CESAR*.

551 See in particular: AACC, Music Collection, Ms 280 (manuscript score of the duet 'Serait-il vrai').

552 AACC, Manuscripts, 29/10.

553 AACC, Annual accounts of the caissiers, 64/1-7 (account of Jacques Gaillard, 1759), f. 104r: payment on 12 November of 9 florins 16 sols to Étienne 'pour avoir relié des Inventaires pour les archives d'Enghien'.

554 AACC, Annual accounts of the caissiers, 64/1-7 (account of Jacques Gaillard, 1769), f. 66r: payment on 3 July to Étienne of 249 florins 13 sols 6 deniers 'au sujet des armes qu'il a mises sur les Livres de la Bibliotheque'.

555 AACC, Music Collection, I 1051 (RISM G/GG 3049).

556 Cornaz, *L'édition et la diffusion*, pp. 174-175. See G7 in Cornaz, *Les éditions musicales publiées à Bruxelles au XVIIIᵉ siècle (1706-1794)*.

557 AACC, Music Collection, I 1059 (RISM M/MM 3259).

558 *Ibid.*, I 1056 (RISM M/MM 3159); *ibid.*, I 1057 (RISM M/MM 3264). The second print is listed in the Duchess of Arenberg's library catalogue of 1769, under the heading 'Operas Bouffons en Partitions'. We may note that Boucherie also published a libretto containing two *ariettes* and a vaudeville, together with their musical notation (see Cornaz, *L'édition et la diffusion*, p. 170). *Le Maître en droit* premiered in Brussels on 29 January 1761, *Le Cadi dupé* on 16 February 1765, and *On ne s'avise jamais de tout* on 9 February 1765 (see entry 'Monnaie', *CESAR*).

559 A score printed in 1764 is listed in the Duchess of Arenberg's library catalogue of 1769, in the section 'Operas Bouffons en Partitions'; see also entry 'Rose et Colas', *CESAR*.

560 AACC, Music Collection, I 1029 (RISM P/PP 1800). This print is listed in the Duchess of Arenberg's library catalogue of 1769 under 'Operas Bouffons en Partitions'.

561 *Ibid.*, I 1046 (RISM P/PP 1847). This print is listed in the Duchess of Arenberg's library catalogue of 1769 under 'Operas Bouffons en Partitions'.

562 *Ibid.*, I 1048 (RISM P/PP 1048).

563 *Ibid.*, I 1049 (RISM P/PP 1049). This print is listed in the Duchess of Arenberg's library catalogue of 1769 under 'Operas Bouffons en Partitions'.

564 *Ibid.*, I 1047 (RISM P/PP 1785).

565 *Blaise le savetier* was first staged in Brussels in January 1760, *Le Jardinier et son seigneur* on 11 April 1763, *Le Maréchal ferrant* on 3 February 1765, *Sancho Pança dans son île* on 24 February 1770, and *L'Amant déguisé ou le Jardinier supposé* on 12 December 1769.

566 AACC, Manuscripts, 29/12.

567 Entries 'Le Bûcheron ou les Trois souhaits', 'Le Sorcier', and 'Tom Jones', *CESAR*. Boucherie also published a libretto of *Le Sorcier* with some airs and their music (see Cornaz, *L'édition et la diffusion*, p. 173).

568 AACC, Music Collection, I 1066 (RISM M/MM 3011).

569 *Ibid.*, I 1060 (RISM D/DD 1095); this is currently the only copy recorded for Belgium.

570 The premiere of *L'Île des fous* took place in Paris on 29 December 1760 and in Brussels on 17 January 1765 (see entry 'L'Ile des fous', *CESAR*).

571 *Mazet* was first staged in Paris on 24 September 1761 and in Brussels on 24 January 1765 (see entry 'Mazet', *CESAR*).

572 The first performance of *Les Deux chasseurs et la laitière* took place in Paris on 23 July 1763 and in Brussels on 7 February 1765 (see entry 'Les Deux chasseurs et la laitière', *CESAR*). In 1763 Boucherie produced a libretto with three airs plus their music (see Cornaz, *L'édition et la diffusion*, p. 172).

573 *Le Milicien* was performed in Versailles on 29 December 1762 and in Brussels on 14 February 1765 (see entry 'Le Milicien', *CESAR*).

574 *La Fée Urgèle ou Ce qui plaît aux dames* was first given at Fontainebleau on 26 October 1765 and in Brussels on 12 December 1766 (see entry 'La Fée Urgèle ou Ce qui plaît aux dames', *CESAR*). In 1766 Boucherie published – probably for the first performance in Brussels – a libretto containing two airs and a romance with their music (see Cornaz, *L'édition et la diffusion*, p. 174).

575 The premiere of *La Clochette* took place in Paris on 14 July 1766 and in Brussels on 18 January 1767 (see entry 'La Clochette', *CESAR*). A Brussels edition of the libretto was printed by Boucherie in 1766 (see Cornaz, *L'édition et la diffusion*).

576 *Les Moissonneurs* was first performed in Paris on 17 January 1768 and in Brussels on 26 July 1769 (see entry 'Les Moissonneurs', *CESAR*). Boucherie published a libretto containing an air with its music in 1768.

577 AACC, Music Collection, I 1054; the title page is unfortunately too damaged to reveal the publisher's name.

578 *Ibid.*, I 1030 (RISM K/KK 1287). *Le Serrurier* was first staged in Paris on 20 December 1764 and in Brussels on 19 May 1765 (see entry 'Le Serrurier', *CESAR*).

579 *La Servante maîtresse* was first given in Paris on 14 August 1754 and in Brussels on 12 July 1755 (see entry 'La Servante maîtresse', *CESAR*).

580 *Le Tonnelier* was staged in Paris on 28 September 1761 and in Brussels on 20 April 1767 (see entry 'Le Tonnelier', *CESAR*).

581 *Toinon et Toinette* was first performed in Paris on 20 June 1767 and in Brussels on 29 June 1767 (see entry 'Toinon et Toinette', *CESAR*).

582 See above.

583 Boucherie is cited for the first time in the account book of 1762, in connection with the delivery of gazettes (AACC, Annual accounts of the caissiers, 64/1-7 (account of Jacques Gaillard, 1762), f. 121v).

584 Cornaz, *La vie musicale à Bruxelles*, p. XXXVIII.

585 *Gazette des Pays-Bas*, Thursday 16 August 1764; cited in Cornaz, *loc. cit.*

586 *Gazette des Pays-Bas*, Monday 15 April 1765; cited in Cornaz, *ibid.*, p. XL.

587 In the *Gazette des Pays-Bas* of Monday 14 March 1763, Boucherie specifies that he 'vient de recevoir des nouvelles Musiques de Paris' (cited in Cornaz, *ibid.*, p. XXXV).

588 AACC, Annual accounts of the caissiers, 64/1-7 (account of Jacques Gaillard, 1766), f. 60r: payment on 24 March of 7 florins 19 sols 'pour la voiture et droit d'une caisse de Livres venue de paris'.

589 Cornaz, *L'édition et la diffusion*, pp. 222-253.

590 Cited in Cornaz, *La vie musicale à Bruxelles*, p. XLVI. Jean-Louis de Boubers does not appear, though, in the Duke's accounts until 1771 (see below).

591 AACC, Music Collection, Ms 341, Ms 403 and Ms 427. These were the airs 'Quand un amant', 'On doit en aimer davantage', and 'Un mot d'amour'.

592 *Ibid.*, I 1073 (RISM B/BB 79).

593 *Ibid.*, I 811 & I 908/5 (RISM S 1945).

594   *Ibid.*, I 718 (RISM D 1186). B. Dünner, 'Davesnes, Pierre Just', in *Dictionnaire de la musique en France aux XVIIe et XVIIIe siècles*, p. 208.

595   AACC, Music Collection, Ms 61.

596   *Ibid.*, Ms 60.

597   *Ibid.*, Ms 85.

598   M. P. McClymonds, 'Jommelli, Niccolò', in *Grove Music Online. Oxford Music Online* (consulted 12 March 2015), article 14437.

599   AACC, Music Collection, Ms 93.

600   *Ibid.*, Ms 168.

601   *Ibid.*, Ms 157.

602   *Ibid.*, Ms 330.

603   *Ibid.*, Ms 57; G. T. Hollis, 'Bertoni, Ferdinando', in *Grove Music Online. Oxford Music Online* (consulted 12 March 2015), article 02933.

604   *Ibid.*, Ms 126. Y. Gérard, *Thematic, Bibliographical and Critical Catalogue of the Works of Luigi Boccherini* (London, 1969), pp. 37-38.

605   AACC, Annual accounts of the caissiers, 64/1-7 (account of Jacques Gaillard, 1770), f. 81r: payment on 5 April of 315 florins for 'trois mois de clarinettes'; this sum, paid every three months, appears in the accounts from 1770 to 1778.

606   AACC, Annual accounts of the caissiers, 64/1-7 (account of Jacques Gaillard, 1771), f. 69v: disbursement on 12 January of 630 florins to Vitzthumb 'pour ses soins de la Comedie pendant l'année 1770'.

607   SAB, Administration du théâtre de Bruxelles, registers 117 and 118; SAB, Tribunaux auliques, 3156; SAB, Conseil privé, 1054.

608   AACC, Accounts of the caissiers trésoriers généraux, 65/3/I (information and receipts of the accounts of Jacques Gaillard, 1771 and 1772): Mechtler's receipt for the sum of 6 pistoles signed on 19 March 1771.

609   Cornaz, *L'édition et la diffusion*, pp. 244-245.

610   AACC, Accounts of the caissiers trésoriers généraux, 65/3/I (information and receipts of the accounts of Jacques Gaillard, 1771 and 1772): Jean-Louis de Boubers's receipt for the amount of 16 florins 2 sols signed on 16 March 1771. This receipt does not give any details about the volumes delivered.

611   AACC, Annual accounts of the caissiers, 64/1-7 (account of Jacques Gaillard, 1771), f. 59v: payment to Staes on 23 May of 83 florins 6 sols for three months of harpsichord lessons to the two princesses and 14 escalins 'pour des copies'. The receipt is preserved (AACC, Accounts of the caissiers trésoriers généraux, 65/3/I (information and receipts of the accounts of Jacques Gaillard, 1771 and 1772)).

612   AACC, Annual accounts of the caissiers, 64/1-7 (account of Jacques Gaillard, 1771), f. 64r: payment on 11 December of 80 florins 6 sols 6 deniers 'pour avoir mis en Etat le Clavecin de son Altesse Madame et de la princesse'. The receipt specifies that E. Borremans tuned instruments, but also made some small repairs, providing jacks, tuning pins, and strings (AACC, Accounts of the caissiers trésoriers généraux, 65/3/I (information and receipts of the accounts of Jacques Gaillard, 1771 and 1772)). E. Borremans would continue working for the family over the subsequent years. We do not know what the family connection was between the tuner Borremans and the musician brothers from Brussels Charles (1769-1827) and Joseph Borremans (1775-1858).

613   Borremans's name appears again in the list of musicians of the Théâtre de la Monnaie orchestra from 1772 (SAB, Administration du théâtre de Bruxelles, register 119).

614   AACC, Annual accounts of the caissiers, 64/1-7 (account of Jacques Gaillard, 1771), f. 60r: payment on 25 May of 88 florins 18 sols to Antoine Pallet 'pour trois mois de la harpe aux deux princesses et autres debours'. The receipt signed on 25 May is preserved (AACC, Accounts of the caissiers trésoriers généraux, 65/3/I (information and receipts of the accounts of Jacques Gaillard, 1771 and 1772)).

615   P. Gilson, 'harpe (répertoire)', in *Dictionnaire de la musique en France aux XVIIe et XVIIIe siècles*, p. 337. Marie Antoinette married the future King of France, Louis XVI, on 16 May 1770; Duke Charles-Marie-Raymond d'Arenberg was among the wedding guests.

616   AACC, Accounts of the caissiers trésoriers généraux, 65/3/I (information and receipts of the accounts of Jacques Gaillard, 1771 and 1772): statement of disbursements of 8 August 1771 detailing the hiring of a harp and repairs made on the small harp.

617   These details are given on the receipt of 25 May 1771 (see above).

618   AACC, Music Collection, I 1076: 'Paris, auteur (gravé par Gerardin)' (RISM B VI¹, p. 349).

619   F.-J. Fétis, *Biographie universelle des musiciens* (Paris, 1873), II, p. 416.

620   AACC, Annual accounts of the caissiers, 64/1-7 (account of Jacques Gaillard, 1771), f. 62r: payment on 22 August of 22 florins 1 sol to Pallet for lessons given to 'la princesse'.

621   Neu, p. 234.

622   *Journal secret de Charles de Lorraine 1766-1779*, p. 209: evening of 29 April 1771.

623 AACC, Annual accounts of the caissiers, 64/1-7 (account of Jacques Gaillard, 1771), f. 83r; the Duke's payment request is preserved (Accounts of the caissiers trésoriers généraux, 65/3/II (information and receipts of the accounts of Jacques Gaillard, 1771 and 1772)).

624 AACC, Annual accounts of the caissiers, 64/1-7 (account of Jacques Gaillard, 1771), f. 83v: remuneration on 18 June to Antoine Cardon of 14 florins for the printing of 850 entrance tickets 'de la Comedie D'Everléz'. The receipt indicates that the performance took place in June (AACC, Accounts of the caissiers trésoriers généraux, 65/3/II (information and receipts of the accounts of Jacques Gaillard, 1771 and 1772)).

625 A. Devriès and F. Lesure, L'édition musicale dans la presse parisienne au XVIIIᵉ siècle. Catalogue des annonces (Paris, 2005), p. 64.

626 The Baron de Poederlé, who had made a similar visit to France in 1769, published in Brussels in 1772 a Manuel de l'arboriste et du forestier belgiques.

627 Mons, State Archives, Famille d'Olmen de Poederlé, 78bis.

628 E. Croft-Murray and S. Mc Veigh, 'London', in Grove Music Online. Oxford Music Online (consulted 12 March 2015), article 16904pg5.

629 Mons, State Archives, p. 4.

630 Ibid., p. 5.

631 Ibid., p. 47.

632 AACC, Music Collection, I 985 (RISM B II, p. 177). This is the only example currently listed for Belgium. This score may also have been added to the collection at the same time as other London editions acquired after 1771 in the generation of Duke Louis-Engelbert (see below).

633 AACC, Music Collection, Ms 365.

634 See entry 'Sylvain', CESAR.

635 AACC, Annual accounts of the caissiers, 64/1-7 (account of Jacques Gaillard, 1771), f. 84v: payment on 25 September of 37 florins 16 sols 'pour un abonnement suspendu en faveur de Madame Verteuil'; the receipt, as well as a small printed poster, has been preserved (AACC, Accounts of the caissiers trésoriers généraux, 65/3/II (information and receipts of the accounts of Jacques Gaillard, 1771 and 1772)).

636 M. Galand, 'Artistes du Grand Théâtre cités dans le "journal intime" de Charles de Lorraine', in Le théâtre de la Monnaie au XVIIIᵉ siècle, p. 325.

637 Eugénie D'Hannetaire (1746-1775) was the elder daughter of Jean-Nicolas Servandoni D'Hannetaire.

638 See entry 'Jean Mauduit dit Larive', CESAR. M. Couvreur, 'Un amateur de ballets longs et de jupons courts. Le prince Charles-Joseph de Ligne', in Le théâtre de la Monnaie au XVIIIᵉ siècle, p. 214.

639 AACC, Annual accounts of the caissiers, 64/1-7 (account of Jacques Gaillard, 1771), f. 86r: payment on 22 December of 75 florins 12 sols 'pour deux abonnements suspendus, en faveur de Mrs. Dugué et de la Rive'. The receipt is preserved (AACC, Accounts of the caissiers trésoriers généraux, 65/3/II (information and receipts of the accounts of Jacques Gaillard, 1771 and 1772)). Governor Charles of Lorraine was also in the audience that evening: see Galand, 'Artistes du Grand Théâtre', p. 324.

640 See entry 'Monnaie', CESAR.

641 AACC, Annual accounts of the caissiers, 64/1-7 (account of Jacques Gaillard, 1772), f. 86v: payment on 1 February of 75 florins 12 sols for two 'abonnements suspendus'. The receipt states that this is to help Grandmesnil and Compain (AACC, Accounts of the caissiers trésoriers généraux, 65/4/I (account of Jacques Gaillard, 1772)).

642 AACC, Annual accounts of the caissiers, 64/1-7 (account of Jacques Gaillard, 1772), f. 87r: disbursement on 2 March of 151 florins 4 sols for 4 'abonnements suspendus'. The preserved receipt gives the names of Dubois, Larive, Vitzthumb and Defoye (AACC, Accounts of the caissiers trésoriers généraux, 65/4/I (account of Jacques Gaillard, 1772)).

643 AACC, Annual accounts of the caissiers, 64/1-7 (account of Jacques Gaillard, 1771), f. 85r: payment on 21 October of 585 florins 18 sols 6 deniers for the third and fourth quarters of the annual subscription. The printed receipt, with the signatures of Vitzthumb and Compain, is preserved (AACC, Accounts of the caissiers trésoriers généraux, 65/3/II (information and receipts of the accounts of Jacques Gaillard, 1771 and 1772)). At the beginning of May 1772, the Duke's theatre boxes were re-upholstered by the master-upholsterer C. Goossens: AACC, Annual accounts of the caissiers, 64/1-7 (account of Jacques Gaillard, 1772), f. 87v: payment on 4 May of 31 florins 6 sols 'au Tailleur de la Comedie'; the receipt specifies that C. Goossens was asked to 'garnir deux loges a la comedie N. 17 au premier rang' (AACC, Accounts of the caissiers trésoriers généraux, 65/4/I (account of Jacques Gaillard, 1772)).

644 AACC, Annual accounts of the caissiers, 64/1-7 (account of Jacques Gaillard, 1773), f. 84r: payment of 31 florins 10 sols 'pour la Comedie et abonnement suspendu des dames deussin et grammont'. Many 'abonnements suspendus' were mentioned in the account books of the 1770s.

645 AACC, Annual accounts of the caissiers, 64/1-7 (account of Jacques Gaillard, 1774), f. 83r: payment on 15 December of 18 florins 18 sols for the box of the Duchess on 7 December 'jour du Concert de M.r Gervasio'.

646 See entry 'Lucile', CESAR.

647 See entry 'André-Ernest-Modeste Grétry', CESAR.

648   Cornaz, *L'édition et la diffusion*, p. 207. This is the oldest Brussels print containing music by Grétry.

649   AACC, Music Collection, I 967 (RISM G 3920/GG 3920).

650   *Ibid.*, I 1032; the first pages, which are severely damaged, do not allow us to determine which edition it is.

651   AACC, Annual accounts of the caissiers, 64/1-7 (account of Jacques Gaillard, 1772), f. 58v: payment on 5 May of 14 florins 4 sols 6 deniers for the books. The receipt is preserved and mentions in particular the delivery of *Les Deux avares* (AACC, Accounts of the caissiers trésoriers généraux, 65/3/II (information and receipts of the accounts of Jacques Gaillard, 1771 and 1772)).

652   AACC, Music Collection, Ms 312, 331, 336, 374, 375, 387, 388, 391, 436, 442, 452, 546, and 556.

653   AACC, Annual accounts of the caissiers, 64/1-7 (account of Jacques Gaillard, 1772), f. 87v: payment on 30 April of 35 florins 14 sols 'pour les fraix du Concert'.

654   Cornaz, 'Le Concert Bourgeois', pp. 119-120.

655   AACC, Accounts of the caissiers trésoriers généraux, 65/4/I (account of Jacques Gaillard, 1772): receipt signed Giron from Brussels on 24 April 1772 concerning the subscription to the Concert Bourgeois that commenced on 11 December 1771.

656   AACC, Accounts of the caissiers trésoriers généraux, 65/3/II (information and receipts of the accounts of Jacques Gaillard, 1771 and 1772); printed in red, the greetings card with the musical instrument design, although not dated, must have referred to New Year 1771, as it is slipped into a list of the presents made that year.

657   AACC, Music Collection, folder 'divers musique/1': this greeting card presents on its verso four red diamonds as well as the handwritten note in black ink '1772'. Note that the Prints and Drawings Division of the Royal Library of Belgium also once owned a greetings card of this type – one that has unfortunately disappeared from its album (classmark Divers 4° format C (album Outtelet) S II 121766).

658   A receipt dated 28 August states that Pallet was remunerated for harp lessons, providing strings, copying some music, and carrying out certain repairs on an instrument (SAB, Arenberg Collection, SA 2nd series 14026).

659   I would like to thank Peter Parren (Thorn, Netherlands) for telling me about the existence of several documents related to music preserved in the archives of the Windisch-Graetz family (Léopoldine married Count Joseph Ludwig von Windisch-Graetz in 1781) deposited in Nepomuk (Czech Republic). Written in Brussels on 8 March 1775, one receipt confirms the payment to 'Flament' of 14 florins 11 sols for a month of singing lessons. We may note that Léopoldine d'Arenberg would become Canoness of the Chapter of Thorn from 1779 to 1781.

660   AACC, Annual accounts of the caissiers, 64/1-7 (account of Jacques Gaillard, 1772), f. 61r: payment of 10 florins 10 sols 'pour un mois de Leçon de Chant au prince Charles'. In the *Journal* of Jacques Gaillard for the year 1772, we find the entry 'au nommé dewinne pour un mois de leçon de chant au prince Charles' (AACC, Journal of receipts and expenses of Jacques Gaillard, 1772, 64/1-7). The receipt is preserved and is signed 'j. f. Dewinne' (AACC, Accounts of the caissiers trésoriers généraux, 65/4/I (account of Jacques Gaillard, 1772)). Dewinne gave lessons in 1772 only.

661   AACC, Annual accounts of the caissiers, 64/1-7 (account of Jacques Gaillard, 1772), f. 62r: payment on 11 February of 13 florins 1 sol 4 deniers 'pour un mois de Leçon de flute du prince Charles'. The receipt, signed 'R. J. Gehot', is preserved (AACC, Accounts of the caissiers trésoriers généraux, 65/4/I (account of Jacques Gaillard, 1772)). Gehot taught the Prince between 1772 and 1774.

662   AACC, Annual accounts of the caissiers, 64/1-7 (account of Jacques Gaillard, 1773), f. 66v: disbursement on 10 December of 64 florins 8 sols 'au Sr. Rottenbourg pour les flutes du prince Charles'.

663   AACC, Annual accounts of the caissiers, 64/1-7 (account of Jacques Gaillard, 1772), f. 69r: payment on 19 November of 26 florins 2 sols 8 deniers for two months of lessons. The receipt, signed Bocquet, is preserved (AACC, Accounts of the caissiers trésoriers généraux, 65/4/I (account of Jacques Gaillard, 1772)); Van Aelbrouck, *Dictionnaire des danseurs*, p. 80.

664   AACC, Annual accounts of the caissiers, 64/1-7 (account of Jacques Gaillard, 1773), f. 61r: payment on 20 March of 19 florins 12 sols for 12 dancing lessons given to Prince Charles.

665   AACC, Annual accounts of the caissiers, 64/1-7 (account of Jacques Gaillard, 1772), f. 70r: payment on 10 December of 6 florins 6 sols for the copying of music scores. The preserved receipt states that Hinne copied 'plusieurs cahiers d'airs de musique avec accompagnement de la harpe' (AACC, Accounts of the caissiers trésoriers généraux, 65/4/I (account of Jacques Gaillard, 1772)). A receipt from September 1774 states that the copies made by Hinne are 'tant pour la harpe que pour le clavecin' (AACC, Accounts of the caissiers trésoriers généraux, 65/4/II (information and receipts of Jacques Gaillard, 1774)); the payment of 5 florins 5 sols corresponding to this receipt was made on 15 September (AACC, Annual accounts of the caissiers, 64/1-7 (account of Jacques Gaillard, 1774), f. 63v). Hinne is not cited in the accounts after 1775.

666   AACC, Annual accounts of the caissiers, 64/1-7 (account of Jacques Gaillard, 1774), f. 62r: payment on 3 June of 23 florins 12 sols 'pour racomodage de clavecin'. The receipt, signed Borremans, indicates that the latter had 'mie le clavecin et forte piano de la princesse D'arenberg d'accord'.

667   P. Raspé, 'Van Casteel, Henri-Joseph', in *Dictionnaire des facteurs d'instruments de musique*, pp. 414-415.

668   *Gazette des Pays-Bas*, supplement of Thursday 23 August 1770; cited in Cornaz, *La vie musicale à Bruxelles*, p. XLVII.

669 AACC, Annual accounts of the caissiers, 64/1-7 (account of Jacques Gaillard, 1772), f. 88r: payment on 9 June of 392 florins to Dubois. The actor and decorator's bill is preserved (AACC, Accounts of the caissiers trésoriers généraux, 65/4/I (account of Jacques Gaillard, 1772)).

670 Liebrecht ('La comédie de salon', p. 300) cites a letter of 19 October 1772 (written at Heverlee) from the Count of Figuerola to Vitzthumb, referring to this incident. This letter is kept at the SAB, Manuscrits divers, 1808.

671 AACC, Annual accounts of the caissiers, 64/1-7 (account of Jacques Gaillard, 1773), f. 85r: payment of 35 florins 14 sols for the concert of 'Mr. Albanese'.

672 K. Langevin, 'Albanese, Antoine', in *Grove Music Online. Oxford Music Online* (consulted 12 March 2015), article 00414.

673 Albanese's name appears on a manuscript of the aria 'Sol in bracio al mio periglio' from *Fra i due litiganti il terzo gode*, a 'dramma giocoso' by Giuseppe Sarti first staged in Milan in 1782 (AACC, Music Collection, Ms 54). We may note that Prince Charles-Joseph de Ligne would also call on Albanese for the marriage of his eldest son Charles to Princess Hélène Massalska, on 29 July 1779, during the celebrations at the Château de Belœil (Couvreur, 'Un amateur de ballets longs et de jupons courts', pp. 220 and 237).

674 AACC, Annual accounts of the caissiers, 64/1-7 (account of Jacques Gaillard, 1774), f. 79r: payment on 11 April to Petit; the receipt is preserved (AACC, Accounts of the caissiers trésoriers généraux, 65/4/II (information and receipts of Jacques Gaillard, 1774)).

675 AACC, Annual accounts of the caissiers, 64/1-7 (account of Jacques Gaillard, 1772), f. 63v: payment on 4 April of 15 florins 15 sols 'pour la part du prince Charles dans la mascarade du huit mars par ordre de son Altesse Madame'; AACC, Annual accounts of the caissiers, 64/1-7 (account of Jacques Gaillard, 1773), f. 60v: payment on 6 March of 51 florins 4 sols 'pour la mascarade du prince Charles'.

676 AACC, Annual accounts of the caissiers, 64/1-7 (account of Jacques Gaillard, 1774), f. 62v: payment on 21 July of 68 florins 2 sols 'pour l'habit de mascarade, ou de Bal du prince Charles'.

677 *Journal secret*, p. 298.

678 This oil painting on canvas of the French school today forms part of the Arenberg Collection of the Katholieke Universiteit Leuven.

679 Dujardin, 'La direction artistique', p. 161.

680 Cornaz, 'Le Concert Bourgeois', p. 127.

681 AACC, Annual accounts of the caissiers, 64/1-7 (account of Jacques Gaillard, 1775), f. 66v: payment on 19 April of 13 florins 1 sol 4 deniers 'Au Concert Bourgeois pour les fraix au sujet de la statue de S: A: R:'.

682 *Journal secret*, p. 336: 'Eté au bal chez le duc d'Aremberg, où la jeunesse a voulu une mascarade et décidé les Vigneront'. Van Aelbrouck, *Dictionnaire des danseurs*, p. 229: this was the masquerade *Les Vendangeurs*.

683 Couvreur, 'Un amateur de ballets longs et de jupons courts', p. 207.

684 Cornaz, *L'édition et la diffusion*, p. 80.

685 AACC, Music Collection, I 949/1.

686 Indeed, the Duke paid 'pour une souscription de musique' on 16 May 1775 (AACC, Annual accounts of the caissiers, 64/1-7 (account of Jacques Gaillard, 1775), f. 47r).

687 Cornaz, *L'édition et la diffusion*, p. 104.

688 AACC, Music Collection, I 611, 949/2, I 950-1, 2 (first volume); I 950-1, 2 (second volume); I 950-1, 2, I 951, I 612 (third volume).

689 SAB, Arenberg Collection, SA 2nd series 14026.

690 The Brussels première of *La Belle Arsène* took place on 19 February 1776 (see entry 'La Belle Arsène', *CESAR*).

691 The Brussels première of *Les Mariages samnites* was on 4 November 1776 (see entry 'Les Mariages samnites', *CESAR*).

692 Cornaz, 'La collection musicale du château des princes de Ligne à Belœil', in *Hainaut terre musicale*.

693 AACC, Music Collection, Ms 5 and Ms 22.

694 *Ibid.*, I 616.

695 *Ibid.*, I 868 (RISM B 4523).

696 Cornaz, *L'édition et la diffusion*, p. 95.

697 *Ibid.*, p. 100.

698 The accounts specify, from 1776 onwards, 'la loge de Mgr' and that of the Duchess (AACC, Annual accounts of the caissiers, 64/1-7 (account of Étienne Lecocq, 1776)).

699 AACC, Annual accounts of the caissiers, 64/1-7 (account of Jacques Gaillard, 1775), f. 67r: payment to Lekain on 20 May of 107 florins 2 sols.

700 AACC, Annual accounts of the caissiers, 64/1-7 (account of Étienne Lecocq, 1777), f. 50r: payment of 18 florins 18 sols for the Duchess's box at the theatre during the 'abonnement suspendu' (benefit evening) for Angélique D'Hannetaire on 15 February.

701 See entry 'Monnaie', *CESAR*.

702 AACC, Annual accounts of the caissiers, 64/1-7 (account of Étienne Lecocq, 1778), f. 62v: payment of the 630 florins, following the wishes of the late Duke.

703 *Ibid.*, f. 59v: payment on 16 November 1778 of 315 florins for the 5 clarinets 'en les remerciant jusques a nouvel ordre'.

704 AACC, Annual accounts of the caissiers, 64/1-7 (account of Étienne Lecocq, 1776), f. 46r: payment to Le Clerck on 11 December of 11 florins 15 sols.

705 AACC, Annual accounts of the caissiers, 64/1-7 (account of Étienne Lecocq, 1777), f. 37v: payment on 21 October of 147 florins 10 sols to the binder De Groot. He would still be active in 1783 (AACC, Annual accounts of the caissiers, 64/1-7 (account of Étienne Lecocq, 1783), f. 35v).

706 *Ibid.*, f. 38r: payment at the end of the year of 147 florins to Grosfils 'pour sept mois d'occupation a la Bibliothèque'. We may note that from 1777 the costs related to the library were grouped, in the account books, under a specific category.

707 AACC, Manuscripts, 29/10.

708 F. Sabatier, 'Bédos de Celles, dom François', in *Dictionnaire de la musique en France aux xviie et xviiie siècles*, p. 64.

709 AACC, Manuscripts, 29/13, p. 269.

710 AACC, Manuscripts, 29/10, p. 273.

711 This publication is cited in the 1778 catalogue under the subject heading 'Musique'.

712 C. Chevrolet, 'Essai sur les révolutions de la musique en France', in *Dictionnaire de la musique en France aux xviie et xviiie siècles*, p. 278.

713 For precise references to these lessons in the account books, see the previous chapter.

714 X. Duquenne, *Le voyage du duc d'Arenberg en Italie en 1791* (Brussels, 2013), p. 7.

715 Tytgat, 'Een blinde hertog', p. 11.

716 Louis-Léon de Brancas made headlines all over Europe because of the relationship he had for a time with the Comédie-Française actress Sophie Arnould. He wrote a play in three acts: *Les Originaux* 'luë et reçuë a la comedie Française en mai 1782' (AACC, Manuscripts, 27/A).

717 G. Lernout, 'Louise Pauline de Brancas-Villars, gravin van Lauraguais, hertogin van Arenberg', in *Arenberger Frauen*, ed. by P. Neu (Koblenz, 2006), p. 234.

718 P. Duchaine, *La franc-maçonnerie belge au xviiie siècle* (Brussels, 1911), p. 387: Louis-Engelbert appears on a list of 1777; E. Verschueren, *Louis-Engelbert d'Arenberg (1750-1820), Le 'duc aveugle', ses intérêts scientifiques et artistiques y compris le mécénat*, unpublished undergraduate dissertation, Université Libre de Bruxelles, 1994-1995, p. 120; Tytgat, p. 12.

719 AACC, Annual accounts of the caissiers, 64/1-7 (account of Jacques Gaillard, 1774).

720 Van Aelbrouck, p. 229.

721 Tytgat, pp. 12-13.

722 AACC, Annual accounts of the caissiers, 64/1-7 (account of Étienne Lecocq, 1779), f. 62r: payment of 806 florins 8 sols for the Duchess's theatre box and 365 florins 8 sols for the 'loge basse de Mgr'.

723 *Ibid.*, f. 78v: payment to Mechtler on 17 January of 297 florins 10 sols for 'une année de leçon donnée à S: A: Mad.e la Duchesse'; f. 80v: payment on 24 March of 13 florins 1 sol 4 deniers to Mechtler for a month of lessons for Princess Léopoldine.

724 The firm took the name 'Van Ypen et Mechtler' from 11 January 1779 (see Cornaz, *L'édition et la diffusion*, pp. 87-88).

725 For the details of the classmarks and separate parts preserved, see Cornaz, 'Inventaire complet', p. 201.

726 AACC, Annual accounts of the caissiers, 64/1-7 (account of Étienne Lecocq, 1778), f. 77v: payment on 19 December of 326 florins 13 sols 4 deniers 'pour un fortepiano livré à S: A: Sme Mgr. Pour S: A: Madame et par ses ordres'; the receipt is preserved (SAB, Arenberg Collection, LA 10361).

727 AACC, Annual accounts of the caissiers, 64/1-7 (account of Étienne Lecocq, 1779), f. 35v: payment of 619 florins for the purchase of a harpsichord and furniture during the public sale of 20 February 1779.

728 T. Bauman, 'Weidmann, Paul', in *The New Grove Dictionary of Opera. Grove Music Online. Oxford Music Online* (consulted 12 March 2015), article O905686.

729 AACC, Biography Louis-Engelbert d'Arenberg (box 43/2): *Journal de mon voyage de Vienne 1779*, [p. 6].

730 *Ibid.*, [p. 8]: 'on alla après à la Comedie où l'on donna la fausse Magie en Allemand qui fut parfaitement exécutée, la Cavaglieri actrice me charma par son gout du chant, et je ne me rappelle pas en verité d'avoir vu mieux chanter'.

731 AACC, Music Collection, Ms 155 and Ms 156. The title pages of these manuscript scores both bear, in their right upper-hand corner, the detail 'no. 23'. Beethoven would compose a new version of the aria 'Soll ein Schuh nicht drücken' (WoO 91/2) for the revival of *Die schöne Schusterin* in 1795.

732 Fétis, *Biographie universelle des musiciens*, III, p. 194.

733 AACC, Annual accounts of the caissiers, 64/1-7 (account of Étienne Lecocq, 1779), f. 62r and f. 85v.

734 AACC, Annual accounts of the caissiers, 64/1-7 (account of Étienne Lecocq, 1780), f. 52v.

735 AACC, Music Collection, Ms 364; we read on the page 'Accompagnement de E. Gio. Ben: Lang 1780'.

736 AACC, Annual accounts of the caissiers, 64/1-7 (account of Étienne Lecocq, 1781), f. 45v: payment on 30 November to Boutmy of 13 florins 1 sol 4 deniers for a month of harpsichord lessons. Boutmy would remain in the family's service until 1789.

737 AACC, Annual accounts of the caissiers, 64/1-7 (account of Étienne Lecocq, 1780), f. 46v: payment of 29 florins 8 sols 'au maître de clavessin d'Enghien' for 45 lessons.

738 AACC, Annual accounts of the caissiers, 64/1-7 (account of Étienne Lecocq, 1781), f. 44v: payment on 27 January of 39 florins 4 sols to the 'petit Mechtler' for 60 lessons given to the Princess. F. Mechtler may have been a pupil of Vitzthumb (see Vander Straeten, *La musique aux Pays-Bas avant le xixᵉ siècle*, IV, p. 412).

739 *Ibid.*, f. 44v: payment on 9 March of 29 florins 8 sols to a dancing master.

740 AACC, *Maison*, Accounts of Louis-Engelbert, 1782 (file 35). Van Aelbrouck, *Dictionnaire des danseurs*, p. 202.

741 François Gehot, son of Baudouin Gehot, had married Anne Vitzthumb on 28 January 1777 (see P. de Zuttere, 'Les musiciens Ignace Vitzthumb (1724-1816) et Joseph-Henri Mees (1777-1858) et leur postérité', *L'intermédiaire des généalogistes*, no. 188 (1977), p. 111). F. Gehot appears in the list of musicians in the orchestra of the Théâtre de la Monnaie during the 1781-1782 season (see Van Aelbrouck, *Composition des troupes*, Wikipedia article 'La Monnaie', <http://fr.wikipedia.org/wiki/La_Monnaie>).

742 AACC, Annual accounts of the caissiers, 64/1-7 (account of Étienne Lecocq, 1781), f. 54v: payment of 458 florins 6 sols 6 deniers to Gehot 'pour la musique des 6 bals donnés à l'hôtel d'Arenberg du 20 février au 3 mars'; f. 55r: payment of 124 florins 8 sols 6 deniers to Gehot 'pour la musique du bal donné a l'hotel d'Arenberg le 16 juillet' and 50 florins 8 sols for the ball given in Brussels on 21 November.

743 *Ibid.*, f. 55r: payment on 9 October of 247 florins 16 sols 'pour la musique a heverlé le 17 septembre et les deux jours suivants'.

744 SAB, Arenberg Collection, SA II 4941.

745 R. Würth and P. Corneilson, 'Allegranti, Maddalena', in *Grove Music Online. Oxford Music Online* (consulted 12 March 2015), article 00599.

746 SAB, Arenberg Collection, SA II 4941, p. 31.

747 *Loc.cit.*

748 *Ibid.*, pp. 47-48.

749 *Ibid.*, p. 51.

750 C. Hogwood and S. McVeigh, 'Giardini, Felice', in *Grove Music Online. Oxford Music Online* (consulted 12 March 2015), article 11083.

751 SAB, Arenberg Collection, SA II 4941, p. 51.

752 D. DiChiera and J. J. Robinson, 'Sacchini, Antonio', in *Grove Music Online. Oxford Music Online* (consulted 12 March 2015), article 24251.

753 SAB, Arenberg Collection, SA II 4941, p. 116.

754 AACC, Biography Louis-Engelbert d'Arenberg (box 43/2), accounts of M. Simmons.

755 AACC, Music Collection, Ms 137, Ms 138 and Ms 160; under the two latter classmarks are 'Quel caro amabil volto' and 'Porterò nell'alma impressa'.

756 *Ibid.*, Ms 414.

757 *Ibid.*, I 762 (violin part) (RISM H 3896/HH 3896).

758 *Ibid.*, I 715 (RISM C 4605).

759 Curtis's multi-volume collection *The Jessamine* had been initiated around 1765.

760 AACC, Music Collection, I 788 (RISM M 2813/MM 2813). A second series of *Six songs* dates from 1774.

761 *Ibid.*, I 687 (the keyboard and first horn parts are missing) (RISM B 282/BB 282). This print was published around 1777, John Welcker going bankrupt in 1778.

762 *Ibid.*, I 738 (RISM E 545/EE 545).

763 *Ibid.*, I 813 (*Six sonatas for the piano forte or harpsichord with accompanyments for a violin and bass*) (RISM S 2163; the keyboard part is missing); I 812 (*Six concertos for the harpsichord or pianoforte with an accompanyment for two violins and a bass*) (RISM S 2172; the keyboard part is missing); I 814 (*Six sonatas for the pianoforte or harpsichord with an accompanyment for a german flute or violin dedicated to Miss Scott*) (RISM S 2182; the keyboard part is missing).

764 *Ibid.*, I 751 (RISM G 2118/GG 2118). *Il barone di Torre Forte* is an opera by Piccinni. The AACC Music Collection also holds a manuscript of the pieces for soprano and keyboard *Queen Mary's Lamentation* and *Auld Robin Gray* by Giordani (Ms 67).

765 *Ibid.*, I 750 (RISM G 443; the keyboard and first violin parts are missing).

766 S. Wollenberg and S. McVeigh, *Concert Life in Eighteenth-Century Britain* (Aldershot, 2004), p. 107.

767 AACC, *Maison*, Accounts of Louis-Engelbert, 1782 (file 35).

768 AACC, Annual accounts of the caissiers, 64/1-7 (account of Étienne Lecocq, 1782), f. 52v: payment on 31 December to

Gehot of 112 florins 16 sols 'pour les musiciens employés au bal donné à l'hôtel le 27 courant'. Gehot was also involved in a series of balls at the beginning of the year 1786 (AACC, Annual accounts of caissiers, 64/8-14 (account of Étienne Lecocq, 1786), f. 52v (payment of 815 florins 17 sols)) and a concert in the summer of 1786 on the Brussels canal with 25 musicians (SAB, Arenberg Collection, SA 6510, p. 65: payment dated 31 July of 98 florins 15 sols).

769   A. Verbrugge, 'De garderobe', in *De blinde hertog*, pp. 151-159. The Arenberg Collection at the Katholieke Universiteit Leuven preserves an exceptional collection of around 250 articles of clothing belonging to the family from the 18th and 19th centuries, among which are a number of disguises that will have been used during the blind Duke's generation.

770   AACC, Annual accounts of the caissiers, 64/1-7 (account of Étienne Lecocq, 1783), f. 46v: payment to Mechtler on 13 September of 364 florins 13 sols for 'deux concerts donnés a l'hôtel le 13 fev.r et le 15 mars', and also for several scores provided and seven days spent at Enghien and Heverlee.

771   Cornaz, 'La circulation de la musique', p. 191.

772   SAB, Arenberg Collection, MG 3701: receipt signed by Mechtler dated 24 January 1784. The four musicians played in the Monnaie orchestra until 1789.

773   P. de Zuttere, 'La direction des frères Alexandre-Florentin et Herman Bultos (1777-1794)', in *Le théâtre de la Monnaie*, p. 55; see List of those in possession of a box on 26 December 1785 (SAB, Secrétairerie d'État et de Guerre, file no. 447).

774   AACC, Annual accounts of the caissiers, 64/1-7 (account of Étienne Lecocq, 1783), f. 46v: disbursement, for the first quarter, of 326 florins 11 sols for two boxes, 'ayant été augmentées de 33 florins 12 sols par quartier'; payment of 448 florins for the second and third quarters for a new box, 'Son Altesse ayant repris la loge de Madame Deveau balcon a gauche'.

775   SAB, Arenberg Collection, MG 1448 H: several receipts from 1785 give the number and location of the box.

776   SAB, Arenberg Collection, LA 9927, chapter 21, list of the New Year gifts, 1784.

777   *Loc. cit.*: the two societies each received 8 florins 18 sols 6 deniers.

778   SAB, Conseil privé, 251/B: extract of the minutes of the Privy Council of 5 September 1781 (see Cornaz, 'Le Concert Bourgeois', pp. 129-130).

779   The AACC Music Collection holds a previously unknown printed composition by Julie Candeille (1767-1834), the *Choix de morceaux détachés faciles et brillans parmi lesquels se trouve la Walze de Mozart* Op. 7, which was published in Paris by Imbault between 1798 and 1802 (I 923/5). Julie Candeille married the Belgian, Simons, in 1798.

780   Cornaz, 'Lieux de concerts publics et privés', *Études sur le 18ᵉ siècle* (2007), p. 104; Duquenne, 'La salle du Concert noble construite à Bruxelles en 1779', *Cahiers bruxellois*, 45 (2013), pp. 167-190.

781   [Baron De Vinck d'Orp], *Le Concert Noble: ses origines et ses membres* (Brussels, 1879), pp. 19-22.

782   This print, published by Mme Le Menu, was announced in an issue of the *Journal de Paris* of 1784.

783   SAB, Arenberg Collection, LA 9927: in the chapter concerning the expenses of the Duchess, a memorandum states that on 8 March, the Duchess paid two crowns 'pour l'opera de Mlle De Vacqueras', the accountant writing down very approximately the name of Mlle de Walckiers.

784   AACC, Music Collection, Ms 292.

785   *Ibid.*, I 891 and I 956.

786   AACC, Music Collection, I 911/3. M. Cornaz, 'Les romances publiées à Bruxelles à la fin du xviiiᵉ siècle', *Revue Belge de Musicologie*, 55 (2001), pp. 180-183.

787   SAB, Arenberg Collection, MG 3701.

788   Cornaz, *L'édition et la diffusion de la musique*, pp. 97-98.

789   *Ibid.*, p. 118.

790   *Ibid.*, pp. 117-118.

791   These four prints no longer form part of the AACC Collection.

792   Cornaz, p. 258.

793   *Ibid.*, p. 267.

794   A. van Hoboken, *Joseph Haydn: Thematisch-bibliographisches Werkverzeichnis* (Mainz, 1957), I, p. 49.

795   AACC, Music Collection, I 945/4 (RISM H 2853), I 945/10 (RISM H/HH 3094) and I 945/5 (RISM H 3110); van Hoboken, *Joseph Haydn: Thematisch-bibliographisches Werkverzeichnis*, I, pp. 88, 92 and 108.

796   AACC, Music Collection, I 583, 932/3 (RISM H/HH 3314); van Hoboken, *Joseph Haydn: Thematisch-bibliographisches Werkverzeichnis*, I, p. 823.

797   Cornaz, pp. 281-282.

798   SAB, Arenberg Collection, MG 1448 H: memorandum signed P. Mechtler on 28 October 1785.

799   *Loc. cit.*; reference to '6 Sinphonies par Haÿden op. 35'. Cornaz, *L'édition et la diffusion*, pp. 267-268. This Paris print contains the *Sei sinfonie a grand orchestra* whose original print appeared in Vienna from Artaria in 1782.

800   *Ibid.*: reference to '6 Trios par jadin op. 5'. Cornaz, *ibid.*, p. 98.

801   *Ibid.*: reference to '6 Duos par Redin op. 2' and '6 Duos par Redin op. 3'. Cornaz, *ibid.*, pp. 110-111.

802 *Ibid.*: reference to 'Ouverture de Zémire et Azor'. Cornaz, *ibid.*, p. 116.

803 SAB, Arenberg Collection, LA 9927: in the section relating to the Duchess's expenses these concern, on several occasions, Boutmy's travelling expenses in coming by coach to Heverlee.

804 AACC, Annual accounts of the caissiers, 64/8-14 (account of Étienne Lecocq, 1784), f. 66r: payment of 31 florins to a certain Prins 'pour avoir accordé deux Clavessins et un forté piano a Mgr. a Heverlé du mois de mars 1783 au dit mois 1784'.

805 AACC, Music Collection, I 895/11 (RISM H/HH 3843); van Hoboken, *Joseph Haydn: Thematisch-bibliographisches Werkverzeichnis*, I, p. 807.

806 SAB, Arenberg Collection, LA 9927: in the section relating to the Duchess's expenses we find a receipt dated 30 November 1784 showing that Boutmy paid 'au copiste de la part de Madame la Duchesse pour L'Ouverture du Seigneur Bienfaisant la somme de 17 sols et demi'.

807 See entry 'Le Seigneur bienfaisant', *CESAR*; the work does not seem to have been performed at the Théâtre de la Monnaie.

808 AACC, Music Collection, Ms 266. On the title page we see the inked inscription 'Pour Madame la Duchesse D'Arenberg'.

809 *Ibid.*, I 743. This print 'Paris, auteur, M. Le Marchand' is not listed by RISM and therefore is among the *unica* in the Collection.

810 AACC, Annual accounts of the caissiers, 64/8-14 (account of Étienne Lecocq, 1785), f. 68v: payment of 31 florins 10 sols 'aux trompettes et Timballes qui ont joués a l'hotel a l'occasion de la naissance du Prince Prosper'.

811 AACC, Music Collection, Ms 63.

812 *Ibid.*, Ms 64, Ms 372, Ms 420 and Ms 490.

813 AACC, Music Collection, Ms 64: 'Ouverture du Songe de Sarti arrangée pour le piano' mentions the manuscript; *Scipione* was composed by Sarti on Metastasio's libretto *Il sogno de Scipione*.

814 RISM BB 3946 I, 1.

815 Vander Straeten, *La musique aux Pays-Bas avant le XIXᵉ siècle*, I, p. 293.

816 AACC, Annual accounts of the caissiers, 64/8-14 (account of Étienne Lecocq, 1785), f. 70v: payment of 18 florins 18 sols 'au Musicien Van Casteels […] pour accordages de forte-piano pendant l'année 1784'; we encounter Van Casteel's name a final time in 1788, in connection with a repair: AACC, Annual accounts of the caissiers, 64/8-14 (account of Étienne Lecocq, 1788), f. 58v: payment of 12 florins 12 sols for the 'reparation de forte-piano'.

817 AACC, Annual accounts of the caissiers, 64/8-14 (account of Étienne Lecocq, 1785), f. 39v: payment on 10 December to Borremans of 79 florins 10 sols for four months of lessons. Until 1794 Borremans was regularly cited in the accounts for harpsichord tuning as well as providing music scores and violin strings.

818 *Ibid.*: payment to 'Perolle' of 52 florins 5 sols 4 deniers for four months of dancing lessons. Van Aelbrouck, *Dictionnaire des danseurs*, p. 193. Perolle remained in the family's service until 1789.

819 AACC, Annual accounts of the caissiers, 64/8-14 (account of Étienne Lecocq, 1787), f. 44v: payment of 108 florins 13 sols 6 deniers to Boutmy 'pour des leçons de composition données à la princesse'.

820 *Ibid.*, f. 44r: payment of 33 florins 1 sol 6 deniers for twenty-one singing lessons.

821 This letter, preserved at the AACC, was reproduced in Cornaz, 'Le fonds musical', p. 209. Could this Amantini be the Giuseppe Amantini, a singer at La Scala in Milan, who performed in Pasquale Anfossi's *Cleopatra* in 1779 (see Sartori 5849)?

822 AACC, Music Collection, Ms 35. P. Holman and T. Gilman, 'Arne, Thomas Augustine', in *Grove Music Online. Oxford Music Online* (consulted 12 March 2015), article 40018.

823 AACC, Annual accounts of the caissiers, 64/8-14 (account of Étienne Lecocq, 1785), f. 70v: illuminations and fireworks were organized in Brussels on 21 June, when the Duchess returned to Enghien 'apres ses Couches'.

824 *Ibid.*, f. 36v: payment of 30 florins 7 sols 8 deniers (55 livres 16 sols) for the Charpentier Collection which the Duchess 'fait venir de Paris'. AACC, Music Collection, I 708 (RISM B 1491). This represents the sole recorded copy in Belgium.

825 AACC, Annual accounts of the caissiers, 64/8-14 (account of Étienne Lecocq, 1787): payment of 31 florins 18 sols for a box of music 'venant de Mr. D'Arconati pour S: A: Mad.'. In 1796 Paul Arconati would inherit the Château de Gasbeek, near Brussels.

826 AACC, Annual accounts of the caissiers, 64/8-14 (account of Étienne Lecocq, 1784), f. 42v: payment of 1353 florins 7 sols 9 deniers to the bookseller Dujardin for all the books bought with him during the year. Only one document relates to a musical purchase from Dujardin: a receipt dated 5 March 1784 indicating the purchase, for 9 florins 16 sols, of the score of *Les Deux tuteurs* by Dalayrac (Katholieke Universiteit Leuven, Arenbergarchief: cited in *De blinde hertog*, p. 174). This score is no longer held by the AACC Collection.

827 SAB, Arenberg Collection, LA 9368: this dossier contains a 'Liste des livres achetés pour M. Gendebien à la vente du 12. fev.r 1787'.

828 SAB, Arenberg Collection, SA 6510, p. 103: membership payment of 9 florins 9 sols to a man named Cusener.

829 An *Amman* is the head of a district, with particular responsibility for the police.

830 Regarding Marie-Caroline Murray, see C. Lepeer, *Marie-Caroline Murray. Une romantique des Lumières*, unpublished undergraduate dissertation, Vrije Universiteit Brussel, 1980.

831 J. Vercruysse, 'Les projets d'un nouveau théâtre de la Monnaie au XVIIIᵉ siècle. Le duc d'Arenberg, la 'Muse Belgique' Marie-Caroline Murray et l'amman Rapédius de Berg: l'alliance de la finance, de la culture et du pouvoir urbain', in *Le théâtre de la Monnaie*, pp. 111-115; Duquenne, *Le parc de Wespelaar* (Brussels, 2001), pp. 44-45, suggests that the plans for this concert hall, published in the brochure *Projet de construction*, are the work of the Dinant architect Ghislain Joseph Henry.

832 Cornaz, 'Le Concert Bourgeois', pp. 128-129.

833 SAB, Arenberg Collection, MG 1448 H: document stating that 'L'ouvreuse des loges du second rang est prévenue que la petite loge de S.A.S. Mgr. le duc d'Arenberg est à la disposition de M.lle Murray et sa compagnie aujourdhuy Vendredy 23. Xbre 1785'.

834 *Ibid.*: receipt dated 21 December: payment of 10 crowns for the 'louage de deux loges' during a performance of *Le Barbier de Séville*.

835 AACC, Music Collection, I 579; this edition is not listed by RISM. G. Yeats, 'Carolan, Turlough', in *Grove Music Online. Oxford Music Online* (consulted 12 March 2015), article 04978.

836 *Ibid.*, Ms 10: on the inside of the back cover we find: 'Anne Catherine Savage à Douai'; and on the inside of the cover page:'C'est livre appartient A Marie caroline murray'.

837 *Ibid.*, Ms 434; for details concerning the airs, see Cornaz, 'Inventaire complet', pp. 132-133. 'Muray' appears in the margin of the final page.

838 See Van Aelbrouck, entry 'Colette-Marie-Françoise Cifolelli', *CESAR*.

839 SAB, Arenberg Collection, SA 6510, p. 55.

840 *Ibid.*, p. 84: payment of 31 florins 10 sols for twenty tickets to this concert. Cornaz, 'Le Concert Bourgeois', pp. 132-134. Mees would compose several patriotic works when Belgium came under the Dutch rule of William I of the Netherlands, notably a *Cantate à grand orchestre piano ad libitum composée à l'occasion du Congrès d'Aix la Chapelle exécutée le 3 nbre 1818* (AACC, Music Collection, I 781). He would also publish some airs in the *Journal de chant dédié à la Princesse d'Orange* published in Brussels by Weissenbruch (AACC, Music Collection, Ms 26).

841 SAB, Arenberg Collection, SA 6510, p. 88: payment on 23 April 1787 of 113 florins 8 sols to Joseph Gorner.

842 AACC, Biography Louis-Engelbert d'Arenberg (box 43/2): *Voyage dans les Provinces méridionales de la France*.

843 *Ibid.*, f. 26r.

844 AACC, Biography Louis-Engelbert d'Arenberg (box 43/2): *Voyage dans les Provinces méridionales de la France*, letter of 8 March from Marseille.

845 *Ibid.*, letter of 20 March from Marseille.

846 This was Anne-Marie Simonet, wife of Crêtu. I have not been able to identify precisely the other artists mentioned.

847 *Ibid.*, letter from Lyon.

848 SAB, Arenberg Collection, LA 10375: handwritten note detailing the cost of the tuning of the 'forte piano' and the harpsichord at Heverlee. The Prins in question, who carried out the tuning on 20 November and 14 and 28 December 1788, was probably the same person upon whom the family had called in 1783 (see above).

849 Tytgat, 'De blinde hertog', p. 18.

850 AACC, Annual accounts of the caissiers, 64/8-14 (account of Étienne Lecocq, 1789), f. 36r: payment of 81 florins 19 sols 6 deniers to Godecharle for 72 lessons given to the Princess.

851 AACC, Music Collection, I 690, I 935/9 (Paris, Sieber) and I 692 (London, J. Fentum). These two editions are not listed by RISM. See *The Analytical Review*, 1788, I, pp. 570-571.

852 AACC, Manuscripts, 27/A: the manuscript volume *Suite de Pasquinades N° 3* includes the texts of a series of odes and epistles linked to the revolutionary period, one being an *Ode à son altesse Monseigneur le duc d'Arenberg*.

853 Apart from the Duke and Bosschaert, the group included two other companions and seven servants.

854 AACC, Biography Louis-Engelbert d'Arenberg (box 43/2): *Journal d'un voyage en Italie par Antibes, Nice, Monaco, Gênes, Lerici, Lucques, Livourne, Pise, Sienne, Radicofani et à Rome. Dicté par Monsieur Guillaume de Boschaert, l'un des voyageurs*. I would like to thank Xavier Duquenne who very kindly showed me the blind Duke's travel accounts – particular that concerning Italy.

855 *Ibid.*, p. 3 (9 and 10 February).

856 M. R. Moretti, 'Genoa', in *Grove Music Online. Oxford Music Online* (consulted 12 March 2015), article 10871; J. L. Jackman, K. Lipton, and M. Hunter, 'Guglielmi', *ibid.*, article 42287pg2.

857 AACC, Biography Louis-Engelbert d'Arenberg (box 43/2): *Journal d'un voyage en Italie par Antibes*, pp. 11-12 (28 February).

858 G. Fleischhauer, 'Rome', in *Grove Music Online. Oxford Music Online* (consulted 12 March 2015), article 23759.

859 A second manuscript collection describing the same trip gives a few details about the sojourn in Rome (AACC, Biography Louis-Engelbert d'Arenberg (box 43/3)).

860 *Ibid.*, Sunday 3 [April]. Fleischhauer, 'Rome'.

861 *Ibid.*, Thursday 7 [April].

862 *Ibid.*, Thursday 10 [April], Thursday 21 [April] and Friday 22 [April].

863 *Ibid.*, Sunday 17 [April].

864 B. Carr, 'Banti, Brigida Giorgi', in *Grove Music Online. Oxford Music Online* (consulted 12 March 2015), article 01964.

865 AACC, Biography Louis-Engelbert d'Arenberg (box 43/2): *Journal d'un voyage en Italie par Antibes*, p. 20 (22 April).

866 J. Roche, 'Bergamo', in *Grove Music Online. Oxford Music Online* (consulted 12 March 2015), article 02774.

867 R. Stevenson and M. C. De Brito, 'Todi, Luísa', in *Grove Music Online. Oxford Music Online* (consulted 12 March 2015), article 28044.

868 AACC, Biography Louis-Engelbert d'Arenberg (box 43/2): *Journal d'un voyage en Italie par Antibes*, p. 45 (10 September).

869 *Ibid.*, p. 50 (17 September). This work had seen its first performance in Naples during the spring of 1786.

870 AACC, Music Collection, Ms 178, Ms 179, Ms 180, Ms 181, Ms 183, Ms 379 and Ms 450.

871 The painter Vigée-Lebrun painted a portrait of Paisiello in 1791.

872 Cornaz, 'Inventaire complet', pp. 109-111.

873 AACC, Music Collection, Ms 92.

874 Mamy, *La musique à Venise*, pp. 143-151.

875 AACC, Music Collection, Ms 184.

876 *Ibid.*, Ms 264.

877 Tytgat, 'De blinde hertog', p. 19.

878 AACC, Correspondence Louis-Engelbert, 421: letter of November 1801.

879 *Ibid.*, letter of 2 May 1801.

880 *Ibid.*, Ms 11. This manuscript would next be held by the music library of Prince Paul, son of the Duke (see below). We may note that a second manuscript copied by Sukowaty exists in the AACC Collection: a score of a *Rondo* by Carl Ditters von Dittersdorf (1739-1799) (AACC, Music Collection, Ms 43).

881 AACC, Music Collection, I 931/1 (RISM H/HH 3719) and I 931/2 (RISM H/HH 3726); van Hoboken, *Joseph Haydn: Thematisch-bibliographisches Werkverzeichnis*, I, pp. 703 and 706.

882 AACC, Music Collection, I 939/8; see G. Kinsky, *Das Werk Beethovens* (Munich, 1955), p. 67.

883 *Ibid.*, I 939/13 and I 939/16; Kinsky, pp. 69 and 84.

884 *Ibid.*, I 925/17, I 939/7, 11; Kinsky, p. 75.

885 *Ibid.*, I 939/3 (RISM M/MM 5124).

886 *Ibid.*, I 939/6 (RISM M/MM 6087).

887 Cornaz, 'Inventaire complet', pp. 85-86.

888 AACC, Music Collection, Ms 25.

889 *Ibid.*, I 922/1.

890 *Ibid.*, Ms 36.

891 *Ibid.*, Ms 16.

892 *Ibid.*, I 938/6 (RISM M/MM 6313).

893 *Ibid.*, I 897/10, I 898/7, I 899/2 (RISM M/MM 5208).

894 *Ibid.*, I 792 (RISM M/MM 6801), 916/1 (RISM M/MM 7313), 938/1 (RISM M/MM 6523), I 938/2 (RISM M/MM 6470), I 938/3 (RISM M/MM 6495).

895 *Ibid.*, I 790 (RISM M/MM 5040).

896 *Ibid.*, I 935 (RISM M/MM 4780).

897 *Ibid.*, I 791 (RISM M/MM 7130).

898 *Ibid.*, I 904/8, 906/6 (RISM H/HH 3776).

899 *Ibid.*, I 763 (RISM H/HH 3636); van Hoboken, *Joseph Haydn: Thematisch-bibliographisches Werkverzeichnis*, I, p. 685.

900 *Ibid.*, I 860, I 917 (RISM H/HH 3647; RISM H 3934).

901 *Ibid.*, I 939/10; Kinsky, p. 99.

902 *Ibid.*, I 939/14; Kinsky, p. 107.

903 *Ibid.*, I 939/9; Kinsky, p. 86.

904 *Ibid.*, I 939/15; Kinsky, p. 88.

905 *Ibid.*, I 939/12; Kinsky, p. 515.

906 Quenedey produced several profiles of the blind Duke in the first few years of the nineteenth century. The AACC Collection possesses a copy of the Parisian edition of *La musique, étudiée comme science naturelle, certaine, et comme art ou Grammaire et Dictionnaire musical* by Chrétien; a hand-written annotation tells us that this copy belonged to Prince Paul (I 978).

907 AACC, Music Collection, box XXIX.

BIBLIOGRAPHY

SOURCES

Arenberg Archives and Cultural Centre (AACC)

Accounts of the caissiers trésoriers généraux:
> 64/25 (1706-1709), 64/26 (1717), 64/27/II (1719), 64/28 (1703-1705), 64/29 (1711-1722), 64/31 I and II (1733-34, 1743), 64/32 (1744), 64/33 (1744-46), 64/34 (1742-43, 1748-49), 64/35 (1746), 65/1 (1747-1748), 65/2 (1747-1749), 65/21 (1696-1702), 65/22 (1722-27, 1783, 1786-87, 1789), 65/3 (1771-1772), 65/4 (1765-1783, 1772, 1774)

Annual accounts of the caissiers:
> 63/22-28 (accounts of Pascal Henrion, 1729-1730), 63/29-35 (accounts of Pascal Henrion, 1731-1733; accounts of Philippe Vandermale, 1733-1737; accounts of Jacques Gaillard, 1742-45, 1749; accounts of Philippe Vandermale, 1744-1749; accounts of Jacques Gaillard, 1750-51), 64/1-7 (accounts of Jacques Gaillard, 1752-1775; accounts of Étienne Lecocq, 1776-1783), 64/8-14 (accounts of Étienne Lecocq, 1784-1793)

Annual accounts of the trésoriers généraux:
> 63/15/1 (1602), 63/15/2 (1620-22), 63/15/3 (1622-25), 63/22-28 (accounts of Albert Ignace Delaunoy, 1708-1710; accounts of Jean-Baptiste Deschamps, 1712-1714; accounts of Théodore Frantzen, 1716-1717, 1720; accounts of André Bureau de St André, 1720, 1722-1727)

Biographies of musicians: 9/1

Biography Charles-Marie-Raymond: 35/23-24

Biography Léopold-Philippe: 35/25-28

Biography Louis-Engelbert d'Arenberg (box 43/2): *Journal de mon voyage de Vienne 1779*; Accounts of M. Simmons; *Voyage dans les Provinces méridionales de la France*; *Journal d'un voyage en Italie par Antibes, Nice, Monaco, Gênes, Lerici, Lucques, Livourne, Pise, Sienne, Radicofani et à Rome. Dicté par Monsieur Guillaume de Boschaert, l'un des voyageurs*

Biography Louise-Marguerite de La Marck: 80 (box 36-28)

Correspondence Charles-Marie-Raymond: box 40/26, folder 41/7/I/3 (1766-1778)

Correspondence Léopold-Philippe: 1, 8, 69, 175, 188, 207

Correspondence Louis-Engelbert: 107-108, 136-138, 315, 342, 421, 434

Correspondence Louise-Pauline de Brancas: 1-4, 10-11, 18, 100

Correspondence Marie-Françoise Pignatelli: 40/25 (1738-1762)

Maison, Accounts of Louis-Engelbert: 1782 (file 35)

Manuscripts: 27/A, 29/10, 29/11, 29/12, 29/13, 29/23

Music Collection

State Archives in Mons

Famille d'Olmen de Poederlé: 78bis

State Archives of Belgium (Brussels) (SAB)

Administration du théâtre de Bruxelles: 117, 118

Arenberg Collection, series LA (Laloire): 725, 2140, 4323, 4480, 5112, 5219, 5504, 6031, 6607, 6746, 7442, 7487, 7542, 7924, 8165, 8210, 8464, 8752, 8769, 8867, 8905, 9228, 9229, 9368, 9425, 9451, 9927, 9993, 10117, 10322, 10360, 10361, 10375

Arenberg Collection, series MG (Moreau de Gerbehaye): 1104, 1448, 1890, 2111, 2112, 3172, 3383, 3558, 3647, 3701, 3814

Arenberg Collection, series SA (Sabbe): 1598 I-8 (1822-1825), II 4941, II 13307, II 14026, 5262, 6510

Conseil des Finances: 2074

Conseil privé: 251 B, 1054, 1090 (Comédies et Théâtres)

D'Ursel Collection: R 48

Manuscrits divers: 1808, 2663

Notariat du Brabant: 1617

Secrétairerie d'État et de Guerre: file no. 447

Tribunaux auliques: 3156

Books and articles

Ágústsson, J., "'Zu *Lippiza* den *venetian*: Ersten *Musico* eine *Medalie*': Vivaldi meets Emperor Charles VI, 9 September 1728", *Studi vivaldiani*, 14 (2014), pp. 27-38.

Almanach historique et chronologique de la comedie françoise etablie à Bruxelles (Brussels, 1754).

Arouet, F.M., known as Voltaire, *Correspondance*, ed. by T. Besterman (Oxford, 1968-1977).

Awouters, M., 'Jean-Hyacinthe II-Joseph Rottenburgh', in *Dictionnaire des facteurs d'instruments de musique en Wallonie et à Bruxelles du 9ᵉ siècle à nos jours*, ed. by M. Haine and N. Meeùs (Liège, 1986), pp. 351-352.

Bain, S., and Vanhulst, H., 'Phalèse', in *Grove Music Online. Oxford Music Online* (accessed 12 March 2015), article 21541.

Bauman, T., 'Weidmann, Paul', in *The New Grove Dictionary of Opera. Grove Music Online. Oxford Music Online* (accessed 12 March 2015), article O905686.

Bellina, A. L., Brizi, B., and Pensa, M. G., *I libretti vivaldiani. Recensione e collazione dei testimoni a stampa* (Florence, 1982).

Benoit, M. (ed.), *Dictionnaire de la musique en France aux XVIIᵉ et XVIIIᵉ siècles* (Paris, 1992).

Birkner, G., 'La tablature de luth de Charles, duc de Croÿ et d'Arschot (1560-1612)', *Revue de Musicologie*, 49/1 (1963), pp. 18-46.

Bosmans, J., 'L'ameublement du château d'Enghien au commencement du XVIIᵉ siècle', *Annales du Cercle archéologique d'Enghien*, vol. 1 (1880), pp. 407-463.

Brown, H. M. (ed.), *Didone abbandonata: Leonardo Vinci* (New York-London, 1977).

Bucciarelli, M., Dubowy, N., and Strohm, R. (eds.), *Opera in Central Europe, Volume I: Institutions and Ceremonies* (Berlin, 2006).

Calendrier électronique des spectacles sous l'ancien régime et sous la révolution - CESAR, electronic publication (<www.cesar.org.uk>).

Carr, B., 'Banti, Brigida Giorgi', in *Grove Music Online. Oxford Music Online* (accessed 12 March 2015), article 01964.

Chanson nouvelle à l'occasion du jubilé de S. A. R. chanté au Concert Bourgeois le 31 Mars 1769 (Brussels, [1769]).

Chevrolet, C., 'Essai sur les révolutions de la musique en France', in *Dictionnaire de la musique en France aux XVIIᵉ et XVIIIᵉ siècles*, ed. by M. Benoit, p. 278.

CHIEROTTI, C. M., 'La *Musurgia Universalis* di Athanasius Kircher', electronic publication (<http://www.chierotti.net>).

CLAEYS, P., *Histoire du théâtre à Gand* (Ghent, 1892), 3 vols.

CLERCX, S., 'Les clavecinistes belges et leurs emprunts à l'art de François Couperin et de J.Ph. Rameau', *La Revue musicale*, 192 (1939), pp. 11-22.

Clori. Archivio della Cantata italiana, electronic publication (<http://cantataitaliana.it>).

COPPIETERS, J., *Brieven in tijden van verandering. De correspondentie van Louise Margareta van der Marck (1730-1820), douairière van Arenberg*, unpublished undergraduate dissertation, Katholieke Universiteit Leuven, 2005.

--------, 'Louise Margareta van der Marck (1730-1820)', in *Arenberger Frauen*, ed. by P. NEU (Koblenz, 2006), pp. 221-231.

CORNAZ, M., 'Charles de Lorraine et l'édition musicale bruxelloise', *Bulletin de Dexia Banque* (special issue ed. by C. SORGELOOS: *Autour de Charles de Lorraine, gouverneur général des Pays-Bas autrichiens, 1744-1780 Culture et Société*), 54th year, no. 212 (2000/2), pp. 71-78.

--------, 'Deux arias de l'opéra perdu *L'inganno trionfante in amore* RV 721 et autres découvertes vivaldiennes dans les archives privées de la famille d'Arenberg à Enghien', in *'La la la…Maistre Henri': mélanges de musicologie offerts à Henri Vanhulst*, ed. by C. BALLMAN and V. DUFOUR (Turnhout, 2010), pp. 341-346.

--------, 'Ignace Vitzthumb et les opéras de Grétry', in *Grétry. Un musicien dans l'Europe des Lumières*, ed. by B. DEMOULIN, J. DURON, J.-P. DUCHESNE, C. PIRENNE, and F. TILKIN, *Art & fact*, 32 (2013), pp. 124-128.

-------- (ed.), *Ignace Vitzthumb, Recueils d'ariettes (1775-1777)* (Brussels, 2011), 2 vols.

--------, 'Inventaire complet du fonds musical des archives privées de la famille d'Arenberg à Enghien', *Revue Belge de Musicologie*, 58 (2004), pp. 81-202.

--------, 'La cantate italienne et française au sein de la collection musicale des archives d'Arenberg: nouvelles perspectives', in *Music and Musicians in Europe from the late Middle Ages to Modernism. Essays in Memory of Frank Dobbins*, ed. by M.-A. COLIN (Turnhout, 2015, forthcoming).

--------, 'La circulation de la musique et des musiciens entre Bruxelles et Vienne durant le gouvernement de Charles de Lorraine', *Études sur le 18e siècle* (2004), pp. 187-201.

--------, 'La collection musicale du château des princes de Ligne à Belœil', in *Hainaut terre musicale*, ed. by F. THORAVAL and B. VAN WYMEERSCH (Turnhout, 2015, forthcoming).

--------, 'La Monnaie et le commerce des ouvrages lyriques à Bruxelles', in *Le théâtre de la Monnaie au XVIIIe siècle*. ed. by M. COUVREUR (Brussels, 1996), pp. 275-297.

--------, *La vie musicale à Bruxelles et dans les villes des Pays-Bas autrichiens vue par le biais de la* Gazette de Bruxelles *et de la* Gazette des Pays-Bas (unpublished undergraduate dissertation, awarded a prize by the Royal Academy of Belgium, 9 November 1993).

--------, 'Le Concert Bourgeois: une société de concerts publics à Bruxelles durant la seconde moitié du XVIIIe siècle', *Revue Belge de Musicologie*, 53 (1999), pp. 113-136.

--------, *L'édition et la diffusion de la musique à Bruxelles au XVIIIe siècle* (Brussels, 2001).

--------, 'L'édition musicale à Tournai aux XVIIe et XVIIIe siècles', *Le livre & l'estampe*, 53 (2007), pp. 61-78.

--------, 'Le fonds musical des archives privées de la famille d'Arenberg à Enghien', *Revue Belge de Musicologie*, 49 (1995), pp. 129-210.

--------, *Les ducs d'Arenberg et la musique au XVIIIe siècle* (unpublished PhD thesis, awarded a prize by the Royal Academy of Belgium, 22 November 2008).

--------, *Les ducs d'Arenberg et la musique au XVIIIe siècle. Histoire d'une collection musicale* (Turnhout, 2010).

--------, *Les éditions musicales publiées à Bruxelles au XVIIIᵉ siècle (1706-1794). Catalogue descriptif et illustré* (Brussels, 2008).

--------, *Les Princes de Chimay et la musique* (Brussels, 2002).

--------, 'Les romances publiées à Bruxelles à la fin du XVIIIᵉ siècle', *Revue Belge de Musicologie*, 55 (2001), pp. 179-192.

--------, 'Lieux de concerts publics et privés à Bruxelles au XVIIIᵉ siècle', *Études sur le 18ᵉ siècle* (2007), pp. 97-106.

--------, 'Monteverdi de Mantoue à Bruxelles. Les voyages de l'archiduc Albert en Italie (1598) et de Vincenzo Gonzaga dans les anciens Pays-Bas (1599)', *Orfeo son io* (Brussels, 2008), pp. 31-72.

--------, *Nouvelle Biographie Nationale*, vol. 9 (Brussels, 2007), pp. 62-65: 'Josse Boutmy'.

--------, 'Spectacles privés chez les ducs d'Arenberg', *Études sur le 18ᵉ siècle* (2005), pp. 87-98.

--------, 'Un Belge à la rencontre d'Antonio Vivaldi: le voyage musical de Corneille van den Branden de Reeth en France et en Italie', *Studi vivaldiani*, 13 (2013), pp. 53-83.

--------, 'Unknown sources of Italian baroque music and new Vivaldi operatic discoveries in the Montagu Music Collection (Boughton House, UK)', *Revue Belge de Musicologie*, 66 (2012), pp. 249-268.

--------, 'Un opéra retrouvé d'André Vaillant: *Le Retour des plaisirs*', in *Hainaut terre musicale*, ed. by F. THORAVAL and B. VAN WYMEERSCH (Turnhout, 2015, forthcoming).

COUVREUR, M., 'Joseph-Clément de Bavière, Pietro Torri et le développement de l'oratorio dramatique en France (1707-1714)', in *Noter, annoter, éditer la musique. Mélanges offerts à Catherine Massip*, ed. by C. REYNAUD and H. SCHNEIDER (Geneva, 2012), pp. 73-90.

--------, 'Le séjour de Desmarest à Bruxelles. Aperçu de la vie artistique dans la capitale des anciens Pays-Bas espagnols à la fin du XVIIᵉ siècle', in *Henry Desmarest (1661-1741): exils d'un musicien dans l'Europe du Grand Siècle*, ed. by J. DURON and Y. FERRATON (Liège, 2005).

-------- (ed.), *Le théâtre de la Monnaie au XVIIIᵉ siècle* (Brussels, 1996).

--------, 'Pietro Antonio Fiocco, un musicien vénitien à Bruxelles (1682-1714)', *Revue Belge de Musicologie*, 55 (2001), pp. 147-163.

--------, 'Un amateur de ballets longs et de jupons courts. Le prince Charles-Joseph de Ligne', in *Le théâtre de la Monnaie au XVIIIᵉ siècle*, ed. by M. COUVREUR, pp. 197-239.

COUVREUR, M., and VAN AELBROUCK, J.-P., 'Gio Paolo Bombarda et la création du Grand Théâtre de Bruxelles', in *Le théâtre de la Monnaie au XVIIIᵉ siècle*, ed. by M. COUVREUR (Brussels, 1996), pp. 1-27.

CROFT-MURRAY, E., and MC VEIGH, S., 'London', in *Grove Music Online. Oxford Music Online* (accessed 12 March 2015), article 16904pg5.

DANGREAU, S., *Gilles-Joseph de Boussu, dramaturge (1681-1755)*, unpublished undergraduate dissertation, Université Libre de Bruxelles, academic year 2005-2006.

D'ARENBERG, J.-E., 'De heren, graven, prins-graven en hertogen van Arenberg', in *Arenberg in de Lage Landen*, ed. by J. ROEGIERS (Leuven, 2002), pp. 13-51.

DEAN, W., 'Antinori, Luigi', in *Grove Music Online. Oxford Music Online* (accessed 12 March 2015), article 01021.

--------, 'Dotti, Anna Vincenza', in *Grove Music Online. Oxford Music Online* (accessed 12 March 2015), article 08055.

DE BOUSSU, G.-J., *Histoire de la ville de Mons ancienne et nouvelle* (Mons, 1725).

--------, *Le Retour des plaisirs* (Mons, 1719).

DE CHESTRET DE HANEFFE, J., *Histoire de la Maison De La Marck y compris les Clèves de la seconde race* (Liège, 1898).

DE HAAS, F., and SMETS, I. (eds), *Mozart en Belgique* (Antwerp, 1990).

DE LA BORDE, J.-B., *Essai sur la musique ancienne et moderne* (Paris, 1780).

DELANNOY, Y., 'In memoriam Jean-Pierre Tytgat', in *Annales du Cercle archéologique d'Enghien*, vol. 39 (2005), pp. 177-183.

DE LIGNE, C.-J., *Fragments de l'histoire de ma vie* (Paris, 2000).

DELPECH, L., 'Le Hainaut "au centre des affaires". Circulation des troupes et mobilité des musiciens entre la France et la Saxe (1700-1710)', in *Hainaut terre musicale*, ed. by F. THORAVAL and B. VAN WYMEERSCH (Turnhout, 2015, forthcoming).

DE MÉRODE-WESTERLOO, H., *Mémoires du Feld-Maréchal Comte (Johann Philipp Eugen) de Mérode-Westerloo, Capitaine des Trabans de l'Empereur Charles VI* (Brussels, 1840).

DE MOREAU DE GERBEHAYE, C., DEREZ, M., and MERTENS, A., 'Het archief', in *Arenberg in de Lage Landen*, ed. by J. ROEGIERS, pp. 378-383.

DE PLACE, A., 'Quinault, Jean-Baptiste Maurice', in *Dictionnaire de la musique en France aux XVIIe et XVIIIe siècles*, ed. by M. BENOIT (Paris, 1992), p. 585.

DE REIFFENBERG, Baron, *Une existence de grand seigneur au seizième siècle. Mémoires autographes du duc Charles de Croy* (Brussels, 1845).

DEREZ, M., NELISSEN, M., TYTGAT, J.-P., and VERBRUGGE, A. (eds), *De blinde hertog* (Leuven, 1996).

DESCHEEMAEKER, J., *Histoire de la Maison d'Arenberg d'après les archives françaises* (Neuilly-sur-Seine, 1969).

Description de toutes les fêtes [...] qui ont parus à l'occasion du Jubilé de vingt-cinq ans de Gouvernement de S.A.R. Charles-Alexandre Duc de Lorraine (Brussels, [1769]).

DEUTSCH, O. E., *Mozart: Die Dokumente seines Lebens* (Kassel, 1961).

[DE VINCK D'ORP, Baron], *Le Concert Noble: ses origines et ses membres* (Brussels, 1879).

DEVRIÈS, A., and LESURE, F., *L'édition musicale dans la presse parisienne au XVIIIe siècle. Catalogue des annonces* (Paris, 2005).

DE ZUTTERE, P., 'La direction des frères Alexandre-Florentin et Herman Bultos (1777-1794)', in *Le théâtre de la Monnaie au XVIIIe siècle* (Brussels, 1996), ed. by M. COUVREUR (Brussels, 1996), pp. 133-155.

--------, 'Les musiciens Ignace Vitzthumb (1724-1816) et Joseph-Henri Mees (1777-1858) et leur postérité', *L'intermédiaire des généalogistes*, no. 188 (1977), pp. 98-113.

--------, 'Notes sur quelques décorateurs', in *Le théâtre de la Monnaie au XVIIIe siècle*, ed. by M. COUVREUR (Brussels, 1996), pp. 249-274.

D'HOORE, W., *Le Palais d'Egmont-Arenberg à Bruxelles* (Louvain-la-Neuve, 1991).

DICHIERA D., and ROBINSON, J. J., 'Sacchini, Antonio', in *Grove Music Online. Oxford Music Online* (accessed 12 March 2015), article 24251.

DUCHAINE, P., *La franc-maçonnerie belge au XVIIIe siècle* (Brussels, 1911).

DUFOURCET, M.-B., MAZOUER, C., and SURGERS, A. (eds), *Spectacles et pouvoirs dans l'Europe de l'Ancien Régime (XVIe – XVIIIe siècle)* (Tübingen, 2011).

DUJARDIN, D., 'La direction artistique d'Ignace Vitzthumb', in *Le théâtre de la Monnaie au XVIIIe siècle*, ed. by M. COUVREUR (Brussels, 1996), pp. 157-195.

--------, 'Vitzthumb, Ignaz', *Grove Music Online. Oxford Music Online* (accessed 12 March 2015), article 29540.

DÜNNER, B., 'Davesnes, Pierre Just', in *Dictionnaire de la musique en France aux XVIIe et XVIIIe siècles*, ed. by M. BENOIT (Paris, 1992), p. 208.

DUQUENNE, X., 'La salle du Concert noble construite à Bruxelles en 1779', *Cahiers bruxellois*, 45 (2013), pp. 167-190.

--------, *Le parc de Wespelaar* (Brussels, 2001).

--------, *Le voyage du duc d'Arenberg en Italie en 1791* (Brussels, 2013).

DURON, J., 'Moreau, Jean-Baptiste', in *Dictionnaire de la musique en France aux XVIIe et XVIIIe siècles*, ed. by M. BENOIT (Paris, 1992), p. 477.

DUVOSQUEL, J.-M., and MORSA, D. (eds), *La Maison d'Arenberg en Wallonie, à Bruxelles et au G.-D. de Luxembourg depuis le XIVe siècle. Contribution à l'histoire d'une famille princière* (Enghien, 2011).

FABER, F., *Histoire du théâtre français en Belgique depuis son origine jusqu'à nos jours* (Brussels-Paris, 1878-1880), 5 vols.

FAGON, R., 'Matho, Jean-Baptiste', in *Grove Music Online. Oxford Music Online* (accessed 12 March 2015), article 18069.

FÉTIS, F.-J., *Biographie universelle des musiciens* (Paris, 1873-1880), 2nd edition, anastatic reprint (Brussels, 1963), 8 vols. and 2 supplements.

FÉVRIER, P., *Second livre de pièces de clavecin*, introduction to the facsimile by M. CORNAZ (Brussels, 'Musica Bruxellensis' series, I, 2000).

FIOCCO, J.-H., *Pièces de clavecin opus 1*, introduction to the facsimile by H. VANHULST (Brussels, 'Musica Bruxellensis' series, IV, 2009).

FLEISCHHAUER, G., 'Rome', in *Grove Music Online. Oxford Music Online* (accessed 12 March 2015), article 23759.

FORMENT, B., 'Italian Opera "Under the Belgian Climate": the 1727-30 Seasons at the Monnaie', *Journal of the Alamire Foundation*, 4 (2012), pp. 259-280.

FRANÇOIS-SAPPEY, B., 'Principes de l'accompagnement du clavecin', in *Dictionnaire de la musique en France aux XVIIe et XVIIIe siècles*, ed. by M. BENOIT (Paris, 1992), p. 574.

FREEMAN, D. E., *The Opera Theater of Count Franz Anton von Sporck in Prague* (New York, 1992).

GAGNEPAIN, B., 'Gobert, Thomas', in *Dictionnaire de la musique en France aux XVIIe et XVIIIe siècles*, ed. by M. BENOIT (Paris, 1992), p. 322.

GALAND, M., 'Artistes du Grand Théâtre cités dans le "journal intime" de Charles de Lorraine', in *Le théâtre de la Monnaie au XVIIIe siècle*, ed. by M. COUVREUR (Brussels, 1996), pp. 323-325.

---------, *Charles de Lorraine, gouverneur général des Pays-Bas autrichiens (1744-1780)* (Brussels, 1993).

--------- (ed.), *Journal secret de Charles de Lorraine 1766-1779* (Brussels, 2000).

---------, 'Relations et liens financiers entre le gouvernement et le théâtre de la Monnaie sous le régime autrichien', in *Le théâtre de la Monnaie au XVIIIe siècle*, ed. by M. COUVREUR (Brussels, 1996), pp. 117-131.

GÉRARD, Y., *Thematic, Bibliographical and Critical Catalogue of the Works of Luigi Boccherini* (London, 1969).

GILSON, P., 'harpe (répertoire)', in *Dictionnaire de la musique en France aux XVIIe et XVIIIe siècles*, ed. by M. BENOIT (Paris, 1992), p. 337.

GROOTE, I. M., *Pietro Torri. Un musicista veronese alla corte di Baviera* (Verona, 2003).

HAAS, R. (ed.), *Ignaz Umlauf. Die Bergknappen*, in *Denkmäler der Tonkunst in Österreich*, vol. 36 (1959).

HAINE, M., and MEEÙS, N. (eds), *Dictionnaire des facteurs d'instruments de musique en Wallonie et à Bruxelles du 9e siècle à nos jours* (Liège, 1986).

HANSELL, S., and FREEMAN, D. E., 'Bioni, Antonio', in *Grove Music Online. Oxford Music Online* (accessed 12 March 2015), article 03111.

HANSELL, S., and TERMINI, O., 'Bigaglia, Diogenio', in *Grove Music Online. Oxford Music Online* (accessed 12 March 2015), article 03066.

HASQUIN, H., *Joseph II. Catholique anticlérical et réformateur impatient* (Brussels, 2007).

HEARTZ, D., 'Farinelli revisited', *Early Music*, 18/3 (1990), pp. 430-443.

HERNEUPONT, A., 'Musicisti italiani nel Belgio nel secolo XVIII: Pietro-Antonio, Giovanni Giuseppe e Giuseppe Ettore Fiocco', *Rivista Musicale Italiana*, 47 (1943), fasc. I-II, pp. 1-23.

HILL, J. W., 'Pescetti, Giovanni Battista', in *Grove Music Online. Oxford Music Online* (accessed 12 March 2015), article 21408.

--------, 'Veracini, Francesco Maria', in *Grove Music Online. Oxford Music Online* (accessed 12 March 2015), article 29178.

HILL, J. W., and GIUNTINI, F., 'Orlandini, Giuseppe Maria', in *Grove Music Online. Oxford Music Online* (accessed 12 March 2015), article 20473.

HOGWOOD, C., and MCVEIGH, S., 'Giardini, Felice', in *Grove Music Online. Oxford Music Online* (accessed 12 March 2015), article 11083.

HOLLIS, G. T., 'Bertoni, Ferdinando', in *Grove Music Online. Oxford Music Online* (accessed 12 March 2015), article 02933.

HOLMAN, P., and GILMAN, T., 'Arne, Thomas Augustine', in *Grove Music Online. Oxford Music Online* (accessed 12 March 2015), article 40018.

HOWARD, P., *The Modern Castrato: Gaetano Guadagni and the Coming of a New Operatic Age* (New York, 2014).

HUYBENS, G., 'Leonardus Nervius, *Cantiones sacrae…*', in *Antwerpse Muziekdrukken. Vocale en instrumentale polyfonie (16de-18de eeuw)*, exhibition catalogue (Antwerp, 1996), pp. 77-78.

HUYS, J.-P., 'Princes en exil, organisateurs de spectacles. Sur le séjour en France des électeurs Maximilien II Emmanuel de Bavière et Joseph-Clément de Cologne', in *Spectacles et pouvoirs dans l'Europe de l'Ancien Régime (XVIe – XVIIIe siècle)*, ed. by M.-B. DUFOURCET, C. MAZOUER, and A. SURGERS (Tübingen, 2011).

ISNARDON, J., *Le théâtre de la Monnaie depuis sa fondation jusqu'à nos jours* (Brussels, 1890).

JACKMAN, J. L., LIPTON, K., and HUNTER, M., 'Guglielmi', *ibid.*, article 42287pg2.

JACKMAN, J. L., and MAIONE, P. G., 'Falco, Michele', in *Grove Music Online. Oxford Music Online* (accessed 12 March 2015), article 09254.

JONÁŠOVÁ, M., 'I Denzio: tre generazioni di musicisti a Venezia e a Praga', *Hudební věda*, 45 (2008), pp. 57-114.

KING, R. G., PIPERNO, F., and WILLAERT, S., 'Laschi, Filippo', in *The New Grove Dictionary of Opera. Grove Music Online. Oxford Music Online* (accessed 12 March 2015), article O902804.

KINSKY, G., *Das Werk Beethovens* (Munich, 1955).

KOCEVAR, E., 'Parfaict', in *Dictionnaire de la musique en France aux XVIIe et XVIIIe siècles*, ed. by M. BENOIT (Paris, 1992), p. 526.

LALOIRE, É., *Généalogie de la maison princière et ducale d'Arenberg (1547-1940)* (Brussels, 1940).

--------, *Histoire des deux hôtels d'Egmont* (Brussels, 1952).

LANGEVIN, K., 'Albanese, Antoine', in *Grove Music Online. Oxford Music Online* (accessed 12 March 2015), article 00414.

LEMAIRE, C., 'La bibliothèque des ducs d'Arenberg, une première approche', in *Liber Amicorum Herman Liebaers* (Brussels, 1984), pp. 81-106.

LEPEER, C., *Marie-Caroline Murray. Une romantique des Lumières*, unpublished undergraduate dissertation, Vrije Universiteit Brussel, 1980.

LERNOUT, G., 'Louise Pauline de Brancas-Villars, gravin van Lauraguais, hertogin van Arenberg', in *Arenberger Frauen*, ed. by P. NEU (Koblenz, 2006), pp. 233-243.

--------, 'Notities over belangrijke gebeurtenissen tussen 1760 en 1786, opgesteld door Jérôme Debiefve, eerste secretaris van de hertog van Arenberg', *Het oude land van Edingen en omliggende*, 37/1 (2009), pp. 7-35.

LESURE, F., 'La facture instrumentale à Paris au seizième siècle', *The Galpin society journal*, 7 (1954), pp. 11-52.

LIBBY, D., 'Fontana, Giacinto', in *The New Grove Dictionary of Opera. Grove Music Online. Oxford Music Online* (accessed 12 March 2015), article O003247.

--------, 'Paita, Giovanni', in *The New Grove Dictionary of Opera. Grove Music Online. Oxford Music Online* (accessed 12 March 2015), article O008210.

---------, 'Pasi, Antonio', in *The New Grove Dictionary of Opera. Grove Music Online. Oxford Music Online* (accessed 12 March 2015), article O007396.

LIBBY, D., and ROSSELLI, J., 'Peruzzi, Anna', in *The New Grove Dictionary of Opera. Grove Music Online. Oxford Music Online* (accessed 12 March 2015), article O007438.

Libretti d'opera italiani, electronic publication (<http://www.librettidopera.it>).

LIEBRECHT, H., *Histoire du théâtre français à Bruxelles au XVIIᵉ et au XVIIIᵉ siècle* (Paris, 1923).

LORIDAN, J., 'L'Électeur de Cologne à Valenciennes (1708-1714)', *Revue de Lille*, 18th year, 3rd series, vol. I (May 1907), pp. 570-595.

MABILLE, J. A., *Mémoires touchant mes voyages, négociations, entremises pour la très illustre maison d'Egmont* (Paris, 1909).

MAILLARD, J.-C., 'vielle à roue (répertoire)', in *Dictionnaire de la musique en France aux XVIIᵉ et XVIIIᵉ siècles*, ed. by M. BENOIT (Paris, 1992), pp. 712-713.

MAMY, S., *La musique à Venise et l'imaginaire français des Lumières* (Paris, 1996).

MARKSTROM, K. S., *The Operas of Leonardo Vinci* (New York, 2007).

MAROY, C., 'Les séjours de Voltaire à Bruxelles', *Annales de la Société d'archéologie de Bruxelles*, 19/3 and 4, 1905, pp. 11-12.

MATHIEU, E., *Histoire de la ville d'Enghien* (s.l., 1876).

McCLYMONDS, M. P., 'Jommelli, Niccolò', in *Grove Music Online. Oxford Music Online* (accessed 12 March 2015), article 14437.

MEEÙS, N., 'Mahieu, Jérôme', in *Dictionnaire des facteurs d'instruments de musique en Wallonie et à Bruxelles du 9ᵉ siècle à nos jours*, ed. by M. HAINE and N. MEEÙS (Liège, 1986), p. 274.

MONSON, D. E., 'Galuppi, Baldassare', in *Grove Music Online. Oxford Music Online* (accessed 12 March 2015), article 50020.

MORETTI, M. R., 'Genoa', in *Grove Music Online. Oxford Music Online* (accessed 12 March 2015), article 10871.

NESTOLA, B., 'Spoglio dei volumi di "Meilleurs airs italiens" pubblicati da Christophe Ballard (1699-1708)', Cahiers Philidor 26, Versailles, 2004, 9 p., electronic publication (<http://www.cmbv.fr>).

NEU, P. (ed.), *Arenberger Frauen* (Koblenz, 2006).

---------, *Die Arenberger und das Arenberger Land* (Koblenz, 1995), vol. 2.

---------, 'Marie Henriette Félicité del Carretto / d'Alcaretto, Marquise de Savona y Grana (1671-1744)', in *Arenberger Frauen*, ed. by P. NEU (Koblenz, 2006), pp. 161-179.

PUGET DE LA SERRE, P., *Le Roman de la cour de Bruxelles, ou les advantures des plus braves cavaliers qui furent jamais, et des plus belles dames du monde* (Spa, Keulen [Liège], 1628).

POMEAU, R., *Voltaire et son temps* (Paris-Oxford, 1995).

RASCH, R., 'Italian Opera in Amsterdam 1750-1756: The Troupes of Crosa, Giordani, Lapis, and Ferrari', in *Opera in Central Europe, I: Institutions and Ceremonies*, ed. by M. BUCCIARELLI, N. DUBOWY, and R. STROHM (Berlin, 2006), pp. 118-119.

---------, 'Opera in a Different Language. Opera Translations in the Dutch Republic in the Eighteenth Century', in *Music and the City*, ed. by S. BEGHEIN, B. BLONDÉ, and E. SCHREURS (Leuven, 2013), pp. 39-57.

RASPÉ, P., 'Van Casteel, Henri-Joseph', in *Dictionnaire des facteurs d'instruments de musique en Wallonie et à Bruxelles du 9ᵉ siècle à nos jours*, ed. by M. HAINE and N. MEEÙS (Liège, 1986), pp. 414-415.

RENIEU, L., *Histoire des théâtres de Bruxelles depuis leur origine jusqu'à ce jour* (Paris, 1928), 2 vols.

RISM Online Catalogue of Musical Sources (<www.rism.info>).

ROBINSON, M. F., and MONSON, D. E., 'Latilla, Gaetano', in *Grove Music Online. Oxford Music Online* (accessed 12 March 2015), article 16071.

ROCHE, J., 'Bergamo', in *Grove Music Online. Oxford Music Online* (accessed 12 March 2015), article 02774.

ROCHE, J., and CARTER, T., 'Mortaro, Antonio', in *Grove Music Online. Oxford Music Online* (accessed 12 March 2015), article 19172.

ROEGIERS, J. (ed.), *Arenberg in de Lage Landen* (Leuven, 2002).

---------, 'De bibliotheek', in *Arenberg in de Lage Landen*, pp. 358-369.

---------, 'De bibliotheek. Boeken om te lezen', in *De blinde hertog. Louis Engelbert & zijn tijd. 1750-1820* (Leuven, 1996), pp. 175-176.

ROMAGNOLI, A., 'Mancini, Francesco', in *Grove Music Online. Oxford Music Online* (accessed 12 March 2015), article 17594.

ROOSE, P., 'Langhedul', in *Dictionnaire des facteurs d'instruments de musique en Wallonie et à Bruxelles du 9ᵉ siècle à nos jours*, ed. by M. HAINE and N. MEEÙS (Liège, 1986), pp. 242-243.

ROUX, O., 'Vaucanson, Jacques de', in *Dictionnaire de la musique en France aux XVIIᵉ et XVIIIᵉ siècles*, ed. by M. BENOIT (Paris, 1992), p. 699.

SABATIER, F., 'Bédos de Celles, dom François', in *Dictionnaire de la musique en France aux XVIIᵉ et XVIIIᵉ siècles*, ed. by M. BENOIT (Paris, 1992), p. 64.

SALVETTI, G., and KEAHEY, T. H., 'Besozzi', in *Grove Music Online. Oxford Music Online* (accessed 12 March 2015), article 02957.

SARDELLI, F. M., *Catalogo delle concordanze musicali vivaldiane* (Florence, 2012).

SARTORI, C., *I libretti italiani a stampa dalle origini al 1800* (Cuneo, 1991), 7 vols.

SCHLAGER, K. (ed.), *Répertoire International des Sources Musicales, Einzeldrucke vor 1800* (Kassel, 1971-1999), 9 vols + 4 suppls.

SCHNEIDER, H., 'Traité de l'harmonie réduite à ses principes naturels', in *Dictionnaire de la musique en France aux XVIIᵉ et XVIIIᵉ siècles*, ed. by M. BENOIT (Paris, 1992), p. 687.

SELFRIDGE-FIELD, E., *The Calendar of Venetian Opera. A New Chronology of Venetian Opera and Related Genres, 1660-1760* (Stanford, 2007).

STELLFELD, C., *Les Fiocco. Une famille de musiciens belges aux XVIIᵉ et XVIIIᵉ siècles* (Brussels, 1941).

STEVENSON, R., and DE BRITO, M. C., 'Todi, Luísa', in *Grove Music Online. Oxford Music Online* (accessed 12 March 2015), article 28044.

STROHM, R., *The Operas of Antonio Vivaldi* (Florence, 2008), 2 vols.

SUTTON, E. L., *The Solo Vocal Works of Nicola Porpora: An Annotated Thematic Catalogue*, University of Minneapolis (dissertation), 1974.

TALBOT, M., 'Girò [Tessieri], Anna', in *Grove Music Online. Oxford Music Online* (accessed 12 March 2015), article 40662.

---------, *The Vivaldi Compendium* (Woodbridge, 2011).

TALBOT, M., and WHITE, M., 'A Lawsuit and a Libretto: New Facts Concerning the Pasticcio *La ninfa infelice e fortunata*', *Studi vivaldiani*, 14 (2014), pp. 69-81.

TERMINI, O., 'Pollarolo, Antonio', in *Grove Music Online. Oxford Music Online* (accessed 12 March 2015), article 22024.

THIEFFRY, S., 'La chapelle royale de Bruxelles de 1612 à 1618 d'après les *Libros de la Razon* de l'archiduc Albert', *Revue Belge de Musicologie*, 55 (2001), pp. 103-125.

TIMMS, C., 'Ristorini, Antonio Maria', in *Grove Music Online. Oxford Music Online* (accessed 12 March 2015), article 40863.

---------, 'Ungarelli, Rosa', in *Grove Music Online. Oxford Music Online* (accessed 12 March 2015), article 40864.

TYTGAT, J.-P., 'Een blinde hertog', in *De blinde hertog*, pp. 11-27.

---------, 'Nota over het archief van Arenberg', internal note preserved in a file at the AACC.

VAN AELBROUCK, J.-P., *Dictionnaire des danseurs à Bruxelles de 1600 à 1830* (Liège, 1994).

--------, *Livrets de ballets, opéras et pièces de théâtre imprimés ou représentés à Bruxelles (1600-1800)*, Brussels, 1993 (unpublished).

VANDER STRAETEN, E., *La musique aux Pays-Bas avant le XIXe siècle* (Brussels, 1867-1888, anastatic reprint, New York, 1969), 4 vols.

VAN EVEN, G. E., 'Notice sur la bibliothèque de Charles de Croÿ, duc d'Aerschot (1614)', *Bulletin du Bibliophile belge*, 9 (1852), pp. 380-393 and 436-451.

VAN HOBOKEN, A., *Joseph Haydn: Thematisch-bibliographisches Werkverzeichnis* (Mainz, 1957-1971), 2 vols.

VENDRIX, P., 'Francisque, Antoine', in *Dictionnaire de la musique en France aux XVIIe et XVIII^ee siècles*, ed. by M. BENOIT (Paris, 1992), p. 303.

VERBRUGGE, A., 'De garderobe', in *De blinde hertog*, pp. 151-159.

VERCRUYSSE, J., 'Les projets d'un nouveau théâtre de la Monnaie au XVIIIe siècle. Le duc d'Arenberg, la 'Muse Belgique' Marie-Caroline Murray et l'amman Rapédius de Berg: l'alliance de la finance, de la culture et du pouvoir urbain', in *Le théâtre de la Monnaie au XVIIIe siècle*, ed. by M. COUVREUR (Brussels, 1996), pp. 111-115.

VERSCHUEREN, E., *Louis-Engelbert d'Arenberg (1750-1820), Le 'duc aveugle', ses intérêts scientifiques et artistiques y compris le mécénat*, unpublished undergraduate dissertation, Université Libre de Bruxelles, 1994-95.

WALKER, F., '"Tre giorni son che Nina": An Old Controversy Reopened', *The Musical Times*, 90, no. 1282 (1949), pp. 432-435.

WANGERMÉE, R., 'Du divertissement de cour à l'opéra-comique', in *Le théâtre de la Monnaie au XVIIIe siècle*, ed. by M. COUVREUR (Brussels, 1996), pp. I-XX.

WILLAERT, S., 'Crosa, Giovanni Francesco', in *Grove Music Online. Oxford Music Online* (accessed 12 March 2015), article 51571.

WOLLENBERG, S., and S. MCVEIGH, S., *Concert Life in Eighteenth-Century Britain* (Aldershot, 2004).

WOOD, C., 'Desmarest, Henry', in *Grove Music Online. Oxford Music Online* (accessed 12 March 2015), article 07630.

WÜRTH, R., and P. CORNEILSON, P., 'Allegranti, Maddalena', in *Grove Music Online. Oxford Music Online* (accessed 12 March 2015), article 00599.

YEATS, G., 'Carolan, Turlough', in *Grove Music Online. Oxford Music Online* (accessed 12 March 2015), article 04978.

ZASLAW, N., 'Leclair's "Scylla et Glaucus"', *The Musical Times*, 120, no. 1641 (1979), pp. 900-904.

--------, 'Some notes on Jean-Benoît Leclair', *Revue Belge de Musicologie*, 19 (1965), pp. 97-101.

--------, 'Postscript on Jean-Benoît Leclair', *Revue Belge de Musicologie*, 21 (1967), pp. 124-125.

INDEX OF PERSONAL NAMES

Contents

PHOTOGRAPHIC CREDITS

Archives of the City of Brussels (Brussels): 30, 104

Bibliothèque Nationale de France (Paris): 72, 88, 127

British Library (London): 159

Centre de recherche du château de Versailles, château de Versailles: 166

IRPA (Brussels): 129, 153

Mozarteum Foundation (Salzburg): 109, 111

Museo internazionale e biblioteca della musica (Bologna): 50, 126

Museum of the City of Brussels-The King's House (Brussels): 81

Musical Instruments Museum (Brussels), Luc Schrobiltgen: 13, 27, 99, 117, 118, 128, 135

Muzeul Naţional de Artă al României (Bucharest): 65

Pjerpol Rubens (Tielt): 8

RMN /Agence Bulloz: 28

RMN / Daniel Arnaudet: 132

RMN / Hervé Lewandowski: 165

RMN / René-Gabriel Ojéda: 110,113

Royal Library of Belgium (Brussels): 14, 23, 37, 39, 42, 43, 46, 51, 52, 59, 76, 77, 78, 80, 82, 86, 87, 95, 100, 103, 106, 107, 108, 112, 114, 119, 131, 137, 139, 142, 148, 150, 160, 162, 164, 168, 171, 174, 177, 179, 180

State Archives of Belgium (Brussels): 7, 10, 12, 146, 155, 156

Studio Berger (Enghien): 1, 4, 5, 6, 9, 15, 16, 18, 21, 22, 24, 25, 26, 29, 31, 32, 33, 34, 38, 40, 41, 44, 45, 47, 48, 49, 53, 54, 55, 56, 57, 58, 60, 61, 62, 63, 64, 66, 67, 68, 69, 70, 71, 73, 74, 75, 79, 83, 84, 85, 89, 90, 91, 96, 97, 98, 101, 102, 105, 115, 116, 120, 121, 122, 123, 124, 125, 130, 133, 134, 136, 138, 140, 141, 143, 144, 145, 147, 149, 151, 152, 154, 157, 158, 161, 163, 167, 169, 170, 172, 173, 175, 176, 178, 181, 182, 183, 184

University of Leuven, B. Vandermeulen (Leuven): 2, 3, 17, 19, 35, 36, 92, 93